Essays in Economic Theory, Growth and Labor Markets

Essays in Economic Theory, Growth and Labor Markets

A Festschrift in Honor of E. Drandakis

Edited by

George Bitros

Professor of Economics, Department of Economics, Athens University of Economics and Business, Greece

Yannis Katsoulacos

Professor of Economics and Director of Postgraduate Studies, Department of Economics, Athens University of Economics and Business, Greece

Edward Elgar
Cheltenham, UK • Northampton, MA, USA

Published by
Edward Elgar Publishing Limited
Glensanda House
Montpellier Parade
Cheltenham
Glos GL50 1UA
UK

Edward Elgar Publishing, Inc.
136 West Street
Suite 202
Northampton
Massachusetts 01060
USA

A catalogue record for this book
is available from the British Library

ISBN 1 84064 739 6

Printed and bound in Great Britain by MPG Books Ltd, Bodmin, Cornwall

Contents

About the Authors

BETH ALLEN

Beth Allen works in economic theory, in particular, on asymmetric information and strategic behavior, and on engineering design theory; she is Professor of Economics at the University of Minnesota.

COSTAS AZARIADIS

Currently Professor of Economics and Director, Program for Dynamic Economics, UCLA.

Born in Athens, 15/2/1943. Dipl. Eng., (National Technical University) 1969. MBA and PhD (Carnegie-Mellon), 1971 and 1975. Assistant Professor, Brown University, 1973-77. Associate Professor and Professor, University of Pennsylvania, 1977-83 and 1983-92. Professor, UCLA, since 1992. Visiting appointments at Hebrew University, Princeton, Montreal, EHESS and DELTA (Paris), IMPA (Rio De Janeiro), Mannheim, Lisbon, Autonoma de Barcelona, Carlos III, LSE and elsewhere.

Fellow of the Econometric Society, elected 1989. Other research and teaching activities since 1975 include one textbook and 40 articles in scientific journals, and the supervision of 25 doctoral dissertations.

DAVID W. BERNOTAS

David Bernotas is a PhD candidate at the University of Illinois at Urbana-Champaign, USA.

GEORGE C. BITROS

He obtained his PhD in Economics from New York University in 1972 and stayed on for teaching and research until 1976. In that year he returned to Greece in the position of Senior Research Associate in the Research Department of the Bank of Greece and three years later he moved on to the Athens University of Economics and Business where he serves as Professor of Economics to the present day. He has published extensively in major scholarly journals. He has served as research associate in the National Bureau of Economic Research (USA). He has been co-founder, co-manager and co-editor of the *Greek Economic Review*. He has held advisory posts in government, official commissions, as well as major business concerns, and he serves as referee for several domestic and international journals.

AMITAVA BOSE

Amitava Bose is the Director of the Indian Institute of Management, Calcutta, India. He received his PhD from the University of Rochester in 1974. He has been a faculty member at the Indian Institute of Management, Calcutta, since 1974, and has also taught as a visiting professor at the Indian Statistical Institute, Calcutta, and the Center for Development Studies, Trivandrum.

His research work has focused on macroeconomics and monetary theory, the theory of economic growth and development, and aspects of economic liberalization in India.

He is a co-editor of two collections of papers, *Contemporary Macroeconomics* and *Issues in Economic Theory and Public Policy*, both published by Oxford University Press.

SWAPAN DASGUPTA

Swapan Dasgupta is Professor of Economics at Dalhousie University, Canada, which he joined in 1977. He received his PhD from the University of Rochester in 1980, and has taught at the Université Catholique de Louvain, Belgium, and the University of Rochester as a visiting professor. He has also held visiting positions at Cornell University and Instituto Torcuato di Tella, Buenos Aires, Argentina.

His research work has focused on the theory of optimal economic growth, especially on aspects of global asymptotic stability, comparative dynamics and inter-temporal decentralization of optimal paths. He has applied this theory to the economics of exhaustible resources and sustainable development.

JAYASRI DUTTA

Jayasri Dutta works in economic theory and, in particular, on economic growth and political economy; she is Professor of Economics at the University of Birmingham.

STANLEY L. ENGERMAN

Stanley L. Engerman is John H. Munro Professor of Economics and Professor of History at the University of Rochester, Rochester, NY, USA. He is co-author (with Robert W. Fogel of *Time on the Cross: The Economics of American Negro Slavery*, and co-editor (with Seymour Drescher) of *A Historical Guide to World Slavery*, (with Seymour Drescher and Robert Paquette) of *Slavery: A Reader*, and (with Robert Gallman) of *The Cambridge Economic History of the United States*.

ELIAS G. FLYTZANIS

Professor of Mathematics at the Athens University of Economics and Business, Department of Informatics, since 1986. Previously he has held teaching positions at the Polytechnic School of the University of Thessaloniki (1974-1986) and at Georgetown University in USA (1968-70). Also he was visiting fellow at Warwick University UK (1979) and at the University Paris VI (1991,1995). He has a Bachelor degree in Physics from Harvard University, USA (1963), a Master degree in Physics and a Master and PhD degrees in Mathematics from the University of Wisconsin(Madison) USA (1968). His research interests lie in the fields of Functional Analysis and Ergodic Theory, and in Applications of Mathematical Analysis to Economics. His research articles have appeared in the journals Trans.Amer.Math.Soc., Proc.Amer.Math.Soc., J.Func.Anal., J.Geom.Func.Anal., Monatsh.Math., J.Austr.Math.Soc., Math.Japan., J.Diff.Int.Eq., Act.Math.Hung.

JAMES W. FRIEDMAN

James Friedman is Kenan Professor of Economics Emeritus at the University of North Carolina at Chapel Hill, North Carolina, USA. He received his BA from the University of Michigan in 1959 and his PhD from Yale University in 1963. He was Assistant Professor of Economics and Staff Member of the Cowles Foundation at Yale University from 1963 to 1968, Associate, then full Professor of Economics at the University of Rochester from 1968 to 1983, Professor of Economics at the Virginia Polytechnic University from 1983 to 1985, and Kenan Professor of Economics at the University of North Carolina from 1985 to 2001.

DIONYSIUS GLYCOPANTIS

Dionysius Glycopantis is a Professor of Economics at the City University, London, England. He holds a PhD from the London School of Economics and he is a former graduate of the Athens School of Economics.

YANNIS M. IOANNIDES

Yannis M. Ioannides, (Dipl. Eng., 1968, National Technical University, Greece; MS, 1970 and PhD, 1974, Stanford University), is the Max and Herta Neubauer Professor of Economics at Tufts University, Massachusetts. He was born in Kyparissia, Greece, and lives in Lincoln, Massachusetts. He has held faculty appointments at Brown, Boston University, the Athens School of Economics and Business, and Virginia Polytechnic Institute and State University before he joined Tufts in 1995. Ioannides is an applied theorist with interests in urban economics (and, in particular, housing economics), labor economics and macroeconomics.

He has published more than 60 scientific articles, theoretical and empirical, in top international scholarly journals, including the *American Economic Review*, the *Journal of Economic Theory*, *Quarterly Journal of Economics*, *Regional Science and Urban Economics*, and the *International Economic Review*, and in international conference proceedings. His research has been funded by grants from the US National Science Foundation and the John D. and Catherine T. MacArthur Foundation. He has served as consultant to the US Department of Housing and Urban Development, the Government of Greece, and the European Investment Bank. His current research focuses on social interactions, technological progress and economic inequality.

NEELAM JAIN

He received his PhD degree in Economics from the University of Minnesota in 1995. Currently he is at the Jones Graduate School of Management at Rice University. His research interests are financial economics and industrial organization. His research has focused on the relationship between real and financial decisions, for example the effect of insider trading on prices and outputs in different market structures. He has also worked on the relationship between financial contracting and entry-deterrence. Currently he is at working on the effect of debt on managerial compensation in a dynamic model under asymmetric information and uncertainty.

RONALD W. JONES

Ronald W. Jones is the Xerox Professor of Economics and chairman of the economics department at the University of Rochester. He has been in that department since 1958. He is a Fellow of the Econometric Society, of the American Academy of Arts and Sciences and of the National Academy of Sciences. He is the author of over 100 articles on the pure theory of international trade. His textbook, *World Trade and Payments*, co-authored with Richard Caves and Jeffrey Frankel, is in its 9th edition. His latest book, *Globalization and the Theory of Input Trade*, extends trade theory to encompass mobility of factors and exchange of intermediate and capital goods.

YANNIS KATSOULACOS

Professor of Economics at AUEB and Chairman of CERES, Athens. He has been Associate Professor of AUEB between 1990-93 and of the University of Liverpool (1985-1992), taught at the Universities of Bristol, Southampton and the LSE. He got his PhD from the LSE in 1984. He has published over 45 articles in international refereed journals and five books.

Visiting Professor of the University of Pittsburgh (1992-93) at the Center of Economic Research and Graduate Education, Charles University (Prague), Visiting Research Fellow (1994) at CREST-ENSAE (Paris), and Director of the Institute of Economic Policy Studies (Athens), 1993-95.

He has acted as advisor to the OECD and the European Commission since 1986 and has coordinated or has been principal investigator in 23 projects funded by the EU since 1989.

LIONEL MCKENZIE

His university education includes an AB degree (1939) from Duke University, a BLitt. degree (1946) from Oxford, and a Ph D degree (1956) from Princeton. In addition he has two honorary degrees: an LLD from Chicago (1991) and an Econ. D. from Keio (Tokyo) (1995). He was a Rhodes Scholar (1939) and he is a member of the National Academy of Sciences (1978), a fellow of the American Academy of Arts and Sciences (1967), a fellow of the Econometric Society (1958), a Guggenheim fellow (1973), and a Distinguished Fellow of the American Economic Society (1993). Two books, *Classical General Equilibrium Theory* and *Selected Papers* are due for publication in the Spring of 2001 by the MIT Press. They will contain his contributions to economics.

CLAUDIO MEZZETTI

Claudio Mezzetti is Professor of Economics at the University of North Carolina at Chapel Hill, North Carolina, USA. He received his laurea in Political Science from the University of Pisa in 1981, Doctorate in Political Economy from the University of Siena in 1987, and DPhil. in Economics from the University of Oxford in 1988. From 1988 to 1990 he was Visiting Assistant Professor, University of California, Davis. Since 1990 he has been on the faculty of the University of North Carolina.

LEONARD J. MIRMAN

Leonard J. Mirman is the Paul Goodloe McIntire Professor of Economics at the University of Virginia and is a Fellow of the Econometric Society. He got his PhD from the University of Rochester, and has made contributions in numerous fields in the economics discipline. Among his contributions is his work on uncertainty and growth, for both positive and optimal growth. He has applied growth theory to learning, experimentation, games, natural resources and trade theory. He has also used lattice theory techniques to study nonclassical growth. Other contributions include work in the field of uncertainty and information, the study of multidimensional risk aversion, as well as general equilibrium with asymmetric information. He has studied the exploitation of natural resources, industrial organization, cost allocation, contract theory, international trade and corporate finance – the effect of insider trading on real decisions of the firm. His recent research is on growth and macroeconomics in distorted economies and banking – using agency models to study the informational effects of financial intermediation in the face of entry.

TAPAN MITRA

Tapan Mitra is Professor of Economics and the Chairman of the Department of Economics at Cornell University. He received his PhD from the University of Rochester in 1975, and taught at the University of Illinois at Chicago and the State University of New York at Stony Brook before joining Cornell University in 1981.

His research work has focused on the theory of efficient and optimal intertemporal allocation, with applications to economic growth and development, and the economics of renewable and exhaustible resources.

He was awarded the Alfred P. Sloan Fellowship in 1981, and was elected a Fellow of the Econometric Society in 1997.

WALTER Y. OI

Walter Y. Oi is the Elmer B. Milliman Professor at the University of Rochester where he works in the fields of labor economics, industrial organization, and applied price theory. He is a Fellow of the Econometric Society 1976, American Academy of Arts and Sciences 1993, Distinguished Fellow of the American Economic Association 1995, President of the Western Economics Association 1992, and recipient of the Secretary of Defense Medal for Outstanding Public Service 1999 for his work on the staff of the President's Commission on an All-Volunteer Force. He resides in Rochester, New York with his wife, Marjorie Robbins Oi.

EDMUND S. PHELPS

Edmund Phelps holds a PhD from Yale University (1959) and joined the Department of Economics at Columbia in 1971 after several years at Pennsylvania and earlier Yale. He was named McVickar Professor of Political Economy in 1982. Alongside his recent research on capitalism Phelps has also done research on the causes and cures of joblessness and low wages among disadvantaged workers. Phelps recently served as Senior Advisor to the project Italy in Europe at the Consiglio Nazionale delle Ricerche, Italy, for three years until May 2000. Phelps was elected to the National Academy of Sciences (USA) in 1981 and was made a Distinguished Fellow of the American Economic Association in 2000. In 1985 he was awarded an honorary degree from his alma mater, Amherst College, and in June 2000 he received honorary degrees from the University of Mannheim and the University of Rome 'Tor Vergata'.

HERAKLES POLEMARCHAKIS

Herakles Polemarchakis works in economic theory and, in particular, on the theory of economic policy; he teaches at Brown University.

DAVID ULPH

Professor David Ulph is Director of Analysis and Research in Inland Revenue and Professeur Invité, Université de Paris I.

He has been Professor of Economics at University College London (UCL), 1992-2001, Executive Director, ESRC Centre for Economic Learning and Social Evolution, Head of Department of Economics, UCL, Professor and Head of Department of Economics at the University of Bristol.

He has acted as a Member of the Editorial Boards of the *Review of Economic Studies*, *Journal of Industrial Economics* and the *European Economic Review*.

He has been Member of the ESRC Committees: Economics Board, Research Grants Board and Council Member of European Economic Association and Royal Economic Society.

NICHOLAS C. YANNELIS

Nicholas Yannelis is Commerce Distinguished Alumni Professor of Economics at the University of Illinois at Urbana-Champaign.

Also he is currently co-editor of *Economic Theory*, associate editor of the *Journal of Mathematical Economics* and editor of the book series, *Studies in Economic Theory*. Professor Yannelis is a graduate of the Athens School of Economics and a former student of Professor Drandakis.

GYLFI ZOEGA

Gylfi Zoega is a Senior Lecturer at Birkbeck College, University of London. He has a doctorate from Columbia University, New York, and has been employed at Birkbeck since 1993. He is an affiliate of the CEPR and a fellow of the Institute of Economic Studies, University of Iceland. His research is in the areas of macroeconomics and labor economics. In macroeconomics he has published papers on unemployment dynamics and the macroeconomics of natural resources. In labor economics, he has published papers on training and wage compression.

Preface

Emmanuel Drandakis, or simply Manos, as his friends and colleagues call him, retired from the Economics Department of the Athens University of Economics and Business in the summer of 2000. Thus he closed the circle of his academic career in the same place from where he began his professional journey more than four decades ago. As his curriculum vitae reveals, this long journey was full of accomplishments. After his graduation from the then Athens School of Economics and Business, he left in 1957 for postgraduate studies in the USA. Within five years he received an MA and a PhD in Economics from the University of Rochester and in 1962 he was appointed Assistant Professor in the Department of Economics of Yale University and the prestigious Cowles Foundation for Research in Economics. In the four years that he stayed in this position he managed to publish most of the papers for which he is known in the literature and established his reputation as a very promising young economist. Such were his prospects at the time that the University of Rochester attracted him back with an appointment to Associate Professor in Economics in 1966 and a quick promotion to Full Professor in 1968. In short, in just six years he reached at the top of the academic hierarchy in one of the best universities in the world. This was a feat few economists of Greek descent had accomplished until then and this is the reason why many students of economics in Greece considered him as a model of choice for their own professional lives.

Manos returned to the Athens School of Economics and Business Science in 1972. In the three decades since then, he educated several generations of Greek economists. With his standing in the profession he contributed significantly to the international reputation of our Economics Department. When nobody dared think of the possibility of starting programs of postgraduate studies, he was instrumental in 1978 in the establishment of the first MA program in Economics, a program that he worked hard to develop and establish in the next 22 years he stayed in the University. His success is evident from the fact that this has become since then the model for many of the postgraduate programs that have been established in Greece. So, even if it were not for the tradition to honor in some way those colleagues who distinguish themselves in service to the university and to our department, Manos would have deserved an exception. Not only for what he contributed to the well being of each one of us, but also because we all now feel his absence.

As a result we can hardly express how pleased and honored we felt when our Economics Department decided to assign to us the task of putting together the present volume. Besides his professional stature, Manos is a very likable person and we know that there were many friends and colleagues who would have loved to offer essays for this occasion. But we had only so many pages available from the publisher and to our regret we had to be selective. For this reason, while we apologize to all whose essays could not be included for lack of space, we express our sincere appreciation to the contributors for their support and collaboration.

When we sent out the invitation letters, we did not expect the essays to fall into any kind of uniform areas of economics. Judging from the research interests of the invitees we entertained only some slight hope that we might get certain loose concentrations in the theories of economic growth, general equilibrium, labor economics, and games. To our surprise, most of the contributed essays fall into these four areas and that is why we decided to arrange them accordingly.

Lastly, we would like to thank the publisher, Edward Elgar, for the trust he placed in our efforts; the Center of Economic Research of the Athens University of Economics and Business for a small grant which made it possible to typeset and deliver the manuscript in camera ready form; our assistants Maria Zanti and Irene Leftaki who saw the project to completion with impeccable professionalism; and Stelio Michailidi who prepared the volume in time despite the difficulties of having to streamline heavily mathematical texts from different word processors.

GEORGE C. BITROS and YANNIS KATSOULAKOS
    Athens

PART I

Economic Growth

1. Some Early Conferences on Growth Theory

Lionel McKenzie

The first conferences on the theory of economic growth known to me were these:

1. Activity Analysis in the Theory of Growth and Planning, held in Cambridge, England, at the University of Cambridge, July, 1963, sponsored by the International Economic Association, led by Edmond Malinvaud.
2. The Econometric Approach to Development Planning, held in Rome, Italy, at the Vatican, October, 1963.
3. Mathematical Models of Economic Growth, held in Rochester, New York, at the University of Rochester Department of Economics, July, 1964, sponsored by the Social Sciences Research Council, led by Lionel McKenzie.
4. Optimal Growth, held in Stanford, California, at the Center for Advanced Study in the Behavioral Sciences, July, 1965, sponsored by the Mathematical Social Sciences Board, led by Kenneth Arrow.

Of these conferences the first two were not confined to growth theory but also included papers concerned with economic planning, in the case of the Cambridge conference, and with econometrics and planning, in the case of the Vatican conference. I attended the conferences in Cambridge, Rochester, and Stanford, but I was not present at the Vatican. The papers presented to the Cambridge and Vatican conferences were published in volumes of proceedings which included reports of the discussions. These conferences were relatively short, lasting about one week, and papers prepared in advance were presented and discussed. The Rochester and Stanford conferences on the other hand were workshops. The Rochester conference lasted six weeks and the Stanford conference lasted at least four weeks. Thus much work was done at these conferences. Indeed some of the papers which were begun at the Rochester conference continued to be worked on at the Stanford conference and were published in a special issue of the *Review of Economic Studies*, January, 1967. However not all of the papers originating in these conferences were published in this issue and some papers were included there which did not originate in the conferences.

To understand the proceedings of the conferences we should consider some of the immediately preceding events. A summer institute lasting eight weeks was held at Stanford in 1957 on Applications of Mathematics in Social Science Research. It was sponsored by the Committee on Mathematical Training of Social Scientists of the Social Science Research Council. The workshops devoted to economics were one on Linear Economic Models led by Robert Dorfman and one on International Trade and Taxation led by me. Neither of these paid much attention to growth theory, although Dorfman devoted a few days to the von Neumann model. The Rochester conference was also held under the auspices of the SSRC and the design of the conference was in imitation of the 1957 SSRC conference. The Mathematical Social Science Board was in effect the successor of the SSRC committee and held four conferences subsequently devoted to economic growth, beginning with the Stanford conference in 1965.

Two events may have aroused the interest that led to these conferences. One was the publication in 1958 of the book by Dorfman, Samuelson, and Solow, or for short, DOSSO, entitled *Linear Programming and Economic Analysis*. This book contained studies in the context of Leontief type models, without utility functions, and gave a turnpike theorem for a two sector model without presenting a fully rigorous proof. Of course the book was known to Dorfman at the time of his 1957 workshop. It was the direct stimulus to my work and led me to prove a turnpike theorem for a simple Leontief model with variable coefficients. My paper was read to the Econometric Society in December, 1960. Unfortunately I submitted the paper to *Metroeconomica* which then stopped publication for an extended period following the death of the editor. After a wait of many months I resubmitted my paper to *The Review of Economic Studies* where it was published in 1963, well after the publication in 1961 of a paper by Morishima. His paper gave a similar turnpike theorem for a Leontief model with a finite number of activities. My paper was entirely independent of Morishima's but in view of the priority of his publication I acknowledged his paper in mine. *Metroeconomica* also published an earlier version some time later, without showing me a galley proof, despite my attempt to withdraw it.

The other stimulus was a trip by John Hicks to the United States and Japan in 1960. He had been struggling with the DOSSO turnpike theorem in the context of a simple Leontief model. Among the places he visited were Berkeley and Osaka. In Berkeley he spoke with Radner among others and at Osaka with Nikaido and Morishima. These conversations stimulated Morishima and Radner to write the papers that were published, together with one by Hicks, in *The Review of Economic Studies*, February, 1961. I believe the papers by Morishima, Radner, and me gave the first fully proved turnpike theorems for multisector models. They all proved Samuelson turnpikes in von Neumann type models where there were no utility functions, but where the objective was to achieve the largest terminal stocks in certain ratios over a fixed time period. This is the way the problem had been put by Dorfman, Samuelson, and Solow. You will note that these papers did not consider infinite programs and thus did not consider the existence of optimal programs over the infinite horizon. The existence of optimal programs for finite periods was not questioned.

It should also be mentioned that a symposium on production functions and economic growth appeared in the *Review of Economic Studies*, June, 1962, before the conferences occurred. This group of papers contained Arrow's paper on learning by doing and Joan Robinson's paper on the Golden Age that maximizes consumption per capita. Of course the Golden Age was also described by others in this same period. Arrow's paper has had a significant influence on the development of the New Growth Theory. However the important idea for the conferences we are concerned with was the Golden Age which turned out to provide a turnpike for a growth model which combined the Ramsey objective of maximizing a utility sum over an infinite horizon with the multisector production model of von Neumann. Finally, Uzawa published two papers on deterministic economic growth in the two sector neoclassical model in 1962 and 1963 in the *Review of Economic Studies* and a paper on optimal growth in this model in the same journal in 1964. These papers had an influence on both the Rochester and the Stanford conferences. Notice how many of the early papers were published in the *Review of Economic Studies*. The editorial advisors in those years were Nicholas Kaldor and Ursula Hicks and the chairman of the Economic Studies Board was Ian Little. John Hicks was in the background.

Altogether five papers on economic growth were presented to the Cambridge conference held in 1963. The papers labeled as studies on growth theory were given by Koopmans, Allais, and me. They were in the style of the von Neumann model. The paper of Koopmans was entitled Economic Growth at a Maximal Rate. It was largely concerned with presenting in diagrammatic form the turnpike theory for von Neumann models stemming from the papers of Radner, Morishima, and me. The von Neumann model is not easy to illustrate with diagrams since it involves at least two capital goods located at two different times, so the model is at least four dimensional. However by a clever device of representing inputs summing to one by their ratios and outputs by their quantities, Koopmans was able to reduce the dimensionality to three.

Then the diagram could be projected on the plane of the paper. With this diagram he was able to illustrate both the Radner turnpike theorem and the complications that I had found when the assumption of strict convexity of the production set near the von Neumann ray was not met. I am not sure how much of new material on von Neumann facets was available at the conference but it was mentioned in the published paper. Koopmans pointed out the lack of economic realism in the von Neumann model, even after the objective of maximal accumulation from given initial stocks had been introduced by DOSSO. He expected this deficiency to be overcome eventually.

My paper in the Cambridge conference was devoted to establishing a turn-pike theory in the maximal accumulation problem where all the possible complications were present, not only the lack of strict convexity of the production set but also the presence of subeconomies with different maximal growth rates depending on the set of goods to be accumulated. I also showed that the possibility existed that the supremum of the rates of growth for a certain subset of goods might not be attainable, but that this did not invalidate the turnpike theorem. Perhaps I made the mistake of burying my most interesting result in a lemma. My Lemma 11 asserts that the supremum of the rates at which the ith good appears in a feasible path of balanced growth is the growth rate of a von Neumann equilibrium. It is critical that the definition of the equilibrium contains the condition introduced by Kemeny, Morgenstern, and Thompson in 1956 that the output have a positive value at the equilibrium prices. My theorems were stated in terms of the von Neumann facet.

The paper of Allais gave a detailed exposition of his version of the Golden Rule or as he termed it the capitalistic optimum. In his statement the capitalistic optimum is realized at an interest rate equal to the rate of growth of primary income. Then the maximal sustainable output of consumption goods will be realized per unit of primary income, that is, income derived from labor and natural resources.

Radner's paper was classified as planning theory rather than growth theory but it is actually concerned with planning for optimal growth. Thus his discussion introduces a social utility function. He used Bellman's optimality principle to characterize the value function when certain boundedness conditions are satisfied. He is able to give methods for approximating optimal policies in models with infinite horizons by means of stationary policies. In the case of a linear logarithmic economy the procedure was made explicit. In the discussion Radner seems to have conjectured the result recently achieved by Kaganovich that in a closed model with a homothetic utility function and no joint production the von Neumann ray would be a turnpike. It is not clear that the printed paper included everything he presented orally in the conference.

The final paper on growth theory was given by Chakravarty. It is devoted to the question of a proper preference function over investment programs which are essentially of infinite or at least indeterminate length. There is a suggestion of maximizing over finite periods where the terminal objective is to reach a capital stock that will allow the maintenance of some chosen rate of growth for all future time. There was only one paper given in Cambridge which achieved fame. This was not on economic growth. It was the paper of Malinvaud on a planning procedure that became the inspiration for a literature on that subject.

The Vatican conference, which involved some of the same people as the Cambridge conference, was held only three months later. Just as in Cambridge many of the papers were not directly concerned with economic growth and *a fortiori* not with optimal economic growth. The papers of most interest to us were given by Koopmans, Malinvaud, Morishima, and Allais. Since I did not attend this conference, I will not discuss it in any detail. However, just as in the case of the Cambridge conference one paper, by Koopmans, achieved fame and, together with the 1966 paper of David Cass, inspired a literature on what came to be called the neoclassical model of optimal growth. In this model there is only one good which serves both as capital good and consumption good, the horizon is infinite, and utility may be either discounted or undiscounted. The novelty as compared with Ramsey is that population is growing, and the criterion that is adopted for optimality is the maximization of the sum of the utility of per capita consumption over the infinite horizon. In the one sector model they prove convergence of the capital stock to the stock of the Golden Age.

A paper to much the same effect was given by Malinvaud, but it was quickly overshadowed by the Koopmans paper. Malinvaud considered the case of utility which might be either discounted or not and proposed a criterion which is very close to the overtaking criterion proposed later by Atsumi and Weizsacker. He defines a program as optimal if there is no alternative program which achieves a larger utility sum (perhaps discounted) in some finite initial period and gives no less utility in any subsequent period. In the 1964 paper of Uzawa the model was extended to two goods, one a capital good and one a consumption good. He made use of the condition that the consumption sector is more capital intensive than the capital goods sector.

Morishima gave a paper describing a log linear model which bears some resemblance to Radner's paper in Cambridge but suffers from the weakness that the amount of consumption is set equal to the wage bill. Morishima says 'The purpose of this study is to extend the recent results of growth economics (especially the turnpike theorem) to a model with population growth and flexible consumption demands'. The most interesting feature is to relate the rate of growth of population to levels of consumption and therefore to the interest rate, since real wages are inversely related to the interest rate. The rate of growth of population must equal the interest rate in equilibrium. The consequence is that the turnpike is a balanced path whose growth rate is endogenous. The highest equilibrium growth rate also has the highest equilibrium consumption level. Under rather artificial assumptions on the determination of the wage rate Morishima shows that the highest equilibrium growth path is locally stable. He also considers the effect on the equilibrium balanced growth path of technical progress. For modern interests such a theory suffers from the fact that the optimal program is not likely to be relevant to a competitive equilibrium, since consumer tastes only affect current consumption, not the choice between consumption today and consumption later.

Pasinetti in his contribution is very critical of the students of balanced growth for failing to allow for technical progress and a biased change in consumer demand as income increases. However, so far as I can see, he does not model these factors, though he talks about linear models of Leontief or Sraffa type, and goes on at great length about the things that such models should allow for, and do not. Allais presents a paper of immense length, nearly three hundred pages, with about the same message as his Cambridge talk. I was impressed by his attempt to provide an empirical basis for the contention that physical capital saturation is present in all countries and the differences in income are explained by differences in social institutions and culture.

The Rochester conference in 1964 was organized by me. I was given this opportunity by Tjalling Koopmans through the Social Science Research Council. Tjalling was scheduled to run a conference, but some difficulty arose which Tjalling felt compromised his position and left him unable to continue. This conference was not a short meeting such as we now have, where only papers already prepared are presented, but a six week workshop where people collaborated and held discussions following presentations of preliminary research. It is my impression that the most successful interaction took place between Nikaido, Gale, and McFadden. Nikaido presented a working note at the very beginning on a Samuelson turnpike, that is, a turnpike in the simple Leontief model with a terminal objective. He introduces a feasible program of exogenous demand and proves a strong turnpike theorem. This is in the spirit of DOSSO. Very quickly Gale and then McFadden added short comments using a one sector model. McFadden showed that the necessary and sufficient condition for feasibility of an infinite consumption path c_t is that $\sum c_t / \rho^t$ be less or equal to the initial stock where ρ is the growth factor. Two weeks later he introduced a utility function and (he says on the suggestion of Mirrlees and Gale) defines a maximal path with an overtaking criterion and proves that in the one sector model the necessary and sufficient condition for the path to be maximal is that it satisfy a feasibility condition with equality and the condition that $\rho^t u'(c_t) = u'(c_0)$ for all t. Later, giving credit for assistance to Gale, Mirrlees, and Nikaido, he provided a note in which he proved for a continuous time version of this model that the necessary and sufficient condition for the existence of a maximal path is that the utility function be bounded above. This is as far as he got in the workshop, but this research was continued and eventuated in his contribution to the Symposium on Optimal Infinite Programmes in the *Review of Economic Studies*, January, 1967, where the results were extended to general linear models. He showed *inter alia* that good programs in Gale's sense exist if and only if the welfare function is bounded above.

Gale presented a discussion which clearly prefigured his classic paper in the 1967 Symposium, but I do not have a paper for him. Jim Mirrlees presented two papers. He offered an extension of the Ramsey argument to a two sector model like that used by Uzawa in his 1964 optimal growth paper. Mirrlees' innovation is to use a concave utility function in place of the quantity consumed of the consumption good. This allows him to avoid bang-bang solutions. He also attempted to extend the Ramsey model to the case of uncertainty but apparently met a snag he was unable to overcome. I tried to discover from him by E-mail what the difficulty was, but he could not recall, and had lost the paper. He was interested in determining the conditions under which the introduction of uncertainty would cause the level of consumption in the present period to decrease. In a two period model he derives the condition that the product of consumption and the marginal utility of consumption $u'(c)$ should be a convex function. This follows if $2u''(c) + cu'''(c)$ is nonnegative. His difficulty seemed to arise in attempting to extend this criterion to the infinite optimal path. The role of the third derivative has since been widely recognized in the literature on saving by individuals.

Inada, Tsukui, and Kurz also presented papers. Of course, everyone gave talks, including Hiroshi Atsumi, who was a Rochester graduate student, and Emmanuel Drandakis. They both published papers which must have benefited from their attendance in the conference. Atsumi on optimal growth in a two sector model with the overtaking criterion and an infinite horizon, with the first turnpike theorem where a method was used that could be generalized to n-sectors. His paper appeared in the *Review of Economic Studies*, April, 1965. Drandakis' paper, on a generalization of my turnpike theorem for a generalized Leontief model to an infinite horizon, appeared in *Econometrica*, April, 1966.

To continue with the account of papers presented in the conference. Inada gave papers concerned with the stability problem in the two sector model which Uzawa had described in his articles in the *Review of Economic Studies*, 1961 and 1963, mentioned above. Inada abandons the neoclassical assumption of a constant savings ratio by supposing that the savings ratio depends on social preferences given the production possibility frontier for consumption goods and capital goods. He requires this choice to satisfy the weak axiom of revealed preference. However the method of explicitly maximizing a utility sum is not used. In a second paper he deals with two sector models with irreversible investment where it is necessary to explain the distribution of investment between sectors. He assumes that only rental income is saved and gives a rule for the distribution of rental income in one sector over the two sectors.

Tsukui proved a Samuelson turnpike theorem in a similar way to my model in *Econometrica*, 1963. He assumes a finite number of processes and proves that the optimal path will actually enter the von Neumann facet after some time and will converge to the unique von Neumann equilibrium under his assumptions. Tsukui's paper appeared in the Symposium issue. Tsukui also applied this argument to a planning model of Japanese growth in *Econometrica*, April, 1966.

The papers offered by Kurz referred back to the article by Uzawa on optimal growth in two sector models. He replaced the objective of maximizing the discounted sum of per capita consumption by that of maximizing the discounted sum of the utility of per capita consumption over the infinite future. He proves stability of the Golden Age under the assumption that the consumption sector is relatively more capital intensive. It is worth noting the role of the papers of Uzawa on the two sector model in preparing the groundwork for several of these papers.

Gale and I did not present papers. However it is clear from the summary of the presentations that we began the research on the papers which eventually appeared in the Symposium issue in Gale's case and in the Hicks festschrift, *Value, Capital, and Growth*, 1968, in my case.

Koopmans and Chakravarty were visitors to the conference. Koopmans repeated his paper on the Concept of Economic Growth. I do not have enough information to report on the two talks of Chakravarty. John Chipman and Hugh Rose were also visitors.

The third conference in which I participated in this early period was held in Stanford at the Center for Advanced Research in Behavioral Sciences under the leadership of Kenneth Arrow. This conference was also a workshop which lasted about four weeks. I was the initiator of the workshop as the economics member on the Mathematical Social Sciences Board, or MSSB. The MSSB was administered by Preston Cutler of the Center, but the project was initiated by Duncan Luce and Patrick Suppes. National Science Foundation (NSF) provided the money over a period of years. I expected that the research begun at Rochester would be continued in the Stanford workshop and many of the participants in the Rochester workshop did in fact attend the Stanford workshop, in particular, Gale, McFadden, and me, who worked at completing the papers begun in Rochester and later published. Kurz and Mirrlees also attended both workshops, and Koopmans, who was a visitor in Rochester, came full time to Stanford. Newcomers were Arrow, Hahn, Radner, Srinavasan, Uzawa, and Weizsacker. Visitors were Bruno Horvat, Allen Manne, and Hans Vosgerau.

Gale and I presented models which had benefited from a year's further study. The summaries by the conference reporter were as follows:

> Gale presented a multisectoral activity model, including labor as an input. He defined utility as a function of activity levels and assumed strict concavity at a point. He then proved that any good program (not infinitely worse than the optimal stationary program) approaches the optimal stationary programs.

> McKenzie presented a model for considering asymptotic properties of optimal paths under general assumptions about technology. He proved convergence in two stages: convergence of the optimum path to a path in the von Neumann facet is proved, and convergence of paths lying in the facet.

Arrow discussed the problem of choosing a discount factor for use in the public sector. He supposes that if the capital market were perfect it would be appropriate simply to adopt the discount factor prevailing in the private sector. However he believes this to be unrealistic. He defines a natural rate of interest equal to the sum of a utility rate of interest plus the elasticity of marginal utility of consumption times the rate of increase of income. By use of both fiscal policy and monetary policy it may be possible to arrange to have the appropriate rate of investment in both public and private sectors.

Uzawa presented a long paper on optimum fiscal and monetary policy in a two sector model where one good is a private good available for either consumption or investment and the other good is a public consumption good. I do not have a copy of his paper but I recall that Arrow was impressed by the presence of 125 numbered equations. This corresponds exactly to his paper in a book of Adelman and Thorbecke, published in 1969.

McFadden presented a paper on the existence of efficiency prices. I only have the summary but it is clear that this was material included in his article for the Symposium issue of the *Review of Economic Studies*.

Von Weizsacker gave a paper which was intended to address the problem of uncertainty about the future. He suggested setting an accumulation target, for a long enough horizon, lying between 0 and the Golden Rule, and argues that this is sufficient to insure that the path chosen will be close to the optimal path. Of course, this is similar to the type of planning suggested by Tsukui for Japan.

Koopmans spoke on future directions of research. The summary of his talk follows:

> Koopmans discussed some troublesome aspects of optimal growth models: (1) crucial assumptions are not verifiable, (2) problems with infinite horizons, (3) distortions of the distant future due to uncertainty, (4) models cannot incorporate all available information, and (5) the need for clarification of the axiomatic basis for preference orderings.

Manne and Srinivasan gave a paper on the formation of the Fourth Indian Five Year Plan. It really amounted to showing that no effective planning was occurring partly because adequate information was not available, but also because the goal of improving the living standards of the poorest people was not taken seriously. Also there were no provisions for revising the plan when aspects of the plan did not materialize. Moreover the material balances are described only for the final year of the plan and not on an annual basis. One critical paragraph reads as follows:

> All who have read the various documents have been shocked by the vagueness, ambiguity and unwonted eloquence of these documents. One constantly feels that there is an attempt at soft-pedalling all the failures of the past, a shirking from a frank discussion of the fundamental issues of policy, and an attempt to promise everything to everybody, as in an election manifesto of a political party. The publication of a plan coincides with the tension-charged campaign for the general election in the country.

Mirrlees gave a paper discussing planning in mixed economies with 'surplus labor'. The summary reads

> He analyzed the significance for investment planning of sub-optimum levels of aggregate investment and of non-optimum distribution of consumption. The criterion function to be maximized is a function of consumption, with different accounting prices for the consumption of different groups, and of the value of savings, valued at an accounting price. Estimation of the accounting prices is then discussed.

This research foreshadows his joint brochure with Ian Little on criteria for choosing investment projects in developing countries.

Sheshinski and Burmeister gave a paper on the non-switching controversy treating the case of fixed capital. Also several technical papers were presented with, I assume, an educative purpose. Arrow spoke on duality in Hamilton-Pontryagin theory deriving the differential equations for p and k. Kalman talked about control theory, deriving the conditions for controllability, reachability, constructability, and observability. Finally at the start of the conference there were two round tables, one on population and growth led by Mirrlees and one on uncertainty and growth led by Radner.

In the round table on population and growth Mirrlees chose two criteria. If population is determined exogenously Mirrlees favored the criterion to maximize the integral over the planning period of population size times the utility of per capita consumption. However, if population is a policy variable he favored an objective equal to this integral divided by the integral of population size over the period. His periods were finite. The discussion was extensive. I was surprised to see the part I played in the discussion. I first suggested that the criterion should yield decisions on the rate of growth of population which would be made by free choice if individuals bore the full social cost of having children. I also gave a discussion of the consequence of purely selfish behavior by the present population. This might approximate maximizing the sum of per capita utility discounted by the rate of population growth, which we were tending to use in our models. I also suggested that continuity of generations might be enough to keep the optimal path under selfish optimization close to that under unselfish optimization. Koopmans noted that if population was a policy variable it would be necessary for a planner to choose a zero for the utility function.

In the round table on uncertainty and growth one might expect to find some signs of Radner's classic paper on asymptotic properties with uncertainty in *Econometrica*, 1972, but they are hard to find. However, he did present a recursive formulation of a competitive equilibrium. The summary reads

> Suppose we deal with a finite horizon T, and look at period $T - 1$. Then all decision-makers have (different amounts of) information on the past actions of others, and the only remaining uncertainty is about the environment. The extended Arrow-Debreu model applies, yielding a definition of efficiency. By considering periods $T - 2$, $T - 3$, ...1, we get recursive definitions of equilibrium and efficiency.

There is no sign of the definition of asymptotic properties of optimal paths in terms of distribution functions in the manner of Brock and Mirman. The only turnpike discussed is for a Samuelson type theorem where the analog to the von Neumann coefficient of expansion is the maximum over goods of the expectation of the log of the expansion factor over the period.

Further conferences on growth theory were held on the initiative of the MSSB in subsequent years. In 1967 a Symposium on Economic Growth led by Uzawa was held at the University of Chicago. This was a short conference in the style of our conference here. Papers delivered included Uzawa's paper on the Penrose effect, a paper by Foley and Sidrauski on Government Debt, Stabilization Policies, and Economic Growth, and a paper by Goldman on Successive Planning and Continual Planning Revision. In 1968 another short conference was held at Brown University on Money and Growth led, I believe, by Jerome Stein. Papers were read by S.C. Tsiang, Stein, Hahn, Levhari and Patinkin, Foley and Sidrauski, and others. In the summer of 1971 a conference on Uncertainty in Markets was held in Berkeley led by Roy Radner, which included some papers on optimal growth, in particular, the two papers of Brock and Mirman on growth with uncertainty, the undiscounted and the discounted cases. This is also where Bernt Stigum's papers on competitive equilibrium with infinitely many commodities appeared, papers later published in *Econometrica*, but overlooked by Mas-Colell in his survey of this subject in the *Handbook of Mathematical Economics*, Volume 4. Two further conferences were held in the period before 1976 sponsored by MSSB on the Hamiltonian approach to economic dynamics, at Squam Lake in New Hampshire, in facilities owned by Dartmouth College, and at the University of Pennsylvania. These were led by David Cass and Karl Shell.Their accomplishment will be described shortly.

Let us consider how the research program initiated by Ramsey and von Neumann and further defined by Samuelson and Solow, and Uzawa, was promoted by these conferences. The first conference, in Cambridge, is the only one that devoted much of its attention to the Samuelson turnpike theorem in the von Neumann model, although the inadequacy of the objective function was recognized. However there were two papers where the Ramsey objective of maximizing a sum of utilities over the infinite horizon was used. Radner uses the optimality principle of Bellman to approximate the State Valuation function, as he calls it, or simply the value function in the modern terminology. He proves that a stationary policy exists that comes arbitrarily close to generating an optimal path. Under his assumptions the finite initial utility sums are uniformly bounded. He considers both finite and infinite paths, and both open and closed, that is, von Neumann style, models. He gives an algorithm for finding the optimal policy in his linear logarithmic economy, which is a multisector model with a discount factor. Finally Chakravarty discussed the problem of preference functions for investment programs. But the turnpike problem for optimal paths was not addressed in a model with an infinite horizon and a utility function.

In the conference at the Vatican a stability problem was addressed by Morishima in a multisector model of the linear logarithmic type developed by Radner. However the decision to consume or to save was not solved by maximizing utility but by the arbitrary rule that workers only consume and capitalists only save. So his results do not refer to the modern turnpike notion. Of course, the papers of Koopmans and Malinvaud essentially solved the problem of the optimality turnpike for one sector deterministic models with exogenous population growth, strictly concave utility, and strictly convex technology, with or without a discount factor.

Finally in the Rochester conference the modern view of the existence of optimal paths and their asymptotic properties in multisector models was clearly recognized. Of course, the turnpike problem was only addressed in models without a discount factor. However between this conference and its successor at Stanford the problems which had been solved by Koopmans and Malinvaud at the Vatican were solved for the case of many goods and no discounting using the overtaking criterion. I suspect the overtaking criterion was brought to the Rochester conference by Mirrlees who had seen the paper of Weizsacker that was published in the *Review of Economic Studies*, April, 1965. Weizsacker used the one sector model. Thus in these four conferences we had passed from problems defined by the von Neumann closed model with a terminal objective to open Ramsey models with infinite horizons and the objective of maximizing the sum of utility over time. Several further major developments were to occur before reaching the current period in this research program, the proof of stability theorems in multisector models when discount factors are present and utility sums are maximized, the proof of these existence and stability theorems when uncertainty is present, the establishment of the relation of the theorems in optimality models to the properties of competitive equilibria over time, and determining conditions that lead to complex optimal paths. Most recently the so-called New Economic Growth has appeared where there is unbounded growth in the manner of von Neumann models and turnpike theorems like the Samuelson turnpike are proved, but with infinite paths and Ramsey objectives rather than terminal objectives.

Turnpike theorems in multisector models with more than two sectors and discount factors were first reported in the conference held at Squam Lake. The critical papers were given by José Scheinkman, Cass and Shell, and William Brock and Scheinkman. They established the turnpike theorem for models satisfying some strict convexity conditions, that is, no nontrivial von Neumann facets were allowed. These papers were published in a symposium issue of the *Journal of Economic Theory*, February, 1976.

The problem of proving a turnpike theorem with uncertainty was addressed

by Leonard Mirman and William Brock and reported to the Berkeley conference. Their papers were published in the *Journal of Economic Theory*, 1972,
and the *International Economic Review*, October, 1973. The key innovation
was to describe the turnpike in the one sector case as a distribution function
of capital stocks rather than as a particular capital stock. They first dealt with
the discounted case and then in the later paper with the undiscounted case.
The discounted case was extended to the multisector case in 1978 by Brock
and Majumdar.

These were the researches in which the conference series begun by the
SSRC and continued by the MSSB were important. However, one further
development in this research program was made in which these conferences
were not active. This is to establish the relevance of the turnpike in optimal
growth models for asymptotic competitive equilibrium. The problem was addressed by Robert Becker and by Truman Bewley. Important further results
were reached by Makoto Yano. This completes the story for the model that
marries the Ramsey objective with the von Neumann model.

However, in the tradition of the two sector model an Endogenous or New
Growth Theory was initiated by Paul Romer and Robert Lucas, following in
the footsteps of Uzawa. This has served to re-ignite the interest of the wider
public in the subject of growth economics. Finally the study of chaotic optimal paths in one sector models was begun by Michele Boldrin and others,
carried further by Mitra, Yano, Nishimura, and Majumdar and others. The
literature is surveyed by Boldrin and Woodford in the *Journal of Monetary
Economics* in 1990. Perhaps this brings us up to the papers that are being
presented at this conference.

*This paper was presented to a conference on Complex Economic Systems
held at Meiji Gakuin University in June 1998. It was published in the *Meiji
Gakuin Review*, No. 113 (1998). There are slight changes in this version.

REFERENCES

Allais, Maurice (1965), 'The Role of Capital in Economic Development', in *The
    Econometric Approach to Development Planning*, Pontificae Academiae
    Scientiarum Scripta Varia No. 28. North Holland, Amsterdam.
Allais, Maurice (1967), 'Some Analytical and Practical Aspects on the Theory of
    Capital', in *Activity Analysis in the Theory of Growth and Planning*, edited by E.
    Malinvaud and M.O.L. Bacharach, 43-63. Macmillan, London.
Arrow, Kenneth J. (1962), 'The Economic Implications of Learning by Doing', *Re-
    view of Economic Studies*, **29** (3), 155-74.

Atsumi, Hiroshi (1965), 'Neoclassical Growth and the Efficient Program of Capital Accumulation', *Review of Economic Studies*, **32**, 127-36.

Becker, Robert A. (1980) 'On the Long-run Steady State in a Simple Dynamic Model of Equilibrium with Heterogeneous Households', *Quarterly Journal of Economics*, **94**, 375-82.

Bewley, Truman. F. (1982), 'An Integration of Equilibrium Theory and Turnpike Theory', *Journal of Mathematical Economics*, **10**, 233-68.

Boldrin, Michele and Michael Woodford (1990), 'Equilibrium in Models Displaying Fluctuations and Chaos', in *Economic Complexity: Chaos, Sunspots, Bubbles, and Nonlinearity*, ed. by W. A. Barnett, J. Geweke, and K. Shell, Cambridge University Press, Cambridge, England.

Brock, William A., and Mukul Majumdar, (1978), 'Global Asymptotic Stability Results for Multisector Models of Optimal Growth with Uncertainty When Future Utilities Are Discounted', *Journal of Economic Theory*, **18**, 225-43.

Brock, William A., and Leonard J. Mirman (1972), 'Optimal Economic Growth and Uncertainty: the Discounted Case', *Journal of Economic Theory*, **4**, 479-513.

Brock, William A. and Jose Scheinkman (1976), 'The Global Asymptotic Stability of Optimal Control with Applications to the Theory of Economic Growth', *Journal of Economic Theory*, **12**, 164-90.

Cass, David, and Karl Shell (1976), 'The Structure and Stability of Competitive Dynamical Systems', *Journal of Economic Theory*, **12**, 31-70.

Chakravarty, Sukhavoy (1967), in *Activity Analysis in the Theory of Growth and Planning*, edited by E. Malinvaud and M.O.L. Bacharach, 43-63. Macmillan, London.

Dorfman, Robert, Paul A. Samuelson, and Robert Solow (1958), *Linear Programming and Economic Analysis*, McGraw-Hill, New York.

Hicks, John R. (1961), 'The Story of a Mare's Nest', *Review of Economic Studies*, (2), 77-88.

Kaganovich, Michael (forthcoming), 'Sustained Endogenous Growth with Decreasing Returns and Heterogeneous Capital', *Journal of Economic Dynamics and Control*.

Kemeny, John G., Oskar Morgenstern, and Gerald L. Thompson (1956), 'A Generalization of the von Neumann Model of an Expanding Economy', *Econometrica*, **24**, 115-35.

Koopmans, Tjalling C. (1960), 'Stationary Ordinal Utility and Time Perspective', *Econometrica*, **28**, 297-309.

Koopmans, Tjalling C. (1965), 'The Concept of Optimal Economic Growth', in *The Econometric Approach to Development Planning*, Pontificae Academiae Scientiarum Scripta Varia No. 28., North Holland, Amsterdam.

Lucas, Robert E., Jr. (1988), 'On the Mechanics of Economic Development', *Journal of Monetary Economics*, **22**, 3-42.

Malinvaud, Edmond (1965), 'Croissances Optimales dans un Modele Macroeconomique', in *The Econometric Approach to Development Planning*, Pontificae Academiae Scientiarum Scripta Varia No. 28, North Holland, Amsterdam.

Malinvaud, Edmond (1967), 'Decentralized Procedures for Planning, in *Activity Analysis in the Theory of Growth and Planning*, edited by E. Malinvaud and M.O.L. Bacharach, 43-63, Macmillan, London.

McFadden, Daniel (1967), 'The Evaluation of Development Programmes', *Review of Economic Studies*, **34**, 25-51.

McKenzie, Lionel W. (1963), 'Turnpike Theorem of Morishima', *Review of Economic Studies*, **30**, 169-76.

McKenzie, Lionel W. (1963), 'Turnpike Theorems for a Generalized Leontief Model', *Econometrica*, **31**, 165-80.

McKenzie, Lionel W. (1967), 'Maximal Paths in the von Neumann Model', in *Activity Analysis in the Theory of Growth and Planning*, edited by E. Malinvaud and M.O.L. Bacharach, 43-63, Macmillan, London.

McKenzie, Lionel W. (1968), 'Accumulation Programs of Maximum Utility and the von Neumann Facet', *Value, Capital, and Growth*, edited by J. N. Wolfe, 353-83, Edinburgh University Press, Edinburgh.

Morishima, Michio (1961), 'Proof of a Turnpike Theorem: The No Joint Production Case', *Review of Economic Studies*, **28**, 89-97.

Morishima, Michio (1965), 'Balanced Growth and Technical Progress in a Log-linear Multisectoral Economy', in *The Econometric Approach to Development Planning*, Pontificae Academiae Scientiarum Scripta Varia No. 28, Amsterdam: North Holland, 1965.

Pasinetti, L. L. (1965), 'A New Theoretical Approach to the Problems of Economic Growth', in *The Econometric Approach to Development Planning*, Pontificae Academiae Scientiarum Scripta Varia No. 28, North Holland, Amsterdam.

Radner, Roy (1961), 'Paths of Economic Growth that Are Optimal with Regard Only to Final States', *Review of Economic Studies*, **28**, 98-104.

Radner, Roy (1967), 'Dynamic Programming of Economic Growth', in *Activity Analysis in the Theory of Growth and Planning*, edited by E. Malinvaud and M.O.L. Bacharach, 43-63, Macmillan, London.

Radner, Roy (1972), 'Existence of Equilibrium of Plans, Prices, and Price Expectations in a Sequence of Markets', *Econometrica*, **40**, 289-304.

Ramsey, Frank (1928), 'A Mathematical Theory of Savings', *Economic Journal*, **38**, 543-59.

Robinson, Joan (1962), 'A Neo-Classical Theorem', *Review of Economic Studies*, **29** (3), 219-26.

Romer, Paul M. (1986), 'Increasing Returns and Long-Run Growth', *Journal of Political Economy*, **94** (5), 1002-37.

Scheinkman, Jose (1976), 'On Optimal Steady States of n-Sector Growth Models when Utility Is Discounted', *Journal of Economic Theory*, **12**, 11-70.30

Uzawa, Hirofumi (1962), 'On a Two-Sector Model of Economic Growth I', *Review of Economic Studies*, **29**, 40-47.

Uzawa, Hirofumi (1963), 'On a Two-Sector Model of Economic Growth II', *Review of Economic Studies*, **30**, 40-47.

Uzawa, Hirofumi (1964), 'Optimal Growth in a Two-Sector Model of Economic Growth', *Review of Economic Studies*, **31**, 1-24.

Uzawa, Hirofumi (1968), 'The Penrose Effect and Optimum Growth', *Economic Studies Quarterly*, **19**, 1-14.

Uzawa, Hirofumi (1969), 'Optimum Fiscal Policy in an Aggregative Model of Economic Growth', in *The Theory and Design of Economic Development*, 113-39, Baltimore, The Johns Hopkins Press.

Weizsacker, C. C. von (1965), 'Existence of Optimal Programs of Accumulation for an Infinite Time Horizon, *Review of Economic Studies*, **32**, 85-104.

Yano, Makoto (1984), 'The Turnpike of Dynamic General Equilibrium Paths and Its Insensitivity to Initial Conditions', *Journal of Mathematical Economics*, **13**, 235-54.

2. Discounting and the Growth of Net National Product[*]

Amitava Bose[§], Swapan Dasgupta[†] and Tapan Mitra[‡]

1. INTRODUCTION

National Income is a normative concept. Moreover, the concept belongs to economic dynamics and not statics, for it evaluates the potential of current production to contribute to social welfare over time.[1] While this much is taken for granted, there have been relatively few attempts to establish rigorously the precise relation between current production and future welfare. The notable exception to this is the work of Weitzman (1976). Using a dynamic optimization framework, Weitzman showed that when future utilities are discounted, Net National Product at any date along an optimal path, measures the annuity equivalent of the social welfare of the economy, starting from that date.[2]

The purpose of this paper is to extend the scope of Weitzman's analysis to cover the case of undiscounted utilities. We then demonstrate the following: discounting future utilities is a necessary condition for growth of Net National Product, as defined by Weitzman (1976). We establish this by showing that when future utilities are *not* discounted, Net National Product is constant over time along every competitive path.[3]

This observation can be seen as an interpretation of the *Keynes-Ramsey rule* of optimal saving (see Ramsey (1928), Koopmans (1965)), extended from the set of 'optimal paths' for which it was originally derived, to the larger set

* This paper is dedicated, with respect, to Professor Emmanuel Drandakis.
§ Indian Institute of Management, Joka, Calcutta 700027, India; Phone: (91) 33 467-8310; Fax: (91) 33 467-8307; E-mail address: abose@iimcal.ac.in
† Department of Economics, Dalhousie University, Halifax, Nova Scotia, Canada, B3H 3J5; Phone: 902-494-2026; Fax: 902-494-6917; E-mail address: dasgupta@is.dal.ca
‡ Department of Economics, Cornell University, Ithaca, NY 14853, USA; Phone:(607) 255-4062; Fax:(607) 255-2818; E-mail address: tm19@cornell.edu

of 'competitive paths'. Equivalently, our observation is a reinterpretation of
the result that the *Hamiltonian* is constant along a competitive path when
future utilities are not discounted (see Samuelson (1965), Dasgupta (1969)):

$$H(k(t), p(t)) = u(k(t), \dot{k}(t)) + p(t)\dot{k}(t) = \text{constant} \qquad (1.1)$$

where k is the vector of capital goods and p the vector of prices of investment
goods (in terms of current utility). The original Keynes-Ramsey rule follows
from (1.1) by noting that (a) on the 'bliss' path ('golden rule' path), we have
$\dot{k}(t) = 0$, so on paths converging to the bliss point, the Hamiltonian is constant at the bliss level of utility; and (b) the utility price of an investment good
is the current marginal disutility of that investment. In what follows, by the
Keynes-Ramsey rule, we shall mean the constancy over time of the Hamiltonian.

In Weitzman (1976), Net National Product (or NNP) is defined as the value
of the Hamiltonian along a competitive path.[4] We accept this definition since
it is our view also that NNP seeks to capture welfare *potential* and competitive conditions, being necessary conditions for optimality, are indicative of
potentiality. However, Weitzman uses a positive discount rate and so in his
framework NNP is not constant. As noted in Dasgupta and Mitra (2001),
Weitzman's result is actually a reinterpretation of the Bellman equation of
optimality in dynamic programming:

$$V'(k(t))\dot{k}(t) = u(k(t), \dot{k}(t)) - rV(k(t)) \qquad (1.2)$$

where V is the value function associated with the dynamic optimization problem, and therefore satisfies:

$$V(k(t)) = \int_t^\infty e^{-r(s-t)} u(k(s), \dot{k}(s)) ds = Max \int_t^\infty e^{-r(s-t)} u(k'(s), \dot{k}'(s)) ds \qquad (1.3)$$

and the maximization in (1.3) is understood to be over all feasible paths
$(k'(s), \dot{k}'(s))$ with $k'(t) = k(t)$. Weitzman (1976) established that for each t:

$$Y(t) = r \int_t^\infty e^{-r(s-t)} u(k(s), \dot{k}(s)) ds \qquad (1.4)$$

where $Y(t)$ is NNP at time t, defined as $H(k(t), p(t))$. His result (1.4), which
we will refer to as *Weitzman's Rule*, can be seen as following from (1.2) and
(1.3), by recognizing that along optimal paths, the derivative of the value

function, $V'(k(t))$, equals the (shadow) price of investment, $p(t)$.

The validity of the Keynes-Ramsey Rule is demonstrated in the literature, in closely related one-sector models of optimal growth, by Ramsey (1928) and Koopmans (1965). The result that the Hamiltonian is constant along an optimal path, is established by Samuelson (1965) in a one-sector model, and by Dasgupta (1969) in a two-sector model with non-shiftable capital. On the other hand, the result of Weitzman, referred to above, is a perfectly general one, holding for a model of capital accumulation with heterogeneous capital goods (some of which can be non-renewable resources). Thus, it is important to demonstrate the Keynes-Ramsey Rule (under a zero discount rate) for a comparably general model of inter-temporal allocation. This is a fairly straight-forward task.

Ensuring the existence of an optimal path (in the zero discount rate case) is a well-known difficult problem. But, it does not have a direct bearing on the point we wish to make. To emphasize this, we will find it more convenient to establish that the Keynes-Ramsey rule holds for any 'competitive path', whether optimal or not. In this respect, our result for the undiscounted case is actually simpler than the corresponding result for the discounted case, since the valid-ity of Weitzman's Rule along a competitive path requires that (see Dasgupta and Mitra (1999)) an *investment value transversality condition* holds on the path.

The demonstration of the Keynes-Ramsey Rule for optimal paths, in more specific models, as discussed above, relies on the (myopic) competitive prop-erties of an optimal path, and not on its asymptotic (transversality) behavior. Thus, our approach is an extension of the method already employed in the literature, but it clarifies the essential argument involved in arriving at the result. If an optimal path does exist, then it will turn out to be competitive in our sense (see, for example, Takekuma (1982)) and so it will satisfy the Keynes-Ramsey Rule.

2. THE FRAMEWORK

Consider a general framework of capital accumulation along the lines of Cass and Shell (1976). We assume that population and technology are stationary, and individuals at each date are identical in all respects (so one can think in terms of a representative agent and ignore distribution considerations).

Denote by $k_i \geq 0$ the stock of the i th capital good, where $i = 1, \ldots, n$ and by z_i the investment flow, net of depreciation, of the i th capital good. Denote the vectors $(k_1, \ldots, k_n)$ and $(z_1, \ldots, z_n)$ by k and z respectively. The *technology set*, denoted by Λ, is a set of pairs (z, k) in $R^n \times R^n_+$. By a typical point (z, k) of Λ we understand that from capital input stock k, it is technologically feasible to obtain the flows of net investment, z. The *utility function* is denoted by a function $u: \Lambda \to R$. We will make the following assumptions[5] on Λ and u:

(A.1) Λ is closed and convex; for each $k \geq 0$, there is a z in R^n such that $(z, k) \in \Lambda$.

(A.2) Given any number $\xi > 0$, there is a number $\eta > 0$ such that $(z, k) \in \Lambda$, and $\|k\| \leq \xi$ implies $|u(z, k)| \leq \eta$ and $\|z\| \leq \eta$.

(A.3) u is continuous on Λ and twice continuously differentiable in the interior of Λ.

(A.4) $u(z, k) \geq 0$ for $(z, k) \in \Lambda$; u is non-increasing in z.

(A.5) u is a concave function on Λ; for each $k \gg 0$, $u(z, k)$ is a strictly concave function of z; in the interior of Λ, the matrix of second-order partials of u with respect to z, $\left[\partial_u^2 (z, k) / \partial z^2 \right]$ is negative definite.

For each $k \geq 0$, defining the set $\Lambda(k) \equiv \left\{ z : (z, k) \in \Lambda \right\}$, we note that $\Lambda(k)$ is a non-empty, compact and convex subset of R^n.

A *path* from initial stock K in R^n_+ is a pair of functions $(z(\bullet), k(\bullet))$, where $z(\bullet): [0, \infty) \to R^n$ and $k(\bullet): [0, \infty) \to R^n_+$, such that $k(\bullet)$ is absolutely continuous and[6]

$$(z(t), k(t)) \in \Lambda \text{ for } t \geq 0, \text{ a.e.; } \dot{k}(t) = z(t) \text{ for } t \geq 0, \text{ a.e.; and, } k(0) = K \quad (2.1)$$

Denote by $\Im(K)$ the set of paths from initial stock K. We will assume:

(A.6) For each K in R^n_+, the set $\Im(K)$ is non-empty.

A path $(z(t), k(t))$ from K is called *optimal* [7] if for every path $(z'(t), k'(t))$ from K, we have:

$$\liminf_{T \to \infty} \int_0^T \left[u(z'(t), k'(t)) - u(z(t), k(t)) \right] dt \leq 0 \quad (2.2)$$

3. COMPETITIVE PATHS AND THE KEYNES-RAMSEY RULE

We will first elaborate on what we mean by a time path of quantities and prices, which evolve along a competitive path. Then, we will show that along such a path, the Keynes-Ramsey rule must hold.

Let $p = (p_1, \ldots, p_n)$ denote the prices of the investment goods. Define a function, $H : R^n_+ \times R^n$

$$H(k, p) = \begin{matrix} Max \\ subject\ to \end{matrix} \left. \begin{matrix} [u(z,k) + pz] \\ (z,k) \in \Lambda \end{matrix} \right\} \tag{3.1}$$

As noted above in Section 2, for each k in R^n_+, $\Lambda(k)$ is non-empty and compact and, therefore, $H(k, p)$ is well-defined. Further, H is convex in p, and (since Λ is convex) concave in k.

By (A.5), for $k >> 0$, $u(z,k)$ is strictly concave in z and, therefore, there is a unique maximizing choice of investment, which solves (7). We can write this maximizing choice of z as a function $g(k, p)$, where $g : R^n_+ \times R^n \to R^n$ satisfies:

$$H(k, p) = u(g(k, p), k) + p\,g(k, p) \text{ and } (g(k, p), k) \in \Lambda \tag{3.2}$$

Remark 3.1: For (k^0, p^0) such that $k^0 >> 0$ and $(g(k^0, p^0), k^0)$ is in the interior of Λ,

(i) $p^0 + \left[\partial u(g(k^0, p^0), k^0) / \partial z \right] = 0$

(ii) By (A.3), the function $F(k, p, z) \equiv p + \left[\partial u(z, k) / \partial z \right]$ is defined in an open neighborhood around $(k^0, p^0, g(k^0, p^0))$, is continuously differentiable, and its derivative matrix with respect to z is non-singular. Thus, by the implicit function theorem, $g(k, p)$ is continuously differentiable with respect to (k, p) in an open neighborhood N of (k^0, p^0) and the range of $(g(k, p), k)$ for (k, p) in N, is an open subset of Λ. It follows that in this neighborhood N of (k^0, p^0), H is continuously differentiable, and by the envelope theorem,

$$\left[\partial H(k, p) / \partial p \right] = g(k, p) \text{ and } \left[\partial H(k, p) / \partial k \right] = \left[\partial u(g(k, p), k) / \partial k \right]$$

A *competitive path* is a path $(z(t), k(t))$ with associated prices, denoted by absolutely continuous functions of time $(p_1(t),\ldots,p_n(t)) \equiv (p(t))$, with $p(t) \geq 0$ for $t \geq 0$, a.e., satisfying the following two conditions:

$$u(z(t),k(t)) + p(t)z(t) = H(k(t),p(t)) \text{ for } t \geq 0, \text{ a.e.} \qquad (3.3)$$

$$\dot{p}(t) = -\left[\partial H(k(t),p(t))/\partial k\right] \text{ for } t \geq 0, \text{ a.e.} \qquad (3.4)$$

Here, $p(t)$ is the vector of (present value = current value) prices of the investment goods, prevailing along a competitive path at date t. Use the notation $(z(t),k(t),p(t))$ to denote a competitive path with its associated prices. Along a competitive path, for $t \geq 0$, denote $H(k(t),p(t))$ by $Y(t)$; that is:

$$Y(t) \equiv H\left(k(t),p(t)\right) \text{ for } t \geq 0 \qquad (3.5)$$

Interpreting utility as output with present value price of unity, (3.3) says that the maximum value of output achievable from capital stocks $k(t)$ at the prices $p(t)$, $\left[\text{that is, } H(k(t),p(t))\right]$ is realized along a competitive path:

$$Y(t) = u(z(t),k(t)) + p(t)z(t) \text{ for } t \geq 0, \text{ a.e.} \qquad (3.6)$$

Equation (3.4) says that asset markets are in equilibrium; that is, no gains can be made by pure arbitrage (see Dorfman, Samuelson and Solow (1958), Weitzman (1976)).

We are now in a position to state and prove the principal result of the paper: competitive paths satisfy the Keynes-Ramsey Rule in the sense that the Hamiltonian is constant over time along the path.

If $(z(\bullet),k(\bullet))$ is a path from K in R_+^n, we shall say that it is *interior* if (i) $(z(t),k(t))$ is in the interior of Λ for $t \geq 0$, a.e., and (ii) $k(t) \gg 0$ for $t \geq 0$.

Theorem 1: If $(z(t),k(t),p(t))$ is an interior competitive path from K in R_{++}^n, then

(i) the function $Y(t)$, defined in (3.5), is an absolutely continuous function of t; and,

(ii) $\dot{Y}(t) = 0$ for $t \geq 0$, a.e.

Proof: Before coming to the proof, note that assertion (ii) of the theorem is the Keynes-Ramsey Rule. Assertion (i) is a technical result which is stated because it ensures that the function $Y(t)$ is differentiable for $t \geq 0$, a.e., and enables us to *state* assertion (ii).

The proof of assertion (i) can be obtained exactly along the lines of Dasgupta and Mitra (1999), and is therefore omitted. We turn now to the proof of assertion (ii).

Since $g(k, p)$ solves the problem (3.1) for $k \gg 0$, we can use condition (3.3) for a competitive path to obtain:

$$g(k(t), p(t)) = z(t) \text{ for } t \geq 0, \text{ a.e.} \tag{3.7}$$

Since the competitive path is interior, $(g(k(t), p(t)), k(t))$ is in the interior of Λ. By (i) above, $Y(t)$ is absolutely continuous, and so for $t \geq 0$, a.e., $Y(t)$ is differentiable. Also, $k(t), p(t)$ are differentiable, and by Remark 3.1, $H(k, p)$ is continuously differentiable at $(k(t), p(t))$. Thus, by differentiating (3.5), and using the formulae derived in Remark 3.1,

$$\dot{Y}(t) = \left[\partial H(k(t), p(t))/\partial k\right]\dot{k}(t) + \left[\partial H(k(t), p(t))/\partial k\right]\dot{p}(t)$$

$$= \left[\partial H(k(t), p(t))/\partial k\right]\dot{k}(t) + g(k(t), p(t))\dot{p}(t) \text{ for } t \geq 0, \text{ a.e.}$$

Thus, we obtain:

$$\dot{Y}(t) = \left[\partial H(k(t), p(t))/\partial k\right]\dot{k}(t) + \dot{k}(t)\,\dot{p}(t) \text{ for } t \geq 0, \text{ a.e.} \tag{3.8}$$

Combining condition (3.4) for a competitive path with (3.8), we have:

$$\dot{Y}(t) = 0 \text{ for } t \geq 0, \text{ a.e.} \tag{3.9}$$

which establishes (ii).

4. MAXIMUM SUSTAINABLE UTILITY AND NET NATIONAL PRODUCT

In this section, we use the Keynes-Ramsey rule to examine the relationship between maximum sustainable utility and the net national product of a dynamic economy. For this purpose, our concept of net national product will be the same as in Weitzman (1976), and we will be concerned about this magnitude along an *optimal* path, when future utilities are *not* discounted.

In order to make our discussion precise, we will conduct our analysis entirely in terms of a one sector neoclassical model. Briefly, the ingredients of this well-known model are a gross production function, $G: R_+ \rightarrow R_+$, a constant exponential rate of depreciation, $\delta \in (0,\infty)$ and a welfare function, $w: R_+ \to R_+$. A net output function, f, can be defined as $f(k) = G(k) - \delta k$ for $k \in R_+$. Along a path $(z(t), k(t))$, we have consumption at date t, denoted by $c(t)$, and defined by $c(t) = f(k(t)) - z(t)$ for $t \in [0,\infty)$. Utility is obtained from consumption, so that $u(z(t), k(t)) = w(f(k(t)) - z(t))$ for $t \in [0,\infty)$. We assume that G, w, and δ satisfy the following standard properties:

(N.1) $G(0) = 0$; G *is continuous on* R_+ and twice continuously differentiable on R_{++}; for $k > 0$, $G'(k) > 0$ and $G''(k) \le 0$; there is $k' > 0$ such that for $k \in (0, k']$, $G'(k) > \delta$; there is $k'' > 0$ such that for $k \in [k'', \infty)$, $G'(k) < \delta$.

(N.2) $w(0) = 0$; w is continuous and concave on R_+; w is twice continuously differentiable on R_{++}; $w'(c) > 0$ and $w''(c) < 0$ for all $c > 0$; $w'(c) \to \infty$ as $c \to 0$. Under these assumptions, it can be verified easily that this one-sector neoclassical model is a special case of the general framework described in Section 2.

In this one-sector model, it is known that an optimal path $(z(t), k(t))$ exists from every initial stock, $K > 0$, and is competitive (see Koopmans (1965)). Thus, by Theorem 1 of Section 3, it must satisfy the property that the Hamiltonian is constant along the path, as noted in (1.1). But, because we are now dealing with an *optimal* path, not just a competitive one, we can say more. It is known that $k(t) \to k^*$ as $t \to \infty$, so that $z(t) \to 0$ and $c(t) \to c^* \equiv f(k^*)$, where k^* is the golden-rule capital stock (and c^* is the corresponding golden-rule consumption). The prices $p(t)$ associated with the program satisfy $p(t) = w'(c(t))$, so that $p(t) \to w'(c^*)$ as $t \to \infty$. Using this in (1.1), we see that the *constant value of the Hamiltonian on an optimal path must be equal to the golden-rule utility level:*

$$H(k(t), p(t)) = u(k(t), \dot{k}(t)) + p(t)\dot{k}(t) = u(0, k^*) = w(c^*) \qquad (4.1)$$

This is, in fact, the original form of the Keynes-Ramsey Rule.

We now turn to a discussion of net national product along an optimal path of this one-sector economy, and its relation to the maximum utility level that it can sustain. Weitzman (1976, p.159) observes that 'a standard welfare interpretation of NNP is that it is the largest permanently maintainable value of consumption'. (Note that Weitzman's 'consumption' is 'utility' in our terminology; see endnote 4). He explains that this conventional wisdom is, in general, flawed and provides a diagram (due to Samuelson (1961)) to illustrate why this is so.

In the context of the one-sector model discussed above, we would like to point out that for a class of initial capital stocks (namely, those at or above the golden-rule capital stock), NNP along an optimal path (in the undiscounted case) measures *precisely* the maximum sustainable utility of the economy. This is because NNP along any optimal path equals golden-rule utility (by (4.1) above). And, from every initial stock at or above the golden-rule stock, the maximum sustainable utility level is also the golden-rule utility level. This last statement can be verified by checking two elementary facts: (a) any higher utility level than the golden-rule utility level *cannot* be maintained forever, and (b) the constant golden-rule utility level *can* be maintained forever.

Our observation should not be taken as defending conventional wisdom, which is clearly incorrect in general, but as a clarification of its relation to Weitzman's contribution. To see the flaw in conventional wisdom in terms of our one-sector model, note that NNP along an optimal path, starting from an initial stock, K, (strictly) below the golden-rule stock, equals golden-rule utility, by (4.1) above. But, the maximum sustainable utility level starting from such an initial stock, K, is precisely $w(f(K))$, which is (strictly) less than the golden-rule utility level of $u(0,k^*) = w(f(k^*)) = w(c^*)$.

The above comments prompt us to examine a bit more closely Weitzman's (1976, p.160) observation that conventional wisdom is valid only if the transformation between z and $u(z, k)$ is linear. Clearly, there is no such linearity in our one-sector model, and yet conventional wisdom does give the right answer for a class of optimal paths. The mystery disappears when one recognizes that Weitzman identifies paths of maximum sustainable utility with paths having stationary capital stocks ($z = 0$). While this is correct for initial stocks below the golden-rule stock, it is not so for initial stocks strictly above the golden-rule stock. In the latter case, paths of maximum sustainable utility will necessarily disinvest ($z(t) < 0$) and approach (or reach) the golden-rule capital stock over time.

It appears, then, that for a complete analysis of the difference between NNP and maximum sustainable utility in our one-sector model, one needs to extend the Samuelson-Weitzman diagram appropriately. We provide this extension in Figure 1. Following Samuelson-Weitzman, the diagram depicts transformation curves between investment (z) and utility ($u(z,k)$), given k.

First consider the transformation curve when the capital stock equals the golden-rule capital stock, k^*. Then, corresponding to $z^* = 0$, we have golden-rule utility, $u(0,k^*)$, depicted by OA. The (negative of the) slope of the tangent to the transformation curve at A denotes the price, p^*, of the investment good (in terms of utility), which equals $w'(c^*)$, where c^* is golden-rule consumption. Note that $NPP = u(0,k^*) + p^*z^* = u(0,k^*)$, so Weitzman's measure of NNP coincides with the maximum sustainable utility.

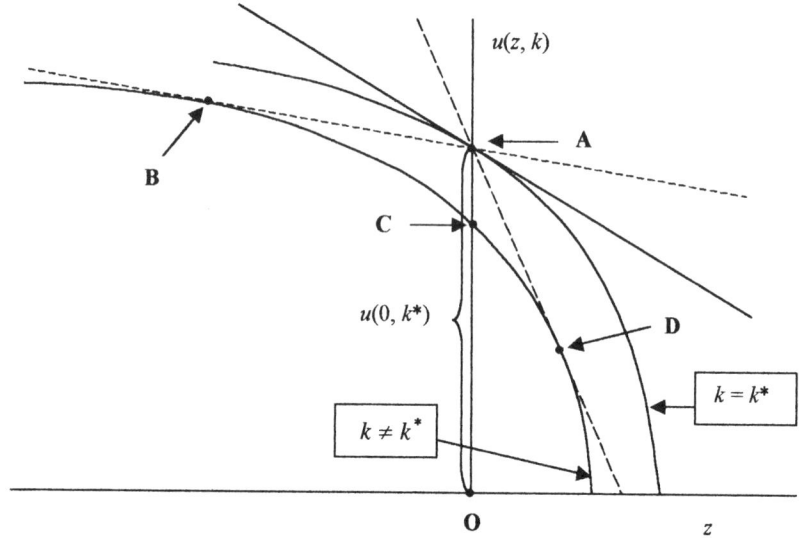

Figure 1

Now, consider a transformation curve corresponding to $k > k^*$. Note that $f(k) < f(k^*)$, recalling that f is the net output function. Thus, the new transformation curve lies wholly *below* the old one. Along an optimal path, one chooses $z < 0$ and $c > c^*$; so B represents a typical optimal point. By the Keynes-Ramsey Rule, we have $u(z,k) + p\,z = u(0,k^*)$, so the tangent to the new transformation curve must pass through the point A. Once again, NNP measures maximum sustainable utility, namely $u(0,k^*)$. Along the optimal path, as k falls, the transformation curve rises (while always remaining below the k^* transformation curve), and each new optimal point on the new transformation curve will have a tangent, which goes through point A (by the Keynes-Ramsey Rule).

Finally, consider a transformation curve corresponding to $k < k^*$. Since $f(k) < f(k^*)$, we can now interpret the lower curve in the diagram as this transformation curve. The difference is that, along an optimal path, we will now have $z > 0$ and $c < c^*$, so a typical optimal point is depicted by D. Now, maximum sustainable utility corresponding to such an initial stock k is given by OC. This falls short of OA, which represents $NPP = u(z,k) + p\,z$. This is the case depicted by Weitzman (1976, p.160) in his diagram.

NOTES

1. Since the focus is on potentials, it is appropriate to consider social welfare on the optimal path.
2. In this framework, social welfare is seen as the present discounted value of the stream of current utilities over time.
3. Optimality requires satisfying both the competitive (myopic) and the transversality (asymptotic) conditions. Our result relies on the former only and is valid for all competitive paths, whether optimal or not.
4. In Weitzman's set up, the consumption level can be represented by a single number, which 'might be calculated as an index number with given price weights, or as a multiple of some fixed basket of goods, or more generally as any cardinal utility function' (see Weitzman(1976), pp. 156-157). Thus, the consumption level is measured at date t by $u(z(t), k(t))$. Adding this to the total valuation of investment at date t, $p(t)\dot{k}(t)$, including possible dis-investments (using up) of non-renewable natural resources, we get Weitzman's notion of Net National Product.
5. For x, y in R^n, $x \geq y$ means $x_i \geq y_i$ for $i = 1,...,n$; $x > y$ means $x \geq y$ and $x \neq y$; $x \gg y$ means $x_i > y_i$ for $i = 1,...,n$. For x in R^n, the sum norm of x, denoted by $\|x\|$ is defined by $\|x\| = \sum_{i-1}^{n} |x_i|$.
6. The notation 'a.e.' stands for 'almost everywhere'; more precisely, if A is a subset of R, then by the expression 'for $t \in A$, a.e.' we mean 'for $t \in B$, where B is a subset of A, such that the complement of B in A is a set of Lebesgue measure zero'; if the set A is an interval $[\alpha, \infty)$, we often use the expression 'for $t \geq \alpha$, a.e.' instead of 'for $t \in [\alpha, \infty)$, a.e.'.
7. Our concept of optimality is due to Brock (1970), who calls it 'weak maximality' in his paper. Gale (1967) calls the path $(z(t), k(t))$ 'optimal' if (2.2) holds with 'lim inf' replaced by 'lim sup'. Since we are concerned with only one concept of optimality, our departure from historical practice is not likely to be a source of confusion. With this notion of optimality, the existence of optimal paths can be shown for the widest class of growth models.

REFERENCES

Brock, W.A. (1970), 'On the existence of weakly maximal programmes in a multi-sector economy', *Rev. Econ. Stud.*, **37**, 275-280.

Cass, D. (1965), 'Optimum growth in an aggregative model of capital accumulation', *Rev. of Econ. Stud.*, **32**, 233-240.

Cass, D. and Shell, K. (1976), 'The structure and stability of competitive dynamical systems', *J. Econ. Theory*, **12**, 31-70.

Dasgupta, P.S. (1969), 'Optimum growth when capital is non-transferable', *Review of Economic Studies*, **36**, 77-88.

Dasgupta, S. and Mitra,T. (1999), 'On the welfare significance of national product for economic growth and sustainable development', *Japanese Economic Review*, **50** (1999), 422-442.

Dasgupta, S. and Mitra,T. (2001), 'National Product, Income Accounts and Sustainable Development', in A. Bose, D. Ray and A. Sarkar (eds), *Contemporary Macroeconomics*, Oxford.

Dorfman, R., Samuelson, P. and Solow, R. (1958), *Linear Programming and Economic Analysis*, McGraw-Hill.

Gale, D. (1967), 'On optimal development in a multi-sector economy', *Rev. Econ. Stud.*, **34**, 1-18.

Koopmans, T.C. (1965), *On the concept of optimal economic growth*, Pontificae Academia Scientiarum, Vatican City, 225-288.

Ramsey, F.P. (1928), 'A mathematical theory of saving', *Economic Journal*, **38**, 543-559.

Samuelson, P.A. (1965), 'A catenary turnpike theorem involving consumption and the golden rule', *American Economic Review*, **55**, 486-496.

Samuelson, P.A. (1961), 'The evaluation of "Social Income": capital formation and wealth', chapter 3 in F.A. Lutz and D.C. Hague (eds), *The Theory of Capital*, London, Macmillan, 32-57.

Takekuma, S.I. (1982), 'A support price theorem for the continuous time model of capital accumulation', *Econometrica*, **50**, 427-442.

Weitzman, M.L. (1976), 'On the welfare significance of national product in a dynamic economy', *Quarterly J. of Econ.*, **90**, 156-162.

PART II

General Equilibrium

3. Equilibrium Selections[*]

Beth Allen,[†] Jayasri Dutta[‡] and Herakles Polemarchakis[††]

1. INTRODUCTION

Multiplicity of equilibria poses a tough problem for economic theory.

Uniqueness of competitive equilibria can be guaranteed only under very restrictive assumptions, introduced by Arrow and Hurwicz (1958) and surveyed in Arrow and Hahn (1974); the alternative that uniqueness may arise from the heterogeneity of the characteristics of individuals, proposed and developed by Hildenbrand (1983, 1994) and by Grandmont (1982) in an explicit general equilibrium framework, is fascinating, yet, still, tentative. Work by Mercenier (1996) demonstrates that non-uniqueness of equilibrium prices also arises empirically, in applied general equilibrium models.

Multiple competitive equilibria do not present any serious problems of interpretation in the framework of Debreu (1959), where all markets are open at the same date and all trading takes place simultaneously. Individuals observe the prices of all contingent commodities at the same time, choose their demands, and markets clear. This does not require any extreme form of rationality from participants in the market, but does impose strong requirements on the market structure. In economies where activity is carried out over time and trading in markets occurs sequentially, individuals need to form expectations

---

[*]   Egbert Dierker, Ed Green, Jim Jordan and Tim van Zandt provided detailed comments on an earlier version.

[†]   Department of Economics, University of Minnesota and Federal Reserve Bank of Minneapolis. This work was supported by the Curtis Carlsson Chair in Economics at the University of Minnesota and by the NSF Grant SBR - 9309854. Any views expressed herein are those of the authors and not necessarily those of the Federal Reserve Bank of Minneapolis or the Federal Reserve System.

[‡]   Department of Economics, University of Birmingham. This work was supported by the ESRC grant R000232865 and by the Institute of Empirical Macroeconomics at the Federal Reserve Bank of Minneapolis.

[††] Department of Economics, Brown University.

about prices that will clear markets in the future. Competitive equilibria in such worlds are equilibria in plans, prices, and price expectations at each trading date, in Arrow (1953) and, more explicitly, in Radner (1972). The presence of multiple competitive equilibria could be problematic in such a situation. There is no theory about which equilibrium will occur, while competitive equilibrium of the artificial economy, where all markets open at the initial date, can only be sustained as an equilibrium in price expectations if individuals agree on which equilibrium will arise at future dates. Indeed, expectations must be single valued and coincident. The argument by Pietra and Siconolfi (1998), according to which prices at the initial date identify the equilibrium, is only a partial solace; it facilitates the coordination of expectations but does not force the choice of equilibrium at subsequent dates. In economies with asymmetric information, where the notion of equilibrium is strengthened to allow individuals to refine their information with the information revealed by prices, as in Radner (1979), the multiplicity of equilibria has been offered as a critique of rational expectations, in Hahn (1992).

In the presence of multiplicity of equilibria, it is natural to explore the consequences of imagining that prices are chosen according to a probability distribution concentrated on equilibrium prices. In the nicest possible case, the probabilistic selection of prices depends continuously on the data and the random selection rule is itself common knowledge among all agents in the economy. Thus, expectations are not single valued, though individuals agree on the probability distribution. According to results of Allen (1985, a, b) and Mas-Colell and Nachbar (1991), generic smooth exchange economies permit continuous random selections from their equilibrium price correspondences. It is, as a consequence, possible to restrict attention to these generic economies, which feature a finite or countable number of equilibria for all possible distributions of the aggregate endowment.

Randomness in the selection of equilibrium causes risk – averse individuals to desire insurance against the price uncertainty induced by the random selection among multiple equilibria. As ultimate consequences of this line of argument, the hypotheses of a complete asset market and the availability of actuarially fair insurance policies are desiderata for an idealized perfectly competitive economy.

Random equilibrium selection generates non-trivial distributions over competitive equilibrium allocations. Due to risk aversion, these distributions fail to satisfy Pareto optimality. The first welfare theorem of Arrow (1951) and Debreu (1951) fails ex ante, when equilibrium prices are randomly selected, even though it holds ex post for any particular competitive price vector and any associated equilibrium allocation. The introduction of the random selection alters the economy: not only does its equilibrium change, but more fundamentally, the entire specification changes to incorporate some risks that were previously absent, but must now be hedged.

There are two alternative approaches to the problem of insuring against equilibria. In the first, assets are traded in a first period, and, in a second period, commodities are traded and then consumption takes place. The only source of uncertainty concerns the presence of multiple equilibria in spot markets for commodities, so that assets serve to insure individuals against a random selection of equilibria. With a complete asset market in the first period, the only outcomes compatible with market clearing correspond to degenerate distributions.

The result follows, fairly straightforwardly, from the ineffectivity of sunspots in Cass and Shell (1983) and, in a more abstract framework, Balasko (1983); earlier work by Arrow and Lind (1970) and Malinvaud (1972, b) anticipated some of the conclusions. This does little to alleviate the problem of multiple equilibria. It does, however, provide a clear answer to the criticism of rational expectations summarized above. Enough markets – in this case, a complete market in securities with payoffs depending on equilibrium selections – yield the coordination of expectations as an outcome. Individuals who are uncertain or uninformed, about the equilibrium that will occur in the future can learn it by observing asset prices, which reveal precisely, before spot markets open, the equilibrium price vector that will arise.

It is probably useful to insist on the crucial role played by the completeness of the asset market. Randomization among equilibria introduces uncertainty that does not affect preferences or aggregate endowments: it is extrinsic, as it does not alter the Pareto optima and therefore the competitive equilibria. Extrinsic uncertainty can matter if the asset markets is incomplete, as in Azariades (1981) and Guesnerie and Laffont (1987), if participation is restricted, as in Cass and Shell (1983), or if traders have prior beliefs that are diverse, as in Kurz (1996, a, b).

Insurance against multiple equilibria can be considered in the framework of market games; Giraud (1998) made such an attempt, but results are tentative.

In the second approach, there is an iterative process of asset trading, as was first introduced in Chichilinsky, Dutta and Heal (1991). Randomization over equilibria introduces uncertainty. Individuals insure themselves in a complete asset market and trade in spot markets; asset trading occurs as long as there are multiple equilibria and consumption takes place only at the end. The end result of this process of recognizing myopically that randomization among competitive equilibria will occur and making fair insurance contracts at each stage is that a distinct and determinate allocation is reached after finitely many steps whenever the original economy features a continuous random selection from its equilibrium price correspondence. This outcome is Pareto optimal. Further, any regular competitive equilibrium allocation of the original economy can be reached in two steps as the unique equilibrium of the iterative process, provided that a suitable continuous random selection, which always exists, is followed.

In work in progress, Ghosal and Morelli (2001) examine convergence to a Pareto optimum in a market game when trading posts reopen and players re-trade.

The convergence of a procedure with arbitrary and not necessarily continuous randomization has been examined in Chichilinsky, Heal, Streufert and Swinkels (1992). Convergence in finitely many steps is demonstrated in Chichilinsky, Dutta and Heal (1992).

A continuous random selection results in the iterative procedure being continuous in endowments as well as monotone in utilities. This ensures convergence for all endowments and allows a partial characterization of the limit points of the trading process.

2. THE ECONOMY

Individuals are $i \in I = \{1,...,I\}$, a non-empty, finite set.

Commodities are $l \in L = \{1,...,L\}$, a non-empty, finite set. A bundle of commodities is[1] $x = (...,x_l,...)'$.

An individual is described by a cardinal utility function, u^i, over consumption bundles, $x >> 0$, and by an endowment, $e^i = (...,e_l^i,...) >> 0$.

The utility function is smooth, differentiably monotonically increasing: $Du^i >> 0$, strictly differentiably concave: D^2u^i is negative definite, and it satisfies a boundary condition: if a sequence of consumption bundles $(x_n : n = 1,...)$ that converges to a commodity bundle, $\bar{x}$, on the boundary of the consumption set, $\lim_{n \to \infty} x_n = \bar{x}$,

then $\lim_{n \to \infty} \|Du^i(x_n)\| = \infty$ and $\lim_{n \to \infty} \|Du^i(x_n)\|^{-1} x_n^i Du^i(x_n) = 0$.

The set of cardinal utility functions that satisfy these properties is U.

An allocation of consumption bundles is $\xi = (...,x^i,...)$.

An economy is described by the profile of utility functions, $\omega = (...,u^i,...)$, and the allocation of endowments, $\varepsilon = (...,e^i,...)$; the aggregate endowment is $e^\alpha = \sum_{i \in I} e^i$.

An allocation, $\xi = (\dots, x^i, \dots)$, is feasible if the aggregate consumption bundle $x^\alpha = \sum_{i \in I} x^i$, coincides with the aggregate endowment: $x^\alpha = e^\alpha$.

An allocation, ξ, Pareto dominates another, $\hat{\xi}$, if $u^i(x^i) \geq u^i(\hat{x}^i)$, for every individual, with strict inequality, $u^i(x^i) > u^i(\hat{x}^i)$, for some. A feasible allocation is Pareto optimal if no feasible allocation Pareto dominates it.

Prices of commodities are $p = (\dots, p_l, \dots)$, and they are normalized to the open simplex: $p \in P = \left\{ p \gg 0 : \sum_{l \in L} p_l = 1 \right\}$.

The optimization problem of an individual at prices p is

$$\max_x u^i(x),$$

$$\text{s.t } p_x \leq pe^i.$$

The solution to the optimization problem, $x^i(p, e^i)$, yields the demand function, x^i, which depends on the utility function, u^i. The demand function is smooth.

A competitive equilibrium allocation is an allocation, $\xi = (\dots, x^i, \dots)$, which is feasible and such that, for every individual, $x^i = x^i(p, e^i)$, for p, competitive equilibrium prices. An economy can have multiple competitive equilibrium allocations.

The Edgeworth box for an aggregate endowment, e^α, is

$$E(e^\alpha) = \left\{ \varepsilon \gg 0 : \sum_{i \in I} e^i = e^\alpha \right\}.$$

An allocation ξ, is feasible for an economy with aggregate endowment e^α if and only if $\xi \in \varepsilon(e^\alpha)$.

In order to consider equilibria that arise following a preliminary trading in assets that induces a reallocations of the endowments of consumers, it is useful to study the equilibrium correspondence, as the allocation of endowments varies, while the aggregate endowment remains fixed: the allocation of endowments varies over $E(e^\alpha)$, the Edgeworth box for the aggregate endowment.

The equilibrium price correspondence

$$\Psi : E(e^\alpha) \to P ,$$

is defined by

$$\Psi(\varepsilon) = \left\{ p \in P : \sum_{i \in I} x^i(p; e^i) = e^\alpha \right\};$$

it associates equilibrium prices with allocations of endowments. If competitive equilibrium prices for the allocation of endowments ε are unique,[2] $\# \Psi(\varepsilon) = 1$.

For each $p \in \Psi(\varepsilon)$, the associated equilibrium allocation is

$$\xi(p; \varepsilon) = (\ldots, x^i(p; e^i), \ldots) \in E(e^\alpha) .$$

The equilibrium allocation correspondence,

$$\Xi : E(e^\alpha) \to E(e^\alpha) ,$$

is defined by

$$\Xi(\varepsilon) = \left\{ \xi \in E(e^\alpha) : x^i = x^i(p; e^i), i \in I, \text{ some } p \in P \right\};$$

it associates equilibrium allocations with allocations of endowments.

Because of the strict concavity of the utility functions, distinct equilibrium prices are associated with distinct equilibrium allocations; because of the smoothness of the utility functions, distinct equilibrium allocations are associated with distinct equilibrium prices.

Continuous random selections

A random selection from the equilibrium price correspondence is a mapping that associates each allocation of endowments, ε, with a probability measure on $\Psi(\varepsilon)$: it represents likelihoods that specific equilibrium prices realize as the allocation of endowments varies. A random selection from the equilibrium price correspondence reflects objective uncertainty about the equilibrium that will realize.

Results often require continuity of the random equilibrium selection. This need not be problematic as it holds for a generic subset of economies: each pure exchange economy in a dense G_δ subset possesses such a continuous random selection from its equilibrium price correspondence as the allocation of endowments varies. Any economy that satisfies the assumptions of the model can be approximated arbitrarily closely by economies with a continuous random selection. This result is the continuous random selection theorem of Allen (1985, a, b). However, one appeals directly to the formulation provided by Mas-Colell and Nachbar (1991), since they perturb utility functions rather than aggregate excess demand functions in the definition of generic subsets of economies. The argument is that, for a countable intersection of open and dense subsets of economies, each distribution of endowments leads to at most countably many competitive equilibrium prices. From this follows the existence of a continuous random selection from the equilibrium price correspondence.

The set of probability measures on Borel subsets of the set of normalized prices is $M(P)$; it is endowed with the topology of weak convergence of probability measures – alternatively, this is the weak* topology and is defined by the condition that $\lim_{n \to \infty} \mu_n = \mu$ if, for all continuous and bounded functions,

$\lim_{n \to \infty} \int f d\mu_n = \int f d\mu$, pointwise.

A continuous random selection from the equilibrium price correspondence is a continuous function

$$\mu: E(e^\alpha) \to M(P),$$

such that

$$\mu(\Psi(E)) = 1, \text{ all } \varepsilon \in E(e^\alpha).$$

For a profile of utility functions, $\omega = (\ldots, u^i, \ldots)$, the Edgeworth box, $E(e^\alpha)$, has the critical property if, for all allocations of endowments, $\varepsilon \in E(e^\alpha)$, the set $\Psi(\varepsilon)$ is at most countable.

According to the critical property, for each feasible redistribution of endowments, the resulting set of competitive equilibria is at most countable, even in economies that fail to be regular in the sense of Debreu (1970). Interest in the critical property derives from the fact that it is generic, and that it suffices to ensure the existence of a continuous random selection from the equilibrium price correspondence.

For a given aggregate endowment, e^α, and utilities functions, $u^i \in U$, for all individuals but one: $i \in I \backslash \{1\}$, for utility functions $\tilde{u}^{-1}$ that belong to a countable intersection of open, dense subsets, in the C^∞, compact – open topology on the set, U, of utility functions, for the profile of utility functions, $\omega = (\tilde{u}^{-1}, u^2, \ldots, u^i, \ldots)$, the Edgeworth box, $E(e^\alpha)$; has the critical property. Moreover, all profiles of utility functions in this generic set possess continuous random selections from their equilibrium price correspondences. This follows from Mas-Colell and Nachbar (1991), together with the observation that differentiable strict concavity is satisfied by a countable intersection of non-empty open subsets of utilities.

The hypothesis that all utilities and demands are infinitely continuously differentiable is needed for the proofs given in Allen (1985, a, b) and in Mas-Colell and Nachbar (1991). Similarly, these methods do not permit one to strengthen the result to yield an open and dense subset of well-behaved profiles of utility functions, rather than a dense G_δ subset. While Allen (1985, a, b) obtains the generic finiteness of the equilibrium price set for all parameters, the framework of Mas-Colell and Nachbar (1991) framework yields only the conclusion that, for all parameter values, the set of equilibria is at most countable for a residual subset of utilities.

The assumption that the set of competitive equilibria is at most countable proves valuable for two reasons. First, it ensures that continuous random selections exist. In addition, it allows for a countable state space for the analysis of asset trading.

Extrinsic uncertainty

An extension allows for extrinsic uncertainty.

States of extrinsic uncertainty are $s \in S = \{1,...\}$, a non-empty set, finite or, at most, countable. A probability measure on S is $\pi = (...,\pi(s),...)$; extrinsic uncertainty is described by the pair $(S; \pi)$.

Across states of extrinsic uncertainty, a bundle of commodities is $\vec{x} = (x(s): s \in S)'$, where $x(s) = (...,x_l(s),...)'$ is a bundle of commodities at the state of extrinsic uncertainty s. The bundle $\vec{x}$ is invariant with respect to extrinsic uncertainty if $x(s) = x, \pi -$ almost surely.

The endowment of an individual is $\vec{e}^i$; the aggregate endowment, $\vec{e}^\alpha$, is invariant with respect to extrinsic uncertainty.

For an individual, the expected utility of a consumption plan, $\vec{x} = (x(s): s \in S)$ with $x(s) \gg 0$, $\pi -$ almost surely, is

$$v^i(\vec{x}) = E_\pi u^i(x(s)),$$

which serves to define the Pareto dominance and Pareto optimality of allocations, $\vec{\xi} = (...,\vec{x}^i,...)$.

Assets are $\alpha \in A = \{1,...\}$ a set that is at most countable; they effect the transfer of revenue across states of extrinsic uncertainty. The payoff of an asset is $r_\alpha = (...,r_{\alpha,s},...)'$. A portfolio of assets is $y = (...,y_\alpha,...)'$, such that $y_\alpha r_\alpha(s) \neq 0$, for at most finitely many $\alpha \in A$, for π – almost all $s \in S$. The payoff of portfolio y is $r_y = \sum_{\alpha \in A} y_\alpha r_\alpha$. An elementary security for state s is an asset, $\alpha = s$, such that $r_s(\hat{s}) = 0$, whenever $\hat{s} \neq s$; and $r_s(s) = 1$.

The asset market is complete if, for any distribution of revenue, $\tau = (...,\tau_s,...)'$, there exists a portfolio, y, such that $r(s)y = \tau(s)$, for π – almost all $s \in S$. By definition, the payoff of each elementary security can be attained by such a portfolio in a complete asset market.

The extreme form of market incompleteness occurs when no assets are available: for every asset, $r_\alpha(s) = 0, \pi$ – almost surely; this is an autarkic asset market.

Prices of commodities are $\vec{p} = (..., p(s),...)$, where $p(s) = (...,p_l(s),...)$ are prices of commodities at spot market at the state s.

Prices of assets are $q = (...,q_\alpha,...)$. In a complete asset market, the price of an elementary security, possibly implicit, is $\tilde{q}_s$.

The optimization problem of an at prices $(\vec{p},q)$ is

$$\max_{\tilde{x}} \upsilon^i(\vec{x}) = E_\pi u^i(x(s)),$$

s.t. $qy \leq 0$,

$$p(s)x(s) \leq p(s)e^i(s) + r(s)y(s), \quad \pi - \text{almost all } s \in S,$$

$$x(s) >> 0, \quad \pi - \text{almost all } s \in S.$$

At a competitive equilibrium, individuals optimize, and markets for commodities and assets clear.

At any competitive equilibrium with a complete asset market, for any individual, the consumption plan, $\vec{x}^{i^*} = (...,x^{i^*}(s),...)$, is invariant with respect to extrinsic uncertainty: $x^{i^*}(s) = x^{i^*}$. This is the ineffectivity of sunspots of Cass and Shell (1983); the prices of commodities, $\vec{p}^* = (...,p^*(s),...)$; are invariant with respect to extrinsic uncertainty: $p^*(s) = p^*$, up to normalization, which is inessential. The prices of elementary securities, which may be only implicit, coincide with the probability measure over the set of states of extrinsic uncertainty: $\tilde{q}^* = \pi$.

Full insurance at actuarially fair prices is feasible as well as desirable. With complete markets, individuals can attain a sunspot – invariant income that is simply the statistical average of the original distribution of incomes. Assets are necessarily priced at their expected payoffs and consequently elementary securities are necessarily priced at the objective state probabilities. This provides a useful algorithm for finding the competitive equilibria of such an economy with complete markets; they necessarily coincide with the equilibria of the artificial economy where each individual has the average endowment in each state of extrinsic uncertainty.

At any competitive equilibrium with an autarkic asset market, the allocation of commodities at any state $\xi^*(s) = (\ldots, x^{i^*}(s), \ldots)$, is a competitive equilibrium allocation for the underlying economy and $p^*(s)$ are competitive equilibrium prices. If the underlying economy has multiple competitive equilibria, a competitive equilibrium allocation with an autarkic asset market need not be invariant with respect to extrinsic uncertainty, and the prices of commodities can vary with extrinsic uncertainty beyond normalization, which is essential.

If the asset market is either complete or autarkic, the distribution of prices and allocations at competitive equilibria are necessarily randomizations among the competitive equilibria for the underlying economy. This need not be the case with intermediate asset structures. Non-degenerate distributions, which correspond to non-trivial equilibria with extrinsic uncertainty, are known to occur with incomplete markets; the point was made by Cass (1989) and was elaborated on in Guesnerie and Laffont (1988), Mas-Colell (1989) and Polemarchakis and Ventura (2001). Importantly, they arise in economies that have unique equilibria with autarkic asset markets – Hens (1991). Moreover, equilibrium distributions can be indeterminate with countable state spaces and incomplete markets – Mas-Colell (1991). Of concern, here, is the role of assets in insuring against multiple equilibria.

3. ASSETS AND EQUILIBRIUM DISTRIBUTIONS

How should one think about multiple competitive equilibria?

One alternative is to start from a distribution over equilibrium prices – that is, a random selection from $\Psi(\varepsilon)$. But, such a distribution introduces a source of uncertainty, additional to the basic structure the preferences and endowments of the economy. It seems reasonable, then, that individuals will wish to insure against such risks. In a competitive economy, asset markets are a natural way to model the possibilities of insurance both individual and the aggregate.

Absent asset markets, randomness in the selection of equilibria persists. With insurance possibilities, risk-averse individuals will typically hold portfolios of assets that insure them to the extent possible. Spot market equilibria must reflect these transfers of revenue, so that alternative asset structures will yield different equilibrium distributions. A full characterization of self-fulfilling equilibrium distributions with competitive asset markets requires a larger family of price distributions, and not just probabilities $\pi \in M(P)$ over the competitive equilibria of the original economy. Thus, one may have $\pi(\Psi(\varepsilon)) \neq 1$. The more restrictive situation, $\pi(\Psi(\varepsilon)) = 1$, arises with extremal asset structures.

Random selections, which give distributions on prices, are associated with states of extrinsic uncertainty, which correspond to distributions on endowments. The equilibrium price and allocation correspondences with aggregate endowment e^{α} are $\Psi: E(e^{\alpha}) \rightarrow P$ and $\Xi: E(e^{\alpha}) \rightarrow E(e^{\alpha})$, respectively.

The Edgeworth box $E(e^{\alpha})$ has the critical property: both $\Psi(\varepsilon)$ and $\Xi(\varepsilon)$ are at most countable for each $\varepsilon \in E(e^{\alpha})$.

States of extrinsic uncertainty, $s \in S(\varepsilon)$, index the elements of $\Xi(\varepsilon)$; for each $\varepsilon \in E(e^{\alpha})$. The map $\vec{\xi}: S(e) \rightarrow \Xi(\varepsilon)$ is one-to-one and onto, by construction, and $S(e)$ is at most countable. If $p(s)$ are the support prices of the equilibrium allocation $\xi(s)$; this defines $\vec{p}: S(\varepsilon) \rightarrow \Psi(\varepsilon)$, also one-to-one and onto. Any random selection π from $\Psi(\varepsilon)$ defines a probability measure on $S(\varepsilon)$ and on $\Xi(\varepsilon)$. One writes π for a probability measure on S, on $\Psi(e)$ and on $\Xi(e)$. Finally, as before, assets are written as $\alpha \in A$, and pay off in states $s \in S(e)$.

For $\varepsilon \in E(e^{\alpha})$, a random selection π from $\Psi(\varepsilon)$ is an equilibrium selection with assets A if $\vec{\xi}^{*} = (...,\xi(p(s);\varepsilon),...)$ is a competitive equilibrium allocation with assets A and sunspots $(\Xi(\varepsilon),\pi)$. An equilibrium selection is degenerate if $\pi(s) = 1$, for some $s \in S(e)$. States of extrinsic uncertainty index competitive equilibria. This implies that distinct states correspond to distinct equilibrium prices and allocations.

As $\varepsilon \in E(e^{\alpha})$, varies, the number of equilibria may change. This necessarily alters the indexing set $S(\varepsilon)$.

For some $\varepsilon \in E(e^{\alpha})$; equilibria are unique. This corresponds to a singleton $S(\varepsilon)$ and, *a fortiori*, a degenerate selection.

Proposition 1. *If the asset market is complete, equilibrium selections are degenerate, every degenerate selection from $\Psi(\varepsilon)$ is an equilibrium selection, and there are no other equilibrium selections. If the asset market is autarkic, every random selection from $\psi(\varepsilon)$ leads to an equilibrium selection, and these are the only equilibrium selections.*

Proof. The first claim follows immediately from the results on competitive equilibria in economies with extrinsic uncertainty and a complete asset market in Cass and Shell (1983). The second claim is evident.

This proposition clearly states that the problem of the multiplicity of competitive equilibria cannot be resolved by opening markets contingent on equilibria, or equivalently, on price-states. With a complete asset market, the competitive equilibria of the original economy remain degenerate equilibria of the economy with asset trading.

The message is different when it comes to justifying equilibria with an incomplete asset market, which requires perfect foresight and coordination. The claim is that sufficiently rich markets achieve the coordination of expectations at equilibrium. With a complete asset markets, elementary securities prices vanish for all but one equilibrium-state. Failing this, the asset market cannot clear. Asset prices reveal the equilibrium choice before spot markets open, so that individuals can learn to foresee the equilibrium arising from these prices.

At an equilibrium with a complete asset market, assets are not traded, even though the potential availability of all assets is important in deriving the conclusions.

A complete asset market, on the one hand, and an autarkic asset market, on the other, are extreme asset structures. Nevertheless, equilibria arising out of these structures have interesting similarities. The distribution of prices and allocations at equilibrium necessarily have support on the competitive equilibria of the underlying economy, so that $\pi(\Psi(\varepsilon)) = 1$. Typically this is not true of intermediate incomplete asset structures. Both structures have the property that at competitive equilibria, assets are, effectively, not traded. Indeed, this is what allows $p(s) \in \Psi(\varepsilon)$ to be in the support of π. The reasons for no effective exchange are different. At autarky, no assets are available. At any non-degenerate equilibrium, individuals are willing but unable to ensure. With a complete asset market, there is no uncertainty about which equilibrium will arise; assets command a positive price if and only if they pay off positive amounts in that equilibrium-state. With the certain knowledge that this state will occur, individuals do not have claims, which they can trade them against. In effect, only one elementary security is available in the first period, so that there is no trade. Finally, complete asset market equilibria are necessarily equilibria under autarky. The reverse is not true, because autarky allows for non-degenerate distributions.

If the asset market is either complete or autarkic, the distribution of prices and allocations at competitive equilibria are necessarily randomizations among the competitive equilibria for the allocation of endowments, (ε). This, typically, fails for equilibria with intermediate asset structures, which are not treated here. Two issues that arise with incomplete asset markets should be mentioned; they concern insurance and the no-exchange result.

First, the question of insurance: The outcome with a complete asset market is paradoxical, because it achieves insurance but not uniqueness. As proposition 1 shows, multiple equilibria necessarily persist with complete markets because every competitive equilibrium of the original economy can be supported as a degenerate equilibrium distribution with a complete asset markets. When assets are traded, equilibrium is fully insured, in the sense that only one of these equilibria will occur and individuals are able to anticipate exactly which one. The question, then, is whether incomplete markets, possibly of very special forms, can lead to a unique degenerate outcome. The answer to this is clearly negative, as long as markets clear and that probabilities are correctly perceived: if the outcome is a degenerate distribution, it must be that $\pi(s) = 1$, for some s. If state s is to occur with certainty, and if all individuals know this, assets cannot trade at equilibrium. With no transfers of revenue, the set of competitive equilibria is unaltered. This is just the argument of proposition 1, which is valid at any degenerate equilibrium, irrespective of A.

Second, the no-exchange result: at equilibrium either with a complete or with an autarkic asset market, assets are not traded. If assets are not traded, equilibrium distributions necessarily assign probability 1 to the original set, $\Psi(\varepsilon)$, of equilibria. The reverse is true as well. If non-trivial assets are traded, some redistribution of revenues must take place, for some individual, in some state. This necessarily changes this individual's budget set. At interior optima, income transfers alter the spot market demands of individuals, resulting in a different price-allocation pair at equilibrium. Assets are only traded in incomplete markets. The reasoning here suggests that equilibrium price distributions with asset trading cannot be supported on $\Psi(\varepsilon)$; typically, then, incomplete insurance against prices would sustain, and even increase price variability.

4. AN ITERATIVE PROCESS

Alternatively, a distribution over equilibrium prices is taken as part of the basic data of the economy. If markets are complete, individuals will insure themselves fully against such uncertainty; which leads to a reallocation of endowments, and, typically, to a different set of equilibrium outcomes. This is an iterative process.

The main result is the convergence of insured allocations in finitely many steps, and the continuous dependence of the limiting allocation on the initial allocation of endowments.

The process writes as the iteration of a map on $E(e^{\alpha})$. The critical property ensures that the map is continuous, which, along with the utility-improving property of competitive trade, allows a simple proof of convergence.

The question of interest is as follows: competitive equilibria often fail to be unique. At the same time, given preferences and the aggregate endowment, there are endowment allocations that lead to unique competitive equilibria. This is clearly true if the endowment allocations happen to be Pareto optimal, and this property is preserved at allocations that are close to optimal. Is it possible, then, that individuals will choose to trade into such reallocations? Asset markets provide a natural way of modeling individually rational reallocations.

For an allocation of endowments, ε, the sets of competitive equilibrium prices and allocations are $\Psi(\varepsilon)$ and $\Xi(\varepsilon)$, respectively. If π is a random selection from $\psi(\varepsilon)$, a redistribution of endowments is defined by

$$\tilde{\varepsilon} = \int_{p} \xi(p; \varepsilon) d\pi(p).$$

Asset trading in a complete asset market achieves this reallocation. By construction, $\tilde{\varepsilon} \in E(e^{\alpha})$, whenever $\varepsilon \in E(e^{\alpha})$.

If $E(e^{\alpha})$ possesses the critical property, a continuous random selection, $\mu : E(e^{\alpha}) \to M(P)$, exists: $\mu(\varepsilon)(\Psi(\varepsilon)) = 1$: Setting $\pi = \mu(\varepsilon)$ defines an iterated map on $E(e^{\alpha})$.

Proposition 2. *For a countable intersection of open and dense subsets of utilities, starting from any allocation of endowments, ε_0, the sequence of redistributions defined inductively by*

$$\varepsilon_{n+1} = \int_{P} \xi(p; \varepsilon_n) d\mu(\varepsilon_n)(p_n), \quad n = 0,\ldots,$$

converges to an allocation of endowments, $\bar{\varepsilon}$, that has a unique competitive equilibrium price vector: $\# \Psi(\bar{\varepsilon}) = 1$. Convergence occurs in finitely many steps, and the terminal allocation, $\bar{\varepsilon}$, varies continuously with ε_0, the initial allocation.

Proof. The closure of the Edgeworth box for the aggregate endowment, e^{α}, is

$$\overline{E}(e^{\alpha}) = \left\{ \varepsilon \geq 0 : \sum_{i \in I} e^i = e^{\alpha} \right\},$$

a compact, convex set.

If $p \in \Psi(\varepsilon_n)$ then, by the feasibility of a competitive equilibrium allocation, $\xi(p; \varepsilon_n) \in \overline{E}(e^{\alpha})$ while, by the convexity of the closure of the Edgeworth box, $\varepsilon_{n+1} = \int_P \xi(p; \varepsilon_n) d\mu(\varepsilon_n)(p_n) \in \overline{E}(e^{\alpha})$. Since the closure of the Edgeworth box is compact, the sequence $(\varepsilon_n : n = 1,...)$ has a convergent subsequence, $(\varepsilon_{n_k} : k = 1,...)$, such that $\lim_{k \to \infty} \varepsilon_{n_k} = \overline{\varepsilon} \in \overline{E}(e^{\alpha})$. Iterated individual rationality of the demands $x^i(p, e^i_{n+1})$ that constitute competitive equilibrium allocations for the economy with utilities $(...,u^i,...)$ and endowments $(...,e^i_n,...)$ implies that, for all individuals and all iterations, $u^i(e^i_{n+1}) \geq u^i(e^i_n) \geq u^i(e^i_n) \geq u^i(e^i_0)$. This, combined with the boundary condition satisfied by the utility function of every individual and the strict positivity of the endowments, implies that $\overline{\varepsilon} \in E(e^{\alpha})$.

Since $\mu : E(e^{\alpha}) \to M(P)$ is weakly continuous while the demand function, x^i, is continuous, in fact C^{∞}, in prices and endowments, $\overline{e}^i = \int_P x^i(p, \overline{e}^i) d\mu(\overline{\varepsilon})(p)$. If $\mu(\overline{\varepsilon})$ is a Dirac measure, then necessarily $x^i(p, \overline{e}^i) = \overline{e}^i$ for $p \in \Psi(\overline{\varepsilon})$ and, because $\overline{\varepsilon} \in E(e^{\alpha})$ implies $x^{\alpha}(p, \overline{\varepsilon}) = \overline{e}^{\alpha}_n = \overline{e}^{\alpha}_0$, it follows from the first welfare theorem that $\overline{\varepsilon}$ is Pareto optimal. If $\mu(\overline{\varepsilon})$ is not a Dirac measure, strict concavity of the utility functions and individual rationality of competitive equilibrium allocations imply that $u^i(\overline{e}^i) = u^i(\int_P x^i(p, \overline{e}^i) d\mu(\overline{\varepsilon})(p)) > \int_P u^i(x^i(p, \overline{e}^i)) d\mu(\overline{\varepsilon})(p) \geq \int_P u^i(\overline{e}^i) d\mu(\overline{\varepsilon})(p) = u^i(\overline{e}^i)$, which is a contradiction. Therefore $\overline{\varepsilon}$ is Pareto optimal.

The entire sequence, $(\varepsilon_n : n = 1,...)$, and not just a subsequence, converges to $\overline{e}$: If not, there are subsequences with distinct limits, $\overline{e}$ and $\overline{\overline{e}}$: Since $x^i(p, e^i_n)$ is the demand of the individual at price and endowment e^i_n; necessarily $u^i(x^i(p, e^i_n)) \geq u^i(e^i_n)$; strict concavity of the utility function then implies that $u^i(\int_P x^i(p, e^i_n) d\mu(\varepsilon_n)(p)) > \int_P u^i(p, e^i_n) d\mu(\varepsilon_n)(p) \geq u^i(e^i_n)$ whenever $\mu(\varepsilon_n)$ is not a Dirac measure. For all individuals, the sequences $(\varepsilon^i_n : n = 1,...)$

of endowments are strictly improving in the sense that $u^i(e^i_{n+1}) \geq u^i(e^i_n)$, with strict inequality unless $\mu(\varepsilon_n)$ is a Dirac measure, which is the case whenever $\psi(\varepsilon_n)$ is a singleton. The Pareto optimality of both $\bar{e}$ and $\bar{\bar{e}}$ implies that there are individuals, $\bar{i}$ and $\bar{\bar{i}}$ for whom $u^{\bar{i}}(\bar{e}^{\bar{i}}) < u^{\bar{i}}(\bar{\bar{e}}^{\bar{i}})$ and $u^{\bar{\bar{i}}}(\bar{\bar{e}}^{\bar{\bar{i}}}) < u^{\bar{\bar{i}}}(\bar{e}^{\bar{\bar{i}}})$. This contradicts the strict improvement along the sequence $(\varepsilon_n : n = 1, \ldots)$, whenever $\bar{e} \neq \bar{\bar{e}}$. If $\Psi(\varepsilon_n)$ is a singleton or, more generally, if $\mu(\varepsilon_n)$ is a Dirac measure, then $e^i_{n+1} = x^i(\Psi(\varepsilon_n); e^i_n)$; for every individual, and, hence, $\varepsilon_{n+1} = \varepsilon_{n+2} = \ldots,$; in this case, $\bar{e} = \bar{\bar{e}}$.

Convergence occurs in finitely many steps. Since $\lim_{n \to \infty} \varepsilon_n = \bar{e}$, for every $\delta > 0$, there exists $M(\delta)$; such that $\|\varepsilon_n - \bar{e}\| < \delta$, for $n = M(\delta), \ldots$. By theorem 4.5.3 and corollary 4.5.4 of Balasko (1988, pp. 104-5), every Pareto optimal allocation $\bar{e} \in \varepsilon(e^\alpha)$ has the property that there is $\delta(\bar{e}) > 0$, such that every $\varepsilon \in \varepsilon(e^\alpha)$ with $\|\varepsilon_n - \bar{e}\| < \delta(\bar{e})$ is regular and has a unique competitive equilibrium price vector. Since ε is Pareto optimal, setting $M(\delta) - 1 = M(\delta(\bar{e}))$ guarantees that $\Psi(\varepsilon_{M(\delta)-1})$ is a singleton, so that $\mu(\varepsilon_{M(\delta)-1})$ must be a Dirac measure. It follows that $\varepsilon_{M(\delta)}$ is Pareto optimal, and therefore $\varepsilon_{M(\delta)} = \varepsilon_{M(\delta)+1} = \ldots = \bar{e}$.

Since the random selection from the equilibrium correspondence is continuous, while convergence occurs in finitely many steps, the terminal allocation varies continuously with the initial allocation of endowments.

Any regular competitive equilibrium can be achieved in two steps by using a continuous random selection that assigns probability one to the competitive equilibrium price vector associated with the desired equilibrium allocation.

Corollary 1. *The convergent sequence* $(\varepsilon_n : n = 1, \ldots)$ *identified in proposition 2 features a Pareto improvement at each step; the limit* $\bar{e}$ *is a Pareto optimal allocation.*

Proof. By the individual rationality of competitive equilibrium allocations and by concavity of the utility functions of individuals,

$$u^i(e^i_{n+1}) = u^i(\int_P x^i(p; e^i_n) d\mu(\varepsilon_n)(p))$$

$$\geq \int_P u^i(x_i(p; e^i_n)) d\mu(\varepsilon_n)(p) \geq u^i(e^i_n),$$

with strict inequality whenever $\#\psi(\varepsilon_n) > 1$. Pareto improvement occurs at each step, except, possibly, if $\#\psi(\varepsilon_n) = 1$; in that case, the iteration moves directly to the contract curve; in symbols, if $M-1$ is defined to be the first integer for which $\#\Psi(\varepsilon_{M-1}) = 1$; then $\mu(\varepsilon_{M-1})$ is precisely the Dirac measure concentrated at the point $\Psi(\varepsilon_{M-1})$ in P; and, by strict concavity, each $x^i(p, \varepsilon^i_{M-1})$ is a singleton when evaluated at $p = \Psi(\varepsilon_{M-1})$. Hence, for all individuals, $e^i_M = x^i(\Psi(\varepsilon_{M-1}); e^i_{M-1})$, which is Pareto optimal by the first welfare theorem.

The procedure analyzed in the proposition can be viewed as the iteration of a map on the Edgeworth box.

The map is continuous. An allocation that is not a fixed point is mapped into a Pareto superior allocation, while an allocation is a fixed point if and only if it is Pareto optimal.

Observations

1. In general, whenever there are multiple equilibria for the original economy that receive strictly positive probability under the continuous random selection, one cannot achieve the limit allocation in a single step except for extraordinarily special configurations. Depending on the probability weights assigned to various equilibria, the first step gives a reallocation that lies in the convex hull of the competitive equilibrium allocations for the original economy; the first reallocation generally is not Pareto optimal and hence requires additional redistributions. The basic problem is that an overall equilibrium need not be achieved in a single step, so that the process must be repeated.
2. The iterative process of redistribution has three elements: (C) finding the set of competitive equilibria for a given endowment allocation, (D) assigning a probability distribution to these prices, and (I) allocating the average (according to the distribution) of the equilibrium allocations to the traders in the economy. Steps D and I can be understood as the outcome of complete insurance against randomization; the reallocation achieved at step I is typically not optimal, leaving room for spot trading, which takes place at the next step C. This occurs until step D chooses a degenerate distribution, which is necessarily the case if the competitive equilibrium is unique.
3. Insurance against price randomization can be achieved by trade in elementary securities, Arrow (1953), in insurance contracts Malinvaud (1972, b) or in price contingent claims Chichilinsky, Dutta and Heal (1992). At each step, individuals are able to insure themselves against randomness in the

equilibrium outcome. At the nth step, the maximum number of elementary securities or basic insurance contracts which must be traded is $\# \Psi(\varepsilon_n)$; the number of competitive equilibria associated with the endowment distribution ε_n. By assumption, the number of these equilibria is at most countable at every step. With finitely many steps, the total number of securities required by the entire process is at most countable, provided that the utilities of the underlying economy lie in the generic set for which our process is defined and converges.

4. One may wonder whether it is possible to characterize the limit points of the process completely. It is not evident how to do this in general, due to the potentially complex nature of the set of Pareto optima in high dimensions and the fact that, by choosing appropriate continuous random selections, one can generate at least the convex hull of the set of regular competitive equilibrium allocations for the original economy in our first step. However, for the 2 x 2 Edgeworth box that is, with I = L = 2, a characterization is possible. As the continuous random selection changes, one can generate a closed subset of the contract curve for a given initial endowment distribution in the original economy. The set of all limit points of the iterative process contains only individually rational and Pareto optimal allocations, but not every such allocation can be reached; for instance, the indifference curve through an original initial allocation may perhaps not contain the original economy's unique competitive equilibrium allocation. Thus, the reallocation process implicitly proposes a refinement of the core, and this refinement of a cooperative solution concept always gives a non-empty closed set of feasible allocations. On the other hand, with an atomless continuum of each type of agent in a 2 x 2 Edgeworth box for which the original initial endowment vector led to exactly three distinct competitive equilibria, relatively open subsets of the contract curve are generally included in our set of limit points of the process. For large economies, the process does not necessarily yield the core or, equivalently, the competitive equilibrium allocations of the underlying economy.

5. One could also ask whether some subset of the competitive equilibria are stable relative to this trading process. Indeed, not all equilibria in $\Psi(\varepsilon_0)$ can emerge as the outcome of iterative asset trading with non-degenerate distributions. This is easy to see in the 2 x 2 Edgeworth box. If there are competitive equilibria, '1', '2' and '3', they are ranked by the individuals in opposite direction: $u^1(x^1(1)) > u^1(x^1(2)) > u^1(x^1(3))$, while $u^2(x^2(1)) < u^2(x^2(2)) < u^2(x^2(3))$. It follows from the individual rationality of competitive equilibrium allocations that the equilibrium 2 can be the limit of

iterative asset trading with non-trivial randomization, while the equilibria 1 and 3 cannot: every allocation in the relative interior of the convex hull of the three equilibria dominates equilibrium 3 for individual 1 and equilibrium 1 for individual 2. In this particular case, the equilibrium 2 is tâtonnement unstable: iterative asset trading imposes different stability requirements.

6. The statement of the proposition 2 is reminiscent of the concept of quasi-stability analyzed in Hahn and Negishi (1962), in that some set – here the set of Pareto optimal allocations – serves as a sink for a discrete-time process that involves trades conducted out of equilibrium prices, where no consumption occurs before the limit of the process has been reached. However, there is no claim of stability or its analogue for the setting here, and questions of how one can find competitive prices are not considered. Instead, the iterative process features competitive equilibrium prices at each stage, even if individuals act myopically, as if the randomization and further redistributions will not occur. In addition, since the limit is attained after a finite number of steps, the common objection that non-tâtonnement processes let individuals agents starve before attaining the limit is alleviated.

7. The convergence of the iterative process to a Pareto optimal allocation in finitely many steps does not require the continuity of the random selection. This is evident from the proof of proposition 2 and was pointed out independently by Jim Jordan and Tim van Zandt; indeed, it was part of the argument in Chichilnisky, Dutta and Heal (1992).

8. A more abstract way to derive the existence of a limit set for all random selections considered together that satisfies Pareto optimality and uniqueness of competitive equilibria could be based on Zorn's lemma. The binary relation $\prec$ on $\widetilde{\varepsilon}(e^{\alpha})$ is defined by $\widehat{\varepsilon} \prec \varepsilon$ if ε belongs to the relative interior of the convex hull of the competitive equilibrium allocations with endowments $\widehat{\varepsilon}$ and there are at least two such equilibria or $\widehat{\varepsilon}$ is a limit of such a chain beginning at $\widehat{\varepsilon}$. The relation $\prec$ is asymmetric and acyclic; it is a subrelation of the strict Pareto dominance relation. Then the partial ordering $\prec$ has a maximal linearly ordered chain which has an accumulation point, since the non-empty set $\widetilde{\varepsilon}(e^{\alpha})$ of feasible and individually rational allocations is compact. A maximal chain has a maximal element, which is an allocation having a unique competitive equilibrium. However, this alternative method does not yield convergence in finitely many steps, nor does it guarantee the equality of all possible limits for a given, continuous random selection.

9. Whenever there are continuous random selections, typically there are uncountably many of them unless, of course, the equilibrium price correspondence is single valued, in which case the equilibrium price function is the only selection continuous or otherwise. All individuals use the same selection, which is common knowledge. This requirement can be weakened somewhat so that it applies only to the finite number of redistribution points that arise during the process, but one must impose the restriction that all of the averages, with respect to the randomization, defining the redistribution process must use the same probabilities for all individuals. Otherwise redistributions need not constitute feasible allocations. Common probabilities also serve to define fair insurance. Lack of agreement in evaluating probabilities leads to outcomes with less than full insurance, even in the standard competitive framework.

10. The iterative process shares with the planning procedure for public goods proposed by Drèze and de la Vallée Poussin (1971) and Malinvaud (1972,a) the property that reallocations are Pareto improving at each step.

11. The iterative asset trading process that insures against multiple competitive equilibria calls for a comparison with the social choice problem the aggregation of data from the economic environment so as to obtain a unique individually rational and Pareto optimal outcome. For generic profiles of utilities, it provides a solution that exhibits continuous dependence on the allocation of endowments and that satisfies uniqueness for a particular continuous random selection. Continuity with respect to utilities must remain a conjecture, since new mathematical machinery appears to be needed to show that there are random selections that depend continuously on preferences.

NOTES

1. ' ´ ' denotes the transpose.
2. '#' denotes the cardinality of a set.

REFERENCES

Allen, B. (1985, a), 'On the finiteness of the equilibrium price set', Working Paper no. 85-03, CARESS, University of Pennsylvania.

Allen, B. (1985, b) 'Continuous random selections from the equilibrium price correspondence', Working Paper no. 85-25, CARESS, University of Pennsylvania.

Arrow, K. J. (1953), Le rôle des valeurs boursieurs pour la repartition la meilleure des risques, *Econometrie, Colloques Internationaux du CNRS*, **11**, 41-47.

Arrow, K. J. and L. Hurwicz (1958), 'On the stability of competitive equilibrium, I', *Econometrica*, **26**, 522-552.

Arrow, K. J. and J. Lind (1970), 'Uncertainty and the evaluation of public investment decisions', *American Economic Review*, **60**, 364-378.

Arrow, K. J. and F. H. Hahn (1971), '*General Competitive analysis*', Holden Day, San Fransisco..

Azariades, C. (1981), 'Self-fulfilling prophecies', *Journal of Economic Theory*, **25**, 380-396.

Balasko, Y. (1983), 'Extrinsic uncertainty revisited', *Journal of Economic Theory*, **31**, 203-210.

Balasko, Y. (1988), *Foundations of the Theory of General Equilibrium*, Academic Press.

Cass, D. (1989), 'Sunspots and incomplete financial markets: the leading example', in G. Feiwel (ed.), *The Economics of Imperfect Competition and Employment: Joan Robinson and Beyond*, Macmillan.

Cass, D. and K. Shell (1983), 'Do sunspots matter?' *Journal of Political Economy*, **91**, 193-227.

Chichilinsky, G., J. Dutta and G. Heal (1991), 'Options and price uncertainty', Discussion Paper no. 574, Department of Economics, Columbia University.

Chichilinsky, G., J. Dutta and G. Heal (1992), 'Price uncertainty and derivative securities in a general equilibrium model', Economic Theory Discussion Paper no. 178, Department of Applied Economics, University of Cambridge.

Chichilinsky, G., G. Heal, P. Streufert and J. Swinkels (1992), 'Believing in multiple equilibria', First Boston Working Paper no. 92-32, Graduate School of Business, Columbia University.

Debreu, G. (1970), 'Economies with a finite set of equilibria', *Econometrica*, **38**, 387 - 392.

Drèze, J. and D. de la Vallèe Poussin (1971), 'A tâtonnement process for public goods', *Review of Economic Studies*, **38**, 133-150.

Ghosal, S. and M. Morelli (2002), 'Retrading in market games', Princeton University, School of Social Sciencs, Institute of Advanced Study, Discussion Paper, No 12.

Giraud, G. (1998), 'Correlated equilibria and strategic incompleteness in competitive market games', mimeo.

Grandmont, J.-M. (1982), 'Transformation of the commodity space, behavioral heterogeneity and the aggregation problem', *Journal of Economic Theory*, 57, 1-35.

Guesnerie, R. and J.-J. Laffont (1988), 'Notes sur les équilibres à taches solaires en horizon fini', *Mélanges Economiques: Essais sur l'honneur de Edmond Malinvaud*, *Economica*, 117-144.

Hahn, F. H. (1992), 'A remark on incomplete market equilibria', mimeo.

Hahn, F. H. and T. Negishi (1962), 'A theorem on non-tâtonnement stability', *Econometrica*, **30**, 463-469.

Hens, T. (1991), 'Sunspot equilibria in finite horizon models with incomplete markets', mimeo.

Hildenbrand, W. (1983), 'On the "law of demand" ', *Econometrica*, **51**, 997-1019.

Hildenbrand, W. (1994), *Market Demand: Theory and Empirical Evidence*, Princeton University Press.

Kurz, M. (1994, a), 'On rational belief equilibria', *Economic Theory*, **4**, 859-876.

Kurz, M. (1994, b), 'On the structure and diversity of rational beliefs', *Economic Theory*, **4**, 887-900.

Malinvaud, E. (1972, a), 'Prices for individual consumption, quantity indicators for collective consumption', *Review of Economic Studies*, **39**, 385-405.

Malinvaud, E. (1972, b), 'The allocation of individual risks in large markets', *Journal of Economic Theory*, **4**, 312-328.

Mas-Colell, A. (1989), 'Three observations on sunspots and asset redundancy', in P. S. Dasgupta, D. Gale. O. D. Hart and E. Maskin (eds), *Economic Analysis of Markets and Games: Essays in Honor of F. H. Hahn*, MIT Press, 465-474.

Mas-Colell, A. (1991), 'Indeterminacy in incomplete market economies', *Economic Theory*, **1**, 45-62.

Mas-Colell, A. and J. Nachbar (1991), 'On the finiteness of the number of critical equilibria, with an application to random selections', *Journal of Mathematical Economics*, **20**, 397-409.

Mercenier, J. (1996), 'Non-uniqueness of solutions in applied general equilibrium models with scale economies and imperfect competition: a theoretical curiosum?' *Economic Theory*, **6**, 161-178.

Pietra, T. and P. Siconolfi (1998), 'Fully revealing equilibria in sequential economies with an asset market', *Journal of Mathematical Economics*, **29**, 211-224.

Polemarchakis, H. M. and L. Ventura (2001), 'The relevance of extrinsic uncertainty', *Annales d' Economie et de Statistique*, forthcoming.

Radner, R. (1972), 'Existence of equilibrium of plans, prices, and price expectations', *Econometrica*, **40**, 289-303.

Radner, R. (1979), 'Rational expectations and the information revealed by prices', *Econometrica*, **47**, 655-678.

4. Extensive Form Implementation of Weak Fine Core Allocations through Penalties

David W. Bernotas[*], Dionysius Glycopantis[†], and Nicholas C. Yannelis[‡]

1. INTRODUCTION

Sections 1 to 4 are based on the discussion in Glycopantis-Muir-Yannelis (2001a,b) where we refer the reader for further information. They are reproduced here for completeness. The analysis in Section 5 is novel. The discussion there shows that an interim weak fine core (i.w.f.c.) allocation can be obtained as a perfect Bayesian equilibrium (PBE) even if the penalties imposed by an exogenous party, such as a court, are not very severe. In fact a unique threshold value for the penalty is calculated.

An economy with differential information consists of a finite set of agents each of which is characterized by a random utility function, a random consumption set, random endowments, a private information set and a prior probability distribution over possible states of nature. Issues in this area are discussed in Allen-Yannelis (2001), Hahn-Yannelis (2001), Krasa-Yannelis (1994) and Yannelis (1991), for example. The w.f.c. of a differential information economy (see Koutsougeras-Yannelis, 1993) is the set of all state-wise feasible and pooled information measurable allocations which cannot be dominated, in terms of ex ante expected utility, by feasible pooled information measurable net trades of any coalition. There is also an analogous definition

[*]   Department of Economics, University of Illinois at Urbana-Champaign, IL61820, USA (dbernota@uiuc.edu)
[†]   Department of Economics, City University, Northamption Square, London, EC1V 0HB, UK (d.glycopantis@city.ac.uk)
[‡]   Department of Economics, University of Illinois at Urbana-Champaign, IL, 61820, USA (nyannelis@uiuc.edu)

of an interim weak fine core, in terms of interim expected utility functions, given below. For private core concepts, we require that allocations are private information measurable.

As in Glycopantis-Muir-Yannelis (2001a, b) we provide a noncooperative, extensive form interpretation of the w.f.c. Generally speaking, we investigate whether or not cooperative core concepts such as the w.f.c. can be supported as a PBE, a variant of the sequential equilibrium of Kreps and Wilson (1982). In our analysis, we introduce game trees to show both the prior probability with which nature chooses and to make explicit the sequential moves of the players. By using game trees, we get a better understanding for the dynamics involved in designing contracts that may or may not be incentive compatible.

We also specify rules, i.e. the terms of a contract, which determine specific redistribution of the random initial endowments in different events. The rules spell out the consequences of each possible action by the players under all possible states of nature. Specifically, the rules give us a recipe for calculating the payoffs for each player as a function of their actions during play of the game.

A PBE consists of a set of players' optimal behavioral strategies and a consistent set of beliefs which attach a probability distribution to the nodes of each information set. Consistency requires that the decision from an information set is optimal given the particular player's beliefs about the nodes of this set and the strategies from all other sets. A player's beliefs are updated using the available information through Bayes' formula wherever possible. If an information set is not reached along the path of play, then appropriate beliefs are assigned arbitrarily to the nodes of the set.

The main results in this paper are the following. Despite the fact that the w.f.c. exists under mild assumptions, we show that, with reasonable rules for calculating payoffs, the w.f.c. cannot be supported as a perfect Bayesian equilibrium. The players have no incentive to share their information with each other, so the optimal path of play will lead to no trade. However, if we allow players to use an outside party, such as a court, which can impose penalties if a player lies, then the w.f.c. can be made incentive compatible, and thus can be reached as PBE.

The paper is organized as follows. Section 2 contains definitions of the differential information economy, incentive compatibility and the w.f.c. Section 3 gives an example of non-implementation of the w.f.c. Section 4 shows that the w.f.c. can be implemented if an outside agent such as a court is used to penalize players for lying. Section 5 calculates optimal penalties, and Section 6 presents some concluding remarks.

2. DIFFERENTIAL INFORMATION ECONOMY

We define below the notion of a finite-agent economy with differential information (see Glycopantis-Muir-Yannelis, 2001a, b). Let (Ω, F, μ) be a complete probability measure space. $\mathfrak{R}^l$ denotes l-fold Cartesian product of the set of reals $\mathfrak{R}$, and $\mathfrak{R}^l_+$ denotes the positive cone of $\mathfrak{R}^l$. Denote by 2^A the set of all non-empty subsets of the set A, and let / denote set theoretic subtraction.

Definition 2.1: *A differential information economy E as a set* $\{((\Omega, F, \mu),$
$X_i, F_i, u_i, e_i): i = 1, \ldots, n\}$ *where*

1. $X_i : \Omega \to 2^{\mathfrak{R}^l_+}$ is the set-valued function giving the random consumption set of player i,
2. F_i is a partition of F, denoting the private information of player i,
3. u_i is the random utility function of player i, endowment of player i,
4. $e_i : \Omega \to \mathfrak{R}^l_+$ is the random intial endowment of player i, where e_i is F_i-measurable with $e_i(\omega) \in X_i(\omega), \mu - \alpha.e.$
5. μ denotes the common prior of all agents.

To simplify notation, we shall denote Player i by Pi.

An interpretation of the model is as follows. In the first period, players must agree to and sign a contract. Agents have no information about the state of nature at this point. In period two, after the contract is agreed to, the state of nature is flashed on a screen for all players to see. However, some agents may not be able to distinguish the true state, and may therefore be uncertain of the actual state of nature. Players must then decide whether or not to renege on the original contract given their new information. All trades are then carried out.

Before agents receive any information about the realized state of nature, they must establish a contract to maximize their *ex ante expected utility:*

$$V_i(x_i) = \int_\Omega u_i(\omega, x_i(\omega)) d\mu(\omega),$$

where $\mu(\bullet) > 0$. The state of nature is then flashed on a screen for the agents to see, but according to their private information, some agents will be confused about what the actual state of nature is. For example, if we let $E_i(\omega)$ denote an element of the partition of F_i that contains the actual state of nature ω, then the agent cannot distinguish between ω and any $\omega' \in E_i(\omega)$.

The agents then decide whether or not they should renege on their contractual agreement according to their *interim expected utility:*

$$V_i(\omega, x_i) = \frac{1}{\mu(E_i(\omega))} \int_{\omega' \in E_i(\omega)} u_i(\omega', x_i(\omega')) d\mu(\omega').$$

It is assumed that $\mu(E_i(\omega)) > 0$. Given that some agents might be confused about which state of nature actually occurred, it may be impossible to detect if another agent has misreported their observed state. This being the case, agents may have an incentive to lie if the allocation resulting from the lie is preferred to the one resulting from telling the truth, and the other agents cannot detect this lie. An allocation is said to be *coalitionally Bayesian incentive compatible* (CBIC) if no coalition has an incentive to misreport the realized state of nature in order to make its members better off.

Let $L_1(\mu, \mathfrak{R}_+^l)$ denote the space of equivalence classes of Bochner integrable functions, and define $L_{x_i} = \left\{ x_i \in L_1(\mu, \mathfrak{R}_+^l) : x_i(\omega) \in X_i(\omega), \mu - \alpha.e. \right\}$.

Let $L_X = \prod_{i=1}^{n} L_{X_i}$.

Definition 2.2: *An allocation* $x \in L_x$ *with* $\sum_{i=1}^{n} x_i = \sum_{i=1}^{n} e_i$ *is CBIC if there do not exist a coalition S and states* ω^*, ω' *with* $\omega^* \neq \omega'$ *and* $\omega' \in \bigcap_{j \notin S} E_j(\omega^*)$,

with $e_i(\omega) + x_i(\omega') - e_i(\omega') \in \mathfrak{R}_+^l$ *such that* $\dfrac{1}{\mu(Z_i(\omega^*))} \int_{\omega \in Z_i(\omega^*)} u_i(\omega, e_i(\omega)$

$+ x_i(\omega') - e_i(\omega')) \, d\mu(\omega) > \dfrac{1}{\mu(Z_i(\omega^*))} \int_{\omega \in Z_i(\omega^*)} u_i(\omega, x_i(\omega)) d\mu(\omega)$, *for all* $i \in S_i$

where $Z_i(\omega^*) = E_i(\omega^*) \cap (\bigcap_{j \notin S} E_j(\omega^*))$ *with* $\mu(Z_i(\omega^*))$ *positive.*

The above definition reduces to the notion of *individual Bayesian incentive compatibility* (IBIC) if we restrict S to be singleton coalitions.

The idea of a fine core allocation (w.f.c.), or more generally pooled information core allocations, is due to Wilson (1978). Different versions of the fine core of Wilson were introduced in Yannelis (1991). The variant of the w.f.c. with ex ante utility functions is taken from Koutsougeras-Yannelis (1993).

Definition 2.3: *An allocation* $x = (x, \ldots, x_n) \in L_X$ *is called a weak fine core (w.f.c.) allocation if it satisfies the following:*

1. each $x_i(\bullet)$ is $V_{i=1}^n F_i$ - *measurable,*[1]

2. $\sum_{i=1}^n x_i = \sum_{i=1}^n e_i$ *(feasibility),*

3. *there do not exist coalition* S *and allocation* $(y_i)_{i \in S} \in \prod_{i \in S} L_{X_i}$ *such that* $y_i(\bullet) - e_i(\bullet)$ *is* $V_{i=S} F_i$ - *measurable for all* $i \in S$, $\sum_{i \in S} y_i(\bullet) = \sum_{i \in S} e_i(\bullet)$ *and* $V_i(y_i) > V_i(x_i), \forall i \in S$.

An interim weak fine core (i.w.f.c.) is defined by replacing condition 3 in definition 2.3 with condition 3′: there does not exist coalition S and allocation $(y_i)_{i \in S} \in \prod_{i \in S} L_{X_i}$ such that $y_i(\bullet) - e_i(\bullet)$ is $V_{i=S} F_i$ - *measurable for all* $i \in S$, $\sum_{i \in S} y_i(\bullet) = \sum_{i \in S} e_i(\bullet)$ *and* $V_i(\omega, y_i) > V_i(\omega, x_i), \forall i \in S$ *and* $\mu - \alpha.e$.

Notice that by replacing the pooled infromation measurability of each agent's allocation in (1) and (3′) by the private information measurability we obtain the definition of an *interim private core (i.p.c.)* allocation.

It should be noted that the w.f.c. is fully Pareto optimal since agents are allowed to share their information. However, the w.f.c. may not be IBIC, since it requires agents to share their private information. Specifically, we need to consider the possibility that the players have an incentive to lie about what they have seen in the interim state. It is this interim stage that the extensive form interpretation analyzes. As we will show in the next section, in the interim stage each player's optimal strategy may be to lie. Therefore, the pooling of information may not take place because of lack of incentive compatibility, as the example below indicates.

3. NON-IMPLEMENTATION OF THE WEAK FINE CORE

In this section, players will move sequentially and we investigate whether a contract between P1 and P2, which results in w.f.c. allocations, will be signed or not. In particular, we consider the following example.

Example 3.1: Consider the following two agent economy, $I = \{1,2\}$ with one commodity, i.e. $X_i = \mathfrak{R}_+$ for each i, and three states of nature $\Omega = \{a,b,c\}$. The agents are characterized by their initial endowments, their private information and their utility functions. For all $i \in I$ define $u_i : \Omega \times \mathfrak{R}_+^I \to \mathfrak{R}$ and $e_i : \Omega \to \mathfrak{R}_+^I$ as follows:

$$u_i(\omega, x_i(\omega)) = \sqrt{x_i}, \ \forall i$$

$$e_1(a,b,c) = (5,5,0), \qquad\qquad F_1 = \{\{a,b\},\{c\}\},$$
$$e_2(a,b,c) = (5,0,5), \qquad\qquad F_2 = \{\{a,c\},\{b\}\},$$
$$\mu_i(\omega) = \frac{1}{3}, \ \forall \omega \in \Omega, \ \forall i \in I.$$

Notice that if P1 and P2 pool their information, they will each know with certainty which state of nature has occurred, i.e. $F_1 V F_2 = \{\{a\},\{b\},\{c\}\}$. This implies that the agents will share risk perfectly, and the resulting w.f.c. allocation will be (5, 2.5, 2.5) for each agent. However, this is not IBIC.

Indeed if Agent 1 sees $\{a,b\}$, he has an incentive to report c. Agent 1 stands to gain if the true state is a and Agent 2 believes the declaration that it is c. In such a case, Agent 1 keeps the 5 units of the initial endowments in state a and also receives 2.5 units from Agent 2. As $u_1(e_1(a) + x_1(c) - e_1(c)) = u_1(7.5) > u_1(5) = u_1(x_1(a))$, it follows that the proposed allocation is not CBIC. Therefore, he has an incentive to lie and say state c occurred, which suggests a difficulty in implementing the proposed allocation by means of a contract.

We construct a game tree and employ reasonable rules for describing the outcomes of combinations of states of nature and actions of the players. We find that, although the Pareto superior allocation (5, 2.5, 2.5) is possible, the optimal strategies of the players imply no trade because of lack of IBIC. Hence, there is no advantage to signing such a contract.

Notice the w.f.c. allocation (5, 2.5, 2.5) for each agent is also an i.w.f.c. allocation. For example, under $\{a,b\}$ for Agent 1 and $\{b\}$ for Agent 2, a new allocation in order to make both players better off must give to Agent 1 more than 5 in a and less than 2.5 in b. However, the same allocation under $\{c\}$ and $\{a,c\}$ must give to Agent 2 more than 5 in a and less than 2.5 in c. It follows that such an allocation does not exist.

We discuss the possible realization of the allocation (5, 2.5, 2.5) through the analysis of a specific sequence of decisions and information sets shown in the game tree in Figure 1. The players are given choices to tell the truth or to lie, i.e., we model the idea that agents truly inform each other about what states of nature they observe, or deliberately aim to mislead their opponent. The issue is what type of behavior is optimal and therefore whether a proposed contract will be signed or not.

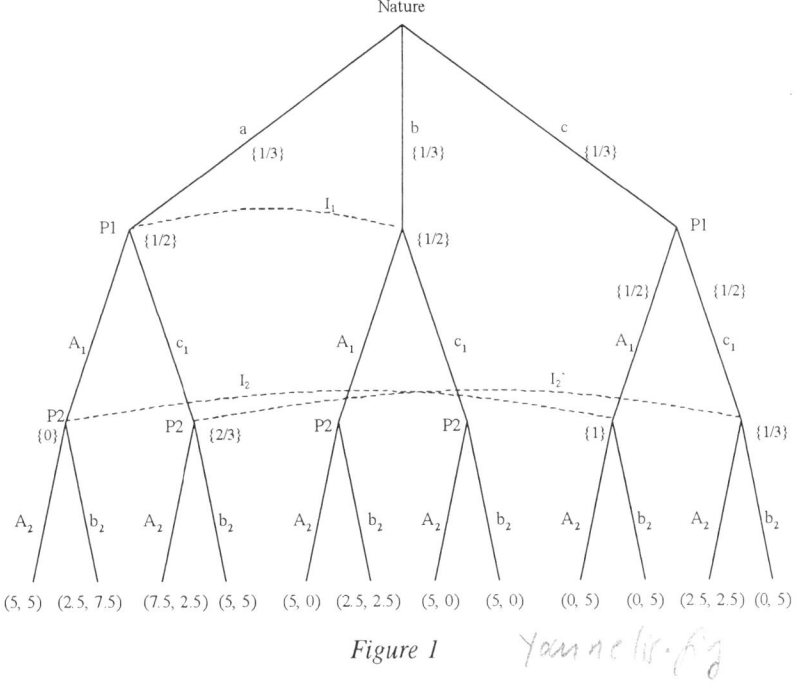

Figure 1

Figures 1 and 2 show that the allocation (5, 2.5, 2,5) will be rejected by the players. It is not IBIC and the proposed contract will not be signed. Notice that vectors at the terminal nodes of a game tree refer to payoffs of the players. The first element will be the payoff of P1, etc.

The explanation of Figure 1 is as follows. Nature chooses states *a*, *b* or *c* with equal probability. This choice is flashed on a screen which both players can see. P1 cannot distinguish between *a* and *b*, and P2 between *a* and *c*. This accounts for the information sets I_1, I_2 and I_2' with more than one node. A player cannot distinguish between the nodes in his information set, and therefore his action must be the same from all such nodes. A behavioral strategy of a player is an assignment of a probability distribution per information set that belongs to him over the choices available from that set. This is irrespective of whether a particular play of the game implies that these choices will have an effect on the payoffs. Indistinguishable nodes imply the F_i - *measurability* of decisions.

P1 moves first. After seeing what is flashed on the screen, P1 has two choices. He can either play $A_1 = \{a,b\}$ by announcing 'I have seen $\{a,b\}$ being unable to distinguish between the two' or he can play $c_1 = \{c\}$ and say 'I have seen $\{c\}$ '. Obviously one of these declarations will be truth and the other a lie. Following the announcement of P1, P2 takes his turn having listened to P1. He can respond by saying that the signal he has seen on the screen is $A_2 = \{a,c\}$ or $b_2 = \{b\}$. Again, one of these statements is a lie.

Next, given the sequence of decisions of the players shown on the tree, we specify the rules for calculating the payoffs, i.e. we specify the terms of the contract. This is a statement of what to do for all possible states of nature and declarations by the players.

The rules are:
(i) If the declarations by the two players are incompatible, that is (c_1, b_2) then at least one of the players is lying and, moreover, the opponent of a lying player detects that lie. This is the case when state c occurs and agent 1 reports state c and agent 2 state b. In state a, both agents can lie and the lie cannot be detected by either agent (the agents are in the events $\{a,b\}$ and $\{a,c\}$, respectively and they get five units of the initial endowments). Therefore, whenever the declarations are incompatible, no trade takes place and the players retain their initial endowments.
(ii) If the declarations are (A_1, A_2) then even if one of the players is lying, this cannot be detected by his opponent who believes that state a has occurred and both players have received endowment 5. Hence no trade takes place.
(iii) If the declarations are (A_1, b_2) then a lie can be beneficial and undetected, and P1 is trapped and must hand over half of his endowment to P2. Obviously if his endowment is zero then he has nothing to give.
(iv) If the declarations are (c_1, A_2) then again a lie can be beneficial and undetected. P2 is now trapped and must hand over half of his endowment to P1. Obviously if his endowment is zero then he has nothing to give.

The calculations of payoffs do not require the revelation of the actual state of nature. Instead, payoffs are based entirely on the announcements of the players according to the above rules. Optimal decisions from an information set will be denoted by a heavy line. Rationality and monotonicity of the utility function require that a player will not lie if he cannot get a higher payoff by doing so.

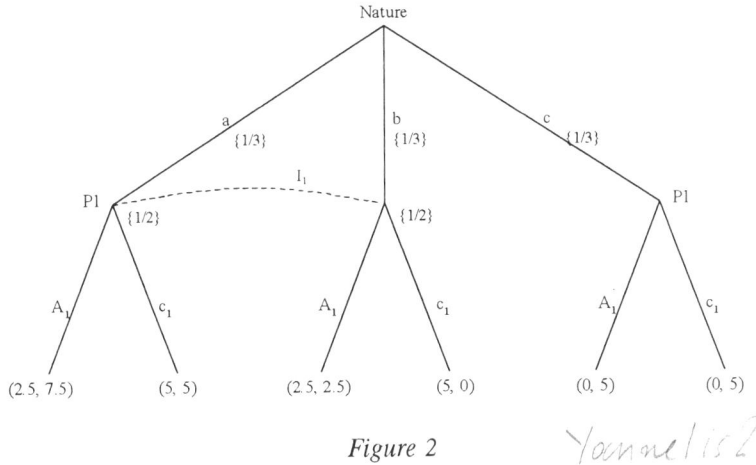

Figure 2

Using backward induction, the game in Figure 1 folds back to the one in Figure 2 in the following manner. In Figure 1, we see that from the information set I_2, P2 will play with probability 1. This accounts for the payoff (2.5, 7.5) and the first payoff (0,5) from left to right in Figure 2. Similarly, we undo all other information sets of P2 and we arrive at the remaining payoffs in Figure 2. Inspection of this figure reveals the optimal strategies of P1.

We now see that the optimal behavioral strategy for P1 is to play c_1 from I_1 i.e. to lie, and from the singleton to play either strategy. For simplicity, we have chosen the mixed strategy $(A_1, \frac{1}{2}; c_1, \frac{1}{2})$ for this node, and indicated this is with the $\frac{1}{2}$ on the branches from the singleton. Optimal behavioral strategy of P2 is to play b_2 with probability 1 from both I_2 and I_2', i.e. to lie, and from the singletons to play either strategy. Again P2 can use a mixed strategy from the singletons with any probability between zero and one.

Finally we point out that in Figures 1 and 2 the fractions next to the nodes in the information sets correspond to beliefs of the agents obtained, wherever possible, through Bayesian updating. Thus, they are consistent with the choice of a state by nature and the optimal strategies of each of the players. Hence strategies and beliefs satisfy the condition of a perfect Bayesian equilibrium.

These probabilities are calculated as follows. We give labels to the nodes of the information sets: from left to right, in I_1 we denote them by j_1 and j_2 in I_2 by n_1 and n_2 and in I_2' by n_3 and n_4. The probabilities attached to the nodes in I_1 follow from the fact that the probability with which nature chooses state a is the same as the one with which it chooses state b. Given the choices by nature, the strategies for the players described above and using the Bayesian formula for updating beliefs we also calculate the conditional probabilities:

$$\Pr(n_1|A_1) = \frac{\Pr(A_1|n_1) \cdot \Pr(n_1)}{\Pr(A_1|n_1) \cdot \Pr(n_1) + \Pr(A_2|n_2) \cdot \Pr(n_2)} = \frac{1 \cdot 0}{1 \cdot 0 + 1 \cdot \frac{1}{3} \cdot \frac{1}{2}} = 0, \text{ and}$$

$$\Pr(n_3|c_1) = \frac{\Pr(c_1|n_3) \cdot \Pr(n_3)}{\Pr(c_1|n_3) \cdot \Pr(n_3) + \Pr(c_1|n_4) \cdot \Pr(n_4)} = \frac{1 \cdot \frac{1}{3}}{1 \cdot \frac{1}{3} + 1 \cdot \frac{1}{3} \cdot \frac{1}{2}} = \frac{2}{3}.$$

Similarly, we obtain $\Pr(n_2|A_1) = 1$ and $\Pr(n_4|c_1) = \frac{1}{3}$.

Therefore, the perfect Bayesian equilibrium obtained above shows that the players' optimal decisions are to lie whenever possible. This implies that the contract $(5, 2.5, 2.5)$ cannot be realized and the players will not sign. In Figure 3 we indicate, through heavy lines, plays of the game which are the outcome of the choices by nature and the optimal behavioral strategies by the players. The interrupted lines at the beginning of the tree signify that nature does not take an optimal decision, as it has no payoff function, but simply chooses among three alternatives with equal probability. From each such choice the play of the game continues through the optimal decisions by the agents to a specific terminal node. The path (a, c_1, b_2) with payoffs $(5, 5)$ occurs with probability $\frac{1}{3}$. The paths (b, c_1, A_2) and (b, c_1, b_2) lead to payoffs $(5, 0)$ and occur with probability $\frac{1}{3}(1-q)$ and $\frac{1}{3}q$ respectively. The values $(1-q)$ and q denote the probabilities with which P2 chooses between A_2 and b_2 from the singleton node at the end of (b, c_1). Of course, no matter what q is selected this does not affect the payoffs. The paths (a, A_1, b_2) and (c, c_1, b_2) lead to payoffs $(0, 5)$ and each occur with probability $\frac{1}{3} \cdot \frac{1}{2}$ as by assumption, from the singleton node at the end of (c), P1 chooses between A_1 and c_1 with probability $\frac{1}{2}$. This of course is not significant because any other probabilities attached to A_1 and c_1 would not affect the payoffs.

Summarizing, we have shown that the implied equilibrium paths for Example 1 are as follows. If nature chooses a or b, P1 lies and plays c_1, P2 will lie from I'_2 with probability one and he will lie from the singleton node at the end of (b, c_1) with some arbitrary probability. The players end up with their initial endowments. If nature chooses c, P1 will lie with some arbitrary probability, and P2 will lie and play b_2 with certainty. Again, the players end up with their initial endowments. It follows that for all choices by nature, at least one of the players tells a lie on the optimal play path. The players, by lying, avoid the possibility of having to make a payment to their opponent.

We have constructed an extensive form game and employed reasonable rules for calculating payoffs and shown that the proposed allocation (5, 2.5, 2.5) will not be realized. The same conclusion would have been reached if P2 were assumed to move first.

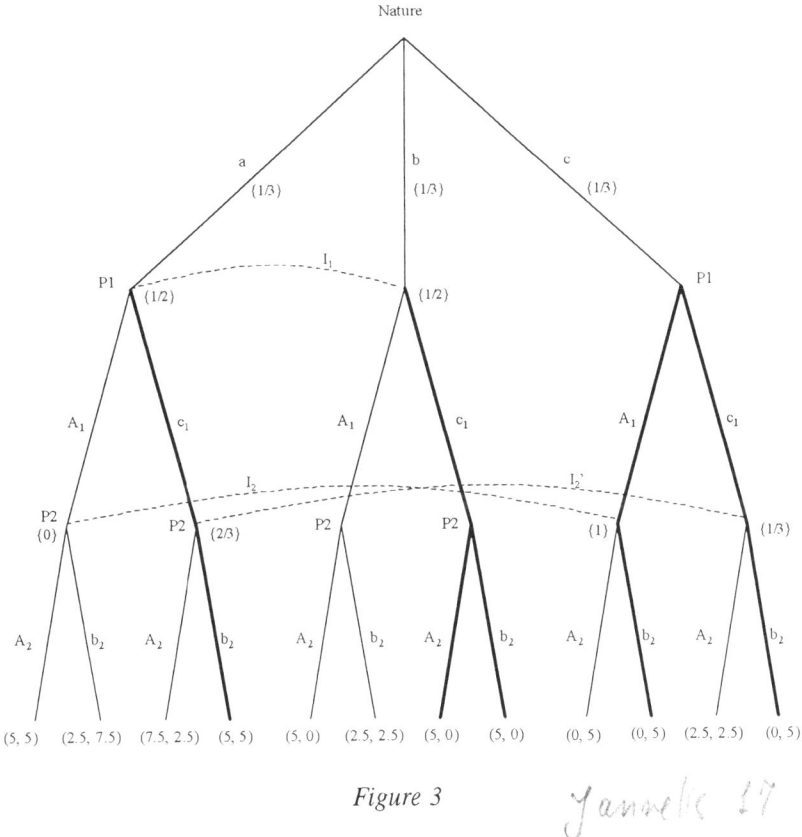

Figure 3

Yannelis 17

4. IMPLEMENTATION OF THE WEAK FINE CORE WITH PENALTIES

In this section, we introduce an exogenous third party in the form of a court, which sees the correct state of nature and has the power to penalize players for misreporting their observed state (or states) of nature. We will again illustrate play on a game tree, and calculate payoffs using specified rules as we did in Section 3.

The main structural difference between the game here and the one game of the previous section is that now, since the court has the power to ensure honest reporting of the state of nature, each player will not pay attention to what the other player reports. In essence, we are assuming that each player reports directly to the court. The court then determines if any penalties for lying are necessary, and the final allocations are then determined. This detail is illustrated in Figure 4. Notice that the first information set for P2 now includes four nodes, since he no longer cares if P1 announced A_1 or c_1.

The rules for calculating payoffs are as follows:

(i) If a player lies about his observation, then his endowment is taken by the court. If both players lie, then they are both penalized. If a player lies and the other agent who has not lied has a positive endowment, then the court keeps the quantity for itself. However, if the other agent has no endowment, then the court transfers to him the goods taken from the player who lied.

(ii) If the declarations of the two agents are consistent, then they divide equally the total endowments in the economy.

In Figure 4, the game tree reflects the severe penalties of the court. Now, P2 will play A_2 from I_2 and P1 will play A_1 from I_1. Thus, both players will tell the truth along the optimal path of play, and the w.f.c. allocation (5, 2.5, 2.5) can now be implemented as a PBE.

The intuition behind this is simple. In Example 3.1, the players lied in order to avoid giving half of their endowment to the other player. However, with the court implementing such severe penalties for lying, the players prefer to surrender 2.5 to the other player than to pay 5 to the court. The penalty made the w.f.c. allocation IBIC. Also notice that the court did not have to take any action in this example. Just the threat of the penalty was enough to ensure that the players reported truthfully their observed state of nature. The court made no redistribution of endowments.

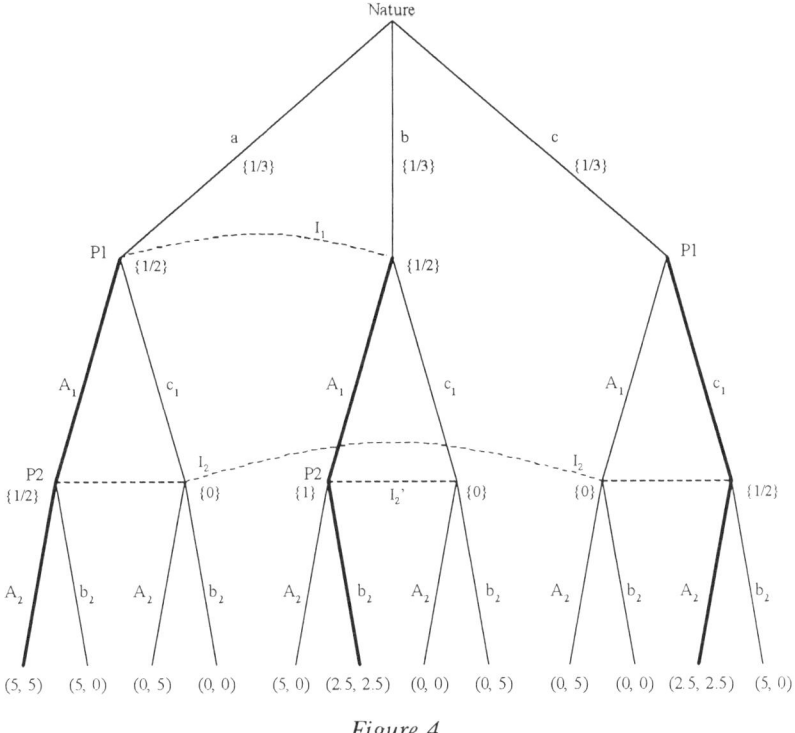

Figure 4

5. OPTIMAL PENALTIES

First we show, in a general static context, that penalties which make an i.p.c. allocation IBIC can be imposed and offer a conjecture concerning i.w.f.c. allocations. We next show that the w.f.c. allocation (5, 2.5, 2.5) can be obtained as a PBE in the presence of penalties even if these are not as severe as in the example in Section 4. Specifically, given our assumptions on the utility function, there exists a unique threshold value for the penalty. Any penalty more severe than this optimal value will result in truthful actions along the path of play. However, if the penalty falls short of this threshold value, then the players will lie, and the court will have to make the necessary redistributions.

We shall assume that, if there exists an ε' less than ε such that ε' eliminates the gain from misreporting, then the penalty will be set at ε'. Otherwise, it will be set at the level of ε. We consider this a reasonable rule for imposing penalties.

We now give a formal definition of the notion of CBIC in the presence of penalties. Again, this definition reduces to the notion of IBIC in the presence of penalties if we consider only singleton coalitions.

Definition 5.1: *An allocation $x = (x_1,\ldots,x_n) \in L_X$ is said to be CBIC in the presence of a penalty $\varepsilon_i \in \Re_+^l$, $(i = 1,2,\ldots,n)$, if the following does not hold:*

there exists a coalition S and states ω^*, ω' with $\omega^* \neq \omega'$ and $\omega' \in \bigcap_{j \in S} E_j(\omega^*)$,

with $e_i(\omega) + x_i(\omega') - e_i(\omega') - \varepsilon_i \in \Re_+^l$ such that $\dfrac{1}{\mu(Z_i(\omega^*))} \displaystyle\int_{\omega \in Z_i(\omega^*)} u_i(\omega, e_i(\omega))$

$+ x_i(\omega') - e_i(\omega') - \varepsilon_i)d\mu(\omega) > K_i(\omega^*, x_i)$, for all $i \in S$, where $K_i(\omega^*, x_i) =$

$\dfrac{1}{\mu(Z_i(\omega^*))} \displaystyle\int_{\omega \in Z_i(\omega^*)} u_i(\omega, x_i(\omega))d\mu(\omega)$ and $Z_i(\omega^*) = E_i(\omega^*) \cap (\bigcap_{j \notin S} E_j(\omega^*))$ with
$\mu(Z_i(\omega^*))$ positive.

We next prove that any interim private core allocation is IBIC in the presence of penalties.

Theorem 5.1: *Let $X(\omega) = R_+^l$ for all $\omega \in \Omega$ and suppose that for each i, with $i = 1,2,\ldots,n$, u_i is monotonic. If $x = (x_1,\ldots,x_n)$ is an interim private core allocation, then there exist penalties such that x is IBIC.*

Proof: We argue by contradiction. Let $x = (x_1,\ldots,x_n) \in L_x$ be an interim private core allocation and suppose that it cannot be made BIC by imposing penalties. Then there exists $i \in I$ and states ω^*, ω' with $\omega^* \neq \omega'$ and $\omega' \in E_k(\omega^*)$ for $k \in I \backslash \{i\}$, such that for alla penalties $\varepsilon_i > 0$ we have

$$\frac{1}{\mu(Z_i(\omega^*))} \int_{\omega \in Z_i(\omega^*)} u_i(\omega, e_i(\omega) + x_i(\omega') - e_i(\omega') - \varepsilon_i)d\mu(\omega) \qquad (1)$$

$$> \frac{1}{\mu(Z_i(\omega^*))} \int_{\omega \in Z_i(\omega^*)} u_i(\omega, x_i(\omega))d\mu(\omega)$$

where $Z_i(\omega^*)$ is defined above and ω^* can be taken to the realized state of nature. Because of the measurability of the measurability of $e_i(\bullet)$ and $x_i(\bullet)$, the above implies $e_k(\omega) + x_k(\omega') - e_k(\omega') - \varepsilon_i > x_k(\omega)$ for all $\omega \in Z_i(\omega^*)$. $^{not}_{correct.}$

We select a particular ε_i and call it ε. We now define the following functions, one per agent, on Ω.

$$y_i(\omega) = e_i(\omega) + x_i(\omega') - e_i(\omega') - \varepsilon, \text{ for all } \omega \in \Omega$$

$$y_k(\omega) = e_k(\omega) + x_k(\omega') - e_k(\omega') + \frac{\varepsilon}{n-1}, \text{ for all } \omega \in \Omega, k \in I\backslash\{i\}.$$

Next we show that $y = (y_1, \ldots, y_n)$ is an allocation in the sense that it is feasible and that also $y_i \in L_{X_i}$, and $y_i(\bullet) - e_i(\bullet)$ is F_i-measurable. These properties are needed in order to satisfy the conditions in Definition 2.3, adjusted for an i.p.c. allocation.

First we check feasibility, $\sum_{k \in I} y_k(\omega) = \sum_{k \in I} e_k(\omega)$ for all ω. This is straightforward. It is obtained by summing up over $k \in I$ per ω. Next, for all the function $y_k(\bullet)$, and hence $y_k(\bullet) - e_k(\bullet)$, is F_k-measurable. This follows from the F_k-measurability of $e_k(\bullet)$. Thus, each $y_k(\bullet) - e_k(\bullet)$, for $k \in I$ is F_k-measurable.

Now we build up (1) into the whole of $E_i(\omega^*)$ ignoring $\dfrac{1}{\mu(Z_i(\omega^*))}$. Player I will be the one-player coalition that will violate the assumption that $x = (x_1, \ldots, x_n)$ belongs to the interim private core. We have

$$\int_{\omega \in Z_i(\omega^*)} u_i(\omega, e_i(\omega) + x_i(\omega') - e_i(\omega') - \varepsilon) \, d\mu(\omega) +$$

$$\int_{\omega \in E_i(\omega^*)\backslash Z_i(\omega^*)} u_i(\omega, e_i(\omega) + x_i(\omega') - e_i(\omega') - \varepsilon) \, d\mu(\omega) > \qquad (2)$$

$$\int_{\omega \in Z_i(\omega^*)} u_i(\omega, x_i(\omega)) \, d\mu(\omega) + \int_{\omega \in E_i(\omega^*)\backslash Z_i(\omega^*)} u_i(\omega, x_i(\omega)) \, d\mu(\omega)$$

This follows by looking at the inequalities per term. The first term is (1) and the second one follows from the fact that $e_i(\omega)$ and $x_i(\omega)$ are constant on $E_i(\omega^*)$. Hence we have obtained a contradiction to the assumption that x is an interim private core allocation. This completes the proof.

Notice that the inequality (2) cannot be built up into the whole of Ω. This is because we cannot argue that $e_i(\omega) + x_i(\omega') - e_i(\omega') - \varepsilon \geq x_i(\omega)$ for $\omega \in \Omega$ $\backslash E_i(\omega^*)$. Therefore we cannot employ the above argument to extend in the theorem 'an i.p.c.' to 'an ex ante p.c.' allocation.

It should be noted that no continuity assumption was used in the above result and therefore it doesn't follow as a corollary from the theorem proved in Hahn-Yannelis (2001) on the incentive compatibility of a related interim private core notion.

Adopting a modification of the above argument, we conjecture that interim and ex ante weak fine core allocations can also be shown to be IBIC in the presence of penalties.

Suppose next that there is only one good. Then given ω^* and ω' a penalty $\varepsilon_i > 0$ can be found such that there is no gain from misreporting. Denote the smallest such penalty for each Agent i as $\varepsilon_i^* = min\{\varepsilon_i\}, \forall i \in I$. Thus, ε_i^* can be interpreted as the threshold penalty value for Agent i, and any penalty greater than or equal to ε_i^* will eliminate the gain from misreporting for that agent i. Finally, choosing $\varepsilon^* = \underset{i}{max}\{\varepsilon_i^*\}$ will result in a single penalty value that is equal to or exceeds the threshold value for all agents $i \in I$ implying that no agent can gain by misreporting in the presence of penalty ε^*. We can call this ε^* the optimal penalty.

It is important to notice that if the court chooses an $\varepsilon > \varepsilon^*$ then it will not have to take action in implementing the contract, i.e. the players will not use the courts along the optimal path. The threat of the penalty will be enough to ensure players do not misreport.

Next we show how the optimal penalty can be calculated in a dynamic setting using our model with sequential decisions. Figure 5 is the same diagram used in the above examples, but the payoffs have been changed to reflect the generalized payoff structure which includes ε, the penalty for lying. Payoffs were calculate using the same rules as above. Thus, a lie results in $5 - \varepsilon$ units of consumption.

The goal of the court should be to set ε such that the benefit of lying is just barely removed. The object of lying is to avoid giving the other player half of your endowment. However, given your incomplete information, you can't be certain if telling the truth will result in surrendering half of your endowment (as in states b for player 2 or c for player 1), or if you will be able to retain the entire endowment (as in state a). Thus, the penalty for lying should be set so that it is better for you to risk transferring half of your endowment than it is to pay the court penalty.

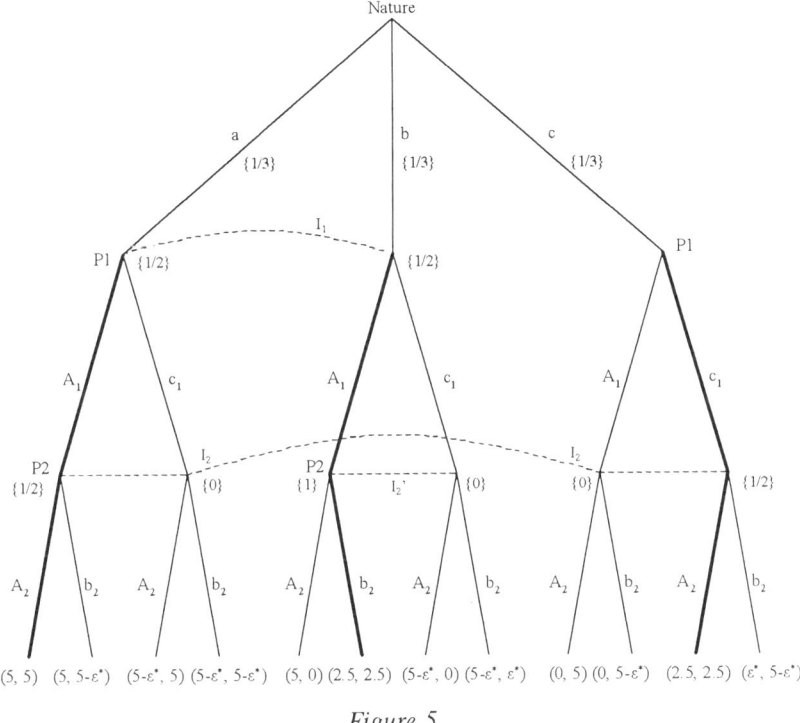

Figure 5

In order to analyze optimal strategies, we argue as follows. From the single-ton, P1 will play c_1 with probability one. Similarly, P2 will play b_2 from I'_2. Consider now the action of P2 from I_2. The first two nodes, from left to right are reached with a sum pf probabilities equal to $\frac{1}{2}$, and the last node with a probability equal to $\frac{1}{2}$. The payoff from A_2 is $\frac{1}{2}\sqrt{5}+\frac{1}{2}\sqrt{2.5}=1.91$ and the payoff from b_2 is $\sqrt{5-\varepsilon}$ which is decreasing in ε. It follows that for $\varepsilon \geq 1.357$ player P2 chooses A_2 and the tree folds back, eliminating I'_2 and I_2. Now for P1, the payoff from A_1 is $\frac{1}{2}\sqrt{5}+\frac{1}{2}\sqrt{2.5}$, and the payoff from c_1 is $\sqrt{5-\varepsilon}$. Again, the critical value of ε is 1.357. Thus, for $\varepsilon \geq 1.357$ both players tell the truth and implement the w.f.c. allocation (5, 2.5, 2.5).

In this particular example, since the endowments are symmetric, both agents have the same threshold value of ε^*. If we allow endowments to be asymmetric, then we may end up in a situation where one player plays truthfully from every node, but the other player lies with probability one. The resulting allocation will not be a w.f.c. allocation. Thus, the court must set the penalty to be above the highest threshold value for all players.

6. CONCLUDING REMARKS

If agents are allowed to pool their information, they can reach a fully Pareto optimal allocation such as the w.f.c. However, it is well known that the w.f.c. may not be IBIC, so there may be problems implementing such a contract as a PBE in a game with differential information. Implementation of the w.f.c. has been considered through sequential moves using game trees. Section 3 shows, using a two agent example, that the w.f.c. allocation will not be reached as a PBE since each player has an incentive to lie along the optimal path of play. However, the examples in Sections 4 indicate that if an exogenous party, such as a court, is allowed to penalize players for lying, then the w.f.c. can be made IBIC and thus implementable as a PBE. For our example, we have shown in Section 5 that, given basic assumptions on the utility functions, a unique threshold value for this penalty exists, and any penalty above this threshold will result in honest play along the optimal path.

NOTE

1.   Notice that $V_{i=1}^{n} F_i$ denotes the 'join', i.e. the smallest σ - field containing each F_i.

REFERENCES

Allen, B., Yannelis, N.C. (2001), 'On differential information economies', *Economic Theory*, **18**, pp. 262-273.

Glycopantis, D. Muir, A., Yannelis, N.C. (2001a), 'An extensive form interpretation of the private core', *Economic Theory*, **18**, pp. 293-319.

Glycopantis, D. Muir, A., Yannelis, N.C., (2001b), *Extensive form implementation of Radner equilibria*, REE and private core allocations, Mimeo.

Hahn, G., Yannelis, N.C. (2001), 'Coalitional Bayesian Nash implementation in differential information economies', *Economic Theory*, **3**, pp. 485-509.

Koutsougeras, L. Yannelis, N.C. (1993), 'Incentive compatibility and information superiority of the core of an economy with differential informations', *Economic Theory*, **3**, pp. 195-216.

Krasa, S., Yannelis, N.C. (1994), 'The value allocation of an economy with differential information', *Econometrica* , **62**, pp. 881-900.

Kreps, M. D., Wilson, R. (1982), 'Sequential equilibrium', *Econometrica*, **50**, pp. 889-904.

Wilson, R. (1978), 'Information, efficiency, and the core of an economy', *Econometrica* **46**, pp. 807-816.

Yannelis, N. C. (1991), 'The core of an economy with differential information', *Economic Theory*, **1**, pp. 183-198.

5. Nonlinear Neighborhood Interactions and Intergenerational Transmission of Human Capital

Yannis M. Ioannides*

1. INTRODUCTION

I develop a model of the evolution of human capital as an outcome of individual choice. A person chooses how much of her own human capital to devote to raising children and how much to allocate for own consumption. Production of offspring human capital is the only means by which individuals save. The model implies that under certain conditions the law of motion for the evolution of human capital exhibits multiple equilibria, two of which are stable and one is unstable. It is thus possible that the distribution of human capital across the population in the long run may not collapse into a single point.

This feature of the model is entirely dependent on two features: first, nonlinear neighborhood interactions must be present; second, the elasticity of substitution between own human capital and the neighborhood interactions must be sufficiently larger than the elasticity of substitution between one's

* Department of Economics, Tufts University, Medford, MA 02155, +1.617.627.3294. Yannis.Ioannides@tufts.edu.

I thank Costas Azariadis, Marcelo Coca, Steven Durlauf, Dennis Epple, Anna Hardman, Michael Kremer, Gib Metcalf, Scotte Page, Steve Ross, Danny T. Quah, Jeff Zabel and seminar participants in the University of Helsinki, the Athens University of Economics and Business, the London School of Economics and the University of Connecticut for useful comments, and Luis Ahn, Marcelo Coca, David Iaia, Pamela Jia and Anne K. Thompson for expert research assistance. Thanks are also due to the PSID staff at the University of Michigan for their help with the data, to Danny T. Quah for giving me access to tSrF and to Henry G. Overman for help with the program. This version is a major revision of my working paper with the same title.

Financial support by the John D. and Katherine T. MacArthur Foundation and the National Science Foundation is gratefully acknowledged.

child's human capital and own consumption. Neighborhood interactions, in general, represent the role of public education in the production of human capital. The model supports the Kuznets hypothesis, namely that the income distribution would worsen before it improves during the process of economic growth (Kuznets (1955)). I obtain a complete characterization of the properties of the intertemporal evolution of human capital, for the family of the functional specifications that I assume, and when it is an outcome of optimization by parents in the presence of neighborhood interactions.

The theoretical assumptions I make in the paper are intended to justify empirical specifications made by several researchers, but especially by Kremer (1997). I also report here empirical findings, which are based on geocoded data from the Panel Study of Income Dynamics and are similar to Kremer's findings of significant linear effects on a person's human capital, measured by years of education, of the average education in the neighborhood suitably defined where he or she grew up. However, my results show that a person's education is nonlinearly related to both father's and mother's education, when both are present in the regression, and to the mean, second and third moments of the distribution of education within the neighborhood where an individual was brought up. These findings are also supported by non-parametric estimates. They confirm a key prediction of the theory in this paper, namely that under certain conditions, the relationship between a child's education and that of his or her parent has a sigmoid shape, although the impact of the education of parents is different from that of education in the census tract where an individual grew up.

The model of the paper allows for the acquisition of human capital to involve both private and publicly provided inputs. Individuals and parents influence the former directly and can exercise some (possibly indirect, through residential choice) control over the latter. Examples of parents' direct choice over inputs into the educational process are sending one's children to private school, spending time helping children with their schoolwork, or paying for private tutors. Even if individuals rely on public education, they still may exercise choice when they decide what schools to send their children to, if there is choice, or where to locate, if that might make a difference, as in societies where the public provision of education is locally controlled, as in the US and other countries. In societies where the provision of education is highly centralized, choice of location may still influence the quality of education via the characteristics of the other students who reside in the same community. The behavioral model of this paper emphasizes how parental choice of human capital investment for their children is affected by their own human capital and by a neighborhood effect.

Formal education, of course, is only one factor in the development of human capital. It is complemented by direct parental inputs and by health, recreation, and culture, all of which are influenced by the choice of community of residence. Similarly, access to information about educational requirements of jobs may be facilitated by social interactions in one's residential community.

The coexistence of individual and social factors in the intergenerational transmission of human capital has been addressed theoretically by Azariadis and Drazen (1990), Benabou (1996a; 1996b) and Durlauf (1996a; 1996b). Benabou and Durlauf, in particular, emphasize the role of an economy's community structure on human capital accumulation in the presence of social spillovers. In the empirical literature, the paper is most closely related to Borjas (1992; 1995) and Kremer (1997).

In the remainder of this paper, I review in Section 2 key empirical findings, obtained by Borjas (1992) and Kremer (1997). In Section 3, I introduce a model that encompasses certain empirical models, including those of Borjas (1992) and Kremer (1997), as special cases. I explore the properties of a family of models, in which both parental and social components contribute to the process of intergenerational transmission of human capital. These models are amenable to empirical testing. I investigate their dynamics, which turn out to be quite rich. In Section 4 I present empirical results which confirm the importance of *nonlinear* effects of parental and neighborhood education. In Section 5 I show that the dynamics of the model may predict intertemporal variations of the income distribution along the lines of the Kuznets hypothesis. I also show how to apply the model to the case of local communities, where individuals' being able to choose where to locate may serve to internalize neighborhood interactions. Section 6 concludes.

2. NEIGHBORHOOD EFFECTS IN THE INTERGENERA-TIONAL TRANSMISSION OF HUMAN CAPITAL

The empirical literature on neighborhood effects construes them literally, that is, as effects on one's decisions of the characteristics and of the decisions of one's neighbors. It also construes them metaphorically, as interactions in a non-geographical sense, such as social interactions. Empirical research in this area is hampered by a paucity of suitable data. The two studies that I review below are significant also for their use of data.

2.1. Kremer's Findings on Neighborhood Effects

I use the term human capital to refer to the educational attainment in years of formal schooling. More generally, let $H_{i,t+1}$ denote human capital of a member of the ith dynasty in generation $t+1$; and let h_{it} denote that of a member of the same dynasty in generation t; agent i' is the spouse of agent i; $v(i)$ denotes the set of neighbors of agents i and i'; and n_i is its size, $n_i = |v(i)|$. In an important empirical paper on neighborhood effects, Kremer (1997) postulates the following law of intergenerational transmission of educational attainment:

$$H_{i,t+1} = \alpha_0 + \frac{\alpha}{2}(h_{it} + h_{i't}) + \beta h_{v(i)t} + \varepsilon_i , \qquad (2.1)$$

where α_0 denotes an exogenous intercept, $h_{v(i)t}$ is average education in the neighborhood of i's upbringing, $h_{v(i)t} = \frac{1}{n_i}\sum_{j \in v(i)} h_{jt}$ and ε_i is a stochastic shock. H_{it+1} is capitalized because it is an endogenous variable. Kremer uses equation (2.1) to obtain estimates of coefficients α and β and to study the intertemporal evolution of the variance of schooling (which may also be interpreted as a measure of the inequality of log earnings).

Kremer's estimates of neighborhood effects are large, when they are compared to the effect of parents' education, although there is no obvious metric. Kremer makes the point, however, that with the observed values for the parameters of the model, sorting of individuals into neighborhoods contributes little to the magnitude of the variance of schooling in steady state, σ_∞^2: specifically, with his findings of $\hat{a} = 0.395$ (0.051), $\hat{\beta} = 0.149$ (0.072), $\hat{\sigma}_\varepsilon = 0.179$ years. As Kremer puts it, 'living in an educated neighborhood increases the expected education for one's child by three-quarters as marrying an educated spouse, since the effect of each parent is half the total parental effect of 0.395.' by only 1.7 per cent, if ρ_v were to go up[1] from 0.2 to 0.4; it will go up by only 0.9 per cent, if ρ_m were to go up from 0.6 to 0.8. Kremer's findings on the importance of neighborhood effects make it even more pressing to explore what sort of behavioral setting would give rise to equations like his key estimating equation (2.1).

2.2. Borjas' Findings on Ethnicity and Neighborhood Effects

Borjas (1992) assumes that individuals value their own consumption and the human capital of their descendant according to a constant elasticity of substitution utility function. He assumes that a child's human capital is expressed as a Cobb-Douglas function first of the fraction an individual allocates of her own human capital to her child's upbringing, and second, of a local interaction effect, represented by the mean human capital of her ethnic group. These assumptions imply an intergenerational human capital (or earnings) mobility equation that relates an individual's human capital, H_{igt+1}, to those of her parent, h_{igt}, and to the mean human capital in the ethnic group g, $\overline{h}_{gt}$ as follows:

$$H_{igt+1} = \gamma_1 h_{igt} + \gamma_2 \overline{h}_{gt} + \xi_{igt} , \tag{2.2}$$

where all variables are measured as deviations from the mean, the shock ξ_{igt} may be decomposed as $\xi_{igt} = e_{igt} + \varepsilon_{gt}$ where the random variables e and ε are uncorrelated; the random variable ξ_{igt} has the stochastic structure of the random effects model. The estimates with (2.2) with log wages data by Borjas range from 0.1829 to 0.2664, for γ_1 and from 0.1455 to 0.4589, for γ_2 ; the estimates with schooling data vary from 0.2566 to 0.3465, for γ_1 ; and from 0.0990 to 0.2983, for γ_2 .[2]

3. NONLINEAR MODELS OF THE INTERGENERATIONAL TRANSMISSION OF HUMAN CAPITAL

The differences between Kremer's and Borjas's results may have rather minor consequences for our understanding of the dynamics of human capital formation in an economy, if one were to rely upon linear dynamic models. Results could differ dramatically if nonlinear processes were at work. Next I explore a class of models of neighborhood interactions and human capital, which imply the models of Borjas and Kremer as special cases. The general model is somewhat related to Azariadis and Drazen (1990) and exploits the behavioral model of Borjas (1992) to its full generality. It allows me to explore some of the same issues as those raised by those two and other researchers.

The economy consists of a large number of agents, each of whom lives for a single period. Each agent has an endowment of human capital, which she must allocate to the production of labor services and of human capital for her offspring. I adopt the assumption of Borjas (1992), equation (2.1) of a utility function for the parent, with a constant elasticity of substitution (CES) between the child's human capital, H_{it+1}, measured in efficiency units, and own consumption, C_{it}:

$$U = U(H_{it+1}, C_{it}) \equiv \left[\zeta(H_{it+1})^{1-\frac{1}{\sigma}} + (1-\zeta)(C_{it})^{1-\frac{1}{\sigma}} \right]^{\frac{\sigma}{\sigma-1}} ; \sigma > 0, \quad (3.1)$$

The parameter σ, which may exceed 1, denotes the elasticity of substitution between human capital stock of the child and own consumption. A parent and her child are always indexed by the same subscript. However, I do not consider marital sorting, and therefore I drop the subscript i from now on, when no confusion arises.

Let s_t denote the savings rate, that is, the fraction of own human capital that a parent devotes to the production of human capital of her child. The remainder is allocated to paying for her own consumption, $(1 - s_t)R_t h_t = C_t$ where R_t denotes the real wage rate per efficiency unit of labor, with consumption as numeraire. A child's human capital is produced by the parent's own input, $s_t h_t$, and the local interaction effect, v_t, from the community where individual i lives. They combine through a constant elasticity of substitution production function to produce the child's human capital, H_{t+1}. This assumption of a CES production rather than of a Cobb-Douglas relationship as in Borjas (1992), combines with (3.1) to enrich the model.[3] It is more convenient for the problem at hand to express this relationship in terms of C_t directly, instead of s_t, as the unknown decision variable:

$$H_{t+1} = \left[\eta(h_t - \frac{1}{R_t}C_t)^{1-\frac{1}{b}} + (1-\eta)(v_t)^{1-\frac{1}{b}} \right]^{\frac{b}{b-1}}, \quad (3.2)$$

where b, $b > 0$, denotes the elasticity of substitution between parental input and the social interaction effect in human capital production, and η, $0 < \eta < 1$ a parameter.

From the first order conditions for the maximization of (3.1) subject to (3.2), we have:

$$
(H_{t+1})^{\frac{1}{\sigma}-\frac{1}{b}} = \frac{\eta\zeta}{(1-\zeta)R_t^{1-\frac{1}{\sigma}}} \frac{\left(h_t - \left[\frac{1}{\eta}(H_{\tau+1})^{\frac{b-1}{b}} - \frac{1-\eta}{\eta}v_t^{1-\frac{1}{b}} \right]^{\frac{b}{b-1}} \right)^{\frac{1}{\sigma}}}{\left[\frac{1}{\eta}(H_{\tau+1})^{\frac{b-1}{b}} - \frac{1-\eta}{\eta}v_t^{1-\frac{1}{b}} \right]^{\frac{1}{b-1}}}
\tag{3.3}
$$

I develop the properties of the solution of (3.3) by working with its inverse, that is, with h_t as a function of H_{t+1} and v_t : simplifying by using the homogeneity of degree 0 of (3.3) yields:

$$
h_t = H_{t+1}\eta^{-\frac{b}{b-1}} \left[1-(1-\eta)\left(\frac{v_t}{H_{t+1}}\right)^{\frac{b-1}{b}} \right]^{\frac{b}{b-1}} + \left(\frac{1-\zeta}{\eta\zeta}\right)^{\sigma}\eta^{-\frac{\sigma}{b}}R_t^{\sigma-1}H_{t+1}\left[1-(1-\eta)\left(\frac{v_t}{H_{t+1}}\right)^{\frac{b-1}{b}} \right]^{\frac{\sigma}{b-1}}
\tag{3.4}
$$

3.1 Law of Motion of the Intertemporal Evolution of Human Capital

A child's human capital follows, from (3.4), as an implicit function of her parent's human capital and of the local interaction effect,

$$
H_{t+1} = \mathcal{H}(h_t, v_t) .
\tag{3.5}
$$

I shall refer to the above equation as the *law of motion* for human capital. My results are summarized in the propositions which follow. Proposition 1 deals with general properties of the law of motion. Proposition 2 deals with properties of specific cases, many of which have been utilized by the empirical literature, but had not been explored as following from the same general behavioral framework. Both proofs are elementary and therefore relegated to the Appendix.

Proposition 1. *The time map associated with the law of motion (3.5) of the evolution of human capital is a monotone increasing function of* (h_t, v_t) ; *with*

$H_{t+1} = (1-\eta)^{\frac{b}{b-1}}v_t$ *if* $h_t = 0$. *It is an increasing (decreasing) function of* R_t *if* $\sigma \leq 1 (>1)$. *In addition:*

1. *If* $\sigma \geq b$ *or* $\sigma < b$, *and* $1 > b - \sigma$ *then the time map is an increasing con-*

cave function of h_t; with $lim_{h_t \to \infty} \frac{\partial H_{t+1}}{\partial h_t} < \eta^{\frac{b}{b-1}} < 1$.

2. *If $\sigma < b$ and $1 < b - \sigma$ then in general there exists an interval, defined by a pair of threshold values for $R_t, [R_{min}(v_t), R_{max}(v_t)]$, within which the time map is an increasing S-shaped (sigmoid) function of h_t; for low values of h_t.*
3. *The time map is an increasing concave function of v_t, if $\sigma < b < 1$, or $\sigma > b > 1$. If $b > \sigma > 1$ and b is sufficiently larger than σ, then the time map may become a convex function of v_t.*

The essence of Proposition 1 may be summarized as follows. Given b, the elasticity of substitution in (home) production between own input and the neighborhood interaction effect, there exists a maximum value of σ, the elasticity of substitution in consumption between the offspring's human capital and own consumption, below which the law of motion is sigmoid. In other words, provided that $\sigma > 1$; own input and neighborhood interaction input are not essential in the production of offspring human capital, the more complementary are own consumption and offspring human capital the more likely it is that the law of motion is sigmoid. This property is subject to a threshold value of the real wage rate and therefore is similar to the emergence of sigmoid time maps in overlapping-generations neoclassical growth models, that also involve thresholds (see Galor and Ryder (1991) and Azariadis (1993), p. 203). However, there is an important difference from Galor and Ryder's finding, where emergence of a sigmoid map requires that the economy be sufficiently productive and that the elasticity of substitution between capital and labor in the aggregate production function be less than 1 (in which case capital and labor are essential). Proposition 1 generalizes in the form of maximum and minimum thresholds for productivity, and of a maximum threshold $b - 1$ for the elasticity of substitution between own consumption and offspring human capital. A notion of complementarity that rests on a comparison of preference and human capital production parameters heeds in part Matsuyama's point that complementarity should *not be assumed* but *derived* (Matsuyama (1995; 1996)). The main model here implies results similar to those of Ciccone and Matsuyama (1999). It is precisely because own input and neighborhood interaction input are not essential in the production of offspring human capital that we may have three positive steady states. In contrast, the fact that inputs are essential in the Galor-Ryder case gives rise to at most two equilibria. This result serves as a specific example of the general possibility of a sigmoid time map, recognized by Galor and Tsiddon (1997) and attributed by them to third derivative properties.[4]

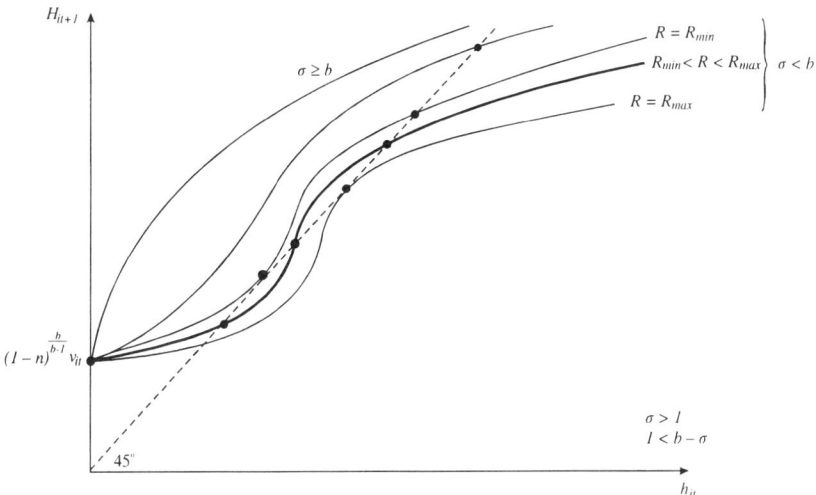

Figure 1

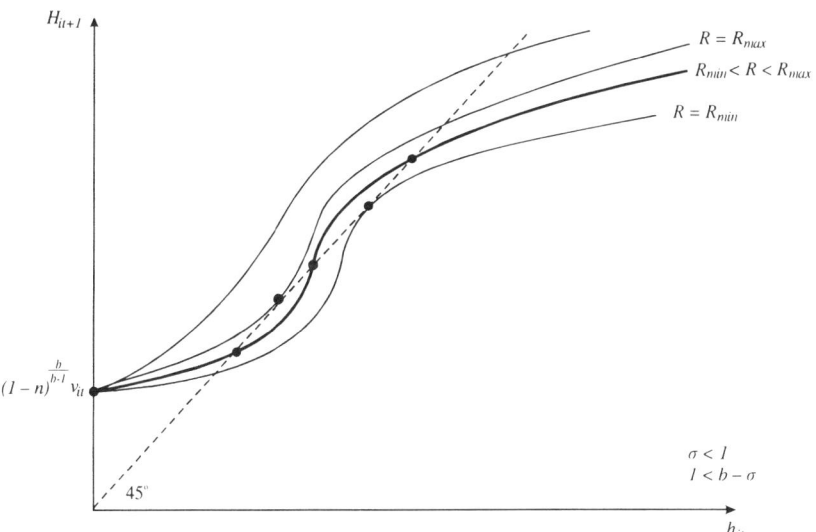

Figure 2

As the above discussion and Figures 1 and 2 make clear, as R_t changes, the dynamical system (3.5) undergoes a *saddle-node bifurcation* (Azariadis (1993), p. 92). The fact that the critical values depend upon the social interaction term v_t makes clear that in general the dynamics of the model are quite complicated, especially when interactions are endogenous. An exhaustive analysis would be based on the properties of H_{t+1} as a function of v_t, which may be obtained from (3.3). However, unlike (3.4), we cannot solve (3.3) in closed form for H_{t+1} as a function of v_t (nor its inverse), a fact that complicates such an analysis. Additional elements of complication are introduced if an individual's own human capital is related to the interaction effect v_t as is likely to be the case in the model of community selection that I briefly touch upon further below. It is straightforward to work out the basic properties of the law of motion for special sets of values of the substitution elasticities. I summarize my results in the following proposition.

Proposition 2. The law of motion (7) encompasses the following as special cases.

1. *If* $v_t = 0$, *or* $\eta = 1$, *no interaction effects, the time map is linear in* h_t :

$$H_{t+1} = \eta^{\frac{b}{b-1}} \left[1 + \left(\frac{1}{\eta}\right)^{\frac{b-\sigma}{b-1}} \left(\frac{1-\zeta}{\eta\zeta}\right)^{\sigma} R_t^{\sigma-1} \right]^{-1} h_t.$$ (3.6)

2. *If the elasticity of substitution in consumption is greater than 1 and in human capital production equal to 1,* $\sigma > 1$ *and* $b = 1$, *then the time map, expressed by its inverse,*

$$h_t = H_{t+1}^{\frac{1}{\eta}} v_t^{1-\frac{1}{\eta}} + \left(\frac{1-\zeta}{\eta\zeta}\right)^{\sigma} R^{\sigma-1} (H_{t+1})^{\frac{\eta+\sigma(1-\eta)}{\eta}} v_t^{\sigma(1-\frac{1}{\eta})},$$ (3.7)

is an increasing concave function of (h_t, v_t). *It follows that,* $H_{t+1} = 0$, *if* $h_t = 0$,

$$lim_{h_t \to \infty} \frac{\partial H_{t+1}}{\partial h_t} = 0.$$

3. *If* $\sigma = 1$ *and* $b > 2$, *the elasticity of substitution in consumption is equal to 1 and in human capital production greater than 2, then the time map*

$$h_t = \left[\frac{1}{\eta}(H_{t+1})^{\frac{b-1}{b}} - \frac{1-\eta}{\eta} v_t^{\frac{b-1}{b}} \right]^{\frac{b}{b-1}} + \left(\frac{1-\zeta}{\eta\zeta} \right)(H_{t+1})^{1-\frac{1}{b}} \left[\frac{1}{\eta}(H_{t+1})^{\frac{b-1}{b}} - \frac{1-\eta}{\eta} v_t^{\frac{b-1}{b}} \right]^{\frac{1}{b-1}} \quad (3.8)$$

may be a sigmoid curve and is independent of R_t. It follows that

$$H_{t+1} = (1-\eta)^{\frac{b}{b-1}} v_t, \text{ if } h_t = 0, \ lim_{h_t \to \infty} \frac{\partial H_{t+1}}{\partial h_t} < \eta.$$

4. *If $\sigma \to \infty$, the utility function is linear, then the time map is given by*

$$H_{t+1} = (1-\eta)^{\frac{b}{b-1}} \left(\frac{\left(\frac{1-\zeta}{\zeta\eta} R_t \right)^{b-1}}{\left(\frac{1-\zeta}{\zeta\eta} R_t \right)^{b-1} - \eta} \right)^{\frac{b}{b-1}} v_t, \quad (3.9)$$

and is a function of v_t, only, and thus independent of h_t.

5. *If $b \to \infty$, the production function for human capital is linear, then the time map is given by*

$$H_{t+1} = \left(1 + \left(\frac{1-\zeta}{\zeta\eta} \right)^{\sigma} \eta^{1-\sigma} R_t^{\sigma-1} \right)^{-1} \left[\eta h_t + (1-\eta) v_t \right] \quad (3.10)$$

and is proportional to a convex combination of (h_t, v_t).

6. *If $\sigma = b$, the elasticity of substitution in consumption is equal to that in human capital production, then the time map is given by*

$$H_{t+1} = \left[\eta \left(\frac{1}{1 + \left(\frac{1-\zeta}{\eta\zeta} \right)^{\sigma} R_t^{\sigma-1}} \right)^{1-\frac{1}{\sigma}} \left[h_t^{1-\frac{1}{\sigma}} + (1-\eta)(v_t)^{1-\frac{1}{\sigma}} \right] \right]^{\frac{\sigma}{\sigma-1}}. \quad (3.11)$$

Borjas (1992) works with a case similar to (3.8) above, except that his Cobb-Douglas production function assumes decreasing returns to scale, whereas mine assumes constant returns to scale. It would be possible to work back-wards from the cases where the model has been solved for explicitly in order to recover the savings rate s_t associated with the behavioral model. For some of these cases, it may be necessary to impose additional restrictions on parameter values, as is typically the case for CES-based models, in order for the value of the savings rate to be between 0 and 1. Kremer (1997) does not assume a specific behavioral model, but the model he estimates, equation (2.1), is reminiscent of (3.10), which is a special case of our general model.

The law of motion for the intergenerational transmission of human capital implies a solution for a child's human capital, H_{t+1} as a function of both the human capital of the parent, h_t and of the interaction effect, v_t. An increase in the interaction effect shifts the entire map upwards. However, the impact of such an increase in the interaction effect upon the steady state depends on whether or not we have multiple equilibria.

This basic model may be adapted to express different institutional environments via the specification of the relationship between one's human capital, h_t, and the interaction effect, v_t. I return below to the role of the specification of v_t. The properties of $\mathcal{H}(\bullet)$ that I have developed allow broad predictions about the dynamic evolution of dynastic, i.e., a family's, human capital. The possibility that the time map has a sigmoid shape leads readily to a multiplicity of steady-state equilibria, where one of these equilibria will be unstable in certain circumstances. Nonlinear dynamics are caused by the dependence of offspring human capital on the interaction effect v_t. In the context of an ethnic capital interpretation of the model (in the style of Borjas), observing the occupational distribution among ethnic groups and applying the standard Roy model of occupational choice would make one conclude that there are intrinsic skill differences across ethnic groups. In contrast, as Matsuyama (1995) notes, 'a theory of pattern formation would suggest that there are some complementarities in the processes of skill acquisition, limited within an ethnic group, so that some small differences in skills or some random events happen to end up sorting different groups into different occupations' (*ibid.*, p. 68). It is precisely such complementarities that my model seeks to articulate. The skill differences do not have to be very large. It suffices, according to Proposition 1, to have an unstable equilibrium that is symmetric (loosely speaking, although it could be rendered precisely so by means of suitable choice of parameter values) relative to two other stable but asymmetric equilibria. Such a variety of outcomes for the intergenerational evolution of human capital depends upon behavioral parameters and the parameters of the production function for human capital, on one hand, and initial conditions (h_0, v_0), on the other.

4. EMPIRICAL RESULTS

Kremer (1997) works with data on years of education from the Panel Study of Income Dynamics (PSID), augmented by means of the geocodes. This additional information in the form of geocodes allows the researcher to identify the census tract in which a respondent lived when the interviews took place. US census tracts typically comprise approximately 5000 people. Education and other data by census tracts is publicly available and reported in terms of brackets (Adams (1991a)). Such a linkage is made possible by means of tract identifiers, which are documented in Adams (1991b) and made available to investigators confidentially by means of special arrangements only. These identifiers allow one to link individuals to the 'neighborhoods' of their residence. I am aware of the fact that years of education is a very restricted measure of human capital but wish to conform to Kremer's choice as well. It is a measure that is particularly relevant for inequality. To give an example, the variance of logarithm of years of education is an important component of the variance of logarithm of earnings.

I follow Kremer (1997) and define the sample within the PSID to include only individuals who have completed their education. I have selected individuals, male or female, who have been interviewed at least once and are at least 28 years of age by 1992 and both of whose parents have been interviewed at least once. That is, I work with the same age cutoff as Kremer (1997), except that he applies it to 1988 only while I extend it to 1992. Kremer defines the neighborhood of upbringing as the census tract where the child lived in 1968. For individuals who became 28 years of age after 1988 I use the 1980 Census Extract Data Sets. About 74 per cent of the sample used in regressions are associated with neighborhood data from the 1970 Census, and the remainder are from the 1980 Census. In spite of this difference, the resulting samples are quite similar. In order to use self-reported data from parents and children I need to use split-offs from the original Panel Study of Income Dynamics (PSID) sample. This renders the sample no longer representative of the US population because it does not include observations added to the PSID to replace respondents lost to attrition. Moreover, the PSID oversamples the poor. I therefore weight observations, using the most recent set of PSID weights as suggested by the PSID staff, just as Kremer (1997), p. 123).

I follow Kremer in defining the values of years of education to associate with each interval. These brackets and the respective means in 1970 and 1980 are as follows:

Age group	Mean 1970	Mean 1980	Value
Percent of age 25 or older with 0-8 years	24.96	16.70	6
Percent of age 25 or older with 9-11 years	20.32	15.99	10
Percent of age 25 or older with 12 years	31.30	33.65	12
Percent of age 25 or older with 13-15 years	11.59	16.63	14
Percent of age 25 or older with 16 + years	11.85	16.98	17

I am interested in exploring further the presence of nonlinearities in the relationship between individuals' education and those of parents and the distribution of education in the neighborhood where individuals were brought up.[5]

I follow Kremer in constructing neighbors' education; see the last column of the above table. In an additional and novel step, I use the frequency distribution for the educational attainment of males over twenty-five years of age in the census tract in which the respondent grew up, to compute the first, second and third moments of the distribution of education in the census tract of respondents' residence. I believe this is the first such use of the frequency distributions for education within census tracts in the context of the neighborhoods effects literature. It appears to be crucial for the appearance of significant nonlinear effects.

4.1 Parametric Estimations

My OLS regressions basically follow equation (2.1) and are reported in Table 1.

It is worth recalling the fundamental identification issues which may in principle affect this model (Manski (1993)). Here as in Manski's equation (3.11), with 'social forces act[ing] on the individual with a lag', the coefficient of neighbors education (the social effect) may be identified if I assume that the process is observed out of equilibrium (*ibid.*, p. 540).

Column 1 reports Kremer's main regression for the purpose of comparison. Columns 2, 4 and 6 report our results for equation (2.1) with a similarly defined sample, based on the random subsample of the PSID. Columns 3 and 5 report our results with the entire PSID sample, which includes oversampling of the poor. All regressions are weighted with the appropriate weight. Columns 1 and 2 are quite similar, broadly speaking, although in my results the total effect of parents' education is numerically less important than that in Kremer, and the opposite is true for the average education in the neighborhood. I do not an explanation for these differences.

A key prediction of Proposition 1, part 2, is that parents' education would have a sigmoid effect on children's education in the presence of an interaction effect. Kremer reports that inclusion of quadratic terms for parents' education, are and neighbors' education, and an interaction term for parents' and neighbors' education is not significant and an F-test cannot reject linearity.[6] I test this prediction by including linear, quadratic and cubic terms for fathers' education and for mothers' education. The results for the polynomial structure, which are reported in Table 1, Columns 3 and 5, respectively, for the random subsample of the PSID include both fathers' and mothers' education. A polynomial structure for fathers' education on its own is significant, but two of the terms lose their significance when the terms for mothers' education are added. The results imply a sigmoid shape for the relationship between parents' education and children's education, with two of the terms for mothers' education being statistically significant and implying an inflection point at 11.75. Mothers generally spend more time with their children, which enables them to instill more of their own values upon their offspring. Moreover, mothers' own educational attainments can also be seen as better proxies for 'social class', especially at the time when the data were collected. Marital sorting suggests that education of spouses are related to one another, and such dependence may cloud the interpretation of the two different coefficients. The data reject the hypothesis that the linear terms for fathers' and mothers' education are equal. Nonetheless, imposing equality and including quadratic and cubic terms yields dynamics very similar to those implied by the terms for mothers' education.

I test the nonlinearity of education within the neighborhood where an individual was brought up by including the second and third *moments* of the distribution of education within the appropriate census tract. These moments are computed directly from the frequency distributions in the data and have not been used before in this literature. Their inclusion as a group is statistically significant overall. The estimated coefficients are not statistically significant for the random sample (Column 13.4) but are more significant and do imply a nonlinear effect for neighbors' education for the entire PSID sample (Column 5). The results of this procedure are very different from those obtained when the square and the cube of the mean neighborhood education are included as regressors.

Table 1: Intergenerational Transmission of Human Capital
Dependent Variable: Educational attainment at 28 years of age (years). Sample restricted to individuals whose parents report their own educational attainment. t statistics in parentheses. All regressions are weighted by latest PSID weights. + denotes the estimate of the coefficient of the interaction term. Column 1 reports Kremer's main regression for the purpose of comparison. Columns 2 and 4 report our results with a similarly organized sample, which is based on the original random sample of the PSID. Columns 3, 5 and 6 report our results with the entire PSID sample. Columns 7 and 8 report results with the same sample as that for Columns 2 and 4, but the dependent variables and all regressors (except for the dummy for 1970 neighbors data) are in logarithms.

Model	1	2	3	4	5	6	7	8
Observations	880	881	1764	885	1764	881	881	881
R^2_{adj}	0.231	0.2385	0.2212	0.2624	0.2033		0.2219	0.2411
F		70.28	126.27	32.48	62.62		63.80	35.98
LLF		-3463.12				-3462.36		
Mean dep.var	13.18	13.96	13.75	13.96	13.75	2.62	2.62	2.62
Intercept	6.96 (7.48)	6.38 (10.83)	7.24 (18.31)	7.19 (0.79)	5.05 (0.80)	2.81 (0.98)	1.32 (12.58)	1.56 (3.96)
Fathers' education (12.11, 3.85)	0.288 (12.11, 3.85)	0.192 (7.38)	0.186 (7.29)	-0.353 (10.33)	-0.263 (1.39)	0.152 (1.50)	0.164 (6.96)	0.671 (6.89) (1.08)
Fathers' education squared				0.035 (1.26)	0.027 (1.44)			-0.436 (1.36)
Fathers' education cubed				-0.0006 (0.67)	-0.0004 (0.66)			0.092 (1.74)
Mothers' education (12.9, 2.85)	0.154 (2.85)	0.166 (4.79)	0.139 (5.88)	-0.643 (1.11)	-1.184 (5.10)	0.110 (3.95)	0.127 (4.21)	-0.573 (1.99)
Mothers' education squared				0.109 (2.06)	0.141 (5.84)			0.483 (2.38)
Mothers' education cubed				-0.004 (2.51)	-0.004 (5.72)			-0.091 (2.29)
Neighbors' education (11.29,1.53)	150 (11.29,1.53)	232 (2.08)	0.191 (4.46)	1.916 (5.27)	3.24 (0.71)	0.159+ (1.68)	0.224 (0.43)	0.193 (4.91) (4.20)
Neighbors' education Second moment				-0.229 (0.91)	-0.344 (1.89)			
Neighbors' education third moment				0.008 (1.13)	0.011 (2.15)			
1970 neighbors data (0.739, 1.532)		0.344 (2.58)	0.365 (3.81)	0.350 (2.63)	0.348 (3.68)		0.027 (2.66)	0.027 (2.61)
Interaction parameter (ι)						0.626 (1.17)		

Comparison of the signs of the coefficients of the polynomial terms for mothers' education with those for the moments of neighbors' education suggests a puzzling asymmetry. The marginal effect of mothers' education, which is quadratic, attains a maximum within the range of values, is positive for most of them but is ultimately decreasing. The marginal effect of neighbors' education, which is also quadratic, attains a minimum within the range of values, and is ultimately increasing. Similar differences are present in all econometric experiments that I performed with both samples. Overall, my results with the random subsample of the PSID are not as statistically significant as those with the entire sample, yet both sets of results are very similar.

In a further attempt to explain the structure of interactions among neighbors I explore another, generally little known (even among researchers who have used the PSID geocoded data), feature of the PSID. That is, PSID employed cluster sampling techniques which result in several observations from each census tract, and within tracts additional groupings, to be referred to as sampling clusters. The number of observations per tract are fairly evenly spread between one and seven. However, there are about 2 per cent of the sample that come from tracts that contribute more than ten observations each, with a maximum of thirty-three. I re-estimated the basic regressions reported in Columns 2 and 4 by allowing for a random effect associated with observations belonging to the same tract, but excluding the dummy indicating whether the neighborhood data come from the 1970 census. There are 227 clusters with an average of 3.9 observations per cluster. The estimated coefficients differ little from those reported, but the random effects structure is significant. The fraction of the variance that is explained by the random effect varies from 11.02 per cent, for Column 2, to 10.83 per cent, for Column 4.[7]

In a further attempt to probe the structure of nonlinearities in the intergenerational transmission of human capital, I estimate the model in logs and report the results on Columns 7 and 8, Table 1. The model in logs also addresses an important concern, namely the numerical significance of the coefficient for the dummy of whether 1970 neighborhood data are used. In contrast to the results in levels, the numerical effect on the mean is an order of magnitude smaller. Also particularly interesting are the results for the effect of parental education, which are both positive and have positive marginal effects and have sigmoid shapes. The terms for fathers' education are more significant than those in Column 4, although still insignificant at conventional levels of significance, and imply different dynamics. The marginal effect of the log of fathers' education is quadratic and ultimately increasing at an increasing rate. The terms for mothers' education are all significant at conventional levels of significance, and imply similar dynamics to those of Column

4. The marginal effect of the log of mothers' education is quadratic, attains a maximum and ultimately decreases. Again, I interpret this asymmetry as evidence of different mechanisms at work. The effect of paternal education may be more likely to reflect income, whereas the maternal one to reflect mothers' own values, in which case it would make sense to be more closely related to her own values. The inclusion of all nonlinear terms is significant. Allowing for a random effect associated with observations from the same sampling cluster, is significant and yields that the fraction of the variance that is explained by the random effect varies from 20.48 per cent, for Column 7, to 18.84 per cent, for Column 8.

I address the question of whether the impact of parental education and of the distribution of educational attainment within a relevant neighborhood is more different than that of either polynomial terms of parents' education or through the first three moments of the distribution of neighbors' education. I work with a CES specification for interaction effects that is similar to the one proposed by Benabou (1996b). Equation (2.1) may be specified more generally as

$$ln H = \alpha_0 + \alpha_p \, ln(Dh^{1-\frac{1}{\phi}}(1-D)h^{1-\frac{1}{\phi}}) + ln v + \in \qquad (4.1)$$

and

$$v = \varpi(\mu_{v(i)}(\bullet)) \equiv (\sum_{j \in v(i)} \mu_{v(i)j} h_j^{1-\frac{1}{\iota}})^{\frac{\iota}{\iota-1}}, \qquad (4.2)$$

where μ^j denotes the frequency of the value h^j within the distribution of educational attainment of population in neighborhood $v(i)$ at time t and μ the entire distribution.[8]

Estimation of the above model with nonlinear interaction structures as in (4.1) and (4.2) by means of nonlinear least squares did not work well. The best of the results I obtained with both parental and neighborhood data are reported on Table 1, column 6, where parental educations enter in logs. Inclusion of a CES structure for neighborhood education according to (4.2) is marginally significant relative to the OLS case with parental education in logs, and their estimated coefficients differ little, and the actual estimate $\hat{\iota} = 0.626$ is not statistically significant. I obtained clearer results when I tried to estimate nonlinear structures with parental education and neighborhood education in separate regressions. A significant CES structure for parental education was estimated with $\hat{\varphi} = -0.415$ (*t*–statistic of 2.45), and $\hat{D} = 0.634$ (*t*-statistic of

8.07), and $R^2_{adj} = 0.224$. A significant CES structure for neighborhood education was estimated with $\hat{\imath} = -0.206$ (*t*-statistic of 1.91, significant at 5.6 per cent), and $R^2_{adj} = 0.115$. Both these results imply that parental educations and neighbors' educations are 'complements', when considered separately. These results are consistent with the notion that parents' education and neighbors' education serve as role models. All of the results taken together suggest that nonlinearities for both parents' education and neighbors' education are important.

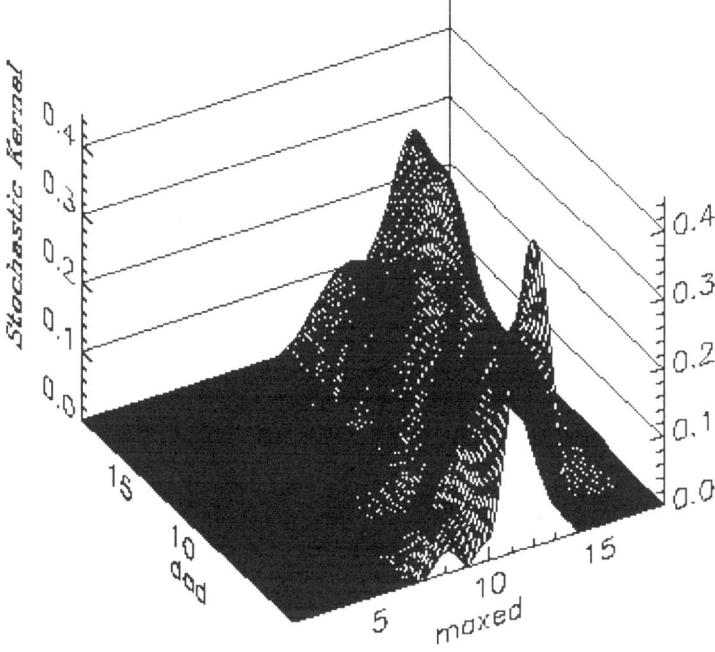

Figure 3a

Stoch. Kernel Contour(s)

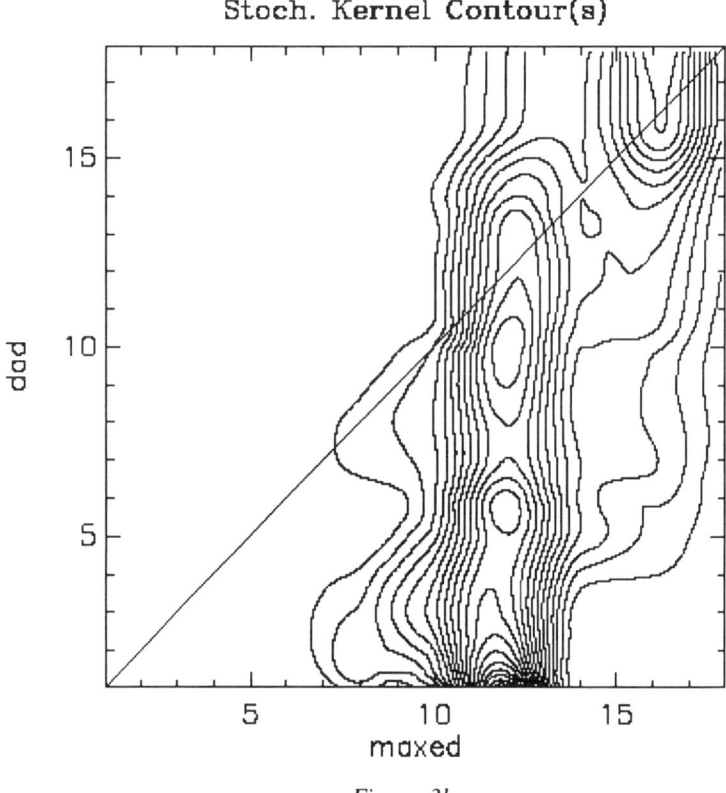

Figure 3b

4.2 Nonparametric Results

While the parametric results do provide support for the nonlinear effects of parental and neighborhood education, they do depend on restricted notions of nonlinearity. Next I turn to discussion of nonparametric estimations of stochastic kernels for various versions of equation (2.1). I use Danny Quah's tsrf program.[9]

To understand the construction of the stochastic kernel, consider the kernel showing the child education conditional on fathers' education, $H_i = G(h_i, \varepsilon_i)$ reported in Figures 3a, b. To estimate that stochastic kernel, the program first derives a non-parametric estimate of the joint distribution $f(h_i, H_i)$. Then it numerically integrates under this joint distribution with respect to H_i to get the marginal distribution of fathers' education $f(h_i)$. Next the conditional distribution $f(H_i/h_i)$ is estimated by $\hat{f}(H_i \mid h_i) = \hat{f}(h_i, H_i) / \hat{f}(h_i)$. Under regularity conditions, this gives us a consistent estimator for the conditional distribution for any value of fathers' education h_i.

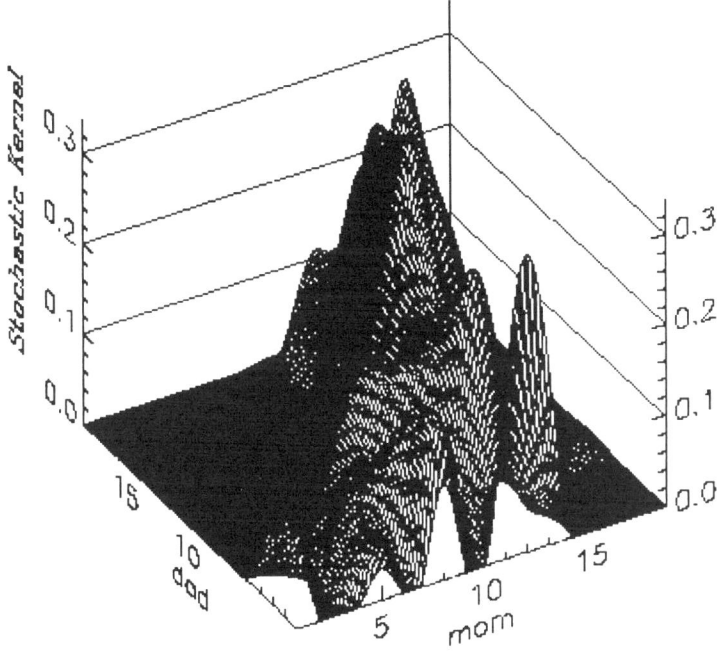

Figure 4a

The stochastic kernels plot this conditional distribution of H_i (maxed) for all values of h_i (dad), Figure 3a, and the corresponding contours are given in Figure 3b. Figures 4a and 4b give a glimpse at marital sorting in terms of education by reporting kernel estimates of mothers' education (mom) conditional on the fathers' $\hat{f}(h_i' \mid h_i)$. In view of the complexity of marital sorting, I examine the dependence, due to selection, between average neighborhood education (nschup) and average parents' education (parent), with the stochastic kernels for $f(h_{v(i)} \mid \frac{1}{2}(h_i + h_i'))$ being reported in Figures 5a, b.

Figures 6a, b report the stochastic kernels for $f(H_i \mid \frac{1}{2}(h_i + h_i'))$; and Figures 7a, b report the stochastic kernels for $\hat{f}(H_i \mid h_{v(i)})$. This last set of estimations provide persuasive evidence of the presence of nonlinear effects of parents' and neighborhood education. To appreciate that, consider drawing a curve connecting the modes of the conditional densities, the 'peaks' in Figures 6b and 7b. The resulting curves once transposed look very similar to Figures 1 and 2. This is a particularly interesting finding, given that the theoretical predictions admit many possibilities.

Stoch. Kernel Contour(s)

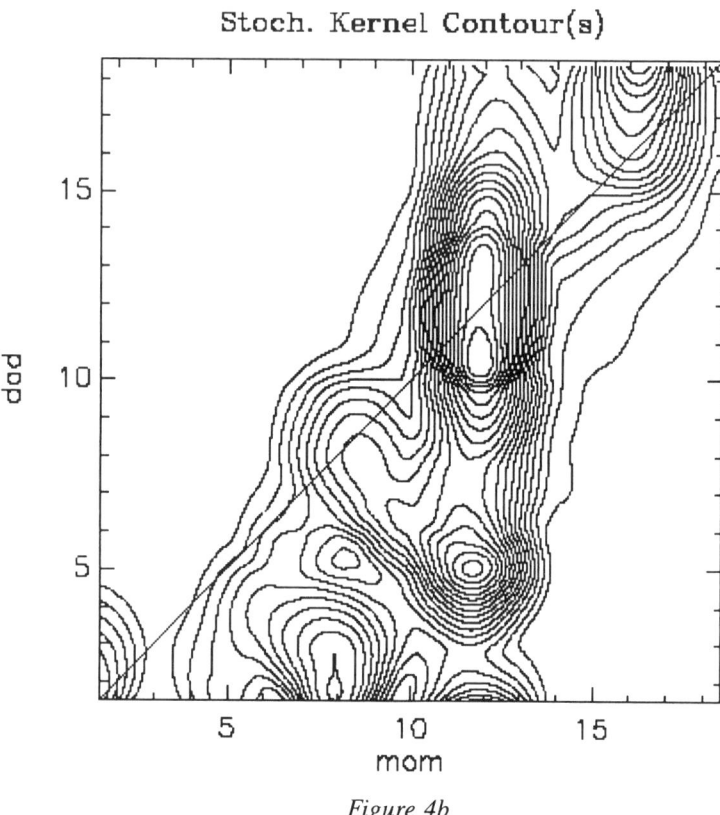

Figure 4b

I also explored the fact that the data on neighborhood education is reported in terms of frequencies. While I have not found a way to build this directly into the nonlinear estimations reported above, I explored the dependence of within neighborhood dispersion on average neighborhood education. A bit to my surprise, there is relatively little variation of within neighborhood dispersion across neighborhoods: its mean standard deviation is 3.12 years, the standard deviation of the standard deviations across all tracts in the data is 0.303, and the respective minimum and maximum values are 2.426 and 4.362. Although it has been suggested to me, I have not tried to estimate an ordered probit model for years of education. This is particularly suitable here, as educational attainment is reported in terms of intervals. However, the nonparametric results reported below have persuaded me on the presence of nonlinearities in general. Nonetheless, a dynamic ordered probit model would be a great improvement over a number of cross-tabulations for the evolution of education, reported by Kremer.

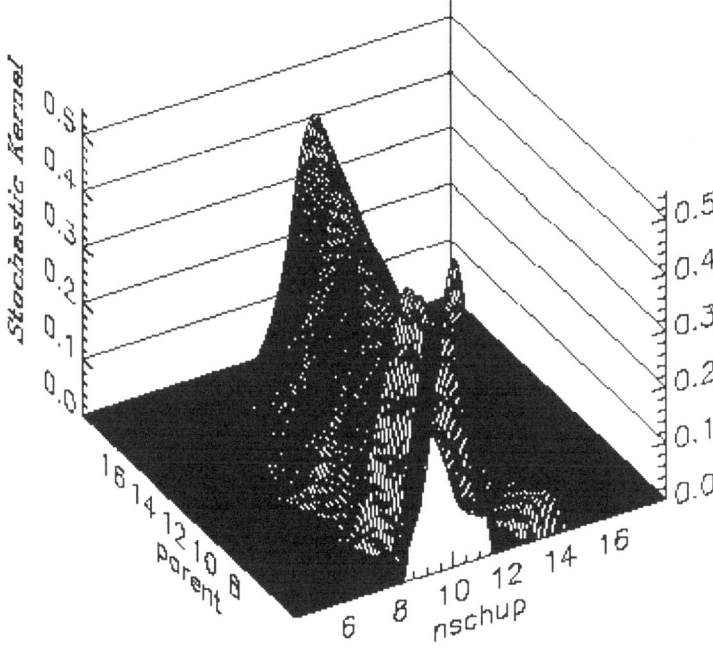

Figure 5a

Stoch. Kernel Contour(s)

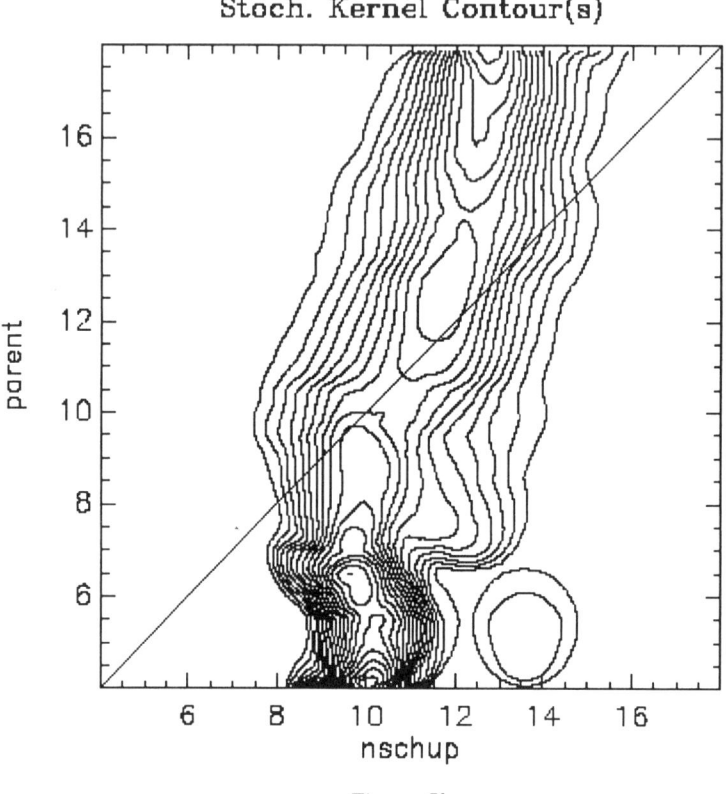

Figure 5b

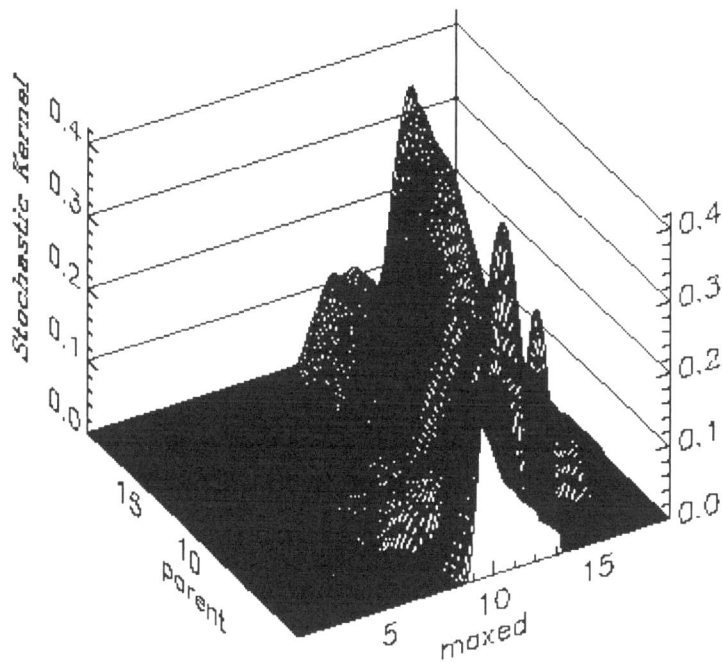

Figure 6a

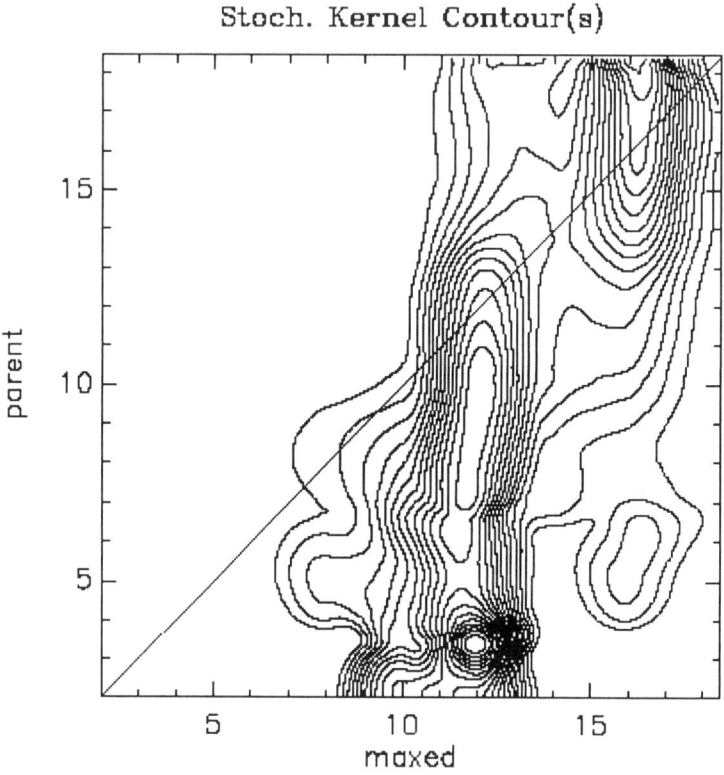

Figure 6b

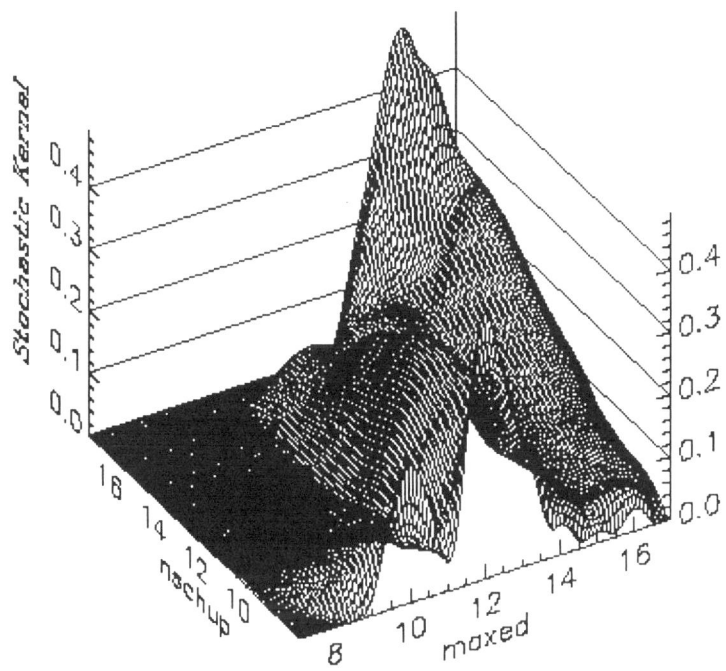

Figure 7a

Stoch. Kernel Contour(s)

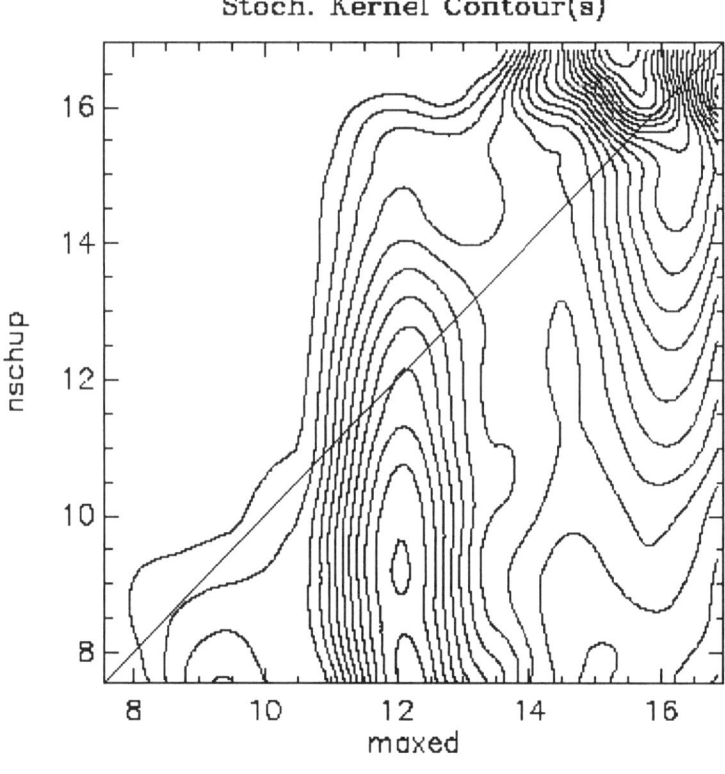

Figure 7b

5. APPLICATIONS

I offer next some applications of the basic model. One explores the properties of distribution of human capital. A second addresses the dynamics of the income distribution and the Kuznets hypothesis. A third allows individuals to choose the community of their residence and therefore neighborhood interactions as well.

5.1 Dynamics of the Distribution of Human Capital

I assume that the entire population benefits from the same interaction effect. I modify the original model slightly. Individuals live for two periods. In the first period of their lives, they are supported by their parents. In the second period, they give birth to offspring (one each) and use some of their labor to bring up their offspring. They supply the remainder of their labor to the labor market, receive earnings and spend them on consumption. Such a simple overlapping-generations model is sufficient for the essential elements of the model (Durlauf (1996b)). I assume an interaction effect as in (4.2).

Let aggregate output be produced by labor only by means of a constant returns to scale aggregate production function $C_t = A \sum_{i \in I} (1 - s_{it}) h_{it}$. Consequently, the equilibrium wage rate is given by $R_t = A$.

If one were to assume the conditions of Proposition 2, part 5, which yield a child's human capital as a linear convex combination of that of the parent's and of the interaction effect, then one could show that however strong the interaction effect might be in the direction of implying diversity as a source of gain, the distribution of human capital will collapse to a single point in the long run. Thus, I concentrate on the case of child's human capital being a nonlinear function of that of the parent's and of the interaction effect.

Recall that under the conditions of Proposition 1, part 2, the time map would be a sigmoid function for low values of h_t. Under those same conditions, it is an increasing concave function of v_t. It follows that in every t, there exist three intersections with the time map with 45-degree line, of which the middle would correspond to an unstable equilibrium for the dynamic evolution of human capital. With $R_t = A$, the time map given by (3.5) is time invariant. Therefore, if the middle of the three intersection points is contained in the interior of the support of the initial distribution then only the stable equilibria will survive in the steady state (Arthur *et al.* (1994)). Theorem 5.1 *ibid.*, p. 193, ensures that the stable equilibria will be attained in the steady state with positive probability. Theorem 5.2, *ibid.*, p. 195, ensures that the unstable equilibrium will be attained in the steady state with zero probability.

A definite statement requires that one examines the role of the interaction term. Since H is increasing concave in v_t it has an equalizing effect on human capital, unless diversity is a source of gain. One would expect that for certain parameter values the equalizing effect of the interaction term, due to concavity, would be offset by the disequalizing effect due to social interactions. Even when diversity is a source of loss, the equalizing effect may be offset by the strength of the instability.

Let $\mathcal{H}_{(1)}(v)$ and $\mathcal{H}_{(2)}(v)$ be the two stable fixed points of $\mathcal{H}(h, v)$, as functions of v and let μ_1, μ_2 be the corresponding population proportions with $\mu_1 + \mu_2 = 1$. At equilibrium,

$$v^{1-\frac{1}{l}} = \mu_1 \mathcal{H}(v)_{(1)}^{1-\frac{1}{l}} + \mu_2 \mathcal{H}_{(2)}(v)^{1-\frac{1}{l}}$$

must be satisfied. Therefore, if the preference for diversity is not too strong, that is, $|l|$ is not very large, then the r.h.s. of the above equation is concave in v and the l.h.s. is convex. Therefore, for given (μ_1, μ_2) a unique equilibrium value of the interaction effect exists and is unique, and the equilibrium values of human capital follow.

Because of the global nature of the interaction effect here, no mechanism exists in this model, through which it may be evaluated, and the population proportions are indeterminate. Therefore, it is interesting to invoke a planner who chooses the population proportions so as to maximize average utility. In the homogeneous case, when all individuals have the same amount of human capital, the interaction effect is also equal to that. If diversity is a source of gain, by creating heterogeneity, the planner could cause the interaction effect to improve utility above what would be its value in the homogeneous case. With this intuition, the heterogeneity associated with the solution to the planner's problem could be interpreted as resulting from competition across the population at the steady state. Such a planner's problem may be stated as follows. Let $V(\mathcal{H}_{(j)})(v)$, $j=1,2$ denote the indirect utility for each type. The planner's problem is to choose (μ_1, μ_2), $\mu_1 + \mu_2 = 1$, $\mu_1, \mu_2 > 0$, so as to maximize $\mu_1 V(\mathcal{H}_{(1)}(v)) + \mu_2 V(\mathcal{H}_{(2)}(v))$, subject to the definition of the interaction effect in (4.2) above. The corresponding first-order condition is:

$$\mu_1 V'(\mathcal{H}_{(1)}(v)) \mathcal{H}'_{(1)} \frac{\partial v}{\partial \mu_1} = \mu_2 V'(\mathcal{H}_{(2)}(v)) \mathcal{H}'_{(2)} \frac{\partial v}{\partial \mu_2}$$

This discussion highlights two important issues pertaining to the persistence of a non-trivial distribution of human capital. One, residential choice is critical for such a persistence; and two, the distribution reflects the nature of social interactions.

5.2 The Kuznets Hypothesis

I consider next the case with an exogenously growing A_t. That is, labor productivity in output production increases, while the productivity of human capital as an input to its own production remains stagnant. As $R_t = A_t$ increases, and depending upon the value of v_{it}, it will at some finite time reach the interval of threshold values $[R_{min}, R_{max}]$. Therefore, as the economy evolves, it will inevitably get into a temporary ('local') tendency for the distribution of human capital to become polarized – which confirms the Kuznets hypothesis. The distribution of income during economic growth will worsen before it improves (Kuznets (1955)).[10]

Depending upon whether $\sigma < 1$ or $\sigma > 1$ the economy will ultimately emerge below or above the area where the time map is sigmoid. Depending upon parameter values, the economy could cycle locally. Finally, I note that even in the case of the previous paragraph when $R_t = A$ and thus constant, and if $A \ni \left[R_{min_0}, R_{max_0} \right]$, the dependence of the threshold values upon the interaction term v_t implies that this region 'moves' and could encompass A in finite time. The economy would again satisfy the Kuznets hypothesis. Which of the two cases of Proposition 1 applies depends upon the magnitude of σ relative to 1 and initial conditions.

I note here the similarity of my finding with that by Galor and Tsiddon (1997), which I was unaware of at the time the first version of the paper was completed. My finding of a Kuznets curve is similar to that of Galor and Tsiddon (1997) but different from that by Glomm and Ravikumar (1998), which rests on short-run increasing returns to scale in learning technology. My finding, like that of Galor and Tsiddon (1997), rests on the complementarity that renders sigmoid the time map of the intertemporal evolution of human capital, and which is endogenous, in that it is defined in terms of certain conditions on preference and human capital production function parameters.

5.3 Neighborhood Choice

Neighborhood effects function as an externality in this model, which could be internalized through choice of community by individuals. Here I consider the same model as in the previous subsections. Individuals' human capital depend on parents' human capital and on the neighborhood effect in the community of their residence, which was chosen by their parents.[11]

Let $\ell_{i,t+1}$ denote the community where individual i, born at time t, chooses to reside when her child is born in period $t+1$, $\mathcal{L} \equiv \{1,...,L\}$ the set of communities in the economy, and $\{\overline{q}_1,...,\overline{q}_L\}$ the land areas they occupy, which are assumed to be given. Individuals choose where to locate so as to maximize utility. I close the model by assuming that each individual receives in the beginning of the second period of her life a lump sum transfer, $\overline{p}_{t+1}$, equal to the aggregate housing rents (across all communities) per capita.

The modification of the behavioral model to allow for land is as follows. Conditional on the choice of a community of residence, individual i's problem is the same as before, except that consumption consists of housing and non-housing consumption, (Q_{t+1}, F_{t+1}), which is evaluated by a subutility function for consumption, $C_{t+1} \equiv \chi^{-\chi}(1-\chi)^{-(1-\chi)}Q_{t+1}^{\chi}F_{t+1}^{1-\chi}$ where parameter χ satisfies $0 < \chi < 1$. With non-housing consumption as the numeraire, and $p_{\ell,t+1}$ the rental rate of housing in community ℓ, labor earnings are denoted by E_{t+1} and consumption expenditure is written as $E_{t+1} + \bar{p}_{t+1} = p_{\ell,t+1} Q_{t+1} + F_{t+1}$. The corresponding indirect consumption subutility function is given by, $C_{t+1} \equiv p_{\ell,t+1}^{-\chi}(E_{t+1} + \bar{p}_{t+1})$ in the absence of tax. The individual pays a tax on his housing expenditure at a community-specific rate $\tau_{\ell,t+1}$. As a result, it is the after tax expenditure $(1 - \chi\tau_{\ell,t+1})(E_{t+1} + \bar{p}_{t+1})$ that enters the indirect consumption subutility function.

By using the consumption subutility C_{t+1} in the utility function (3.1), utility is expressed in terms of offspring human capital and consumption expenditure,

$$U \equiv \left[\zeta(H_{t+1})^{1-\frac{1}{\sigma}} + (1-\zeta_{\ell,t+1})(E_{t+1} + \bar{p}_{t+1})^{1-\frac{1}{\sigma}} \right]^{\frac{\sigma}{\sigma-1}} \qquad (5.1)$$

where $1 - \zeta_{\ell,t+1} \equiv (1-\zeta)(p_{\ell,t+1}^{-\chi}(1 - \chi\tau_{\ell,t+1}))^{1-\frac{1}{\sigma}}$. Conditional on the choice of community an individual is assumed to maximize her utility function (5.1), subject to her nonlinear budget constraint (3.2), except that E_{t+1} takes the place of C_t.

Summarizing, an individual i's choice of community ℓ at time $t+1$ is reflected upon the analytics through: first, the community-specific 'taste' parameter $1 - \zeta_{\ell,t+1}$, defined above, and second, the neighborhood interaction effect in the production of offspring human capital $v_{\ell,t+1}$ which also depends on the community. This is pursued further in Ioannides (2000).

6. CONCLUSIONS

I develop here a model of the evolution of human capital as a result of individual choice. The model implies a law of motion for the evolution of human capital with multiple equilibria that differ in terms of stability properties.

This feature of the model is entirely dependent on two features: first, nonlinear neighborhood interactions must be present; second, the elasticity of substitution between own human capital and the neighborhood interactions must be sufficiently larger than the elasticity of substitution between one's child's human capital and own consumption. Neighborhood interactions in general represent the role of public education in the production of human capital. I show that under certain conditions the economy segregates into two types of human capital. The model also supports the Kuznets hypothesis, namely that the income distribution would worsen before it improves during the process of economic growth. An extension of the model allows one to bring together two strands of the literature, those emphasizing the role of neighborhood effects in growing economies with those examining equilibria in economies with local public goods where individuals have a choice where to locate, and therefore they may segregate according to human capital.

I report empirical findings, which are based on geocoded data from the Panel Study of Income Dynamics and are similar to Kremer's findings of substantial (linear) effects on a person's human capital, measured by years of education, of the average education in the neighborhood where he or she grew up. My results also show that a person's education is nonlinearly related to both father's and mother's education, when both are present in the regression, and to the mean, and the second and third moments of the distribution of education within the neighborhood where an individual was brought up. These findings, and nonparametric estimates that I also report, support key predictions of the theory that under certain conditions, the relationship between a child's education and that of his or her parent and the education level in the neighborhood of upbringing has a sigmoid shape.

NOTES

1. See *ibid.*, fn. 12: the estimates are 0.649, 0.633, and 0.620, for 1940, 1960, and 1980, respectively.

2. Borjas (1995) explores further the nature of the ethnic externality by considering a potential link between parental and ethnic capital, on one hand, and residential segregation, on the other. Borjas estimates a version of equation (2.2) with data that provides for several observations from each residential 'neighborhood' and thus allow him to account for neighborhood effects. All of his estimates of expected skills of individuals (measured by either educational attainment or log wages) against the average skills in the parent's generation, $\varepsilon\left[H_{igt+1}\right] = (\gamma_1 + \gamma_2)\bar{h}_{gt}$ show that accounting for fixed neighborhood effects reduces the estimates of mean convergence, denoted by $\gamma_1 + \gamma_2$ in the skills of ethnic groups. Roughly, the estimates of this effect go down from around 0.45 to 0.20, when neighborhood fixed effects are included and when a small number of neighborhood characteristics are included in the regression (%-age of population, with at least high-school diploma, percentage with at least college diploma, labor force participation rate of men and women, the unemployment rate, %-age of workers in professional occupations, the %-age of families below the poverty level, and the %-age of families with at least $15,000 of income).

3. Borjas (1992) works with a Cobb-Douglas version of equation (3.2): $H_{t+1} = (s_t h_t)^{\delta_1} v_t^{\delta_2}$.

$\delta_1 + \delta_2 < 1$. Borjas assumption of a Cobb-Douglas production function for child quality does exclude complementarity in the production of human capital (*ibid.*, equation (3.1)). Since the endogenous savings function may not be solved in closed form anyway, I think it is interesting to assume the most general framework that involves a CES functional form with complementarity in the production of the child's human capital and thus seek the most general results that might be possible within such a framework.

4.   I was unaware of Galor and Tsiddon (1997) at the time when the first version of the paper was completed.

5.   I am not aware of any previous work on nonlinear interactions between education of parents and their offspring. Eide and Showalter (1999) follow a quantile regression approach to studying the intergenerational evolution of earnings. In one of the regressions of sons' earnings against fathers' characteristics that they report, *ibid.*, Table 3, the quantile effects are roughly similar to the predicted relationships by Proposition 1, Part 2, above.

6.   Kremer also estimates a Markovian model, where he codes educational attainment in terms of six ordered categories and estimates probabilities that a child is in each category conditional on each parent's category. He repeats such an estimation for four educational categories of neighbors. In all cases, the computation of the steady-state distribution of education allows one to examine the impact of parental or neighborhood sorting. The standard deviation of education increases only slightly if the proportion of male population whose spouses with the same education were to increase from 0.6 to 0.8, or if the correlation coefficient between neighbors' education were to increase from 0.2 to 0.4.

7.   Additional evidence of the co-dependence of education of individuals who grew up in the same neighborhood is obtained by regressing an individual's education against neighborhood education and the mean education among all other individuals who grew up in the same neighborhood. The respective coefficients are 0.178 (6.92) and 0.564 (21.81), and R^2=0.225.

8.   See Benabou (1996b). If $\phi < 0$, then parental educations are 'complements', and the corresponding 'isoquants' associated with the r.h.s. of (4.1) (in levels) are concave. If $\phi > 0$, then parental educations are 'substitutes', and the corresponding 'isoquants' associated with the r.h.s. of equation (4.1) (in levels) are convex. Similarly if $\iota < 0$, then individual levels of educational accomplishments are 'complements', ϖ is convex with respect to the educational attainment of the population, and diversity is a source of loss: $\varpi_{v(i)t} < \bar{h}_{v(i)t}$. If $\iota > 0$; then individual levels of educational accomplishments are 'substitutes', ϖ is concave with respect to the educational attainment of the population, and diversity is a source of gain $\varpi_{v(i)t} > \bar{h}_{v(i)t}$. Commonly made assumptions about interaction effects are implied as special cases. That is, if $\iota \to +\infty$, ϖ equals the arithmetic mean, $\varpi_{v(i)t} = \sum_{j \in v(i)t} \mu_j h_{jt}$; if $\iota \to 1$, ϖ coincides with the Cobb-Douglas function and thus equals the geometric mean, $\varpi_{v(i)t} = \prod_{j \in v(i)t} h_j^{\mu_j}$; as $\frac{1}{\iota}$ decreases from $+\infty$ to $-\infty$, ϖ spans the whole range of interaction technologies from Leontief, or 'weakest link - one apple spoils the bunch', $\varpi = min_{j \in I_{v(i)t}} \left\{ \frac{h_j}{\mu_{v(i)j}} \right\}$, which occurs when $\frac{1}{\iota} \to \infty$ to 'best shot', that is, to role models where the best individual sets the standard, $\varpi = max_{j \in I_{v(i)t}} \left\{ h_j \right\}$ which occurs when $\frac{1}{\iota} \to -\infty$.

9.   The program is available at http://econ.lse.ac.uk/~dquah/tsrf.html.

10.   Glomm (1997), the latest review of the evidence on Kuznets' hypothesis, emphasizes that while Kuznets' 'inverted U curve' is consistent with the facts for some countries, it does not describe the evolution of income distribution everywhere.

11. This model combines essential features of the models in Benabou (1996a, 1996b). As a model of growth it resembles the overlapping-generations model in the appendix of Benabou (1996a), although it is somewhat more standard and includes assumptions about the acquisition of human capital which differ from his. E.g., Benabou assumes that local spillovers exhibit a threshold effect. The behavioral model in Benabou (1996a) is more general, but is explored fully in only a two-period setting. Benabou (1996b), on the other hand, explores a richer pattern of interactions, which include both global and local linkages, which are limited to the Cobb-Douglas functional forms only. The model here is conceptually very similar to Durlauf (1996a, 1996b) but involves only deterministic tools.

12. Note that I am interested in drawing conclusions for the curvature properties of the time map but I will be working with its inverse. Therefore, concavity of the time map requires convexity of its inverse and so on.

REFERENCES

Adams, Terry K. (1991a), 'Excerpts from Documentation for 1970 and 1980 Census Extract Datasets', Economics Program, Institute for Social Research, University of Michigan, July.

Adams, Terry K. (1991b), 'Excerpts from Documentation for 1968-1985 PSID-Geocode Match Files', Economics Program, Institute for Social Research, University of Michigan, August.

Arthur, W. Brian, Yuri M. Ermoliev, and Yuri M. Kaniovski (1994), *Path Dependence Processes and the Emergence of Macrostructure*, Ch. 3, 33-48, and *Strong Laws for a Class of Path Dependent Stochastic Processes*, Ch. 10, 185-201, in Arthur W. Brian, *Increasing Returns and Path Dependence in the Economy*, University of Michigan Press, Ann Arbor.

Azariadis, Costas (1993), *Intertemporal Macroeconomics*, Blackwell Publishers, Oxford.

Azariadis, Costas, and Allan Drazen (1990), 'Threshold Externalities in Economic Development', *Quarterly Journal of Economics*, CV, May, 501-526.

Benabou, Roland (1996a), 'Equity and Efficiency in Human Capital Investment: The Local Connection', *Review of Economic Studies*, **63**, 237-264.

Benabou, Roland (1996b), 'Heterogeneity, Stratification and Growth: Macroeconomic Implications of Community Structure and School Finance', *American Economic Review*, **86**, (3), 584-609.

Borjas, George J. (1992), 'Ethnic Capital and Intergenerational Mobility', *Quarterly Journal of Economics*, February, 123-150.

Borjas, George J. (1995), 'Ethnicity, Neighborhoods, and Human Capital Externalities', *American Economic Review*, **85**, (3), 365-390.

Ciccone, Antonio, and Kiminori Matsuyama (1999), 'Efficiency and Equilibrium with Dynamic Increasing Returns due to Demand Complementarities', *Econometrica*, **67**, (3), 499-525.

Durlauf, Steven N. (1996a), 'A Theory of Persistent Income Inequality', *Journal of Economic Growth*, **1**, 75-93.

Durlauf, Steven N. (1996b), 'Neighborhood Feedbacks, Endogenous Stratification, and Income Inequality', in W. Barnett, G. Gandolfo and C. Hillinger, *Dynamic Disequilibrium Modelling*, Cambridge University Press.

Eide, Eric, R., and Mark H. Showalter (1999), 'Factors Affecting the Transmission of Earnings across Generations: A Quantile Regression Approach', *The Journal of Human Resources*, **24**, 2.

Galor, Oded, and Harl E. Ryder (1991), 'Dynamic Efficiency of Steady-State Equilibria in an Overlapping Generations Model with Productive Capital', *Economics Letters*, **35**, 385-390.

Galor, Oded, and Daniel Tsiddon (1997), 'The Distribution of Human Capital and Economic Growth', *Journal of Economic Growth*, **2**, 93-124.

Glomm, Gerhard (1997), 'Whatever Happened to the Kuznets Curve? Is It Really Upside Down?', *Journal of Income Distribution*, **7**, (1), 63-87.

Glomm, Gerhard, and B. Ravikumar (1998), 'Increasing Returns, Human Capital, and the Kuznets Curve', *Journal of Development Economics*, **55**, 353-367.

Ioannides, Yannis M. (2000), 'Neighborhood Interactions in Local Communities and Intergenerational Transmission of Human Capital', working paper, Tufts University, May.

Kremer, Michael (1997), 'How Much Does Sorting Increase Inequality?', *Quarterly Journal of Economics*, February, 115-139.

Kuznets, Simon (1955), 'Economic Growth and Income Inequality', *American Economic Review*, **45**, 1-28.

Manski, Charles F. (1993), 'Identification of Endogenous Social Effects: The Reflection Problem', *Review of Economic Studies*, **60**, 531-542.

Matsuyama, Kiminori (1995), 'Comment on Paul Krugman's *Complexity and Emergent Structure in the International Economy*', in Jim Levinson, Alan V. Deardorff and Robert M. Stern (1995), *New Directions in Trade Theory*, University of Michigan Press, Ann Arbor, 53-69.

Matsuyama, Kiminori (1996), 'Why Are There Rich and Poor Countries? Symmetry-Breaking in the World Economy', *Journal of the Japanese and International Economies*, **9**, 419-439.

APPENDIX

Proof of Proposition 1

The first derivative with respect to H_{t+1} of the r.h.s of (3.3) is given by:

$$\frac{\partial h_t}{\partial H_{t+1}} = \eta^{\frac{-b}{b-1}} \left[1 - (1-\eta)(\frac{\upsilon_t}{H_{t+1}})^{\frac{b-1}{b}} \right]^{\frac{1}{b-1}}$$

$$+\eta^{\frac{-\sigma}{\beta-1}}(\frac{1-\zeta}{\eta\zeta})^{\sigma}R_t^{\sigma-1}\left[1-(1-\eta)(\frac{v_t}{H_{t+1}})^{\frac{b-1}{b}}\right]^{\frac{\sigma}{b-1}}(1+\frac{\sigma}{b}\frac{(1-\eta)(\frac{v_t}{H_{t+1}})^{\frac{b-1}{b}}}{1-(1-\eta)(\frac{v_t}{H_{t+1}})^{\frac{b-1}{b}}})\quad(A.1)$$

and is positive. Therefore, h_t, is an increasing function of H_{t+1}, defined for $H_{t+1} \geq (1-\eta)^{\frac{b}{b-1}}v_t$. The curvature properties of the second term in the r.h.s. of (3.4) depend upon parameter values and the magnitude of H_{t+1}.[12]

Specifically, by differentiating (A.1) with respect to H_{t+1}, we have:

$$\frac{\partial^2 h_t}{\partial H_{t+1}^2} = \frac{\frac{1-\eta}{\eta}v_t^{\frac{b-1}{b}}}{\frac{1}{\eta}(H_{t+1})^{\frac{b-1}{b}}-\frac{1-\eta}{\eta}v_t^{\frac{b-1}{b}}}$$

$$\left\{\frac{1}{\eta b}H_{t+1}^{-1-\frac{1}{b}}\left[\frac{1}{\eta}(H_{t+1})^{\frac{b-1}{b}}-\frac{1-\eta}{\eta}v_t^{\frac{b-1}{b}}\right]^{\frac{1}{b-1}}+\frac{\sigma}{b}(\frac{1-\zeta}{\eta\zeta})^{\sigma}\right.\quad(A.2)$$

$\times$

$$\left.R_t^{\sigma-1}H_{t+1}^{-\frac{\sigma}{b}}\left[\frac{1}{\eta}(H_{t+1})^{\frac{b-1}{b}}-\frac{1-\eta}{\eta}v_t^{\frac{b-1}{b}}\right]^{\frac{\sigma}{b-1}}\times(H_{t+2}^{-1}-\frac{b-1}{b}\frac{\frac{1}{\eta}H_{t+1}^{\frac{b-1}{b}}}{\frac{1}{\eta}(H_{t+1})^{\frac{b-1}{b}}-\frac{1-\eta}{\eta}v_t^{\frac{b-1}{b}}})\right\}$$

Therefore, if $\sigma \geq b$, h_t is an increasing convex function of H_{t+1}, for $H_{t+1} \geq (1-\eta)^{\frac{b}{b-1}}v_t$ which implies that H_{t+1} is an increasing concave function of h_t. This is depicted in Figure 1.

If, on the other hand, $\sigma < b$, the second term within the braces in the r.h.s of (A.2) will be negative for sufficiently low values of H_{t+1}. It is thus possible for that second term to dominate the first in absolute value, conferring a sigmoid shape to the time map.

The two possibilities when the time map is sigmoid have been drawn on: Figure 1, for the case of $\sigma > 1$; and, of Figure 2, for the case of $\sigma < 1$.

The threshold value of $R_{max}(v_t)$ for the case of $\sigma < 1$, is obtained by eliminating $h = h_t = H_{t+1}$ between (3.4) and (3.5), where I set $\dfrac{\partial h_t}{\partial H_{t+1}} = 1$, and ensure that the r.h.s of (A.2) is positive ($\mathcal{H}(h_t, \bullet)$) is concave. The threshold value of $R_{min}(u_t)$ is obtained by eliminating $h = h_t = H_{t+1}$ between (3.4) and (3.5), where I set $\dfrac{\partial h_t}{\partial H_{t+1}} = 1$ and ensure that the r.h.s if (A.2) is negative ($H(h_t, \bullet)$ is convex). It can be shown that both threshold values R_{max} and R_{min} are decreasing functions of u_t. See Figure 1.

For the case of $\sigma < 1$, the conditions are reversed. The threshold value of $R_{max}(v_t)$, for the case of $\sigma < 1$, is obtained by eliminating $h = h_t = H_{t+1}$ between (3.4) and (A.1), where I set $\dfrac{\partial h_t}{\partial H_{t+1}} = 1$ and ensure that the r.h.s of (A.2) is negative ($H(h_t, \bullet)$ is concave). It can be shown that both threshold values R_{max} and R_{min} are increasing functions of v_t. See Figure 2.

Regarding Part 3, by totally differentiating (3.4) we have $\dfrac{\partial H}{\partial v_t} = -\dfrac{\partial h_t}{\partial v_t} \bigg/ \dfrac{\partial h_t}{\partial H_{t+1}}$. This yields:

$$\frac{\partial H}{\partial v_t} = (1-\eta)\frac{(\dfrac{v_t}{H_{t+1}})^{-\frac{1}{b}}}{1 + (1-\dfrac{\sigma}{b})\dfrac{\sigma}{R_t\;^{\frac{b}{n}}\left[\dfrac{1}{\eta} - \dfrac{1-\eta}{\eta}(\dfrac{v_t}{H_{t+1}})^{\frac{b-1}{b}}\right]^{\frac{1-\sigma}{b-1}}} + \dfrac{\sigma}{b}\dfrac{1}{1-(1-\eta)(\dfrac{v_t}{H_{t+1}})^{\frac{b-1}{b}}}} \tag{A.3}$$

By inspection, it follows that if $\sigma > b > 1$ or $\sigma < b < 1$, H is a concave function of the interaction effect. In all other cases, the sign of the second derivative of h is ambiguous. In those other cases, if $\sigma \ll b$, and R_t is sufficiently large, the denominator of (A.3) dominates the magnitude of the derivative.

6. Beliefs and the Neutrality of Money[*]

Costas Azariadis[†]

1. INTRODUCTION

This essay explores the direct link of Robert Lucas classic 'Expectations and the Neutrality of Money' to the subsequent literature on endogenous fluctuations. I reconsider how the neutrality of money is influenced by shared beliefs of the sort that US business people and academics appear to hold in practice; these beliefs associate output booms with monetary expansions and recessions with monetary contractions. Can such anticipations be rational in the Lucas (1972) model?

It is useful now to describe precisely what I mean by the term 'Lucas model' and why it may confirm beliefs of monetary non-neutrality. The economic environment used in this essay is the 1972 paper stripped down to its barest essentials: there is no distinction between local and aggregate information because exchange occurs in one single market and agents are fully informed. Population, tastes and commodity endowments are constant over time. Currency is created in random amounts and given away in the form of stochastic interest payments on existing balances. Since all prices are assumed to be flexible and all agents are rational, the fundamental properties of this economy argue for standard super-neutrality results:[1] the set of equilibrium allocations should be deterministic and independent of the process of money creation. Any deviations from super-neutrality in the simple model economy *must* come from a shared belief that money influences output.

What economic mechanism could possibly validate this belief? Suppose that equilibrium is indeterminate in the sense that, at any point in time, two or more future outcomes are consistent with a given present economic state. Then any mechanism that conditions the selection of equilibrium on the reali-

* February 1995, revised, May 2001.
† Department of Economics, UCLA, 405 Hilgard Avenue, Los Angeles CA 90095-1477. Email: azariadi@ucla.edu. I am grateful to Chris Edmond for constructive criticism without implicating him in the final product.

zation of a monetary aggregate will produce some correlation between money and output. In particular, beliefs that associate monetary expansions with high equilibrium output, and contractions with low output, may emerge in a strategic environment in which money is a correlating device in the manner suggested by Aumann (1987).

Monetary aggregates that are used either as a correlating device by individuals or as an equilibrium selection device by a Walrasian auctioneer seem to provide an interesting avenue for non-neutral behavior, which we explore next. Section 2 lays out the theoretical model and defines rational expectations equilibria. Sections 3 and 4 identify a class of equilibria driven by a particularly simple set of beliefs about the role of money. The main findings accord reasonably well with the traditional monetarist view of fluctuations articulated in Friedman (1968): money is neutral in the long run but not in the short run. More precisely, there exist rational expectations equilibria in which output correlates positively with both monetary aggregates and the inflation rate at high frequencies, and is uncorrelated at low frequencies.

2. THE BASE MODEL

Our starting point is Lucas' (1972) overlapping generations model of fiat money, amended as follows. Population is constant, consisting of two-period-lived individuals who produce a single non-storable consumption good in youth and consume it in old age. The young consume only leisure; the old consume the consumption good. Each person has an endowment vector $(e, 0)$ where $e > 1$ is leisure units in youth and 0 is the consumption good endowment in old age. The production technology converts one unit of a homogeneous labor input into one unit of the consumption good. Young members of generation $t = 1, 2, \ldots$ evaluate potentially risky bundles of youthful leisure and old age consumption by the expected value of the linear-quadratic utility function,

$$v_t = c_{t+1} - (1/2)y_t^2 \tag{1}$$

expressed over consumption at $t + 1$ and production (or labor supply) at t.

There is no capital or other store of value except fiat money, the stock of which evolves according to the law of motion

$$M_t = x_t M_{t-1} \tag{2}$$

The random variable x_t is independent and identically distributed with mean

$\mu > 0$. In what follows, we assume that x_t is uniformly distributed on $[1-a, 1+a]$ for some $a \in [0,1]$. This means that the first two moments of x_t are

$$\mu = 1, \qquad \sigma_x^2 = a^2/3 \qquad (3)$$

More importantly, we assume that newly created or destroyed money is added to or subtracted from the pre-existing stock by positive or negative interest payments on existing balances.

At time t all young people trade their production for money held by the old in a central market at a single price p_t determined by a Walrasian auctioneer. Unlike the original Lucas model, this one has no private information or any scope for confusing local price signals with aggregate ones. The rate of return on saving at time t,

$$R_{t+1} = x_{t+1} p_t / p_{t+1}, \qquad (4)$$

may be random in principle. Whatever it is, equation (4) says that inflation is not a tax on money balances because currency holders are compensated by interest payments.

The real value of saving is simply output; a young person maximizing the expected value of her lifecycle utility index, given by equation (1), will choose at time t to produce

$$y_t = E\left(R_{t+1} | I_t\right) \qquad (5)$$

where I_t is public information at t and E is the expectations operator. Equilibrium requires that the quantity of real goods produced by the young should equal the real value of currency balances held by the old.

If we denote real currency balances by $m_t = M_t / p_t$, competitive equilibria satisfy equations (4), (5) and

$$y_t = m_t \qquad (6)$$

for each $t = 1, 2, \dots$. These three equations are easily reduced to the following first order stochastic difference equation:

$$y_t^2 = E\left(y_{t+1} | I_t\right) \qquad (7)$$

A sequence (y_t) of random variables defined in the interval $[0, e]$ is a *ra-*

tional expectations equilibrium if it solves equation (7). Random variables that may eventually exceed the leisure endowment e cannot be part of an equilibrium sequence.

Deterministic solutions to equation (7) are well known to be super-neutral because they reflect the fundamental forces of this economy. The set of sequences (y_t) satisfying the deterministic difference equation

$$y_t^2 = y_{t+1} \tag{8}$$

is independent of the probability distribution of the transfer variable x. Solutions to equation (8) include the *monetary* steady state $y = 1$, the *non-monetary* steady state $y = 0$, as well as a continuum of sequences starting from any $y_1 \in (0,1)$ and converging monotonically to zero. With the exception of the monetary steady state, competitive equilibrium is indeterminate.

Stochastic solutions to equation (7) respond to beliefs as well as to fundamental forces. Azariadis and Guesnerie (1986) and Peck (1988) propose the following class of solutions:

$$y_{t+1} = \begin{cases} 1 & \text{with probability} \quad \pi_{t+1} = (1-\theta_t)y_t^2 / (1-\theta_t y_t^2). \\ \theta_t y_t^2 & \text{with probability} \quad 1 - \pi_{t+1} \end{cases} \tag{9}$$

For any initial $y_1 \in [0, 1]$ and any arbitrary sequence (θ_t) that remains in the interval $[0, 1]$, it is easy to check that this solution satisfies equation (7) for all $t = 1, 2, \dots$. In particular, both sequences (π_t) and (y_t) stay in the unit interval. Hence the random variables (y_t) defined in equation (9) are indeed a competitive rational expectations equilibrium.

The asymptotic properties of this equilibrium depend very much on the choice of the arbitrary sequence $(\theta_t)_{t=1}^{\infty}$. Let $Q(y_1)$ be the asymptotic probability that the equilibrium will end up in the non-monetary steady state, and $1 - Q(y_1)$ be the asymptotic probability of attaining the monetary steady state from any initial output value $y_1 \in [0, 1]$. There is no other possible attractor because equation (9) defines a sequence (y_t) that shrinks over time.

All but one of the deterministic solutions are attracted to the non-monetary state $y = 0$, i.e.,

$$Q(y_1) = \begin{cases} 1 & \text{if} \quad y_1 \in [0, 1] \\ 0 & \text{if} \quad y_1 = 1 \end{cases} \tag{10}$$

In the stochastic case, the asymptotic probability of the non-monetary state is typically less than one; it is possible for an economy that starts at $y_1 < 1$ to converge with positive probability to the monetary state. The parameter Q in this economy is the probability of keeping out of the monetary steady state forever, that is, the infinite product

$$Q(y_1) = \prod_{t=1}^{\infty} (1 - \pi_{t+1}) = \prod_{t=1}^{\infty} \left(\frac{1 - y_t^2}{1 + y_{t+1}} \right) \tag{11}$$

where $y_{t+1} = \theta_t y_t^2$ for $t = 1, 2, \ldots$. This product is well defined for any exogenous sequence (θ_t) in the unit interval.

Stochastic solutions to equation (7) correspond to equilibria of our model economy in which beliefs matter. But why *should* money matter? Currency will be non-neutral in this economy if its issue influences the beliefs of consumers or producers, that is, if it is believed to have any bearing on the events that condition the choice between the two types of equilibria described in equation (9). Given any $\theta_t \in (0, 1)$ and any $y_t \in (0, 1)$, why would the economy produce at the high output rate $y_{t+1} = 1$ instead of at the lower rate $y_{t+1} = \theta_t y_t^2$?

3. MONEY AND OUTPUT IN THE SHORT RUN

Can the inhabitants of this economy rationally expect output to be relatively high when money growth is relatively rapid and low when money growth is relatively moderate? To explore this possibility we recall that the transfer variable x_t is uniformly distributed on the interval $[1 - a, 1 + a]$ and then modify the solution in equation (9) in the following manner. For each period t we define a critical value $\bar{x}_{t+1}$ for the monetary transfer and assume that output at $t + 1$ will be high if $x_{t+1} > \bar{x}_{t+1}$, low otherwise. In particular, we consider the class of solutions

$$y_{t+1} = \begin{cases} 1 & \text{if } x_{t+1} > \bar{x}_{t+1} \\ min\left[0, (y_t^2 - \pi)/(1 - \pi)\right] & \text{if } x_{t+1} < \bar{x}_{t+1} \end{cases} \tag{12}$$

In this class we assume that $\pi \in [0, 1)$ is an arbitrary parameter, $y_t \in [0, 1]$, and the critical value $\bar{x}_{t+1}$ satisfies

$$\overline{x}_{t+1} = 1 + a - 2 \min\{\pi, y_t^2\} \tag{13}$$

This class of solutions to equation (7) satisfies all boundedness assumptions and defines a family of rational expectations equilibria in which beliefs matter. The state variable y_t behaves differently in the two natural domains of its definition. From equations (12) and (13) it is easy to check that

$$y_t \in \left[0, \sqrt{\pi}\right] (\Rightarrow) \; y_{t+1} = \begin{cases} 1 & \text{if} \quad x_{t+1} > 1 + a - 2y_t^2 \\ 0 & \text{if} \quad x_{t+1} < 1 + a - 2y_t^2 \end{cases} \tag{14a}$$

$$y_t \in \left[0, \sqrt{\pi}\right] (\Rightarrow) \; y_{t+1} = \begin{cases} 1 & \text{w.p.} \quad y_t^2 \\ 0 & \text{w.p.} \quad 1 - y_t^2 \end{cases} \tag{14b}$$

For any y_t smaller than the arbitrary parameter $\sqrt{\pi}$, y_{t+1} must be at either the non-monetary or the monetary steady state. Beliefs *do not matter* beyond $t+1$. Given a large enough y_t, however, beliefs may matter for several more periods. In particular

$$y_t \in \left[\sqrt{\pi}, 1\right] (\Rightarrow) \; y_{t+1} = \begin{cases} 1 & \text{if} \; x_{t+1} > 1 + a - 2a\pi \\ (y_t^2 - \pi)/(1 - \pi) & \text{otherwise} \end{cases} \tag{15a}$$

$$y_t \in \left[\sqrt{\pi}, 1\right] (\Rightarrow) \; y_{t+1} = \begin{cases} 1 & \text{w.p.} \quad \pi \\ (y_t^2 - \pi)/(1 - \pi) & \text{w.p.} \quad 1 - \pi \end{cases} \tag{15b}$$

For any initial value y_1 of the state variable close to 1 and any parameter value π close to zero, the solution in equation (15b) can be expected to stay in the region $\left[\sqrt{\pi}, 1\right)$ a large number of periods and will converge to the monetary steady state with a probability near one. The sequence of (y_t) defined by the second line of equation (15b) is shown in Figure 1.

A useful taxonomy of solutions is to regard those inside the domain $(\sqrt{\pi}, 1)$ to define the 'short run' and reserve the term 'long run' for asymptotic solutions. Within the domain $(\sqrt{\pi}, 1)$ we easily compute the variance of output y_{t+1} to be

$$\sigma_y^2(t+1) = Ey_{t+1}^2 - (Ey_{t+1})^2 = \frac{\pi}{1-\pi}(1 - y_t^2)^2 \tag{16}$$

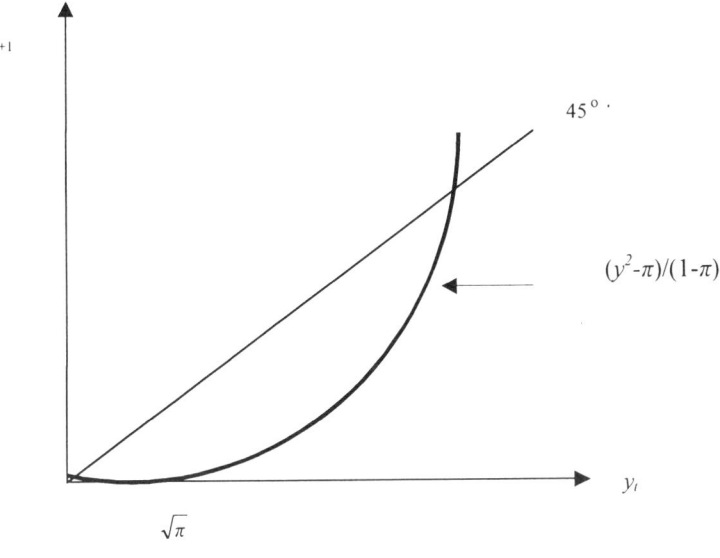

Figure 1

The money-output covariance is

$$cov(x_{t+1}, y_{t+1}) = E(y_{t+1} - y_t^2)(x_{t+1} - 1) = Ex_{t+1}(y_{t+1} - y_t^2) = a\pi(1 - y_t^2) \quad (17)$$

From these two relations and equation (3) we obtain the short-term correlation coefficient between money growth and output

$$\rho(x_{t+1}, y_{t+1}) = [3\pi(1 - \pi)]^{1/2} \quad (18)$$

Figure 2 shows how this coefficient depends on the arbitrary belief parameter $\pi \in [0, 1]$. It is zero at $\pi = 0$ and $\pi = 1$ because in either case beliefs do not matter and output is deterministic; it attains its maximal value of $\sqrt{3}/2$ at $\pi = 1/2$. Values in this range are consistent with what Cooley and Hansen (1995) observe for US time series, 1954:1-1991:2, and with the simulation results obtained by the same authors for a Keynesian model economy with predetermined money wages.[2]

Finally, it is easy to see that equilibria in this economy are consistent with a short-run Phillips relation, that is, with a positive correlation between output and inflation of the sort one finds in the original Lucas model as well as in traditional Keynesian work with nominal rigidities. Let

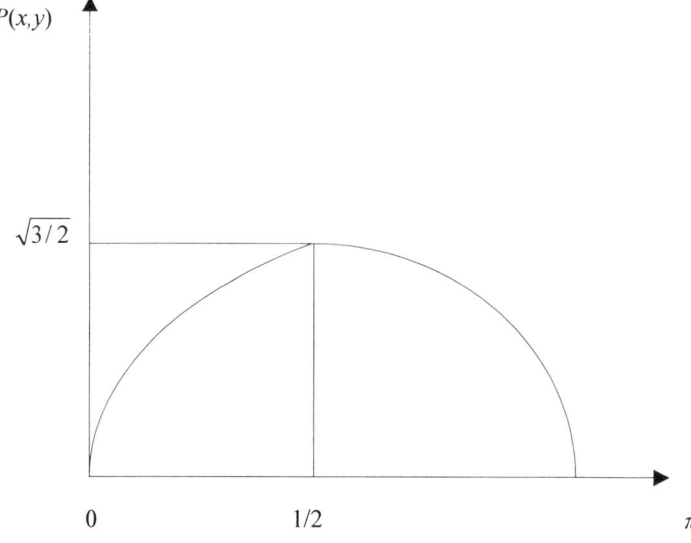

Figure 2

$$z_{t+1} = p_{t+1}/p_t = x_{t+1}y_t/y_{t+1} \qquad (19)$$

define the inflation factor that connects two successive time periods. Then equations (15a) and (19) imply that

$$z_{t+1} = \begin{cases} x_{t+1}y_t & \text{if } x_{t+1} > 1 + a - 2a\pi \\ (1-\pi)x_{t+1}y_t/(y_t^2 - \pi) & \text{otherwise} \end{cases} \qquad (20a)$$

$$z_{t+1}y_{t+1} = x_{t+1}y_t \qquad (20b)$$

This expression directly leads to the following calculation:

$$\begin{aligned} cov(z_{t+1}, y_{t+1}) &= E(z_{t+1} - Ez_{t+1})(y_{t+1} - y_t^2) = E(z_{t+1} - Ez_{t+1})y_{t+1} \\ &= -y_t^2 Ez_{t+1} + Ez_{t+1}y_{t+1} \end{aligned}$$

where

$$Ez_{t+1} = y_t\left[(1+a-a\pi)\pi + (1-a\pi)\frac{(1-\pi)^2 a}{y_t^2 - \pi}\right] \qquad (21)$$

directly from equation (20a). Substituting this relation and (20b) into equation (21) we obtain

$$cov(z_{t+1}, y_{t+1}) > 0$$

$$\Leftrightarrow -y_t^2 E z_{t+1} + y_t E x_{t+1} > 0$$

$$\Leftrightarrow y_t E z_{t+1} < 1$$

$$\Leftrightarrow y_t^2 \left[(1 + a - a\pi)\pi + (1 - a\pi) \frac{(1-\pi)^2 a}{y_t^2 - \pi} \right] < 1 \qquad (22)$$

where $y_t^2 < 1$. Therefore (22) is implied by

$$(1 + a - a\pi)\pi + a(1-\pi)^2(1-a\pi)/(1-\pi) \leq 1 \qquad (23)$$

We conclude that a positive inflation-output covariance is implied by the weak inequalities

$$1 \geq \pi(1 + a - a\pi) + a(1-\pi)(1-a\pi)$$

$$\Leftrightarrow 1 - \pi \geq \pi a(1-\pi) + a(1-\pi)(1-a\pi)$$

$$\Leftrightarrow 1 \geq \pi a + a(1-a\pi)$$

which is satisfied because $a \in (0,1)$. This means that a Phillips relation exists in the short run for any $\pi \in (0,1)$ and any initial output value $y_1 \in (\sqrt{\pi}, 1)$.

4. MONEY AND OUTPUT IN THE LONG RUN

The beliefs that tie output to the inflation rate and to monetary aggregates cannot be rational forever. As the economy chooses between the high-output and low-output alternatives open to it in equation (15a), it is unavoidably driven in finite time to either the monetary or the non-monetary steady state as required by equation (14a). The technical reasons are clear: for any given π and initial y_1, the sequence of non-stationary (y_t) defined by the second line of equation (15a) will shrink below $\sqrt{\pi}$ in finite time. This is also obvious from Figure 1, and it is not difficult to calculate the expected number of periods it takes for that sequence to fall below the critical value $\sqrt{\pi}$. Once that happens, the economy will reach a steady state in one period and the money-output covariance will vanish.

Why beliefs cannot support a long-run correlation of output to fundamentally super-neutral money is closely related to the fact that an indeterminate monetary steady state does not exist in this economy. Other structures with large income effects, stochastic government purchases, non-convexities and similar features will typically admit indeterminate monetary steady states[3] which permit beliefs to create a positive correlation of output to monetary aggregates in the long run as well as in the short run.

5. CONCLUSIONS

This essay has looked at a variant of the Lucas (1972) economy in which money is fundamentally super-neutral but nevertheless causes short-run movements in real economic activity. The transmission mechanism relies on temporary sunspot equilibria that support rational beliefs connecting high output to large realizations of random monetary aggregates. These correlations cannot persist because in the long run the economy converges to a state in which fundamentals uniquely determine economic activity.

The economy we analyze is not rich enough to permit a meaningful distinction between the output effects of monetary aggregates and the output effects of their rates of growth, even though these are considerably different in postwar US time series; see Cooley and Hansen (1995). Neither is the class of rational expectations solutions we study general enough to include the richer correlation patterns that would follow from the non-monotone solutions of Chiappori and Guesnerie (1990). Within these self-imposed limitations, a mild modification of Lucas's original structure will confirm one of the key tenets of traditional monetarism: monetary expansion may influence output favorably in the short run but *cannot* have any impact in the long run.

NOTES

1. See Azariadis (1993), pp. 377-79 for a fuller treatment.
2. The Cooley-Hansen simulations are based on the predetermined wage models of Gray (1976) and Fischer (1977). Other nominal rigidities are studied by Mankiw (1985), Akerlof and Yellen (1985), Farmer and Woodford (1984), and Azariadis and Cooper (1985).
3. Some interesting possibilities are examined in Farmer and Guo (1994). Guesnerie and Woodford (1992) provide a useful survey.

REFERENCES

Akerlof, G. and J. Yellen (1985), 'A Near-Rational Model of the Business Cycle with Wage and Price Inertia', *Quarterly Journal of Economics*, **100** (Supplement), pp. 823-38.

Aumman, R. (1987), 'Correlated Equilibrium as an Expression of Bayesian Rationality', *Econometrica*, **55**, pp. 1-18.

Azariadis, C. (1993), *Intertemporal Macroeconomics*, Oxford: Blackwell Publishers.

_____ and R. Cooper (1985), 'Predetermined Prices and the Allocation of Social Risks', *Quarterly Journal of Economics*, **100**, pp. 495-518.

_____ and R. Guesnerie (1986), 'Sunspots and Cycles', *Review of Economic Studies*, **53**, pp. 725-38.

Chiappori, P.-A. and R. Guesnerie (1990), 'Anticipations, Indetermination et Non-neutralite de la Monnaie', *Annals d'Economie et de Statistique*, **19**, pp. 1-25.

Cooley, T. and G. Hansen (1995), 'Money and the Business Cycle', ch. 7 in T. Cooley (ed.) *Frontiers of Business Cycle Research*.

Farmer, R. and J.T. Guo (1994), 'Real Business Cycles and the Animal Spirits Hypothesis', *Journal of Economic Theory*, **63**, pp. 42-72.

_____ and M. Woodford (1984), *Self-Fulfilling Prophecies and the Business Cycle*, University of Pennsylvania mimeo.

Fischer, S. (1977), 'Long-Term Contracts, Rational Expectations and the Optimal Money Supply Rule', *Journal of Political Economy*, **85**, pp. 163-90.

Friedman, M. (1968), 'The Role of Monetary Policy', *American Economic Review*, **58**, pp. 1-17.

Gray, J.A. (1976), 'Wage Indexation: A Macroeconomic Approach', *Journal of Monetary Economics*, **2**, pp. 221-35.

Guesnerie, R., and M. Woodford (1992), 'Endogenous Fluctuations', ch. 6 in *Advances in Economic Theory*.

Lucas, R. (1972), 'Expectations and the Neutrality of Money', *Journal of Economic Theory*, **9**, pp. 103-24.

Mankiw, G. (1985), 'Small Menu Costs and Large Business Cycles: A Macroeconomic Model of Monopoly', *Quarterly Journal of Economics*, **100**, pp. 529-39.

Peck, J. (1988), 'On the Existence of Sunspot Equilibria in an Overlapping Generations Model', *Journal of Economic Theory*, **44**, pp. 19-42.

7.   Towards a General Theory of Real Capital

George C. Bitros* and Elias G. Flytzanis§

I. INTRODUCTION

A household, a firm or a whole economy owns an assortment of durable goods that are somehow aggregated into what we call capital stock. Apart from its *utilisation*, the owner of this capital stock may alter its state through several decisions. Referring to them by the terms employed to describe the respective activities, these decisions comprise: *expansionary investment,[1] replacement investment, maintenance,[2] overhauling investment, stripping disinvestment, discarding or abandoning*, and *idling*. So far the study of their determinants has been conducted under three fundamental premises. The first is that only a few of these activities carry significant macroeconomic implications to deserve attention. This has led researchers to focus on the analysis mainly of *expansionary* and *replacement investments* and to a much lesser extent on *maintenance* expenditures.[3] The second premise is that each decision is taken at a different point in time during the useful lives of the durables that make up the capital stock, so each can be studied in isolation from the others. With the exception of a few studies stressing the contemporaneous nature of some of these activities,[4] this has allowed researchers to adopt partial equilibrium approaches and single equation estimating techniques. Finally, the third premise is that *investment* is completely reversible (irreversible) in the sense that once put in place it can (cannot) be resold at no (any) economic loss to the investor.

At the time of their introduction these premises were motivated partly by the prevailing stylised facts and partly by the state of economic theory. For example, when Jorgenson (1963) proposed his renowned theory of *expansionary investment*, he was justified in downplaying the importance of *replacement investment* because, even though the latter accounted for over 50 per

*   Athens University of Economics and Business, 76 Patission Street, Athens 104 34, Greece, Tel: (01) 8223545 Fax: (01) 8203301, E-mail: bitros@aueb.gr
§   Athens University of Economics and Business, 76 Patission Street, Athens 104 34, Greece, Tel: (01) 8238804 Fax: (01) 8203235, E-mail: flyt@aueb.gr

cent of gross investment in the United States, it appeared to be a stable proportion of the capital stock. But a few years later Feldstein and Foot (1971),
Eisner (1972), and others, were equally justified in criticising his concep-
tualisations because more recent data from McGraw-Hill surveys and other
sources showed that the ratio of replacement investment to capital stock varied significantly, particularly in the short run. Our view in this chapter is that
both the stylised facts and the state of economic theory have changed significantly so that a major overhaul of the established theory of real capital is
warranted.

To highlight the nature of contemplated changes, consider first the premise
of reversibility (irreversibility). Jorgenson (1963) assumed that the non-
depreciated part of an investment could be resold at the same price that it had
been purchased initially (complete reversibility). This was quite natural at the
time because economic theory was being developed under the presumption
that economic agents operated in complete markets. Then Arrow (1968) came
along and dispensed with the assumption of complete reversibility by postulating that once undertaken investment could not be resold (complete irreversibility). In turn, this meant that investors operated in perfectly incomplete
markets. But whatever the state of second-hand markets might have been in
the late 1960's,[5] their breadth and depth in recent decades has increased significantly under the advancing wave of globalisation. Hence, given that investors may have now the option to resell their investment at some cost,[6] one
necessary generalisation is to account for the implications of this possibility.[7]

Nor is it adequate any more to treat each of the aforementioned decisions
as if they are taken in isolation from the others. For this might have been a
reasonable approximation when the average useful life of capital stock was
20 years and planning of investment in a capital budgeting framework was
little practised. But now the average age of capital stock in all industrial nations has declined dramatically under the influence of rapid technological
advances and ignoring the time profiles of one policy while deciding on the
time profiles of the others may easily turn out to be suboptimal, and hence
costly. Therefore, a general theory of real capital should allow for all possible
interactions among these policies.

Moreover, aside from the generalisations just suggested, the present chapter investigates the consequences of several other extensions. One of them is
the incorporation into the theory of explicit policies for *utilisation* and *maintenance*. Another is the provision for the appearance of minor and major technological changes or breakthroughs. And still another is the provision for
safety in the *operation* and the *disposal* of durables at the end of their useful
lives. Owing to all these revisions and extensions the results that emerge are

quite illuminating. With or without discontinuities, the policies of *utilisation, maintenance*, and *expansionary investment* turn out to be uniquely determined. More specifically, in the absence of linearities, i.e. in the presence of adjust-ment costs, the capital owner is advised to apply the policies so as to equate certain substitution rates to the own price of capital stock. But in the presence of linearities he is told to resort to the *extreme policies* indicated by the solu-tion, prominent among which are the policies of *stopping and idling, stopping and discarding or abandoning*, and *downgrading and depleting*. Additionally we show that, if at any intermediate period the own price of capital stock becomes higher (lower) than the marginal market price of investment, the owner should undertake *overhauling investment* or *stripping disinvestment*, respectively. Last, but not least, it is shown that the optimal service life is uniquely determined and negatively related to the uncertainty due to minor and major technological breakthroughs.

The chapter is organised as follows. In Section II we specify a continuous-time, terminal-horizon real capital problem and derive necessary and almost sufficient conditions for the existence of optimal policies. In Section III we characterise the properties of the optimal policies and trace their interactions. Additionally, in the same section, we extend the model to an infinite-horizon equidistant sequence of replacement investments and investigate the conse-quences of this generalisation on the optimal service life of the capital stock. Then, in Section IV, we obtain a general solution by applying our analysis to a class of operating functions whose elasticities with respect to the policy variables are independent of the capital stock and a specific solution for an indicative but common specification of these functions. Finally, in Section V, we summarise our conclusions.

II. THE MODEL

Consider a capital owner whose operations are designed and implemented on the basis of the following blocks of information:

Capital Stock

$S = S(t)$: *Resale value of capital stock*, expressing the size and state of equipment, structures and generally all real assets owned and used by the capital owner with $S \geq J$, where $J \geq 0$ is some lowest operating capital stock level which we will call safety level.[8]

Utilisation & Maintenance

$u = u(t)$: *Utilisation intensity*, relative to some maximum, with $0 \le u \le 1$.

$m = m(t)$: *Maintenance intensity*, expressed as effort or expense relative to some maximum, with $0 \le m \le 1$. We will be referring to either *utilisation* or *maintenance* as *operating policies* and denote their combination by the vector variable:

$\vec{u}:(u,m)$: *Operating policy pair*.

$r(u,m,S)$: *Current revenue flow*. Strictly increasing in u, strictly decreasing in m, concave in (u, m). It can have either sign, usually positive.

$w(u,m,S)$: *Capital stock deterioration or wear and tear flow*, expressing current deterioration of S due to *usage*. It includes ageing and *current upkeep* due to *maintenance*. Increasing in u, decreasing in m, convex in (u, m). It can have either sign, usually positive. We will be referring to r and w as *operating flow functions*. Of special interest are also the elasticities of these functions with respect to the operating policies.

Expansionary Investment

$i = i(t)$: *Expansionary investment*, with $i(t) \ge 0$.[9]

$c(i)$: *Cost of expansionary investment flow*, convex and strictly increasing, with $c(0) = 0$ and $c(i) \ge i$.

$\dot{S} = -w(u,m,S) + i$: *Current overall rate of capital stock adjustment*.

$q = r(u,m,S) - c(i)$: *Current overall revenue flow net of expansionary investment* cost.

Overhauling Investment or Stripping Disinvestment

$I = \Delta S = S^+ - S$: A finite jump in the capital stock level S, of either sign, usually positive acting like *overhauling investment*, or negative acting like *stripping disinvestment*. Its cost will be represented by

$C(S,I,t)$: *Current cost of overhauling or revenue from stripping*, at time t, with current capital stock S. Convex, strictly increasing in I, with $C(S,0,t) = 0$ and $C \ge I$. Thus, it is positive when I is positive, expressing the cost of *overhauling investment*, and it is negative when I is negative, expressing the revenue from *stripping disinvestment*.[10] Taking into account transaction costs and costly reversibility, we assume that the marginal market cost $C_I(S,0^+,t)$ and revenue $C_I(S,0^-,t)$ are strictly bigger and strictly smaller than I, respectively. Concerning its monotonicity with respect to S, it could be of either sign, usually decreasing: $C_S \leq 0$.

Major Technological Breakthroughs

$F(t)$: Probability of technological obsolescence by time t, with $F(0) = 0$ and $F(t) < 1$. We will examine mainly the usual exponential case:

$$F(t) = 1 - e^{\theta t}.$$

Discounting

Assuming *discount rate* ρ, we will have the *discount factor* $e^{-\rho t}$. Actually, to express *effective current values* where we take also into account the technological obsolescence effect, we will use the terms:

$$\varphi(t) = \left[1 - F(t)\right]e^{-\rho t} : \text{Effective discount factor}$$

$$\sigma(t) = -\varphi'/\varphi(t) : \text{Effective discount rate.}$$

In particular, the exponential case $F(t) = 1 - e^{-\theta t}$ gives $\varphi(t) = e^{-\sigma t}$, where $\sigma \equiv \theta + \rho$ is the *constant effective discount rate*.

Objective

The objective adopted by the capital owner is to maximise the discounted expected total profit from using the stock for a time period T and *selling, discarding* or *idling* what is left from it at the end of this period.[11] Moreover, while pursuing the above, the capital owner is expected to allow for the possibility of *overhauling* or *stripping* at some intermediate time τ.[12]

The Problem

$$\underset{\{u,m,i,I,T,\tau\}}{Max} \left\{ B = Q + R(T,S_T) - E(S,I,\tau) \right\}, \tag{1}$$

where:

$Q = \int_0^T \left[r(u,m,S) - c(i)\right] \varphi(t)d(t)$: *Expected total net revenue* from operation.

$R = \phi(T)S_T$: *Expected revenue from resale*, where $S_T = S(T)$.

$E = \phi(\tau)C(S,I,\tau)$: *Expected cost (revenue) of overhauling (stripping)*.

$\dot{S} = -w(u,m,S) + i$: *Stock adjustment*, with $S(0) = S_0$.

$0 \leq u \leq 1, 0 \leq m \leq 1, S \geq J$: *Operating and stock constraints*.

Remark 1. For the operating policies $\{u,m\}$ we have the natural bounds $0 \le u \le 1$ and $m \ge 0$. In addition, we assumed an upper bound on maintenance, which we normalised to 1. In the absence of such an upper bound, e.g. if m represents actual expense flow, we would have the usual limiting conditions on the derivatives of the operating functions:

$$r_m \to -\infty \text{ or } w_m \to 0 \text{ as } m \to +\infty.$$

Similarly, concerning the investment policy variables $\{i, I\}$ and their cost functions. We note that in particular cases one or both could be absent.

Optimality Conditions

In the setting of optimal control theory we consider the *Hamiltonian* expression:

$$H = \varphi(t)\left[r(u,m,S) - c(i)\right] + \lambda(t)\left[-w(u,m,S) + i\right] \tag{2}$$

where $\lambda(t)$ is a co-state variable, representing the *present own price* of capital stock S. Using *effective current* rather than *present values*, we divide by the strictly positive quantity $\varphi(t)$, and set

$$\mu(t) = \frac{\lambda(t)}{\varphi(t)} : \textit{Current effective own price of } S \Rightarrow \frac{\dot{\mu}}{\mu} = \frac{\dot{\lambda}}{\lambda} + \sigma(t). \tag{3}$$

Without Overhauling or Stripping

As usually we will consider first the case without state discontinuities, i.e. without *overhauling* or *stripping*. According to Seierstad and Sydsaeter (1986, p.335), the assumed convexities give rise to the following almost necessary and sufficient conditions for the optimal solution:

$$\max_{u,m}\left\{H = \varphi(t)\left[r(u,m,S) - c(i)\right] + \lambda\left[-w(u,m,S) + i\right]\,\|\,0 \le u \le 1, 0 \le m \le 1\right\} \tag{4.1}$$

$$\Rightarrow \max_{u,m}\left\{H = \varphi(t)\left[r(u,m,S) - \mu w(u,m,S) - c(i) + \mu i\right]\,\|\,0 \le u \le 1, 0 \le m \le 1\right\}$$

$$\Rightarrow \max_{u,m}\left\{r(u,m,S) - \mu w(u,m,S)\,\|\,0 \le u \le 1, 0 \le m \le 1\right\}, \tag{i}$$

$$\max_{i}\left\{-c(i) + \mu i\right\}, \tag{ii}$$

i.e., given S and μ, the operating and investment policies are decided independently. This is a consequence of the assumed separable forms for the effects of the corresponding policies on the revenue and on the capital stock.

Concerning the time development of capital stock S, we have the state equation:

$$\dot{S} = -w(u, m, S) + i, \text{ with } S(0) = S_0 . \tag{4.2}$$

For the time development of the own price of capital stock μ we have the co-state equation:

Assuming the safety level J is not reached $\qquad\qquad (4.3)$

$$\dot{\lambda} = -\partial H/\partial S = -\varphi r_s + \lambda w_s \text{ with } \lambda(T) = \partial R/\partial S_T = \varphi(T)$$

and $\lambda(t)$ continuous

$$\Rightarrow \dot{\mu} = -r_s(u, m, S) + \mu w_s(u, m, S) + \mu\sigma(t), \text{ with } \mu(T) = 1$$

and $\mu(t)$ continuous.

Assuming the safety level J is reached $\qquad\qquad (4.3')$

$\dot{\lambda} \le -\partial H/\partial S$, and $S \ge J$ with *Complementary Slackness (CS)*,

$\lambda(T) \ge \partial R/\partial S_T$ and $\min S \ge J$ with CS,

and with *downward discontinuities* for λ at the times of hitting and leaving the *safety level*.

$\Rightarrow \dot{\mu} \le -r_s(u, m, S) + \mu w_s(u, m, S) + \mu\sigma(t)$, and $S \ge J$ *with CS* ,

and *downward discontinuities* for μ at the times of hitting and leaving the *safety level J*.

Finally, the total operating period T is determined by the terminal condition:

$$H + \partial R/\partial T\big\|_T = 0 \Rightarrow \varphi(T)[r_T - c_T] + \lambda_T[-w_T + i_T] + \varphi'(T)S_T \Rightarrow \tag{4.4}$$

$r_T - c_T - \mu_T w_T + \mu_T i_T - \sigma(T)S_T = 0$, provided that $T > 0$,

(≤ 0 if $T = 0$), where the T subscript refers to values at the terminal time.

With Overhauling or Stripping

Finally, considering the possibility of spiked investment causing a jump discontinuity in S at time τ , we note that it will be advantageous if the *current effective own price* of capital $\mu(\tau)$ equals the *marginal market price of investment* $C_I(S, I, \tau)$. This means that we will have *overhauling*: $I > 0$, if $\mu(\tau)$ rises above $C_I(S, 0^+, \tau)$, and *stripping*: $I < 0$, if $\mu(\tau)$ falls below $C_I(S, 0^-, \tau)$.

Then, according to Seierstad and Sydsaeter (1987, pp.196 and 207), $\mu(\tau)$ will exhibit a discontinuity determined by the condition:

$$C_S(S,I,\tau) = \Delta\mu \tag{5.1}$$

The amount of *overhauling/stripping* is determined by the condition that the *marginal market price* of I before be equal to the *current effective own price of capital stock* μ after.[13] That is:

$$C_I(S,I,\tau) = \mu^+ , \tag{5.2}$$

assuming, in the case of *stripping*, that this does not drive the stock below its safety level J. Finally, we note the following remarks:

Remark 2. We have assumed that the cost function of *overhauling/stripping* is known in advance. Actually it is only known at the zero time of planning. In the absence of any other information we can assume for convenience that it is constant in time. Also, on general grounds, we can assume that *overhauling/stripping* is not advantageous at the beginning or it would have been incorporated into the initial capital stock level. The above remarks are expressed by the condition:

$$C_I(S,0^-) < \mu_0 < C_I(S,0^+), \text{ where } \mu_0 = \mu(0) . \tag{5.3}$$

Remark 3. Since *overhauling/stripping* changes the values of $\{S,\mu\}$, it necessitates also the modification of the optimal policies as determined above.

III. OPTIMAL POLICIES

In comparing policies $\{u,m,i\}$ for given S, we will call *backward* the direction of decreasing revenue flow r, decreasing deterioration flow w, and increasing investment flow i. We will call *forward* the reverse direction. Thus, in the space of operating policies $\vec{u} : (u,m)$, we distinguish the extremal policies:

$$\vec{u}_0 : (u = 0, m = 1) , \textit{ Backward most extremal.} \tag{6.1}$$

$$\vec{u}_1 : (u = 1, m = 0) , \textit{ Forward most extremal.} \tag{6.2}$$

Also for given S, we can characterise policy triplets (u,m,i) according to their effect on S as follows:

$$\dot{S} = -w(u,m,S) + i = 0 \quad Stock \ equilibrium, \tag{7.1}$$

$$\dot{S} = -w(u,m,S) + i > 0 \quad Upgrading, \tag{7.2}$$

$$\dot{S} = -w(u,m,S) + i < 0 \quad Downgrading, \tag{7.3}$$

Moreover, by considering their effect on the net revenue, we will characterise policies as follows:

$$q = r(u,m,S) - c(i) = 0 \quad Revenue \ equilibrium, \tag{8.1}$$

$$q = r(u,m,S) - c(i) > 0 \quad Profit \ making, \tag{8.2}$$

$$q = r(u,m,S) - c(i) < 0 \quad Loss \ making. \tag{8.3}$$

All above notions could be restricted to apply only to the *operating policy pairs* $\bar{u} : (u,m)$, by considering their effect on the operating functions $r(u,m,S)$ and $w(u,m,S)$. Thus, an *operating policy pair* $\bar{u} : (u,m)$ would be *upgrading (downgrading)* and *profit (loss) making* if $-w(u,m,S)$ and $r(u,m,S)$ are respectively greater (lower) than 0.

S-optimal policies

The *Maximality Principle* (4.1) determines the optimal policy triplet $\{u,m,i\}$ for given $\{S,\mu\}$. Using the convexities of the operating functions and applying the *theory of convex programming*, we find that for each given S the allowed *optimal operating policies* for various μ values are also solutions of the constraint optimisation problem:

$$\max_{u,m}\{r(u,m,S) \| w(u,m,S) \le w, \quad 0 \le u \le 1, \quad 0 \le m \le 1\}, \tag{9}$$

By the strict monotonicity properties of function r we can replace the inequality constraint by the corresponding equality.[14]

Considering the constraint optimisation problem above, we note that for each S the policy pairs $\bar{u} : (u,m)$ maximising revenue for given deterioration, define an upper semicontinuous path of *operating policy pairs* parameterised by w. In practice this means piecewise continuous. We will call these policies **S-optimal policies**. The path will be continuous if the convexity condition is strict for one of the operating flow functions. In this case for each S the optimal policies of *utilisation* and *maintenance* are tied together continuously in a 1–1 fashion, forming a continuous path of *operating policy pairs* represented by:

$$\vec{u} = \vec{u}(w,S) : u = u(w,S), \; m = m(w,S) . \qquad (10)$$

The maximal value function involved measures the maximal operating revenue r for given deterioration w. It is increasing concave in w. The Lagrange multiplier

$$z(\vec{u},S) = \frac{dr}{dw} , \qquad (11)$$

given by the derivative of this maximal function, is the *marginal revenue of capital stock deterioration*. It measures the *substitution rate* between revenue and capital stock deterioration caused by **S-optimal policies**. Moreover, for reasons that will become obvious shortly, we define:

$$z_u = \frac{r_u\{u,m,S\}}{w_u\{u,m,S\}}, \quad z_m = \frac{r_m\{u,m,S\}}{w_m\{u,m,S\}}, \qquad (12)$$

where the subscripts denote indices for z and partial derivatives for $\{r,w\}$. Clearly, for each given S these ratios measure the *substitution* rate between revenue and stock deterioration caused by each operating policy separately. By the convexity properties, z_u is decreasing in u, z_m is increasing in m, and the path of **S-optimal policies** separates the operating policies space into two regions:

$R^+(S) : z_u \le z_m$ *High intensity operating policies,*

$R^-(S) : z_u \ge z_m$ *Low intensity operating policies.*

Using the above definitions, we arrive at the following conclusions:

Conclusion 1: For each given S the *marginal revenue of capital stock deterioration* caused by **S-optimal policies** is positive. Also it is decreasing in the *forward direction* of increasing r and w. If the *operating policies* act independently:

$$\begin{aligned} r(u,m,S) &= \alpha(u,S) - \beta(m,S) \\ w(u,m,S) &= \gamma(u,S) - \delta(m,S) \end{aligned} \qquad (13)$$

then the *forward direction* in the **S-optimal policies** coincides with the direction of increasing *utilisation* and decreasing *maintenance*.

Conclusion 2: The *S*-optimal policies in the interior of the control space are those for which: $z = z_u = z_m$. By implication, in the *high intensity region* we are *over-maintaining* for given *utilisation* or, equivalently, we are *over-utilising* for given *maintenance*, and conversely in the *low intensity region*.

Additionally, for each given *S*, we define the *substitution equilibrium operating policies*:

$$\vec{u} = \vec{u}^*(S) : u = u^*(S), m = m^*(S),\qquad(14)$$

as the *S*-optimal policies for which it holds that: $z^*(S) = 1$. Otherwise, they are the most extremal ones:

$\vec{u}_0 : (u = 0, m = 1), \text{ if } z_0(S) \geq 1$

$\vec{u}_1 : (u = 1, m = 0), \text{ if } z_1(S) \geq 1,$

where $z_0(S)$ and $z_1(S)$ are the *maximal* and the *minimal substitution rates*, respectively.

Next, we define similar notions for *expansionary investment policy*. The *marginal cost of expansionary investment* is given by the derivative of the cost function and depends only on *i*:

$$\xi(i) = \frac{dc}{di}\qquad(15)$$

The *equilibrium expansionary investment policy* is the investment policy for which we have $c'(i^*) = 1$. Otherwise it is the corresponding *most extremal expansionary investment policy*. It follows from our assumptions regarding $c(i)$ that the *equilibrium expansionary investment policy* is always the *extremal*: $i^* = 0$.

Collecting the above, we obtain the following:

Proposition 1. For given *S* and μ:

(i)   The *optimal operating policy pairs* $\vec{u} : (u, m)$ are the *S*-optimal policies for which the *marginal revenue of capital stock deterioration z* equals the *current effective own price of capital stock* μ:

$$z(\vec{u}, S) = \mu \Rightarrow \vec{u} = \vec{u}(S, \mu)\qquad(16)$$

if this rate is attained. Otherwise it is the corresponding *most extremal operating policy* pair.

(ii)   The *optimal expansionary investment policy i* is determined by the *condition that the marginal cost of expansionary investment* equals the *cur-*

rent effective own price of capital stock μ :

$$\xi(i) = \mu \Rightarrow i = i(\mu), \tag{17}$$

if this rate is attained. Otherwise it is the corresponding *most extremal expansionary investment policy.*

(iii) For given S the optimal policies move in the forward direction of increasing revenue, increasing deterioration and decreasing *expansionary investment* when μ decreases, and in the backward direction when μ increases.

(iv) Allowing *overhauling/stripping,* and if the associated cost (revenue) is a decreasing function of the existing stock: $C_S < 0$, then at the appropriate time τ we will observe a forward jump to higher operating flows $\{r,w\}$ and lower investment flow i. The opposite will be observed if $C_S > 0$.

(v) Assuming differentiability, the *interior optimal policies* $\{u,m,i\}$ for given $\{S,\mu\}$ are determined by the equations:

$$\mu = z = \xi \Rightarrow \mu = z_u = z_m = c'(i) \tag{18}$$

Extremal *S*-optimal Policies

Concerning the *extremal **S**-optimal policies* $u = \{0,1\}$ and $m = \{0,1\}$, we mention the following special cases:

1. $z_u \leq z_m$:   *High intensity technology,* i.e. all operating policies are of high intensity. Then the optimal policies are *lower extremal*: $u = 0$ or $m = 0$.

2. $z_u \geq z_m$:   *Low intensity technology,* i.e. all operating policies are of low intensity. Then the optimal policies are *upper extremal*: $u = 1$ or $m = 1$.

Finally we note that, because μ develops continuously, if the substitution rate z is discontinuous at some *operating policy pair* for an interval of S levels, e.g. at extremal policies, then this policy will be *persistent,* if optimal, in the sense that it will be applied for a long period, if applied at all. Similarly, if ξ is discontinuous at some *expansionary investment policy,* e.g. at the extremal values, then these will be also *persistent,* if optimal. We mention now the following important cases where extremal policies are *persistent*:

1. $\vec{u}_0 : (u = 0, m = 1)$. The most backward operating policy pair is *persistent* if it defines finite substitution rate: $z_0 < +\infty$.

2. $\vec{u}_1 : (u = 1, m = 0)$. The most forward operating policy pair is *persistent,* if it defines nonzero substitution rate: $z_1 > 0$.

3. $i = 0$: The zero investment policy is *persistent*, in general.

4. $\vec{u}_- : (u = 0, m = 0)$. The lowest intensity operating policy pair is *persistent* if all operating policies are strictly of high intensity: $z_u < z_m$.

5. $\vec{u}_+ : (u = 1, m = 1)$. The highest intensity operating policy pair is *persistent* if all operating policies are strictly of low intensity: $z_u > z_m$.

Safety Level

The *Maximality Principle* expresses the *optimal policies* $\{u, m, i\}$ as functions of S and the *current effective own price* of capital stock μ. Without *overhauling/stripping*, S develops continuously according to the state equation (4.2). Similarly, the *current effective own price of capital stock* μ develops in time continuously, unless the stock S hits and is operated for a time period at its *safety level* J. In the latter case μ will exhibit a downward discontinuity at the times of hitting and leaving the *safety level*. However, this cannot happen, because:

1. The time movement of S implies that when hitting and leaving the *safety level*, $\dot{S}$ will be increasing going from negative to zero and then to positive values. Since the applied policies will be **J-optimal**, they will be moving necessarily in the *backward direction* of decreasing r, decreasing w and increasing i.

2. The downward discontinuity of μ when S hits and when it leaves the *safety level* implies that in both instances the optimal policies must move in the *forward direction* at capital stock J.

Hence, S is not allowed to hit and be operated at the safety level. Instead we adjust the policies in the backward direction of lower operating rates $\{r, w\}$ and higher investment rate i, just enough so as to stay above the safety level. From these remarks we conclude that:

Proposition 2: Without *overhauling/stripping*, the *current effective own price of capital stock* μ develops in time continuously according to the dynamic equation

$$\dot{\mu} = -r_s(u, m, S) + \mu\left[w_s(u, m, S) + \sigma(t)\right]. \tag{19}$$

(i) If the safety level J is not binding: $\gamma = 0$, we have $\mu(T) = 1$ and the terminal policies $\{u_T, m_T, i_T\}$ are the *substitution equilibrium policies* $\{u^*, m^*, i^* = 0\}$ corresponding to the terminal stock S_T.

(ii) As the safety level J becomes binding: $\gamma > 0$, we have $\mu(T) = 1 + \gamma$ and the *terminal policies* are displaced backward to lower operating rates and higher expansionary investment rate.

Replacement

Taking into account the purchase price P_0 of the initial stock S_0, the total net profit to be maximised becomes:

$$\Pi(T) = B(T) - P_0 = Q + R(T, S_T) - E(S, I, \tau) - P_0 \qquad (20)$$

The terminal condition remains the same as before:

$$\Pi'(T) = 0 \Rightarrow B'(T) = 0 \qquad (21)$$

The above can be extended to a sequence of replacements. Assuming short replacement times relative to the planning period, the sequence can be extended to infinity. Considering equal replacement periods, constant purchase price and exponential probability of obsolescence, we face essentially a problem of constant future revenues with discount rate $\sigma = \theta + \rho$. The objective to be maximised becomes:

$$A(T) = \sum_v \Pi(T) e^{-\sigma v T} = \Pi(T) \frac{1}{1 - e^{-\sigma T}}, \qquad (22)$$

and the terminal condition takes the form:

$$A'(T) = 0 \Rightarrow \Pi'(T) = \Pi(T) \frac{\sigma e^{-\sigma T}}{1 - e^{-\sigma T}}. \qquad (23)$$

We note that since $\Pi(T)$ is assumed positive for profitability, the equation above gives $\Pi'(T) > 0$. This implies that service life in the replacement process becomes shorter as compared to the single operating period without replacement, because Π increases until it reaches $\Pi'(T) = 0$. The remaining optimality conditions remain the same as before. Concerning the new terminal condition, written explicitly it becomes:

$$r_T - c_T - w_T(1 + \gamma) + i_T(1 + \gamma) - \sigma S_T = \left[Q_T + e^{-\sigma T} S_T - e^{-\sigma T} C_T - P_0 \right] \frac{\sigma}{1 - e^{-\sigma T}} \quad (24)$$

When solved for T this gives:[15]

$$\kappa = \sigma K - \kappa e^{-\sigma T} \Rightarrow T = \frac{1}{\sigma} \ln \frac{\kappa}{\kappa - \sigma K} \qquad (25)$$

where:

$\kappa = r_T - c_T - w_T(1+\gamma) + i_T(1+\gamma)$: Terminal profit flow,

$K = Q_T + S_T - e^{-\sigma T} C_T - P_0$: Total profit.

Assuming $\gamma = 0$, the terminal flows $\{r_T, w_T, i_T, c_T\}$ would be determined by the *substitution equilibrium policies* for the terminal stock $\{u^*, m^*, i^* = 0\}$. In fact as indicated below under some general conditions this is independent even of the capital stock, i.e. it depends only on the effectiveness of the existing technology. Then T becomes a function of the observable total quantities, increasing in the revenues $\{Q_T, S_T\}$, and decreasing in the costs $\{C_T, P_0\}$ and in the discount rate σ. Of course T appears implicitly in these total quantities.

IV. APPLICATIONS

We will apply the results derived above so as to obtain the *optimal operating policies* for particular forms of *operating functions* that are of general interest. The existing technology of revenue r, of deterioration w and of expansionary investment cost c allowed us to determine a path of **S-optimal policies** in the control space $\{u, m, i\}$. At any time t, if we know the S and μ, the *optimal operating policies* $\bar{u}:(u,m)$ and i are determined by the condition (16)-(17), requiring that both the *marginal revenue of capital stock deterioration* and the *marginal cost of expansionary investment* be equal to the *current effective own price of capital stock*:

$$z(\bar{u}, S) = \xi(i) = \mu . \qquad (26)$$

In order to find the solution, i.e. the *optimal operating policies* as functions of time, we have to consider the time evolution of S and μ as determined by the dynamical equations (4.2) and (19). We will do this for a general class of problems involving *separable operating functions*, and then we will solve for two specific but quite common analytic forms of these functions.

Solution for Separable Operating Functions

We consider *operating functions* of the *separable* type:

$$r = q(u,m)f(S) \text{ and } w = s(u,m)g(S) \tag{27}$$

i.e., we assume that the elasticities of the *operating functions* $\{r,w\}$ with respect to the *operating policies* $\{u,m\}$ are independent of the capital stock S. Now we will call *forward* the direction of increasing operating rates $\{q,s\}$, and *backward* the opposite direction. The *optimal operating policies* are obtained as solutions of the following equality constraint optimisation problem:

$$\max_{u,m}\{q(u,m)\|s(u,m) = s\} \tag{28}$$

The upper semi-continuous path of *optimal operating policy* pairs is now parameterised by $s:\vec{u} = \vec{u}(s)$. This path is continuous if one of the flow functions satisfies the convexity condition strictly. The Lagrange multiplier defined by the derivative of the maximal value function

$$\zeta(\vec{u}) = \frac{dq}{ds} \Rightarrow \zeta(\vec{u}) = z(\vec{u},S)g(S)/f(S) \tag{29}$$

is positive and decreasing in the forward direction. It expresses the **substitution rate** between revenue and capital stock deterioration rates q and s, with maximal value ζ_0 at the *backward most extremal* policy pair $\vec{u}_0$ and minimal value ζ_1 at the *forward most extremal* policy pair $\vec{u}_1$. For given S and μ the *optimal operating policies* $\vec{u}:(u,m)$ and i are determined now by the conditions:

$$z(\vec{u},S) = \mu \Rightarrow \zeta(\vec{u}) = \mu g(S)/f(S), \xi(i) = \mu. \tag{30}$$

where $\xi(i) = c'(i)$ is always the *marginal cost of expansionary investment*. Also, as before, if any of the terms on the right side of these equations is outside the extremal values of ζ or ξ, respectively, then the *optimal operating policies* are the corresponding most extremal. Since we are considering first the case without *overhauling/stripping*, S and μ develop continuously, i.e., the right sides of the two equations above define continuous functions of time. So, we arrive at the following:

Conclusion 3: For operating functions of the chosen type, an *optimal operating policy* is:
(i)   *Persistent* where the corresponding substitution rate has discontinuity.

(ii) *Skipped* in general where the corresponding substitution rate is constant, i.e. where the operating functions are linear.

Part (ii) implies that, if in time we pass through a region where the operating functions are linear, then we will witness sudden jumps in the policy variables. In particular, if the operating functions are linear everywhere then we will witness only extremal policy values, between *idling* and *full* operation, *discarding* and *full maintenance*, *zero* and *maximum* expansionary investment.

Concerning the time development of *optimal operating policies* we note that they are determined by the factor $\pi = \mu g(S)/f(S)$, while the *expansionary investment policy* by the factor μ. Thus, decreasing π means increasing operating rates $\{q,s\}$, while decreasing μ means increasing operating flows $\{r = qf(S), w = sg(S)\}$ and also decreasing investment flow i.

Solution for a specific type of rate functions

We will apply now the previous results to operating flow functions of the type:

$$r = q(u,m)S^{\varepsilon} \text{ and } w = s(u,m)S . \tag{31}$$

We consider the new variable

$$\pi = \mu \frac{g(S)}{f(S)} = \mu S^{1-\varepsilon} \Rightarrow \frac{\dot{\pi}}{\pi} = \frac{\dot{\mu}}{\mu} + (1-\varepsilon)\frac{\dot{S}}{S} . \tag{32}$$

For the sequel we will consider only technological obsolescence probability of the exponential type, so that $\sigma \equiv \theta + \rho$ is constant so that the dynamical system defined by the optimality conditions becomes autonomous. The optimality conditions take the form:

$$\zeta(\vec{u}) = \pi \Rightarrow \frac{q_u(u,m)}{s_u(u,m)} = \frac{q_m(u,m)}{s_m(u,m)} = \pi = \mu S^{1-\varepsilon} \qquad \text{(i)} \tag{33}$$

$$\xi(i) = \mu \Rightarrow c'(i) = \mu \qquad \text{(ii)}$$

$$\dot{S} = -sS + i \text{ with } S(0) = S_0 \tag{34}$$

$$\dot{\mu} = -\varepsilon q S^{\varepsilon-1} + \mu(s + \sigma) \text{ with } \mu_T = 1 + \gamma \qquad \text{(i)} \tag{35}$$

$$\dot{\pi} = -\varepsilon q + \pi s + \pi\sigma + \pi(1-\varepsilon)\frac{i}{S} \text{ with } \pi_T = \mu_T S_T^{1-\varepsilon} \qquad \text{(ii)}$$

$$r_T - c_T - \mu_T w_T + \mu_T i_T - \sigma S_T = 0 \tag{36}$$

From these conditions we conclude the following:

Conclusion 4:

(i) *The optimal expansionary investment policy i is determined by the value of μ. It moves forward to lower rates when μ decreases and conversely when it increases.*

(ii) *The optimal operating policy pair $\bar{u}:(u,m)$ is determined by the value of $\pi = \mu S^{1-\varepsilon}$. It moves forward to higher revenue rates q and deterioration rates s when π decreases, and conversely when it increases.*

From equation 35(ii) we observe that, if the last term is zero, i.e. if $\varepsilon = 1$ or $i \equiv 0$, π does not involve S. This means that the equation becomes autonomous and therefore π develops monotonously when continuous. We note also that the sign of the time derivative of π gives the monotonicity direction at any time, in particular at the terminal time as determined by conditions (35ii) and (36). Examining these two cases we obtain the following results:[16]

Proposition 3. Assuming constant returns to scale: $\varepsilon = 1$, for $r = q(u,m)S$ and $w = s(u,m)S$, we have:

(i) Without *overhauling/stripping* the optimal policies develop in time as follows:

    1. If the safety level is not binding: $\gamma = 0$ then the *current effective price of capital stock μ* is constant and the *optimal policies* are also constant, equal to the *substitution equilibrium policies*: $(u^*, m^*, i^* = 0)$.

    2. If the safety level is binding: $\gamma > 0$, then the *current effective price of capital stock μ* is time increasing and the optimal policies move in time backward toward decreasing operating flows and increasing investment flow. In the presence of linearities we will witness sudden jumps to lower operating flows and higher investment flow.

(ii) A policy of *overhauling* will be applied provided the safety level is sufficiently high so that $\mu_T = 1 + \gamma > C_I(S,0^+)$.

(iii) A policy of *stripping* will be applied provided the safety level is sufficiently low so that $\mu_T = 1 + \gamma < C_I(S,0^-)$.[17]

Proposition 4. Without *expansionary investment*: $i \equiv 0$, for $r = q(u,m)S^\varepsilon$ and, $w = s(u,m)S$, the *optimal operating policies* move in time in the backward direction of increasing μ and therefore decreasing operating flows $\{r,w\}$ if the safety level is sufficiently high, or if one of the following conditions holds:

decreasing returns to scale: $\varepsilon < 1$ and profit making terminal policies: $r_T > 0$, or increasing returns to scale: $\varepsilon > 1$ and loss making terminal policies: $r_T < 0$.

In both cases considered we found that in general if the *safety level* is sufficiently restrictive, then in time *optimal operating policies* move in the backward direction of lower revenue and lower capital stock deterioration, with sudden jumps where we have linearities.

V. CONCLUSIONS

This paper was motivated by three observations. The first of them has to do with the partial equilibrium approach that the bulk of research has adopted to study the decisions relating to real capital. Clearly, since it is founded on the presumption that each decision is taken in isolation from the others, this approach ignores the interactions among the policy options of capital owners and thus leads to sub-optimal policies. The second observation emanates from the realisation that, even though the more interesting case to study is that of *costly reversibility*, most of the research on real capital continues to be conducted as if investment were either *completely reversible* or completely *irreversible*. Finally, the third observation is that such important issues as uncertainty from minor and major technological breakthroughs, operating safety, friendly environmental disposal, etc. are not considered in a unified theoretical framework. Thus, what we set out to accomplish here was to present a model capable to address the problems of real capital policies as well as their interactions.

To this effect, initially we laid out a continuous-time, terminal-horizon real capital model and used it to trace the properties of *utilisation, maintenance*, and *investment* policies. From its analysis it turned out that these policies are uniquely determined. More specifically, the capital owner should apply the policies so as to equate the substitution rates r_u/w_u, r_m/w_m, and c' to the *current effective own price* of capital stock μ, whereas in the presence of linearities, i.e. in the absence of adjustment and disinvestment costs, he should apply extremal policies. Notable among the latter being the policies of *stopping and idling or mothballing* $(u = 0, m = 1, i = 0)$, *stopping and discarding* $(u = 0, m = 0, i = 0)$, and *downgrading and depleting* or *running down* $(u = 1, m = 0, i = 0)$. Last, but not least, we examined the utilization and maintenance shifts resulting from the procedures of *overhauling* or *stripping* the capital stock.

Then, in order to cast the policy of *optimal service life* in its proper setting, we went on and extended the model to an infinite-horizon equidistant-sequence

of replacement investments. From its analysis, there emerged several important results. For example, *optimal serve life* is uniquely determinate. By comparison to that obtained from the case of single operating period without replacement, the optimal service life is shorter. And the uncertainty due to minor and major technological breakthroughs reduces *optimal service life*, as
does the interest rate.

Finally, to demonstrate the range of its applicability, we solved the model
for a general class of *separable operating functions* and obtained particular
solutions assuming either *constant returns to scale* or absence of *expansionary investment*.

NOTES

1.   We use the term *expansionary* investment to describe the activity of increasing capital stock
through additions of new capital goods that do not affect the state of pre-existing ones. Investment
activities that increase capital stock through modification of pre-existing capital goods are sub-
sumed under the terms of *maintenance*, overhauling investment and stripping disinvestment.
2.   According to the definitions introduced in Bitros and Flytzanis (2000), maintenance may be
distinguished into *regular* and *irregular*, with the former being applied at intervals recommended
by the manufacturers' manuals that relate usually to the intensity with which durables are used. In
turn, *irregular* maintenance may be further distinguished into maintenance proper or just *maintenance*, *upgrading* and *downgrading*. The difference among them being that *maintenance* leaves
the resale value of the durable unchanged, whereas *upgrading* (*downgrading*) increases (decreases)
it.
3.   This statement should not be interpreted to imply that the remaining decisions have not received some attention, albeit scanty. For example, see Rothwell and Rust (1997) on the optimal
stopping of nuclear plants, Das (1991) on the idling of cement kilns, Arnott, Davidson and Pines
(1983) on housing rehabilitation, and Bitros and Kelejian (1974) and Hahn (1995) on capital scrappage.
4.   The studies by Nashlund (1966), Thompson (1968), Kamien and Schwartz (1971) and Ye
(1990) emphasised the simultaneous nature of optimal maintenance and service life decisions.
Bitros (1976) highlighted the simultaneous nature of incremental investment, replacement investment and maintenance expenditures. Roll and Sachish (1978) studied the interrelationship between overhaul and replacement policies, and Bitros and Flytzanis (2000) developed a unified
framework for the analysis of all real capital decisions with the exception of incremental investment.
5.   In his paper Arrow set out to investigate the implications of complete irreversibility for capital
policies. So he was not required to justify his assumption by reference to the range of the then
existing second-hand markets. However, if one cared for the degree to which complete irreversibility was corroborated by reality, one would have concluded that it lacked support because in
such large sectors as housing, shipping, aircraft, medical equipment, trucks, used industrial machinery, etc., the existence of second-hand markets has been always quite robust. For evidence on
this claim see, for example, Sen (1962), Waterson (1964), and Smith (1974).
6.   Abel and Eberly (1996) were the first to investigate the implications for optimal investment of
'costly reversibility', i.e. of the possibility for an investor to purchase capital at a given price and
sell it at a lower price.
7.   In addition, it should be observed that in the absence of some investment reversibility, the
aggregation mentioned above for the derivation of capital stock might be extremely hard to carry

out, if at all possible. To find out how demanding, and hence improbable, the conditions for such an aggregation would be, see, for example, Fisher (1982).

8.   This *safety level* may be imposed by a regulatory agency for various reasons. One such reason is to oblige the owners to maintain certain technical standards for the *safe operation* of their durables. An example in this respect is the conventional requirement that motor vehicles pass a thorough technical examination every so many years or months before they can be issued valid circulation permits. Another reason is to prohibit owners from abandoning their durables and thus generating environmental externalities. Clearly, since due to this constraint the scrap value of durables is kept necessarily positive, for their owners to realise the corresponding revenues they must dispose them properly.

9.   Allowing $i(t)$ to take on negative values does not present analytical difficulties. However, in this paper we decided not to do so for two reasons. First, because expansionary investment as we defined it above is either positive or zero, and, secondly, because reversibility is secured anyway through *stripping disinvestment*.

10.   For example, in the case of complete irreversibility we would have $i \geq 0$ and $I \geq 0$.

11.   Later on we will examine also the option of replacing the capital stock and thus begin a new cycle in the optimal design and application of real capital policies. In fact, we will consider an infinite-horizon, equal service life, sequence of replacement investments.

12.   Dunne (1994), Caballero, Engel and Haltiwanger (1995), Cooper and Haltiwanger (1993), Cooper, Haltiwanger and Power (1999), and others have discovered in recent years 'spiked' patterns of investment at the plant level. Our specification of the problem facing the capital owner is consistent with this literature since it allows for *overhauling*, i.e. spiked investment, at any T during the terminal horizon T. Moreover, notice that that we generalise even further by allowing for *stripping*, i.e. spiked disinvestment.

13.   Abel and Eberly (1996) established that under output demand uncertainty and costly reversibility the optimal investment policy of the firm would be to purchase (sell) capital if its *marginal revenue product* exceeded (fell short of) an upper (lower) value of its usei cost of capital. By con trast, in our model uncertainty springs from technological change and optimal investment policy recommends that the firm purchase (sell) capital when the *marginal market price of investment* is lower (higher) than the *current effective own price of capital.*

14.   In fact this equivalence holds only for $\mu \geq 0$. However if μ is negative then the optimal policy triplet $\{u, m, i\}$ would be necessarily the *forward most extremal,* $\vec{u}_1 : (u = 1, m = 0)$ and $i = 0$, which is included above anyway for $\mu = 0$.

15.   For comparison we note that the terminal condition without replacement is written: $\kappa = \sigma S_T$.

16.   The complete analysis underlying Propositions 3 and 4 is available on request from the authors.

17.   As mentioned earlier, the possibility of *overhauling/stripping* necessitates the recalculation of the *optimal operating policies*, using as final capital stock that one which results from the *marginal cost of overhauling/stripping.*

REFERENCES

Abel, A.B. and Eberly, J.C. (1996), 'Optimal investment with costly reversibility', *Review of Economic Studies*, Vol. 63, pp. 581-593.

Arnott, R., Davidson, R. and Pines, D. (1983), 'Housing, Quality, Maintenance and Rehabilitation', *Review of Economic Studies*, Vol. 50, pp. 467-494.

Arrow, K.J. (1968), 'Optimal Capital Policy with Irreversible Investment', in J. N. Wolfe (ed.), *Value, capital and Growth, Papers in Honour of Sir John Hicks*, (Chicago: Aldine Publishing Company), pp. 1-19.

Bitros, G.C. (1976), 'A Model and Some Evidence on the Interrelatedness of Decisions Underlying the Demand for Capital Services', *European Economic Review*, Vol. 7, 1 pp. 377-393.

_____ and Flytzanis, E. (2000), 'Replacement theory recovered and extended', Athens University of Economics and Business, Department of Economics, unpublished mimeo.

_____ and Kelejian, H.H. (1974), 'On the Variability of the Replacement Investment Capital Stock Ratio: Some Evidence from Capital Scrappage', *Review of Economics and Statistics*, Vol. LVI, pp. 270-278.

Caballero, R.J., Engel, E.M.R.A. and Haltiwanger J.C. (1995), 'Plant level adjustment and aggregate investment dynamics', *Brookings Papers on Economic Activity*, Vol. 2, pp. 1-54.

Cooper, R. and Haltiwanger, J. (1993), 'The Aggregate Implications of Machine Replacement: Theory and Evidence', *American Economic Review*, Vol. 83, pp. 360-382.

Cooper, R., Haltiwanger, J. and Power, L. (1999), 'Machine Replacement and the Business Cycle: Lumps and Bumps', *American Economic Review*, Vol. 89, pp. 921-946.

Das, S. (1991), 'A semiparametric structural analysis of the idling of cement kilns', *Journal of Econometrics*, Vol. 50, pp. 235-256.

Dunne, T. (1994), 'Plant age and technology use in US manufacturing industries', *Rand Journal of Economics*, Vol. 25, 488-499.

Eisner, R. (1972), 'Components of Capital Expenditure: Replacement and Modernization Versus Expansion', *Review of Economics and Statistics*, Vol. 54, pp. 297-305.

Feldstein, M.S., and Foot, D.K. (1971), 'The Other Hall of Gross Investment: Replacement and Modernization Expenditures', *Review of Economics and Statistics*, Vol. 53, pp. 49-58.

Fisher, F.M. (1982), 'Aggregate Production Functions Revisited: The Mobility of Capital and the Rigidity of Thought', *Review of Economic Studies*, Vol. XLIX, pp. 615-626.

Hahn, R.W. (1995), 'An economic analysis of scrappage', *Rand Journal of Economics*, Vol. 26, pp. 222-242.

Jorgenson, D.W. (1963), 'Capital Theory and Investment Behavior', *American Economic Review*, Vol. 53, pp. 247-259.

Kamien, M.I., and Schwartz, N.L. (1971), 'Optimal Maintenance and Sale Age for a Machine Subject to Failure', *Management Science*, Vol. 17, pp. B495-504.

Leonard, D. and Van Long, N. (1992), *Optimal Control Theory*, London: Cambridge University Press.

Nashlund, B. (1966), 'Simultaneous Determination of Optimal Repair Policy and Service Life', *Swedish Journal of Economics*, Vol. 68, pp. 63-73.

Roll, Y. and Sachish, A. (1978), 'Combined overhaul and replacement policies for deteriorating equipment', *Journal of the Operations Research Society of Japan*, Vol. 21, pp. 274-286.

Rothwell, G. and Rust, J. (1997), 'On the Optimal Lifetime of Nuclear Power Plants', *Journal of Business & Economic Statistics*, Vol. 15, pp. 195-208.

Seierstad, A. and Sydsaeter, K. (1987), *Optimal Control Theory*, Amsterdam: North-Holland Publishing Company.

Sen, Amartya, K. (1962), 'On the Usefulness of Used Machines', *Review of Economics and Statistics*, Vol. 44, pp. 346-348.

Smith, M.A.M. (1974), 'International Trade in Second-Hand Machines', *Journal of Development Economics*, Vol. 1, pp. 261-278.

Thompson, G. L. (1968), 'Optimal Maintenance Policy and Sale Date of a Machine', *Management Science*, Vol. 14, pp. 543-550.

Waterson, A. (1964), 'Good Enough for Developing Countries?', *Finance and Development*, Vol. 1, pp. 89-96.

Ye, M.-H. (1990), 'Optimal Replacement Policy with Stochastic Maintenance and Operation Costs', *European Journal of Operations Research*, Vol. 44, pp. 84-94.

PART III

Labor Economics

8. Endowment Changes, Price Response and the Behavior of Wages

Ronald W. Jones[*]

Forty years ago Emanuel Drandakis, in his PhD dissertation at the University of Rochester and subsequently in his published article in the *Review of Economic Studies* (1963), investigated the role of factor substitution in production in the question of convergence of the neo-classical two-sector growth model to the balanced growth path. Shortly before that, Hirofumi Uzawa (1961), had shown that if the capital good is produced by labor-intensive techniques, such convergence would be guaranteed. It was the opposite factor-intensity ranking that would endanger such stability unless market adjustment to price changes could sufficiently dampen the tendency of the production of investment goods to grow more rapidly than the growth of capital when capital is growing more rapidly than labor.[1] It was Drandakis's contribution to show that a simple criterion involving a comparison of the elasticity of factor substitution (in either sector) with unity was sufficient to ensure convergence to balanced growth.

The present chapter combines some of the same features of the neo-classical two-sector model to investigate the fate of real wages when factor endowments change and prices adjust in commodity markets. Once again surprisingly simple results emerge, involving an elasticity of factor substitution and an elasticity of demand. The latter elasticity serves as a generalization of the value of unity found in the Drandakis result, a reflection of his assumption as to savings behaviour.

What happens to a country's wage rate when the endowment of some resource or input expands or an improvement in technology enhances the productivity of factors? The answer to this type of question depends both upon the particular model being considered and to an array of other assumptions concerning the nature of competition, the factor intensities of commodities produced and the response of commodity prices. For example, in the simple

---

* University of Rochester.

textbook competitive framework in which two inputs, labor and land, fixed in total supply, are fully employed to produce two commodities, food and clothing, with food being land intensive, a small price-taking open economy responds to an increase in the endowment of land by producing more food and less clothing, with no adjustment in factor prices required. If, instead, this were an economy closed to trade, the output changes would force an equilibrium downward adjustment in the relative price of food, leading to an unambiguous increase in the real wage. This is the Stolper/Samuelson result associated with the Heckscher-Ohlin 2x2 model.

The sensitivity of such a result to model selection is made abundantly clear when the specific-factors structure is assumed instead. Thus suppose again that two commodities are produced, food and clothing, but that whereas labor is mobile between sectors, the other factor in each sector is specific to that sector, land to produce food and capital to produce clothing. In such a situation an increase in the supply of land would unambiguously improve the real wage rate if this were a small open economy facing given world commodity prices. But suppose, instead, that this were a closed economy, necessitating a fall in food's relative price. Then by a well-known result the change in the relative commodity price ratio by itself leaves the change in the wage rate ambiguous in real terms because it will increase the wage in food units but lower it in clothing units. Combine this, now, with the result that the wage rate unambiguously increases if prices do not change. Under what circumstances will there still emerge an unambiguous increase in real wages despite a rise in clothing's relative price? This is guaranteed if the wage rate rises by relatively more than the price of clothing. In such an event the specific-factors model would resemble the Heckscher-Ohlin model in its income-distribution characteristics for a closed economy.

This type of question is not limited to closed economies. For example, an endowment change in a large economy can be expected to force some change in world prices, and thus to influence the wage rate in that economy. Return to the case of a small open economy, but assume, now, that food represents a non-traded good, whose price must adjust to local conditions to clear the market, whereas 'clothing' now represents an amalgam of all other commodities, goods that are bought and sold at fixed world prices. Will an increase in the endowment of land (or a simple form of technical progress in agriculture) yield an increase in the wage rate relative not only to food but also to 'clothing'? Given the well-understood properties of specific-factors models, the criterion for such a result can easily be derived. In doing so, what struck me was the utter simplicity of the result, reminding me of the conclusions of the Drandakis analysis of convergence. The real wage unambiguously increases if the elasticity of substitution in demand exceeds the elasticity of substitution between labor and land in producing food. In attempting to get a more simple intuitive explanation of this result, I used a technique familiar in much of the standard comparative statics analysis of tariffs or transfers. It is this technique and result that is discussed here.

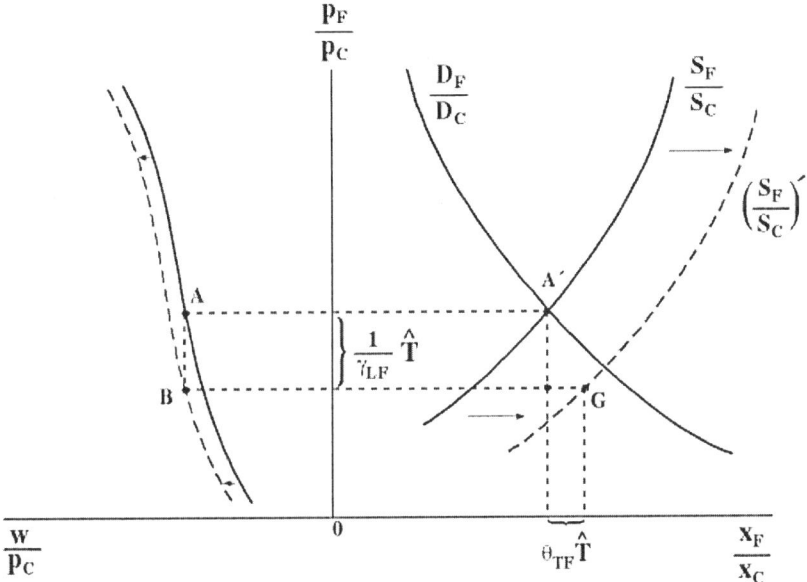

Figure 1. An Increase in Land

A basic supply and demand diagram in Figure 1 is useful in revealing the real wage consequences of an increase in the endowment of land in a small open economy in which clothing is traded (perhaps an amalgam of such traded goods) and food is not. Originally equilibrium is at point A' in the right-hand diagram, showing a balance of relative demand and relative supply. The left-hand diagram needs a bit more explanation. The solid curve shows the initial relationship between the commodity price ratio and the wage rate relative to the price of clothing, with point A corresponding to A'. Note that this curve is drawn so that a given percentage increase in food's relative price increases the wage rate in terms of clothing, but not by as big a percentage. Furthermore, the dashed curve shows that an increase in the endowment of land shifts the curve to the left – it would raise labor's real wage at unchanged commodity prices. Point B on this new curve would exactly balance the effect of land's increase on the ratio of wages to the price of clothing with a drop in food's relative price. As is explicitly shown below, the required drop in food's relative price (or increase in clothing's relative price) to balance the effect of the endowment increase is given by the term $\{1/\gamma_{LF}\}\hat{T}$ where $\hat{T}$ denotes the relative increase in the endowment of land, and the term γ_{LF} indicates the elasticity of the demand curve for labor in the food sector (i.e. the elasticity of the marginal physical product of labor curve). Furthermore, in the right-hand panel of Figure 1 the relative supply curve of food is shifted to the right (as the quantity of land expands) so that in the new equilibrium food's relative price falls. Whereas straightforward comparative statics techniques would lead to solving directly for the price change, and then using the left-hand panel to see whether the wage rate in terms of clothing units has risen (in which case the real wage would unambiguously rise), an alternative procedure asks the question: at the price change which would lead to no change in the wage rate in units of clothing (i.e. point *B*) is there an excess demand or supply in the market for food? The diagram illustrates the case in which there is an excess demand, implying that the real wage would indeed be improved at the new equilibrium. Although excess supply is also possible, the diagram does illustrate that food's relative supply at the lower price shown by point *B* must be higher than initially at *A′*. This increase, shown by $\theta_{TF}T$, the distributive share of land in producing food times the relative increase in land, is derived explicitly below.

A bit of algebra can substantiate these claims. The basic equation of change in the specific-factors model in which labor is the mobile factor shows the relative change in the wage rate as a positive weighted average of the commodity price changes, and increasing with respect to an increase in the endowment of land:[2]

$$\hat{w} = \{\lambda_{LC}\,\gamma_{LC}/\gamma_L\}\,\hat{p}_C + \{\lambda_{LF}\,\gamma_{LF}/\gamma_L\}\,\hat{p}_F + \{\lambda_{LF}/\gamma_L\}\,\hat{T} \qquad (1)$$

or, expressing the wage change in clothing units,

$$(\hat{w} - \hat{p}_C) = \{\lambda_{LF}/\gamma_L\}\{\hat{T} + \gamma_{LF(\hat{p}_F-\hat{p}_C)}\} \qquad (2)$$

In these expressions the term, γ_L, indicates the economy's overall elasticity of demand for labor – the percentage rise in labor's demand if the wage rate were to fall by one percent and commodity prices (and endowments of specific factors) were held constant. Equation (2) confirms what is illustrated in Figure 1, viz. that the drop in food's relative price that would exactly eventuate in no change in the wage rate in clothing units (and thus guarantee a rise in the *real* wage), is shown by the term $\{1/\gamma_{LF}\}\,\hat{T}$.

Turning to supply changes at this price, note that since the wage rate in clothing units is constant at point B in Figure 1, and since the capital endowment is assumed unchanged, so also is the output of clothing. The action comes from the food sector. Let a_{TF} denote the input/output coefficient for land in food production, so that the relative change in food production is shown by equation (3):

$$\hat{x}_F = \hat{T} - \hat{a}_{TF} \tag{3}$$

The change in land's use in food is in turn shown by:[3]

$$\hat{a}_{TF} = \theta_{LF}\,\gamma_{LF}(\hat{w} - \hat{p}_F) \tag{4}$$

Since at point B the term $(w - p_F)$ equals $(p_C - p_F)$,

$$(\hat{x}_F - \hat{x}_C) = \hat{T} - \theta_{LF}\,\gamma_{LF}(\hat{p}_C - \hat{p}_F) = \theta_{TF}\hat{T} \tag{5}$$

This confirms that the increase in food's relative supply from the initial price to the price that keeps the wage rate constant in clothing units (at B) is shown by $\theta_{TF}\hat{T}$.

Now consider the change in the composition of demand at this lower relative price for food. Let σ_D denote the elasticity of substitution in demand (assuming tastes are homothetic). Then the change in the relative demand for food is $\{-\sigma_D\}$ times the price change, or $\{\sigma_D/\gamma_{LF}\}$ times $\hat{T}$. In comparing the changes in relative supplies and demand at this new price, note that the elasticity of the demand curve for labor in the food sector, γ_{LF}, is equal to the elasticity of substitution between inputs in the food sector, σ_F, divided by land's share in food production, θ_{TF}.[4] Therefore the criterion for an increase in the supply of land unambiguously to raise the real wage when food's relative price adjusts is shown by the inequality in (6):[5]

$$\sigma_D > \sigma_F \tag{6}$$

A straightforward solution for the price change would not indicate such a simple procedure. At the initial price the supply curve shifts to the right as the supply of land increases. The extent of this shift depends upon characteristics of production in both food and clothing. This same pair of characteristics is also involved in movements along the new supply curve, so that the solution for the new equilibrium price is somewhat complicated by production characteristics in clothing as well as food. And yet these do not appear in simple criterion (6). For example, suppose that the elasticity of labor demand in the clothing sector were to be larger. How would the shape and shift of the supply curve in Figure 1 be altered? It would shift further to the right but become more elastic, such that it still passes through point G. Thus the criterion for a real wage increase, which depends upon the sign of excess demand at the price shown by point B (or G), would not be affected by this alteration in production conditions in the clothing sector. Analogies abound in trade theory. For example, the criterion for which way the terms of trade are altered by a transfer depends only upon income propensities in the two-country case, and the condition sufficient to avoid a welfare paradox for the giver in the three-country transfer case does not depend on income propensities of the giver. In both these cases the appropriate criterion can be derived by asking about the state of excess demand at a pre-determined crucial price (the original terms of trade in the two-country case and the terms of trade that just leave the real income of the giver unchanged in the three-country case). In the present scenario, the crucial value of the wage change equal to the change in clothing's price guarantees that no change takes place in the clothing sector.

The argument can be summarized by reconsidering Figure 1. The increase in the relative output of food compared with clothing going from initial A' to point G, divided by the relative price change, is $\theta_{TF}\gamma_{LF}$, or σ_F. The increase in the relative demand for food, divided by this same price change, is σ_D. This is the comparison highlighted in inequality (6). Just as in the related question considered by Drandakis, a simple comparison of demand and factor input sensitivity to price changes yields a sufficient criterion to the question posed real wage behaviour in the present case and relative output response in the model so skilfully analysed decades ago by Drandakis.

NOTES

1.   This is a reflection of the *magnification effect* in two-sector models when commodity prices, and therefore factor prices, are fixed, and thus factor substitution frozen out. See Jones (1965).
2.   Derivations are found in Jones (1971) or Caves, Frankel and Jones (1999).
3.   In the food sector changes in input-output coefficients are derived from a pair of equations. One of them states that the distributive share weighted average of the relative change in labor and land coefficients vanishes (as a reflection of costs being minimized), and the other defines the elasticity of demand for labor in the food sector.
4.   This follows from a straightforward comparison of the definitions of the elasticity of substitution in the food sector and the elasticity of demand for labor in that sector.
5.   Drandakis has a slightly different treatment of demand. He assumes that laborers and capitalists each have a *constant* (but different) marginal and average propensity to save. That is, he lets σ_D for each group to be unity.

REFERENCES

Caves, Richard E., Jeffrey Frankel and Ronald W. Jones (1999), World Trade and Payments, (8th Edition), Supplement to Chapter 6, Addison Wesley, Reading, MA.

Drandakis, Emanuel M. (1963), 'Factor Substitution in the Two-Sector Growth Model,' *Review of Economic Studies*, **31**, pp. 217-28.

Jones, Ronald W. (1965), 'The Structure of Simple General Equilibrium Models,' *Journal of Political Economy*, **73**, pp. 557-72.

_____. (1971), 'A Three-Factor Model in Theory, Trade, and History,' Ch. 1 in J. Bhagwati, R. Jones, R. Mundell, and J. Vanek, *Trade, Balance of Payments and Growth*, Amsterdam, North Holland.

Uzawa, Hirofumi (1961), 'On a Two-Sector Model of Economic Growth,' *Review of Economic Studies*, **29**, pp. 40-47.

9. The Pace of Work and Pay

Walter Y. Oi[*]

An employment contract, explicit or implicit, almost always stipulates a rate of pay but is often vague about what constitutes a fair day's work. Output is an increasing function of the effort supplied by a worker. If workers develop habits that 'tend to a maximum of output for a minimum of effort', they ought to produce output at a constant rate per hour. The hourly and daily output curves roundly reject this prediction implying that the flow of effort is variable. A firm can offer incentives that elicit more work effort. When the Safelite Company introduced a piece rate of pay, Edward Lazear (1999) found that the hourly earnings of its employees rose by 9.6 per cent and productivity by 20 per cent. The technology here involved person-specific production functions where self pacing determines the expenditure of energy. At some factories, the employer can exercise some direct control via the machine pacing of the arrival rate of work. It can also indirectly affect the work pace by providing an environment with newer equipment and a safer workplace. Many firms in the service sector confront a production function characterized by the economies of massed reserves. A big hospital realizes a higher bed occupancy rate. It has to pay its nurses higher wages to comply with a faster work pace. A productivity hypothesis can explain a substantial part of the relation of firm size to wages. In passing, a rush of new orders in the upswing creates an effect akin to the economies of massed reserves which could account for the pro-cyclical behavior of labor productivity.

The Bureau of Labor Statistics has recently developed an index of the labor input that is a weighted sum of employee hours where workers are classified by age, education, and gender, variables that are systematically related to differences in labor productivity and pay. To these, one should add the method of pay and certain workplace characteristics that are related to differences in the effort intensity expected of the employee. If person A is prepared to put forth more effort than person B, an hour of A's time should receive a higher

---

*   University of Rochester.

weight in an index of the labor input just as an hour supplied by a male college graduate gets more weight in the BLS index than an hour worked by a
teen-age high school drop-out. Effort and the pace of work are as important as
age, education, and gender in explaining the behavior of labor markets.

1. AN EFFORT BARGAIN

An employment relation involves more than an exchange of money for time.
A labor contract rarely stipulates the effort that the employee is expected to
supply.

> Central to the worktime issue is the concept of a fair day's work. . . The differing
> perspective [between employer and worker] is not resolved by the forging of an
> employment contract. Such an arrangement normally consists of two elements:
> first, an agreement on the wage per unit of time or piece; second, an agreement on
> the amount of work to be undertaken, that is, an effort bargain. It is normal for the
> wage rate to be precisely defined in the employment contract. The effort bargain,
> on the other hand, is generally implicit and indistinct. (Nyland (1989:57))

> . . . the formal wage contract is never precise in stipulating how much effort is
> expected for a given wage (and vice versa). The details of the arrangement are left
> to be worked out through the direct interaction between the partners of the con-
> tract. (W. Baldamus (1961:35))

Indeed, Baldamus believed that 'The organization of industry . . . ultimately
revolves about a single process, the administrative process in which an employee's effort is controlled by the employer.' Although the boundaries are
fuzzy, one can distinguish differences in the effort intensity of work. What is
effort? George E. Johnson (1990:249) wrote, 'Effort is the intensity or pace
of work which may involve the speed of an assembly line, the number of tasks
that each worker is asked to perform, the number and length of coffee breaks,
and a number of other nitty-gritty issues'. It might also include the crew size.
In his model, the labor input in efficiency units is the product of the effort
intensity per worker times the number of employees, $L = eN$. If workers in
factory A actually work 52 minutes each hour, (8 minutes set aside for set-up,
rest, and clean-up), they require 18 hours to assemble one car. At factory B,
workers get 12 minutes for rest and clean-up. A slower work pace increases
the assembly time to 19.5 hours and reduces labor productivity.

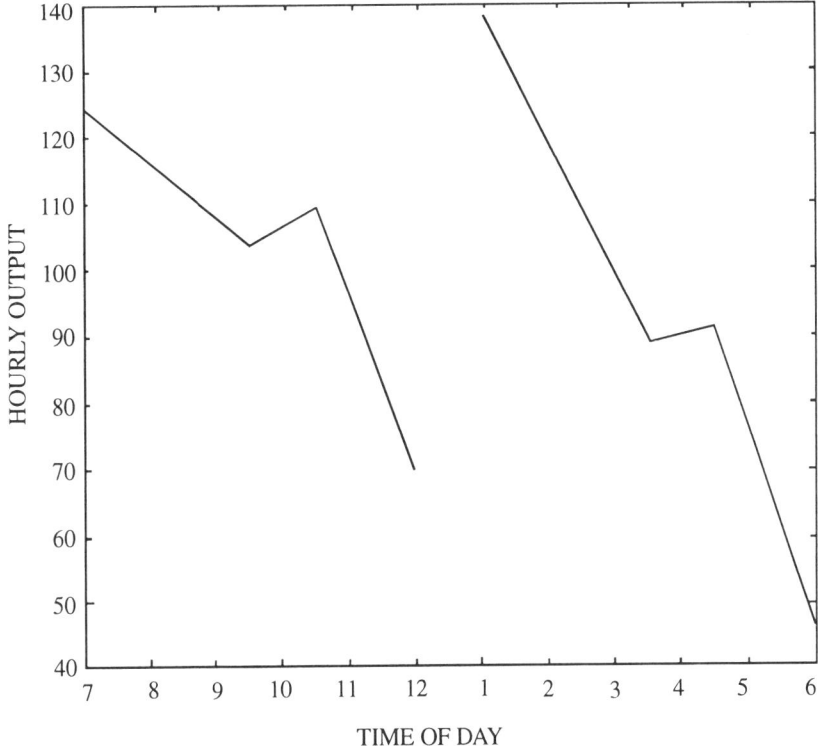

Figure 1. Men polishing metal by hand

2. HOURLY AND DAILY OUTPUT CURVES

'Experienced industrial workers unconsciously adopt habits of work that tend to a maximum of output with a minimum of effort.' (Vernon (1921:27)). Theory implies that an individual with a fixed supply of energy can maximize total output by maintaining a constant rate of output per hour. The output data collected by Vernon and his associates and by the French engineer Abbè roundly rejects the optimality of a flat hourly output curve. For men polishing metal by hand, Vernon observed an output curve exhibiting fatigue. Output was greatest in the first hour and declined steadily, see Figure 1.[1] The modal pattern exhibits what Vernon called practiced efficiency, the case of women covering chocolates, Figure 2. The rate of output initially climbs as the worker gets more efficient with practice, but fatigue and monotony eventually take

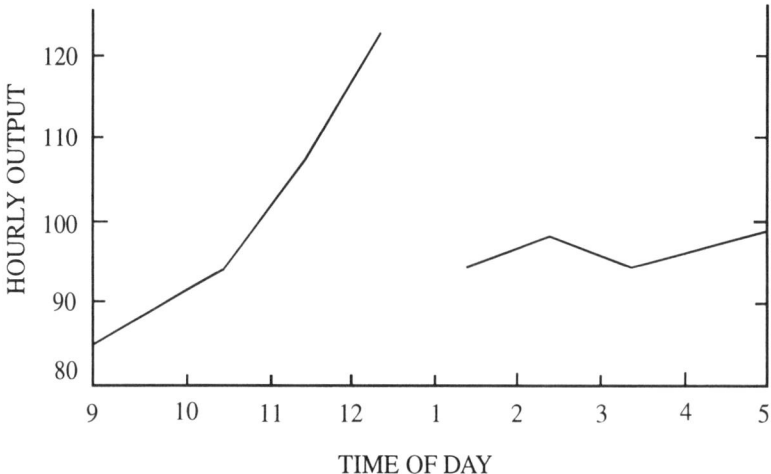

Figure 2. Women covering chocolates

over leading to a decline in the output rate. The cycle is repeated in the afternoon, but the total afternoon output is somewhat smaller than the total morning output. The shape of the daily output curve will depend not only on the
length of the workday but also on working conditions, the strength of employees, and the number and frequency of rest breaks.[2] In addition to output curves
exhibiting fatigue and practice-efficiency, Vernon identified a third curve showing an end spurt, men hand-tapping fuse sockets, Figure 3. 'It looked as if
they were determined to avail themselves of all the physical energy at their
disposal as they knew that an interval of rest was in sight during which they
could recuperate' (Vernon (1921:27)). A piece rate system of pay encourages
behavior producing an end spurt. All three hourly output curves whether they
reflect fatigue, practice-efficiency, or end spurt, depart from the constant output rate of an ideal model. Becker (1985) pointed out that the supply of energy is not fixed, an individual can allocate time and resources into the production of 'effort'. Indeed, many employers provide snacks and food along
with coffee and drinks during rest breaks.

Labor productivity varies not only over the hours in a day but also over the
days of the week. The weekly cycle almost always exhibits the pattern of
practice-efficiency. Daily output is lowest on Monday, rises reaching a peak
on Wednesday or Thursday, and falls off on Friday.

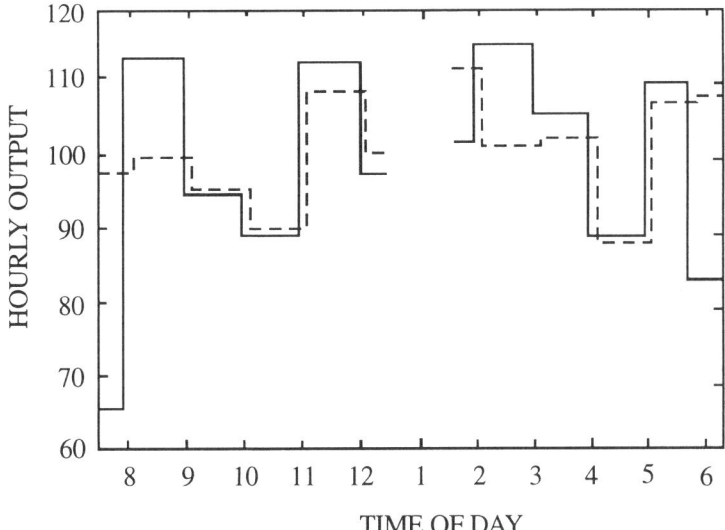

Figure 3. Hourly output of men hand-tapping fuse sockets

'The cessation of work between Saturday afternoon and Monday morning naturally causes a greater loss of neuro-muscular co-ordination than that observed between each week day, and consequently the output on Monday morning tends to be lower than that observed on any other morning of the week. The loss of practice-efficiency owing to the week-end rest is so considerable that the remainder of the week may be needed for recovery, but ... the fatigue induced by the daily round of labour gradually accumulates ... first to neutralize the improvement due to practice-efficiency and then to overpower it.'[3]

Vernon is implicitly appealing to a model where the labor required to produce one unit of output, a fuse cap, is smaller, the larger are the stocks of practice-efficiency capital P and energy E; $L = L(P, E)$ with $L_P < 0$, $L_E < 0$. A worker who produces a fuse cap obtains as a byproduct, an increment to his stock of practice-efficiency capital P. However, P depreciates with work during the week. More importantly, when it is idle, the stock of practice-efficiency capital P depreciates overnight and over a weekend. Hence, at the start of a work-day, P is low and the worker requires more labor time L to produce one fuse cap. The accumulation of output increases his stock of practice-efficiency capital thereby reducing the labor requirement L, but more output reduces his stock of energy which operates in an opposing direction. The labor requirement L thus attains a minimum (and the output rate a maximum) when the two forces are balanced. At the start of a week, the stock of practice-efficiency P is especially small resulting in the *Monday effect*. Although energy is replenished overnight, the accumulation of work over the week de-energizes the employee to the point where it eventually produces the Friday dip in the daily output rate.[4]

3. PERFORMANCE RELATED PAY

An employee can be paid by the hour or by the piece. In addition to piece rates, performance related pay (PRP) includes bonuses and profit sharing. Booth and Frank (1999:446) reported that 'Since 1991, up to 20 per cent of total pay could be fully exempt from income taxes if received in an approved profit related pay scheme'. In five years, there was a ten-fold increase in the number of workers eligible for this tax exemption. The program was too successful. In 1997, the Chancellor of the Exchequer announced the phasing out of this tax exemption.

Consider a model for the choice of a pay system. Utility is assumed to be a function of income and effort, $U = Y - \varphi(E)$. Performance related pay entitles the worker to an income equal to her output, a function of ability and effort, less a fee paid to the firm.

$$Y = Q(A, E) - F. \tag{3.1a}$$

Utility is maximized by equating the marginal product of effort to its disutility.

$$Q_E(A, E) = \varphi'(E). \tag{3.1b}$$

The optimal effort is independent of the fee F and is an increasing function of ability, $E = E(A)$ with $E'(A) > 0$. The utility of a PRP job is thus an increasing function of ability as shown by the curve U^P in Figure 4.

$$U^P = Y - \varphi(E) = \left\{ Q[A, E(A)] - F \right\} - \varphi[E(A)]. \tag{3.2}$$

The alternative to a PRP job is a salary job yielding an income S irrespective of ability or effort. The optimal effort on a salary job is obviously zero, and since $\varphi(0) = 0$, its utility is equal to the salary, $U^S = S$. There is a minimum unobservable ability, $A = m$, such that the two pay systems yield the same utility.

$$U^S = S = \left\{ Q[m, E(m)] - F \right\} - \varphi[E(m)] = U^P. \tag{3.3}$$

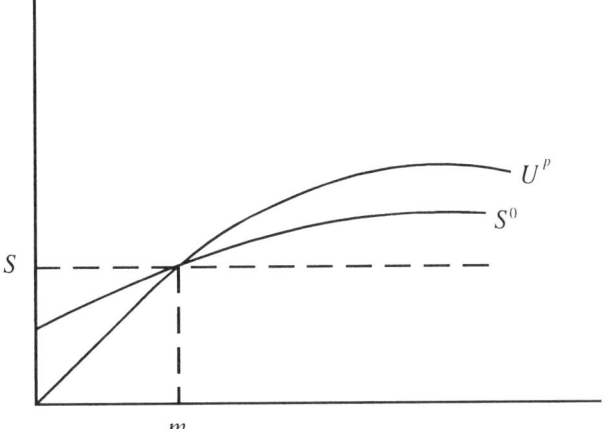

Figure 4

People with high ability levels realize higher utility by taking a PRP job. Others for whom $A < m$ choose a salary job at which they supply zero effort. However, output is still related to ability, $dQ(A,0)/dA > 0$. Let $g(A)$ denote the frequency density of individuals with ability A, while $G(A)$ is the cumulative density. In equilibrium, the zero profit salary S^0 must equal the average product.

$$S^0 = \left[\int Q(A,0)dg(A)\right]\Big/ G(m) \qquad [0 < A < m] \qquad (3.4)$$

The zero profit salary is plotted in Figure 4, it is an increasing function of $A = m$, but its shape and position depends on $g(A)$. A higher fee charged by PRP employers or an increase in the disutility of work effort leads to a downward shift in U^P but no change in S^0. The consequence is a decrease in the fraction of workers on piece rates. An innovation that reduces the marginal product of effort in the individual production function $Q(A, E)$ is likely to shift m to the right because the utility of piece work U^P shifts down by more than the average product S^0 holding m constant, the result is a decrease in the fraction of workers paid by the piece.

The adoption of an incentive pay system raises labor productivity and earnings. The hourly earnings of British female workers on PRP were 5.3 per cent above earnings of those on time rates, it was 9.6 per cent higher for men. But the practice has not spread. Charles Brown (1990) found that the percentage on standard time rates of pay was higher in larger establishments. Large firms are more likely to organize work around teams which makes it hard to measure the contribution of individual effort. The share of employment in large firms with 100 or more employees has been rising, while the incidence of piece rates is falling.

4. THE DISUTILITY AND PRODUCTIVITY OF EFFORT

Workers will allegedly shirk unless they are monitored or given an incentive to comply with some implicit effort bargain. The effort level in the piece rate model is determined by the individual and not by the speed of an assembly line. Alfred Marshall (1952:693) opined, 'As a general though not universal rule, his work is more intense when paid by piece than when paid by time, and insofar as this is the case, shorter hours are especially suitable to industries in which piece work prevails.' An employer can set the speed of an assembly line or establish work norms and performance standards. Bringing the work to the employee instead of letting him fetch the work was the idea that raised productivity in the Josiah Wedgewood pottery factory. In 1790, all but 5 of 270 workers were assigned to specific posts and performed specialized tasks. Pieces of pottery were moved from room to room, and the worker no longer followed his product to the point where it was deposited in the storage room, confer Kranzberg and Gies (1975:99). The slaughter house was the model copied by Henry Ford. Before the assembly line, a worker fetched the 29 pieces needed to make a magneto. The task took an average of 20 minutes. The assembly line reduced the time to 13 minutes. When power was applied to the line, and the height of the table was raised, the time was cut to 5 minutes per magneto, see Kranzberg and Gies (1975:120).

The work pace or the speed of the arrival rate of work S belongs alongside capital K and labor L in the production function, $X = g(L, K, S)$ with $dX/dS = g_s > 0$. Workers have to exert more effort to keep up with a faster pace, $E = E(S)$ with $e'(S) > 0$. At a factory or office, the work pace could be set by the employer or negotiated. The machine pacing of work or explicit norms affect speed, but S also depends on the number and length of rest breaks and downtime caused by machine breakdowns or industrial accidents. A plant that belongs to a multi-establishment firm receives a steadier flow of raw materials and enjoys a lower labor turnover rate which raises labor productivity relative to a stand alone plant. Interest rates are substantially lower for larger firms which respond by adopting more capital intensive methods of production. If capital is divisible, more capital will be allocated to more productive individuals. Differentiated capital presents the firm with an assignment problem. A new computer is allocated to the most efficient operator. Older and less powerful computers are passed down to less productive employees. Sorting and matching of equipment and employees of varying qualities take place within and across establishments. Henry L. Moore (1911:148-9) observed,

> Because of the use of large fixed capital in large establishments, the more efficient workers are more valuable to the large than to the small establishments. We have hitherto supposed that it is a matter of indifference to the employer whether he employs few or many people to do a piece of work provided his total wages-bill for the work is the same. But that is not the case. Those workers who earn most in a week when paid at a given rate for their work are those who are cheapest to their employer and ultimately to the community unless they overstrain themselves and work themselves prematurely for they use only the same amount of fixed capital as their slower fellow workers, and since they turn out more work, each part of it has to bear a less charge on this account. The prime costs are equal in the two cases, but the total cost of that done by those who are more efficient and get the higher time wages is lower than the total cost of that done by those who get the lower time wages at the same rate of piece payment...

Inherent ability and a propensity to work harder are person specific, unobservable traits. Large establishments surely attract and retain more capable workers (Moore 1911:360) claimed that 'Large establishments are able to carry out the work of selection (of more capable individuals) because in consequence of their large capital and better organization, they offer opportunities for more capable individuals to reap the reward of their differential ability'. Individuals surely learn about working conditions including the normal pace of work. Those who are not prepared to supply a high level of effort obtain employment in smaller establishments with slower work paces.

A production function for a retail firm differs from that for a manufacturer in two respects. The customer arrival rate N belongs next to capital and labor, $X = f(N, K, L)$. Customer arrivals are random and delays are costly. Someone is almost always idle, customers waiting to be served or clerks waiting for a customer. Production is characterized by the economies of massed reserves. A two-fold increase in all inputs leads to more than a two-fold increase in output, the flow of transactions X. There are increasing returns to scale. If the largest hospital in a city has 40 per cent of all beds, it will provide more than 40 per cent of all occupied beds. A nurse at a big hospital confronts a higher bed occupancy rate and is thus obliged to put forth more work effort. The work pace at a supermarket is jointly determined by the customer arrival rate and staffing practices. Clerks are busier on weekends than on Tuesday mornings even though the store puts on more part-time employees during peak periods. They also know that they will work harder at a larger supermarket and in return will be paid a higher wage.

The positive association between firm size and wages is regarded by some as a puzzling feature of the labor market. The hourly wages of men employed by small firms with 1-24 employees were $10.289 compared to $14.961 those working at the largest firms with over 1,000 employees. The firm size profile of wages shown in Table 1 is steeper for men and slightly flatter in 1993 than in 1979. Data for supermarkets responding to the 1985 Progressive Grocer survey reveal a similar pattern, see Table 2. Part-time clerks at independent supermarkets earned $3.98 an hour, but their counterparts at stores with annual sales over 12 million dollars were paid $4.71 per hour. The corresponding wages of full-time clerks were $4.84 and $5.63. The slope of the size-wage profile is attenuated when one controls for differences in worker characteristics, but the shape of the relation is retained. The complementarity of capital with skilled labor offers one explanation for this relation. Second, paying a super-normal wage can deter shirking thereby saving on monitoring costs. Third, big firms realize greater profits which they share with their employees. After reviewing a number of theoretical models and the empirical evidence, Charles Brown and James Medoff (1989:1056-7) concluded:

Table 1 Hourly Wages by Firm Size and Sex 1993 and 1979

In firms with an employment of	males 1993	females 1993	males 1979	females 1979
1–24	10.289	8.203	5.646	4.052
25–99	17.381	9.052	6.689	4.239
100–499	13.459	10.114	7.427	4.689
500–999	13.528	10.525	7.820	4.714
1.000+	14.961	10.683	8.452	5.235
ratio	1.453	1.302	1.497	1.292

Source: Current opulation Survey, April 1993 and May 1979.

Table 2 Hourly Wages og Part-Time and Full-Time Clerks: 1985

Sales Volume (in millions of dollars) Independents:	Part-Time Clerks	Full-Time Clerks	Ratio Part-Time/Full Time
2–4	$3.98	$4.84	0.822
4–8	$4.31	$5.11	0.843
8–12	$4.64	$5.35	0.867
> 12	$4.71	$5.63	0.837
Average	$4.18	$5.01	0.834

Source: Progressive Grocer, April 1986.

'Our analysis leaves us uncomfortably unable to explain it, ... In lieu of a more positive conclusion, we offer two observations... First, large employers pay more for their labor but less for their other inputs because of lower interest rates and quantity discounts... Second, large firms are also older firms. Is it possible that the size-wage premium is really a relationship between employer age and wages? ... Thus, the employer size-wage effect remains a fact in need of an empirically based theory.

A productivity hypothesis can, I contend, explain this relation. Labor productivity surely depends on effort. Incentives can elicit more effort raising both productivity and earnings. Output is related to the arrival rate of work which can be partially controlled by the machine pacing of work on an assembly line. In the service sector, the arrival rate of customers, clients, or patients is faster at larger establishments. Workers are busier, have less idle time, and are more productive. A large factory typically owns more and newer equipment. They recruit highly skilled employees who are prepared to comply with a faster work pace. At smaller establishments, the effort bargains are more flexible, breakdowns and disruptions are more frequent, and the work pace can be modified to satisfy varying worker preferences. The reduced form relation is one in which wages are positively related to establishment size. Individuals who experience a smaller disutility from work effort are more likely to be employed by large firms where the speed of the arrival rate of work is faster. They are more productive and are paid higher wages.

5. THE LABOR INPUT

Labor efficiency in cotton mills circa 1910 can be measured by a manning rate, the ratio of machines to operatives. Gregory Clark (1987) found that this index shown in the second column of Table 3 ranged from a high of 2.97 looms per worker in New England to lows of 0.46 in Greece and 0.48 in China. The technology was similar across countries.[5] Output per machine varied little across countries in spite of widely different loom/worker ratios. Indian workers were physically smaller than English workers, but strength is said to be less important than dexterity. Education, experience, nutrition, and culture ought, in principle, to affect labor productivity. Clark concluded that the first three factors could not explain the different staffing practices leaving him to turn to the last. What constitutes a satisfactory manning rate is determined by employer demands and worker preferences. Max Weber observed that people conform to a work norm which prevails in the local economy.

> The same Polish girl who at home was not to be shaken loose from her traditional laziness by any chance of earning money, however tempting, seems to change her entire nature and become capable of unlimited accomplishment when she is a migratory worker in a foreign country. The same is true of migratory Italian labourers. That this is by no means entirely explicable in terms of the educative influence of the entrance into a higher cultural environment, although this naturally plays a part, is shown by the fact that the same thing happens where the type of occupation, as in agricultural labour, is exactly the same as at home. (Max Weber (1958, note 20 at p. 191))

In the cotton mills, it was alleged that workers in foreign countries chose not to mind as many looms or were constrained from doing so. As Pearse (1930: 158) put it, 'They said that they were satisfied with the present wage. There were so many men who wanted to work and can't get it that it would be unfair if they were to attend to more machines.' The interesting fact is that when these workers came to the United States, their productivity and wages rose to the levels prevailing in the local mills. Data shown in Table 4 confirm this fact. The cross-national differences in wages in the home country shown in the first column were substantial, but the wages of immigrants in the US mills, adjusted for the age of the worker converge to the mean of the US workers. Clark (1987:166) reported that the Portuguese workers in Brazil were only a third as productive as the Portuguese workers in New England. Two hypotheses might explain the wide Brazil/US productivity gap of Portuguese immigrants; (a) the labor contracts in New England embraced a far higher effort bargain, or (b) there was considerable selection in which the most productive Portuguese workers migrated to and remained in New England. The latter

Table 3 Machines per Operative. c. 1910

Country or Region	Average Weekly Wage	Loom-Equivalents per Worker
New England	8.8	2.97
Canada	8.8	2.53
United States (South)	6.5	2.65
Britain	5.0	2.04
Germany	3.8	1.28
France	3.7	1.11
Switzerland	3.7	1.40
Austro-Hungary	2.8	1.24
Spain	2.7	0.91
Mexico	2.6	1.15
Russia	2.4	1.10
Italy	2.4	0.88
Portugal	1.72	0.88
Egypt	1.69	0.81
Greece	1.38	0.46
Japan	0.80	0.53
India	0.78	0.50
China	0.54	0.48
Peru		1.17
Brazil		0.88

Notes: The United States and Canada used underpick looms and these were somewhat slower than the standard loom used elsewhere. In Brazil and Peru the nominal wages clearly exceeded the real wage greatly but no price deflator is available.

Table 4 Earnings of US Male Immigrants in Manufacturing, 1910

Country of Origin	Efficiency of Textile Workers (home country)	Average US Wage (England = 100)	Average Age	Age-Adjusted Wage (England = 100)
Canda	124	78	39.0	75
England	100	100	38.7	100
Germany	63	96	40.9	90
France	54	93	36.1	98
Switzerland	39	99		
Austro-Hungary	61	85	31.6	93
Spain	45	106	31.4	115
Mexico	56	90	32.7	102
Russia	54	80	30.7	95
Italy	43	80	29.6	98
Portugal	43	57	26.4	79
Greece	23	60	26.5	83
Japan	26	75	29.5	93

The adjusted earnings are derived by regressing earnings on the average age and then subtracting the estimated effect of age on earnings. Estimated in this way, age explains 44 per cent of the variance of the reported earnings.

hints at the possibility that there is an ethnic component to labor efficiency. I suspect that the former comes closer to the true explanation.

In the upturn of a cycle, a flow of new orders is accompanied by an increase in output per hour, X/H. In British manufacturing, X/H has grown at a rate of 5.2 per cent a year since 1980. Metcalf (1989:4) concluded that 'In the 1980s, people are working harder than they were in the 1970s'. Labor hours are not the same at different points along an expansion path. The effort intensity per hour rises with the arrival rate of work. The labor input can be measured in efficiency units, $L = eH$, where e is the effort intensity per hour. In the upswing, *L* expands at a faster rate than *H* resulting in a pro-cyclical path of labor productivity, *X/H*.

A colorable case can be made to argue that effort and regulation account for much of the cross-national differences in labor efficiency. The US economy is saddled by fewer regulations than most industrialized nations. The Ergonomics Program Standard authorized by Executive Order, OSH190.900 is a policy in the opposing direction. Its premise is that physical exertion and repetitive motions are workplace hazards. These injuries were previously covered under the General Duty clause of the Occupational Safety and Health Act, OSHA. One shipping company found to be in violation was ordered to reduce by half the maximum weight of packages it handled. The purpose of the instant standard is to reduce the number and severity of musculo-skeletal disorders. The remedies imposed on employers include (a) slowing the pace of work so that employees will be engaged in less repetitive motions and less lifting, (b) increase staffing and rest periods so that each employee works less hard, (c) redesign jobs in consultation with employees, and (d) in some exceptional cases, the company may be obliged to give the employee up to six months of leave at 90 per cent of pay to recover.[6] The Ergonomics Program Standard has met with considerable opposition and may be overturned.

The BLS index of labor productivity, *X/H*, measures the labor input by total person hours per period *H*. The methodology has recently been revised to recognize the heterogeneity of hours, at least within the manufacturing sector. A weighted sum of employee hours has been constructed to measure the labor input. An hour of labor time supplied by a male college graduate receives a larger weight than an hour worked by a teen-age high school dropout. Age, education, and gender are the three worker characteristics that are the human capital variables which will hopefully measure differences in labor quality, the rationale is discussed by Edwin Dean (1999). A variety of other factors surely affect labor quality. Effort is a variable that is not accorded the same treatment as other productivity enhancing traits. A person who has the capacity and the willingness to work harder is more productive. If her output depends on a person-specific production function, $Q = Q(A, E)$, payment by results (piece rates or sales commissions) can elicit effort. Jobs that are on performance related pay attract individuals who, on average, will put forth more work effort. The effort intensity implicit in the effort bargain can often be proxied by working conditions such as firm size, machine pacing of work, industry and occupation. The method of pay and workplace characteristics ought to be added to age, education, and gender to construct an index of the labor input.

Work rules and performance standards are jointly determined by firms and employees. A higher effort intensity raises both productivity and pay, but the effort can vary over time due to fluctuations in the arrival rate of work. Hence, effort does not lead to an unobservable, person-specific fixed effect on earnings. Regulations that impede the attainment of an optimal effort intensity will reduce productivity.

NOTES

1.   Earl Alluisi and Ben Morgan (1982:229) reported that mental performance follows the fatigue pattern.
2.   The effect of rest breaks on the productivity of women folding handkerchiefs is depicted in Figure 6.3 of Alluisi and Morgan (1982). Miles and Skilbeck (1923) reported that the output gains from rest breaks are greater when the rest breaks are regularly scheduled rather than left to the discretion of the worker.
3.   Vernon (1921:27-28) goes on to write, 'In industry, it is almost invariably accompanied by low output, which Kent has termed, the Monday effect.' A.S.S. Kent, 'Second Interim Report on Industrial Fatigue' (London: 1915).
4.   Workers on piece rates sometimes exhibit an end spurt and expand their output rates on Friday to meet some target income objective. This behavior is more likely to occur on the Friday before a holiday or vacation.
5.   Automatic looms were being introduced around 1910, but only a few New England mills had acquired these.
6.   In the Pepperidge Farm case, analyzed by Eugene Scalia (2000), slowing the speed of the conveyor belt could lead to burning the cookies in the oven. The number and types of tasks are no longer things to be determined by negotiations between employer and employees (or their agent, a union), but directly regulated. OSHA could insist on a job redesign that moves a worker to light duties.

REFERENCES

Alluisi, Earl A. and Ben B. Morgan Jr. (1982), 'Temporal Factors in Human Performance and Productivity', in *Human Performance and Productivity: Stress and Performance Effectiveness*, E.A. Alluisi and E. A. Fleishman (eds), Hillsdale: Lawrence Erlbaum, 165-237.

Baldamus, W. (1961), *Efficiency and Effort,* London: Tavistock Publications.

Becker, Gary S. (Jan. 1985), 'Human Capital, Effort, and the Sexual Division of Labor', *Journal of Labor Economics*, **3**, Part 2, S33-S58.

Booth, Alison L. and Jeff Frank (July 1999), 'Earnings, Productivity, and Performance Related Pay', *Journal of Labor Economics*, **17** (3), 447-463.

Brown, Charles (Feb. 1990), 'Firms' Choice of Method of Pay', *Industrial and Labor Relations Review*, **43**, S165-S182.

Brown, Charles and James Medoff (Dec. 1989), 'The Employer Size Wage Effect', *Journal of Political Economy*, **97**, 1027-1059.

Clark, Gregory (March 1987), 'Why Isn't the Whole World Developed: Lessons from the Cotton Mills', *Journal of Economic History*, **47**, 141-173.

Dean, Edwin (February 1999), 'The Accuracy of the BLS Productivity Statistics', *Monthly Labor Review*, 24-34.

Johnson, George E. (Jan. 1990), 'Work Rules, Featherbedding, and Pareto Optimal Union-Management Bargaining', *Journal of Labor Economics*, 8 Supplement, S237-S259.

Kranzberg, Melvin and Joseph Gies (1975), *By the Sweat of Thy Brow, Work in the Western World*, New York: G. P. Putnam's Sons.

Lazear, Edward P. (April 1999), 'Personnel Economics: Past Lessons and Future Directions', *Journal of Labor Economics*, **17**, 199-236.

Marshall, Alfred (1952), *Principles of Economics*, New York: Macmillan, fourth printing.

Metcalf, D. (Jan. 1989), 'Water Notes Dried Up: The Impact of the Donovan Reform Proposal and Thatcherism at Work on Labour Productivity in British Manufacturing industries', *British Journal of Industrial Relations*, **27**, 1-28.

Miles, G.H. and O. Skilbeck (1923), 'An Experiment on Change of Work', *Journal of the Institute of Industrial Psychology I*, 263-239, (reprinted in *Occupational Psychology* (1944), 192-195).

Moore, Henry Ludwell (1967), *Laws of Wages: An Essay in Statistical Economics*, New York: Augustus M. Kelley, reprint of economic classics, original publication, 1911.

Nyland, Chris (1989), *Reduced Worktime and the Management of Production*, New York: Cambridge University Press, 857.

Pearse, Arno (1930), *The Cotton Industry of India*, Manchester.

Scalia, Eugene (2000), 'OSHA's Ergonomics Litigation Record: Three Strikes and It's Out', CATO Institute, *Policy Analysis*, No. 370: May 15.

Vernon, Horatio Middleton (1921), *Industrial Fatigue and Efficiency*, London: George Routledge and Sons, Ltd.

Weber, Max (1958), *The Protestant Ethic and the Spirit of Capitalism*, New York: Charles Scribner's Sons.

10. The Incidence of Increased Unemployment in the Group of Seven, 1970-94

Edmund S. Phelps and Gylfi Zoega*

1. INTRODUCTION

A development of major social importance is the fall in the relative wage among men in the lower deciles of the earnings distribution in several G7 countries since the beginning of the 1980s. This development has been most pronounced in the US, the UK and Canada (Gottschalk, 1993). In the United States, for example, the data appear to be consistent with a steady fall in the relative demand for low-paid workers, especially among men, going back to the 1960s; shifts in relative supply generally worked the other way and were either smaller or had a lesser wage effect (Katz and Murphy, 1992; Juhn and Murphy, 1995). A frequently offered explanation is technological progress biased against unskilled workers (e.g. Berman et al., 1994); another is trade with developing countries, most markedly in the past two decades (Sachs and Shatz, 1994; Wood, 1994).

These changes have been less pronounced in France (Davis, 1992) and nonexistent in Germany (Nickell and Bell, 1996; Nickell, 1996) and Italy (Erickson and Ichino, 1992). In France, in fact, the earnings distribution actually became compressed at the bottom, as measured by the 50-10 wage ratio, from 1967 to 1987. In Germany a slight compression also occurred in the 1980s. In Italy, log-wage differentials shrank in the 1970s until 1982-83 and did not undergo significant changes after that. This contrasting wage pattern has implications for changes in relative unemployment. If relative wages in France, Germany and Italy were propped up by non-market institutions such

* We would like to thank Confindustria for financial support. We are grateful to Brian Bell, Luigi Bonatti, Elmar Honekopp, Peter Gottschalk and Roberto Perotti for providing data. We would also like to thank Luigi Bonatti for many helpful comments.

as minimum wages while the pattern of labour demand shifts was broadly similar in the G7 countries, we would expect the relative unemployment of the less advantaged workers in France, Germany and Italy to have increased by more than in Canada, the UK and the US.

The objective of this chapter is to look at changes in relative unemployment across education groups in six of the G7 countries, Japan excluded, and to relate these changes to some of the possible causes of the apparent steady decline in the relative demand for unskilled workers. We write down a set of hypotheses, formulated in terms of an economic model, and test them by estimating a set of structurally shifting expectations-augmented Phillips curves, one for each education group in each of the six countries.

While a considerable literature exists on the nature and causes of changes in the earnings distribution over the past three decades or so, changes in the distribution of employment and unemployment have received less attention. In the case of the United States, Juhn, Murphy and Topel (1991) found that between 1967 and 1989, there was a clear trend towards greater inequality in the distribution of unemployment and nonparticipation across skill levels: the nonemployment rate for the least skilled workers (those in the 1-10 wage percentile) rose by 16 percentage points from 1967-1989, while the nonemployment rate of workers in the top 40 per cent of the wage distribution showed no significant rise.[1]

Nickell and Bell (1996) look at changes in the composition of unemployment across education levels in a group of OECD countries. They find that while relative unemployment of the less educated has risen in the US, this is less so in Canada, Germany, the Netherlands and the UK. In these countries a large part of the increase in aggregate unemployment consists of increases in unemployment rates across skill groups due to neutral shocks.[2]

The following section describes some of the stylized facts of changes in relative unemployment in the six countries. Section 3 has the economic model and our proposed hypotheses. Section 4 describes the estimation results. Section 5 concludes.

2. A QUICK LOOK AT UNEMPLOYMENT BY EDUCATION LEVEL

Charts 1-12 show the rate of unemployment for four education groups in Italy, the UK and the US and five education groups in Canada, France and Germany. The upper charts have the raw unemployment rates and the lower charts have the ratio of unemployment in the lower groups to the general unemployment rate. These should correspond to high school or less in the American education system. Notice the steady upward trend of the relative unemployment rate of the least educated in the US. This applies to both workers without a high-school degree and also to workers who only completed high school. This trend is already visible in the 1970s and accelerates in the 1980s. A similar pattern is visible in Canada although the relative changes are considerably smaller. In the UK, the first three groups have workers with less than high-school education. The rise in their relative unemployment is comparable to that in Canada. These are workers with no formal degree, those with 'O levels' only – acquired at the age of 16 – and those who have some vocational training. The latter two groups have the strongest upward trend.

The situation is somewhat different in France, Germany and Italy. In France, the ratio of unemployment in the bottom two education groups to the general unemployment rate fell from 1971 to 1993. Workers with the lowest degree (CEP) have an unemployment rate in 1971 which is 90 per cent of the aggregate unemployment rate and they end up in 1993 with a rate which is 85 per cent of the aggregate rate. Workers with the degree above (BEPC) also experience a fall in their relative unemployment rate. But this masks a significant development. A large proportion of the French labour force have not declared their educational attainment. These workers had an unemployment rate which was 27 per cent higher than the aggregate in 1971 but 67 per cent higher in 1993. At the same time the number of workers in this category has fallen steadily. In 1970 they were around 39 per cent of all male workers and 35 per cent of female workers and in 1990 only 23 per cent of males and 19 per cent of females. It is likely that workers belonging to this group have low qualifications which makes their unemployment experience look like that of their counterparts in Canada and the US. However, the rise in their rate of unemployment could be due only to a compositional effect – the best workers leave the group raising the unemployment rate of those who stay behind.

In Germany, the relative unemployment rate of the four higher groups remain constant from 1975 to 1994 (Parmentier et al., 1996). These are workers who have gone through the apprenticeship system (lehre/BFS), those who have completed formal vocational school training (fachschule), those with more advanced vocational training (fachhochschule) and those with university degrees. However, workers with no educational or training degrees *did* experience rising relative unemployment rates. Their unemployment rate was 56 per cent higher than the aggregate unemployment rate in 1975 and 138 per cent higher in 1994. Thus workers without any qualifications in Germany have shared the experience of their counterparts in Canada, the UK and the US. Not much attention has been paid to this observation (see Nickell and

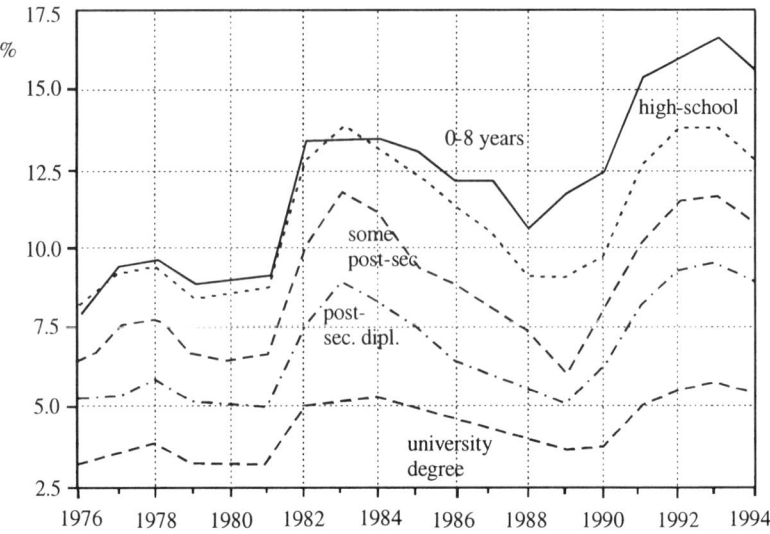

Chart 1. The Rate of Unemployment in Five Education Groups in Canada

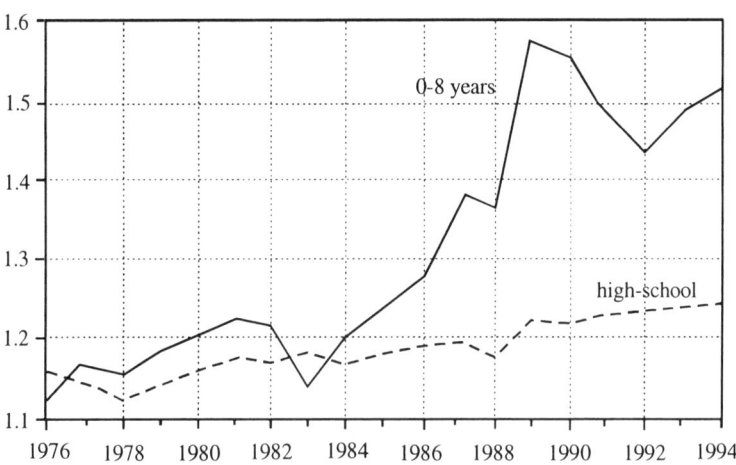

Chart 2. The Ratio of Unskilled to General Unemployment in Canada

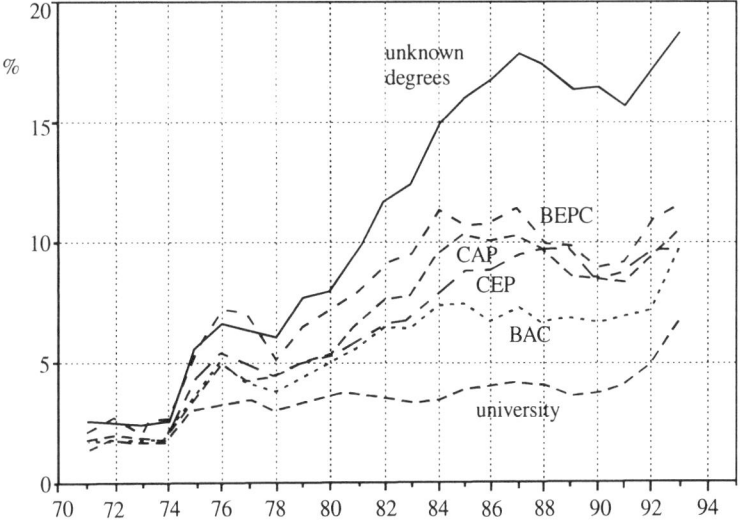

Chart 3. The Rate of Unemployment for Five Education Groups in France

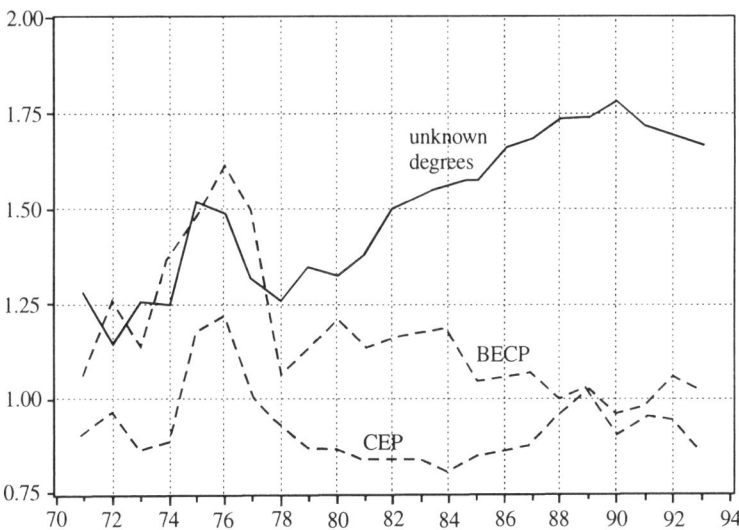

Chart 4. The Ratio of Unskilled to General Unemployment in France

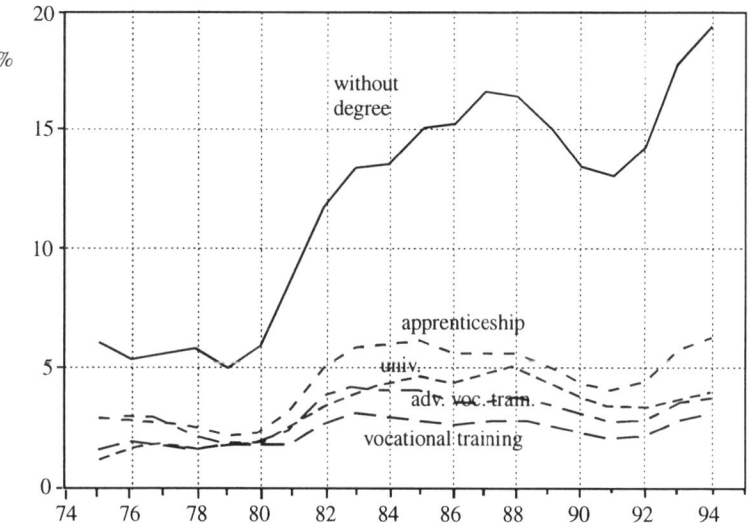

Chart 5. The Rate of Unemployment for Five Education Groups in Germany

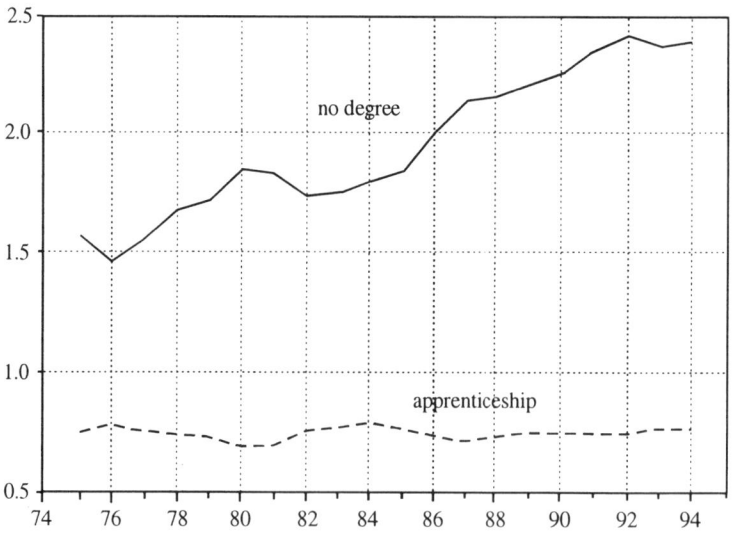

Chart 6. The Ratio of Unskilled to General Unemployment in Germany

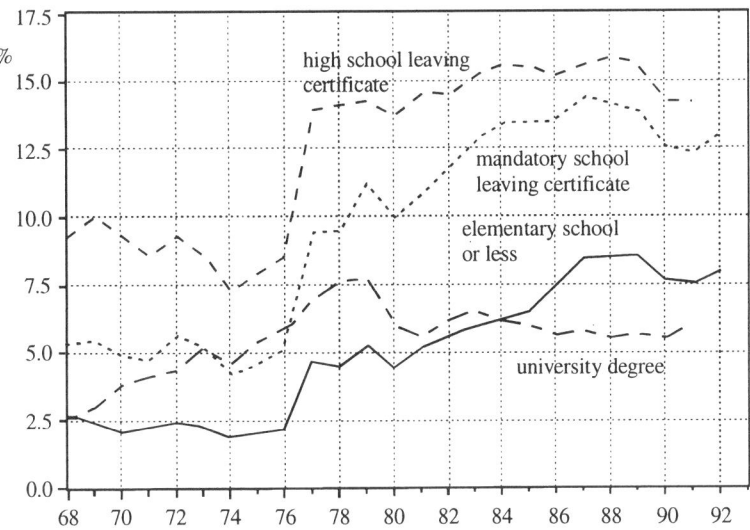

Chart 7. The Rate of Unemployment for Four Education Groups in Italy

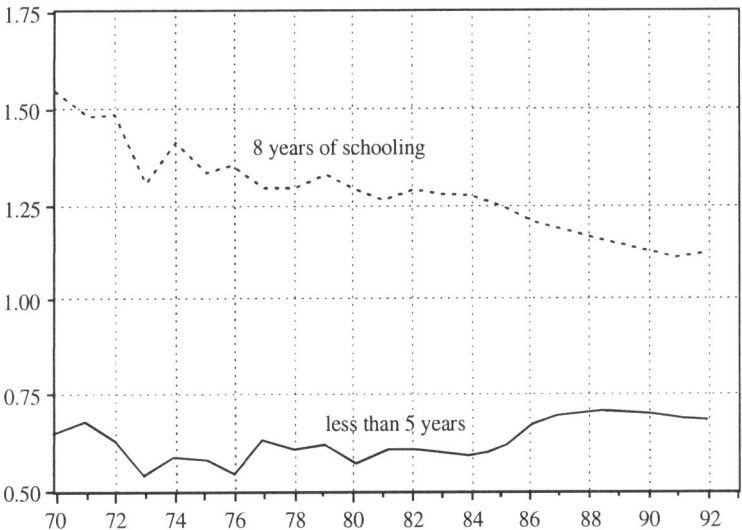

Chart 8. The Ratio of the Rate of Unemployment of Unskilled to the General Unemployment Rate in Italy

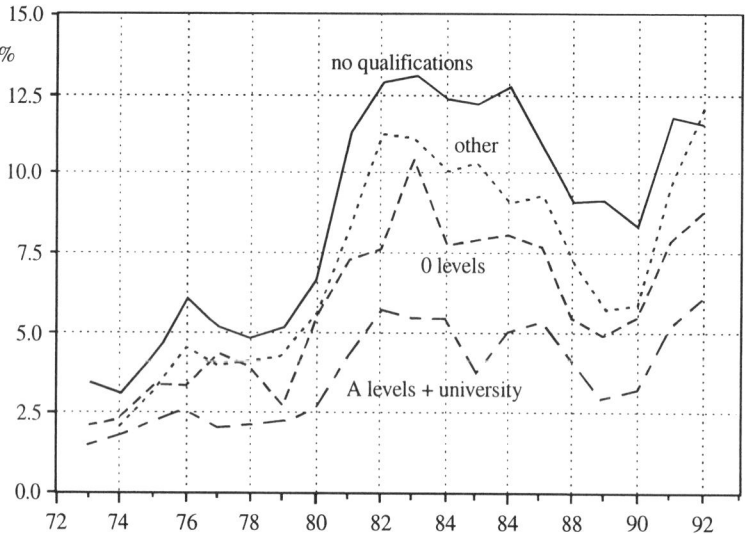

Chart 9. The Rate of Unemployment for Four Education Groups in the UK

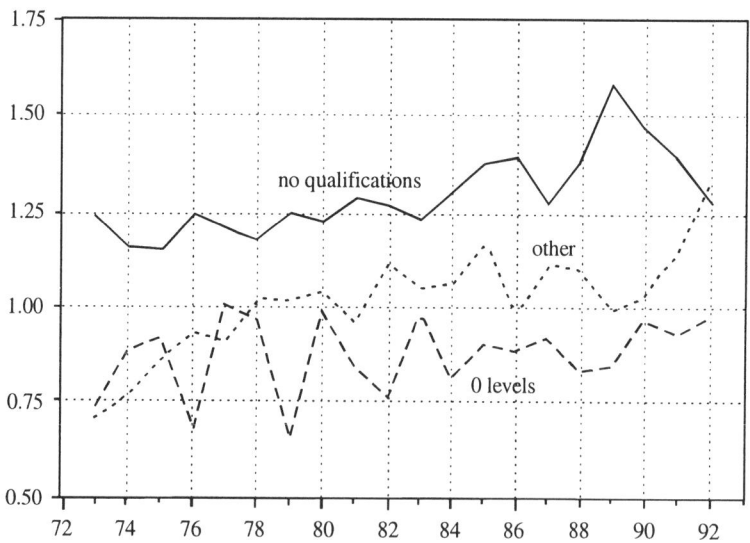

*Chart 10. The Ratio of the Rate of Unemployment of Unskilled to
the General Unemployment Rate in the UK*

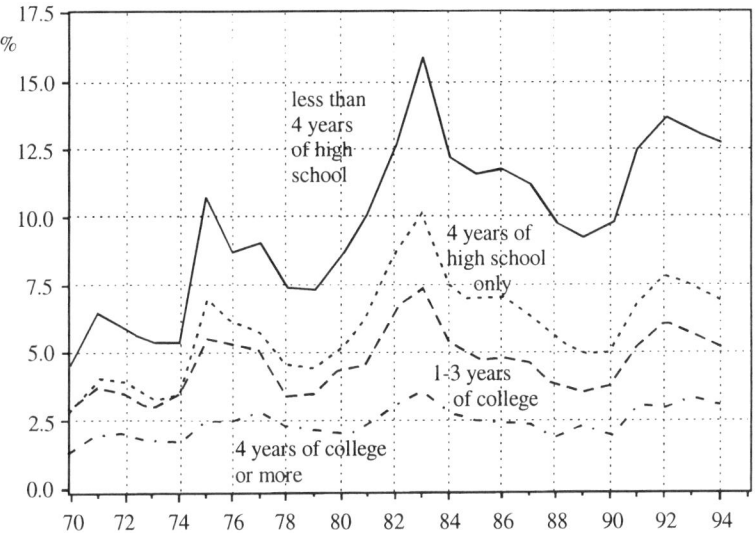

Chart 11. The Rate of Unemployment for Four Education Groups in the US

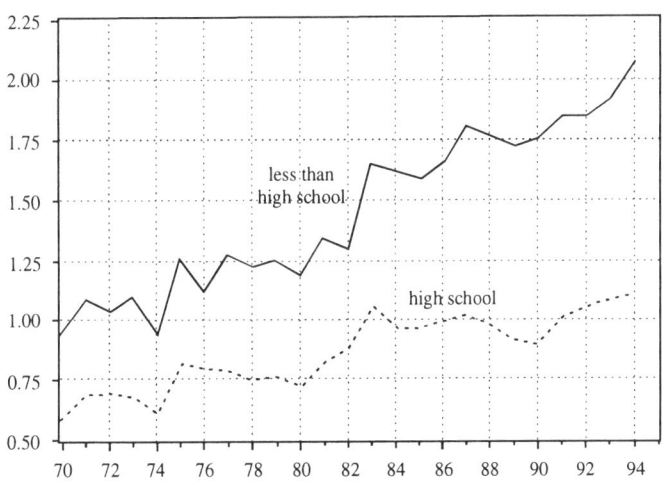

Chart 12. The Ratio of the Rate of Unemployment of Unskilled the General Unemployment Rate in the US

Bell, 1996). The question arises how significant this unskilled German unemployment is. Table 1 shows the proportion of the unemployed belonging to each of the education groups in 1994. The numbers suggest that almost half of all unemployed workers in West Germany belong to this group. In Chart 6 we saw that workers without any degree have had rising relative unemployment rates since 1976 and in Table 1 we see that they account for half of all unemployed. We can only conclude that a fall in the demand for less-educated workers is responsible for some of the rise in aggregate unemployment in Germany.

Table 1 Proportion of the Unemployed Belonging to each of Five Education Groups in Germany

	%		%
Without any degree	46.3	Advanced vocational school	2.0
Apprenticeship training	42.4	University	4.3
Vocational training	2.0		
Vocational school	2.9		

Source: Parmentier et al., 1996.

In Italy, the relative unemployment rate of the two lowest educational categories, namely those with 8 years of schooling – corresponding to the mandatory school-leaving certificate – and those with less than 5 years, have either been declining or remained constant. The unemployment rate of the former group went from being 55 per cent higher than the aggregate rate in 1970 to being only 11 per cent higher in 1992. But young workers (that is under 30 years of age) have much higher unemployment rates than the older ones. Young workers with higher levels of education than previous generations enter the labour market and have difficulty finding jobs. While it is true that those young workers with little education suffer higher rates than those with higher education, the relative number of less-educated workers is much smaller for the young due to the educational upgrading of the labour force. For this reason, the overall rate of unemployment is low for the less educated, although it is high for each age group.[3] For this reason we take a look at the unemployment rates for older workers in Table 2. We find that the composition of unemployment for these workers is indeed similar to that in Canada, the UK and the US. However, there is no apparent deterioration in the relative unemployment of the less educated in the table.

Table 2 The Rate of Unemployment of Workers over 30 Years of Age in Italy

	1977	1982	1987	1992
Elementary school or less	3.11	3.75	5.91	5.70
Mandatory school leaving Certificate	1.89	2.42	4.51	5.71
High school leaving Certificate	1.95	2.36	3.75	4.49
University degree	1.25	1.54	2.25	2.70

Source: ISTAT.

The difference between the unemployment experience of the six countries also becomes apparent when we estimate the persistence of relative unemployment of the different education groups and compare it to the persistence of the general unemployment rate. The following equation was estimated,

$$\Delta\left(\frac{u_{it}}{u_t}\right) = \alpha_i + \beta_i\left(\frac{u_{it-1}}{u_{t-1}}\right) + \varepsilon_{it} \tag{2.1}$$

where u_{it} is the rate of unemployment in group i, time t, u_t is the general unemployment rate and ε denotes the error term. A significant, negative value of β_i indicates stationarity of the unemployment ratio. Persistent changes in the relative unemployment of group i would show up in a value of β_i close to zero.

The estimation results are in Table 3. The first line for each country has the results for the aggregate unemployment rate, u_t. The value of β for the US and Canada indicates stationarity while in the case of France, Germany and Italy β is close to zero.[4] The UK is somewhere between, unemployment is more persistent than in the US and Canada but slightly less than in the European countries. But there is a second difference between the two sets of countries with regard to the ratio u_i/u. While in France, Germany and Italy, the ratio of unemployment of the lower education groups to the general unemployment rate is fairly stationary, it is non-stationary in the case of the US and Canada. An exception is the bottom German group and workers who do not declare their degrees in France. In the United States and Canada, persistent changes in the relative unemployment rate of workers with high-school degrees or less accompany the apparent stationarity of the overall unemployment rate. Again, the UK takes a position somewhere between these two groups of countries.

Table 3 Persistence of Relative Unemployment

	Canada	
	α_i	β_i
u	**2.88 (1.89)**	**−0.29 (−1.79)**
u_1	0.14 (1.06)	−0.09 (−0.89)
u_2	0.07 (0.51)	−0.05 (−0.47)
u_3	0.56 (2.57)	−0.59 (−2.54)
u_4	0.08 (0.66)	−0.10 (−0.60)
u_5	0.11 (1.25)	−0.22 (−1.21)
	France	
	α_i	β_i
u	**0.43 (1.22)**	**−0.01 (−0.16)**
u_0	0.20 (1.38)	−0.12 (−1.26)
u_1	0.38 (2.34)	−0.41 (−2.36)
u_2	0.35 (1.92)	−0.30 (−1.95)
u_3	0.52 (2.98)	−0.55 (−2.97)
u_4	0.25 (2.05)	−0.32 (−2.09)
u_5	0.04 (0.91)	−0.09 (−1.07)

Table 3 continued

Germany	α_i	β_i
u	**0.75 (1.24)**	**−0.09 (−0.92)**
u_1	0.07 (0.70)	−0.02 (−0.30)
u_2	0.34 (2.36)	−0.46 (−2.35)
u_3	0.09 (1.54)	−0.24 (−1.58)
u_4	0.07 (1.19)	−0.15 (−1.47)
u_5	0.26 (4.04)	−0.46 (−3.94)

Italy	α_i	β_i
u	**0.68 (1.48)**	**−0.04 (−0.78)**
u_1	0.19 (1.90)	−0.30 (−1.89)
u_2	0.20 (1.82)	−0.17 (−2.01)
u_3	0.17 (1.73)	−0.14 (−2.66)
u_4	0.05 (0.53)	−0.09 (−0.97)

United Kingdom	α_i	β_i
u	**1.39 (1.84)**	**−0.16 (−1.51)**
u_1	0.41 (1.92)	−0.32 (−1.92)
u_2	0.33 (1.91)	−0.30 (−1.73)
u_3	1.25 (7.24)	−1.43 (−7.21)
u_4	0.41 (3.05)	−0.74 (−3.01)

Table 3 continued

United States

	α_i	β_i
u	**2.49 (2.36)**	**−0.37 (−2.38)**
u_1	0.12 (1.01)	−0.05 (−0.63)
u_2	0.14 (1.65)	−0.14 (−1.42)
u_3	0.18 (1.68)	−0.25 (−1.60)
u_4	0.18 (2.65)	−0.49 (−2.55)

t-ratios in parentheses.

We conclude that while the trend towards increased dispersion of unemployment across education groups appears to be strongest in Canada, the UK and the US, it is by no means confined to these countries. Similar trends can be found in France and Germany. We now turn to the economic model which is the starting point of our empirical analysis.

3. THEORY

3.1 Model

We assume there is a separate labour market for each of the education groups. Corresponding to each group there is an equilibrium rate of unemployment. The determination of this equilibrium rate can be described as follows. There is an equation giving the current real wage, v_i reflecting labour-market equilibrium (meaning correct expectations about upcoming wages). The equation for the supply-wage for education group i takes the form,

$$v_i = V_S^i(1 - u_i; \; x, p, r; Y), \quad V_S^{i'}(1 - u_i; \ldots) \geq 0 \qquad (3.1)$$

where x is a vector of state variables representing the capital stock, customer stock, and the proportion of the labour force belonging to group i, p is a vector of real prices, r is the instantaneous real rate of interest, and Y represents the prevailing set of social policies embodied in tax and welfare legislation. This curve in the $(1-u_i, v_i)$ plane can be derived from incentive-wage models of wage setting based on quitting or shirking, where the curve is up-ward-sloping (as in Shapiro and Stiglitz, 1984).

For equilibrium in the product market (meaning correct expectations about the price level relative to the wage) we need the following equation. This is the real demand price of labour in group i which is a nonincreasing function of the employment rate, $1-u_i$.

$$v_i = V_d^i(1-u_i; x, p, r; Y), \quad V_d^{i'}(1-u_i; ...) \le 0 \qquad (3.2)$$

Among the real prices are asset prices, such as the shadow price of employees and customers. The link between asset prices (interest rates) and the demand wage is implied by recent models of the natural rate (see Phelps, 1994).

The intersection of these two relationships determines the joint-equilib-rium of v_i and $1-u_i$ as a function of p, r, x, Y and the various givens,

$$V_d^i(1-u_i; x, p, r; Y) = V_S^i(1-u_i; x, p, r; Y) \qquad (3.3)$$

The solution for u_i is the equilibrium rate of unemployment. It is a function of a set of real prices and real interest rates as well as various stocks which are the state variables of the system. The equilibrium unemployment rate changes over time until the state variables reach their steady-state values. The steady-state equilibrium is then described as the 'natural rate of unemployment' for each of the education groups. (This is the long-run natural rate in Phelps (1994).)

The natural rate of aggregate unemployment is the weighted average of the equilibrium rates for each of the education groups,

$$u_t = \sum_i^n l_i u_{it} \qquad (3.4)$$

where n denotes the number of education groups and l_i the share of the labour force belonging to group i.

We are interested in finding what could have raised the natural rate of unemployment of the low-education groups relative to the higher ones. Using equations (3.1)-(3.4) we consider the possibilities in the following section.

3.2 Hypotheses

Changes in the Average Level of Education

We note from equation (3.4) that an educational upgrading of the labour force might affect the aggregate rate of unemployment at least for a while, before wealth adjusted to the resulting wage changes. If the rate is lower for the higher groups, the upgrading would reduce the aggregate rate, provided it did not raise the rate in some or all of the groups by enough, if at all, to offset the former effect. But the rate of unemployment in each group may be a function of the size of these groups. This leads us to the first two hypotheses.

- Individual workers differ in their inherent abilities and motivation. Changes in the system of education enable workers to get higher degrees. The best in each group move upwards, leaving the pool of workers in every group with lower average quality. The rate of unemployment now rises in every education group since the best workers leave and inferior workers enter.

- High- and low-education workers are perfect substitutes in production but the high-education ones embody more efficiency units of labour. An increase in the proportion of high-education workers reduces the marginal productivity of an efficiency unit of labour, by increasing their number, and the demand wage of both high- and low-education workers is reduced. The unemployment rate of both is raised (Saint-Paul, 1994). The relative rate of unemployment for the low-education group rises by more, though, because this group finds itself at a higher rate of initial unemployment and hence at a flatter portion of the wage curve.

In both cases we are postulating that the vector of state variables in equations (3.1) and (3.2), x, contains the proportion of the labour force belonging to each group, l_i.

The two hypotheses could help explain the significant rise in unemployment among the less educated in the UK, the US and Canada. If the share of the higher (lower) education groups in the population rose (fell) in these countries, we would also expect relative unemployment among the less educated to have increased. This could also explain why the aggregate rate of unemployment in these countries rose less than in Europe.

The proportion of the labour force with higher degrees could also affect the way in which labour demand responds to biased technological change. This is our third hypothesis.

- A given improvement in technology leads to a greater increase in the supply of effective labour units, the higher (lower) is the proportion of workers in the labour force with more (less) education. Thus the higher is this proportion, the bigger is the increase in the rate of unemployment among all education groups, and especially among the less educated.

This hypothesis draws on the thesis by Nelson and Phelps (1966) that more educated workers are quicker to learn to use new technology.[5]

Youth Unemployment and Insider Power

In the context of Italy it has been claimed that an important characteristics of unemployment is the distinction between young and the older workers (see Bonatti, 1996). If young workers are considerably better educated than the older ones and at the same time disproportionately unemployed, it is possible that even if older workers with low qualifications are losing their jobs, an influx of young workers prevents the relative unemployment rate of the less educated from rising by constantly adding well-educated unemployed workers to the labour force. This gives the following hypothesis.

- The relative rate of unemployment of the low-education workers is a negative function of relative youth unemployment.

But we note that the young unemployed workers will affect the equilibrium rate of unemployment for each skill group of older workers. Because of the young, unemployed workers with good education, the rate of unemployment among older workers in the same education group will be lower since they have more to fear in case of a dismissal.

Public Employment

Changes in the size of the public sector will affect the relative demand for unskilled workers if it hires high- and low-education workers in a different proportion from that of the private sector. Gottschalk (1996) finds that the private sector uses a higher proportion of both high-school dropouts and high-school graduates than both the federal, state and local governments in the US. This difference is particularly significant for male workers. A rise in public employment could thus be expected to work against our low-education groups.

The Welfare State

Changes in the returns to nonwork could affect the groups differently because of differences in their wages. An expansion of the welfare state – defined as the provision of private goods, and transfers to the poor and unemployed – would raise the supply wage of the less educated by more because their marginal utility of consumption is on average higher.

But this explanation runs quickly into trouble. To account for rising relative unemployment among workers with low education, we need to postulate an expansion of the welfare state. But this would affect unemployment only by raising the supply wage of labour, hence narrowing the wage distribution which conflicts with the empirical evidence described above. Moreover, if we believe that low-education labour has been less affected on the continent of Europe, we need a smaller expansion of the welfare state in these countries, which also is not plausible.

International Trade and Capital Movements

Wood (1994) and Minford[6] have recently pointed out that North-South trade and capital movements from the industrial world to the developing countries could affect income distribution in the former by reducing the relative price of manufacturing goods, the production of which tends to be intensive in unskilled labour. Chart 13 (see page 199) is taken from Minford and shows the ratio of developing countries manufacturing export prices to developed countries export prices. There is a clear downward trend after 1981 with a sharp decrease in 1986. This would reduce the demand wage of our low-education groups, hence reducing their relative wage and/or increasing their relative unemployment rates. The hypothesis is then the following:

- Changes in the relative rate of unemployment of workers with little education are negatively correlated with the Minford-index of relative prices of manufacturing goods, the more so the higher is the initial share of the labour force employed in manufacturing.

The Decline in Manufacturing Employment

The decline of manufacturing employment could also be caused by labour-saving technological progress or changes in the composition of demand towards services, as suggested by Krugman (1994). As it is difficult to measure both the level of technology and consumer preferences, we state the following hypotheses.

- A decline in the relative employment share of the manufacturing sector leaves unemployed workers with little formal education and who find it difficult to adjust to different industries, hence remain unemployed for long periods of time.

The converse has also been suggested.[7]

- A decline in the relative share of manufacturing in total employment puts workers into the unemployment pool who, especially in Europe, have relatively high educational attainment. This affects the composition of unemployment across education groups.

We leave it to the data to distinguish between the two conflicting hypotheses.

Antecedent Hypothesis about the General Unemployment Rate

Our analysis extends that in Phelps (1994) where equation (3.3) is also estimated. In that analysis we found four variables to be particularly important.

The first two are the real price of oil, p^{oil}, and the world real rate of interest, r. (Interest rates affect unemployment through asset-price channels in non-monetary natural-rate models (Hoon and Phelps, 1992; Phelps, 1994).) We also include the sum of direct household taxes,[8] dt, and payroll taxes,[9] pt, and the first difference in the domestic inflation rate,[10] π, to allow for the effect of monetary variables.[11]

The intuition behind these relationships is discussed carefully in Phelps (1994). The effect of the interest rate is thought to be mainly through labour demand, equation (3.2). The idea is that labour demand is a function of the shadow price of new workers which reflects discounted future profits of the marginal worker. A rise in the interest rate reduces this shadow price and makes firms invest less in the training of new workers; the rate of employment falls.

The effect of oil prices is more difficult to pinpoint. One possibility is that energy and labour are complements in production so when the use of oil is reduced, the demand for labour is adversely affected. Taxes affect labour demand in the usual way by creating a wedge between the gross wage and the take-home wage. Finally, the inflation term is included to take into account transitory disequilibra around the equilibrium unemployment path described by (3.3).

4. EMPIRICAL TESTS

The basic equations take the following form where (4.1) corresponds to equation (3.3), and (4.2) to equation (3.4).

$$-\frac{\Delta N_{ijt}}{L_{ijt}} = \gamma_{ij} u_{ijt-1} + \alpha_0^{ij} + \beta_j \left[\alpha_1 r_t + \alpha_2 p_t^{oil} + \alpha_3^i \left(dt_{ijt} + pt_{itj} \right) + \alpha_4 \Delta \pi_{ijt} \right] + \varepsilon_{ijt} \quad (4.1)$$

$$\frac{\Delta N_{jt}}{L_{jt}} = \sum_i l_{ijt} \frac{\Delta N_{ijt}}{L_{ijt}}, i = 1, 2, 3, 4, (5), j = 1, 2, 3, \ldots 6 \qquad (4.2)$$

N_i denotes the number of employed workers, L_i the size of the labour force, i is an index for the education groups and j is an index for the country. This is a system of twenty-seven equations (five for Canada, France and Germany; four for Italy, the UK and the US) and five constraints, one for each country. The equations are essentially structurally shifting expectations-augmented Phillips curves since they include both the determinants of the natural rate and an inflation-shock term. The coefficient β_j is a measure of the sensitivity of unemployment in country j to changes in the causal variables.[12]

The results of the estimation are in Table 4, where a time trend is added which has a different coefficient (bold-lettered) for the low-education groups. Note that the coefficient of the time trend for the higher-education groups is below that for the low-education groups. The interest rate variable, the oil price variable and the tax rates have positive coefficients and the inflation variable a negative one. All the coefficients are significant at the 10 per cent level.

Table 4 The Proportion of Workers with less than High-school Education

	1970	1975	1980	1985	1990	1994
Canada	NA	19.1[a]	15.7	11.9	7.9	6.0
France	57.7[b]	47.7	39.1[c]	NA	30.0	NA
Germany	NA	86.7	84.8	83.4	82.2	80.8
Italy	88.3	84.5	78.6	72.6	66.0	64.8[d]
UK	86.6[e]	85.8	80.1	74.0	69.2	66.8[f]
US	36.1	27.5	20.6	15.9	13.4	11.0

a-1976, b-1968, c-1982, d-1992, e-1973, f-1992.

We are interested in changes in the composition of unemployment across education groups. We have to define for each country which groups should be counted as having low-education workers. We group together workers who have received less than or equal to an American high-school degree. For Canada and the US we include workers with no more than a high-school degree (12 years of education), for the UK those who do not have 'A-levels' (also corresponding to 12 years) and for Germany workers who do not have any formal qualifications and those who have only gone through the apprenticeship programme. In Italy we have workers with less than the high school leaving certificate and in France holders of the CEP and the BEPC degrees, in addition to those who do not declare their degrees.

We now move to test the hypotheses in the previous section. First we include the proportion of the labour force belonging to each category, l_i, to test the first two hypotheses. We allow its coefficient to take a different value for the low- and the high-education groups. We then test whether there is a significant difference between the two coefficients. The coefficient is negative, as expected, and fairly significant for the low-education groups but also negative and significant for the higher education groups. The size of the coefficient for the low-education groups is small: a ten percentage fall in the proportion of the labour force belonging to the low-education groups would raise their unemployment rate by about 0.4 per cent or 40 basis points.[13] Moreover, the coefficient for the high-education groups has the wrong sign: the larger the group, the lower is the rate of unemployment. We conclude that the educational upgrading of the labour force would reduce the aggregate rate of unemployment by changing the relative weights of the different groups without notably affecting the unemployment rate of each group.

Turning to the third hypothesis, Table 4 has the proportion of the labour force in the lowest education groups for the six countries. There appear to be three groups in the data. The first has Canada and the US. These two countries start out with a low proportion of low-education workers and then experience a significant fall until the early 1990s. The second group has Germany, Italy and the UK. All have a very high initial proportion and although it does decline over the past twenty years, it does not decline proportionately by as much as in the US. Finally, France also starts out with a fairly high proportion, although lower than in Italy[14] and the UK, but it declines at a more rapid rate. Following the hypotheses above, we would expect the effect of technological progress to be greater in Canada and the US throughout the sample period, since higher education is more widespread there. We would also expect the substantial educational upgrading that took place in those two countries to have kept down the aggregate unemployment rate.

We then include the ratio of youth unemployment to aggregate unemployment, u^y. Table 5 and Chart 14 show the significance of youth unemployment in our six countries. Italy does seem to be a special case: 44 per cent of unemployed workers are between 15 and 24 years of age. The other outlier is Germany where only 13.2 per cent of unemployed workers are in this age category. It is not likely that this variable can explain the low relative unemployment of the less educated in France and Germany. In Table 4 we see that this variable, although significant, has the wrong sign in our unemployment regression.

We next turn to public employment, N^p, and include its ratio to total employment. The coefficient is positive but insignificant for the low-education groups, and negative and significant at the 10 per cent level for the high-education group. This supports the earlier result of Gottschalk. The effect is not insignificant: a 5 per cent increase in the share of public employment would reduce the rate of unemployment among the top groups by about one per cent.

Table 5 Youth Unemployment as Percentage of Total Unemployment in 1991

	%		%		%
Canada	26.7	Germany	13.2	US	33.7
France	24.3	Italy	**44.0**		

Source: OECD Labour Force Statistics.

We then include a measure of the welfare state. This is the ratio of public spending (the sum of public consumption and social assistance expenditures; interest payments and defence expenditures not included), G^w, to *GDP*. Chart 15 shows the variable for the six countries. The coefficients are positive and very significant for both groups. The coefficient is significantly larger for the low-education group. Looking at the size of the coefficients, a 10 point increase in the ratio of public spending as a percentage of *GDP* would raise the rate of unemployment among the low-skilled by 2.3 per cent and by 1 per cent among the top groups. A problem is that the social assistance component includes unemployment benefits and is highly correlated with the aggregate unemployment rate. It is, for that reason, likely that this effect exaggerates the importance of the welfare state due to endogeneity problems.

We now test for the effect of changes in the relative price of manufacturing imports from the developing countries. Chart 13 shows the Minford index. There is a rather abrupt drop in the mid-1980s but this does not seem to correspond to any apparent rise in the unemployment rates. We again estimate a different coefficient for the low education groups and the higher ones, and weigh the Minford-index by the share of manufacturing in total employment in each country at the beginning of the sample period. This gives our explanatory variable p^m. Results are in Table 6. The coefficients for the low- and the high-education groups are both insignificant but their sign implies that a rise in the price of imported manufactures raises unemployment of the low-education group, contrary to our hypothesis. This may be explained by the correlation between oil prices and the price index. Both fall dramatically in 1986 when unemployment was falling in some of the countries. We conclude that this variable is not likely to have caused the rise in relative unemployment among the less educated.

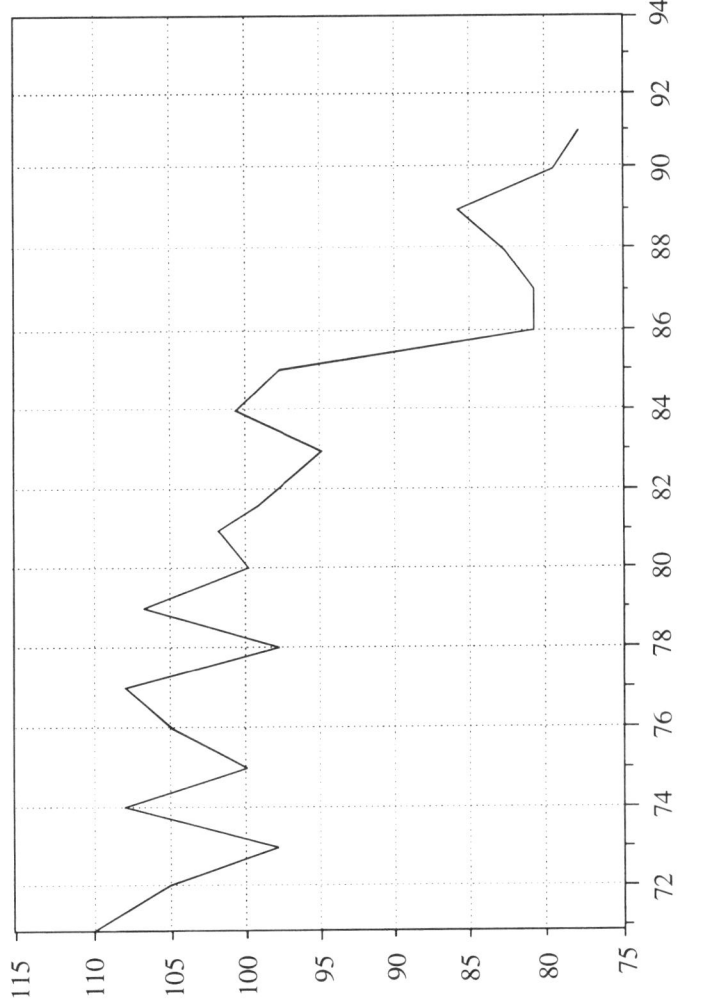

*Chart 13. Ratio of Developing Countries' Manufacturing Export Prices in $ to Developed Countries'
Export Proces of Machinery, Transport Equipment and Services in $*

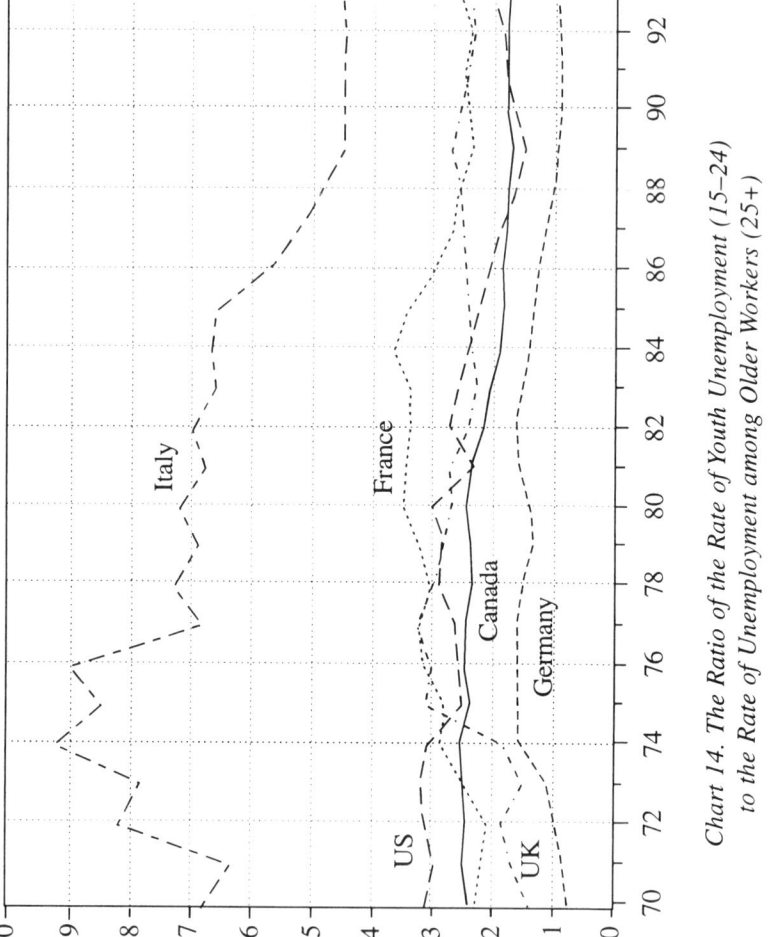

Chart 14. The Ratio of the Rate of Youth Unemployment (15–24)
to the Rate of Unemployment among Older Workers (25+)

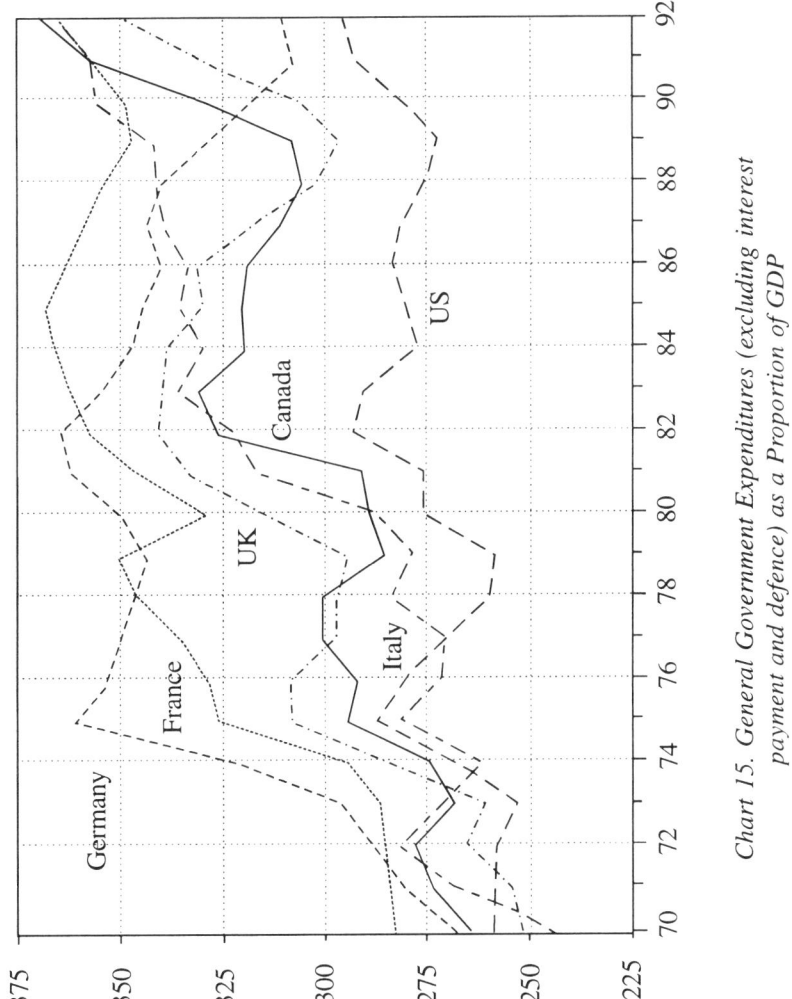

Chart 15. General Government Expenditures (excluding interest payment and defence) as a Proportion of GDP

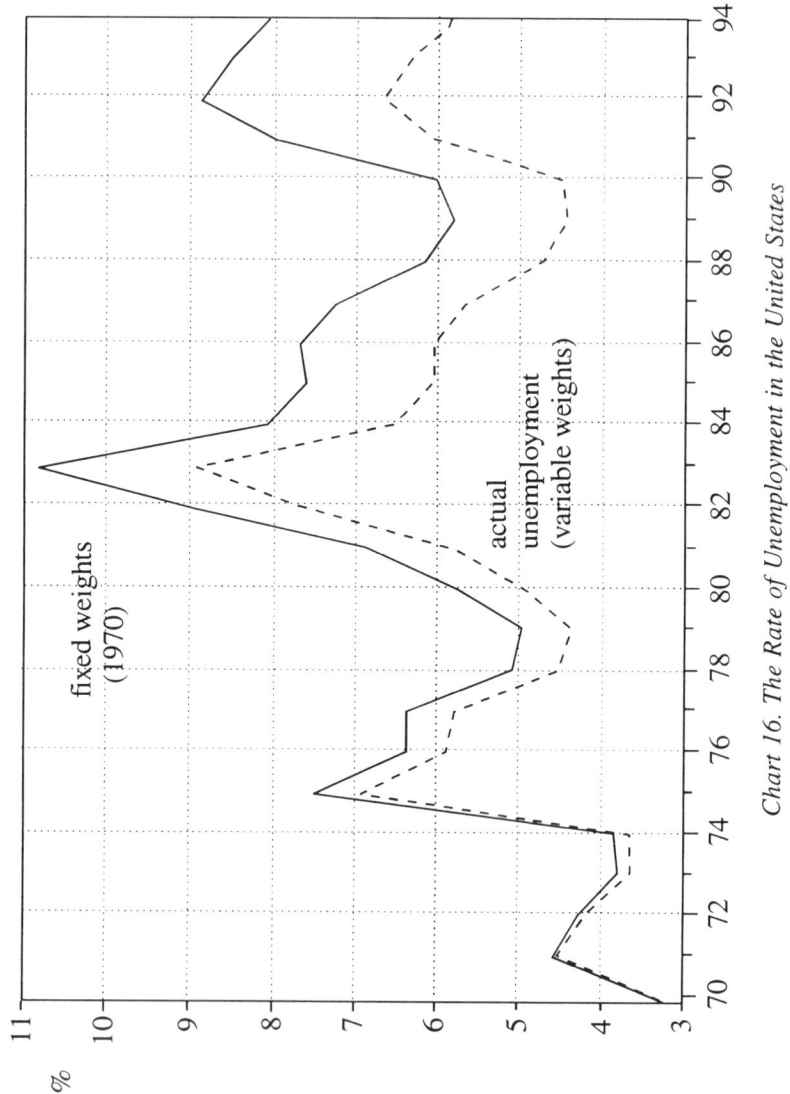

Chart 16. The Rate of Unemployment in the United States

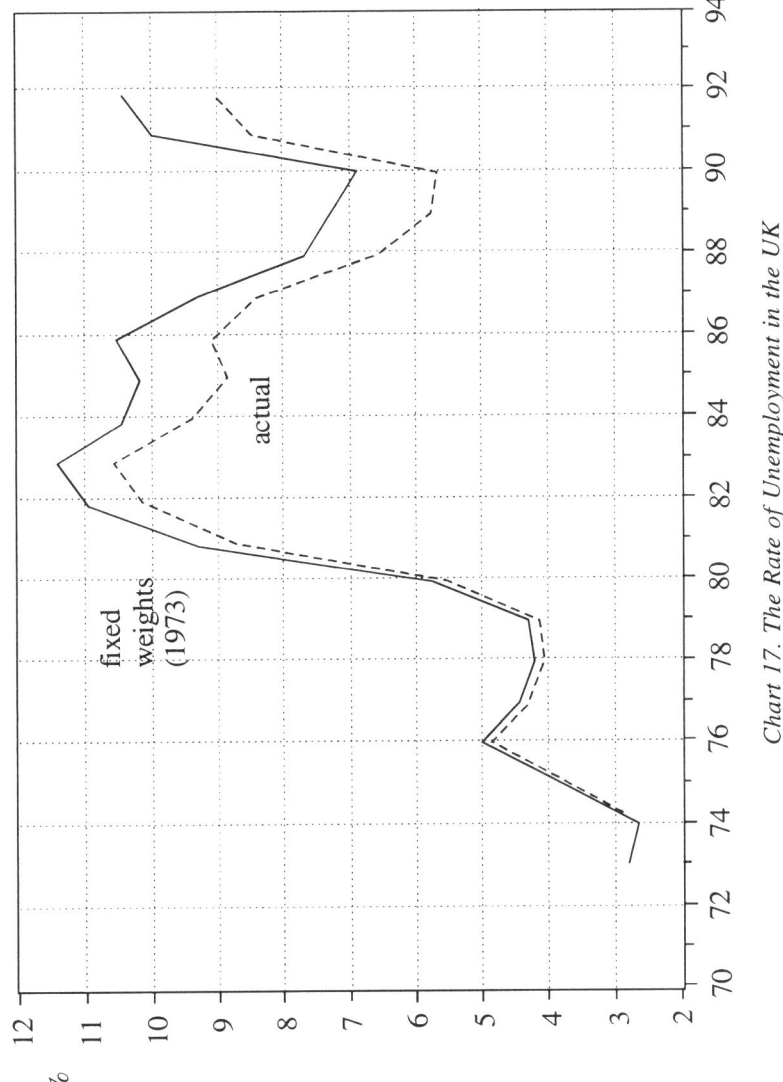

Chart 17. The Rate of Unemployment in the UK

Table 6 Regression results for equation (4.1), 1970-94

r	p^{yil}	$dt+pt$	$\Delta\pi$	trend	l_i	u^y	N^p/N	G^W/GDP
0.026	0.005	0.092	−0.001	**0.0005**				
(1.64)	(2.82)	(3.19)	(−3.94)	(2.98)				
				0.0000				
				(0.18)				
0.033	0.003	−0.047	−0.001	**0.0009**	**−0.042**			
(1.55)	(1.60)	(−1.52)	(−3.57)	(2.86)	(−1.93)			
				0.0014	−0.137			
				(3.14)	(−2.72)			
0.019	0.004	0.104	−0.001	**0.0005**		**0.005**		
(1.46)	(2.92)	(3.31)	(−3.64)	(3.15)		(2.85)		
				0.0000		−0.000		
				(−0.28)		(−0.11)		
0.041	0.005	0.048	−0.001	**0.0005**			**0.055**	
(2.05)	(2.48)	(1.97)	(−3.60)	(2.26)			(0.46)	
				0.0003			−0.184	
				(1.93)			(−1.82)	
0.018	0.002	0.013	−0.001	**0.0008**				**0.235**
(1.29)	(1.61)	(0.68)	(−3.97)	(4.08)				(4.32)
				0.0003				0.102
				(3.02)				(3.74)

t-statistics in parentheses. The bold-lettered numbers refer to the low-education groups while the numbers below refer to the high-education groups.

Table 6 continued

r	p^{oil}	$dt+pt$	$\Delta\pi$	*trend*	p^m	N^m/N	Λ^m/Λ
0.028	0.004	0.078	−0.001	**0.0006**	**0.0003**		
(1.76)	(2.40)	(2.83)	(−3.65)	(2.85)	(1.78)		
				0.0001	0.0001		
				(0.91)	(0.90)		
0.009	0.004	0.093	−0.001	**0.0001**		**−0.0003**	
(0.69)	(2.61)	(2.98)	(−3.29)	(0.90)		(−2.25)	
				−0.0001		−0.0001	
				(−0.78)		(−1.10)	
0.124	−0.002	−0.042	−0.002	**0.0017**			**0.229**
(3.45)	(−0.86)	(−1.05)	(−5.37)	(4.32)			(4.28)
				0.0011			0.147
				(3.34)			(3.85)

t-statistics in parentheses. The bold-lettered numbers refer to the low-education groups while the numbers below refer to the high-education groups.

Throughout these tests, the trend term has had a higher positive coefficient for the low-education groups. This suggests that none of our variables explains fully the changing composition of unemployment across education groups. Our final attempt involves the share of manufacturing in total civilian employment, N^m/N. The coefficients are both negative and significant. Also, there is a significant difference between the two: the decline in manufacturing employment has affected the unemployment of the less educated by more. Moreover, the coefficients of the trend term become insignificant, indicating that changes in the employment share capture the trend towards increased unemployment for the low-education groups.

A problem with this variable is its endogeneity since it is not clear what causes the contraction of manufacturing employment. For this reason we replace the variable with a measure of relative productivity in manufacturing. The variable Λ^m/Λ is equal to the product of the share of manufacturing in total employment and the ratio of manufacturing productivity to overall productivity.[15] This variable comes out significant and positive for both groups but is higher for the low-education groups. Note that the coefficients of the oil price variable and the tax variable become insignificant. However, this could be caused by the endogeneity of the productivity variable since the share of manufacturing in total employment and both productivity measures are likely to change over the business cycle.

5. CONCLUSIONS

We found that the rise in relative unemployment among the less educated is not confined to Canada, the UK and the US. In Germany, those workers with no qualifications have experienced rising relative unemployment rates and account for almost half of total unemployment at the end of the sample period. Thus while workers who have gone through the apprenticeship system appear to do well, this system leaves out a substantial fraction of the labour force which does no better – in employment terms – than their UK and US counterparts. In France, a large fraction of the labour force does not reveal their educational attainment. This group, which probably has mostly workers with low qualifications, has experienced a rise in relative unemployment comparable to that of the bottom groups in the English-speaking countries. In Italy, high unemployment among relatively well educated young workers masks a high relative rate of unemployment among older workers with little education. The distinguishing feature of Italian unemployment is the high rate of youth unemployment, not, as often suggested, low relative unemployment of the less educated.

The most noteworthy finding from our analysis is the implication that the increased educational attainments of the labor force over the past generation have had important effects on the general unemployment rate. Where low education and high unemployment go hand in hand, obviously, a fall in the proportion of workers belonging to the lower educational groups would decrease the general unemployment rate – provided that the rate does not increase within one or more groups so as to offset the former effect. We found that this proviso appears to be satisfied. The statistical results did not show a strong relationship between the relative size of each educational group and its unemployment rate.

To chart this compositional effect, we simulate the evolution of aggregate unemployment in the UK and the US on the counterfactual assumption that the relative size of the different education groups did not change since the beginning of the sample period.[16] Chart 16 has both the actual and our simulated unemployment rate for the US. We see that unemployment would be around 200 basis points higher in 1994 had it not been for the gains in workers' average level of education. The corresponding number for the UK in 1992 is 150 basis points as seen in Chart 17. Although one should not take these simulations too seriously at this very early stage, we would like to point out this potentially very important determinant of medium-term changes in unemployment which has so far been mostly overlooked.[17]

We were not successful in explaining relative unemployment among the less educated by public employment, relative youth unemployment, the relative price of imported manufactures and variables coming from the macroeconomic section. However, our measure of the welfare state was strongly correlated with unemployment of both the high- and the low-education groups and significantly more so in case of the latter. Also, the share of manufacturing in civilian employment and relative productivity in manufacturing, weighted by the share of manufacturing in total employment, appeared to be important.

NOTES

1.   By allowing for different labour-supply elasticities of skilled and unskilled workers, they could explain a 0.7 per cent rise in unemployment of prime-aged males from the early 1970s to the late 1980s by an increase in the relative demand for skills, holding constant the total demand. Allowing for a still larger difference in the elasticities of labour supply, Blanchard (1996) finds that changes in relative demand could have decreased the rate of employment by around 0.5 per cent a year over the same period.

2.   They find that the fall in relative demand for unskilled workers in the UK explains around 20 per cent of the increase in average unemployment from the 1960s to the 1980s.

3.   We are indebted to Luigi Bonatti, Universita degli Studi di Trento, for this point.

4.   The estimate of β is downward biased under the null-hypothesis of unit root. Using the Dickey-Fuller test, nonstationarity is marginally rejected for the US but not rejected for Canada, France, Germany, Italy and the UK.

5.   The hypothesis is supported by empirical estimates in Barro and Sala-I-Martin (1990). They find that the rate of growth of GDP tends to be positively correlated with initial levels of educational attainment, in particular the average years of secondary and higher schooling.

6.   In an article published in the Financial Times, June 1, 1995.

7.   We owe this suggestion to Stanislaw Wellisz.

8.   These are calculated as the ratio of direct taxes to total household income.

9.   Defined as the ratio of social security contributions to the total private sector wage bill.

10. Measured in terms of the GDP deflator.

11. If inflation follows a random walk the (rational and also adaptive) expectation of next years inflation is equal to current inflation and the change in the inflation rate equal to unexpected inflation.

12. This might reflect the slope of the wage curve at the point of equilibrium.

13. This applies to a country where $\beta_j = 1$. We make this restriction for one of the six countries; Italy.

14. Before 1977, the labour force included workers who were 13 years or older. After 1977 the minimum age is increased to 14 years.

15. Productivity in manufacturing is measured by the gross value added per person-hour and overall productivity is measured by real GDP (taken from the Summers-Heston table) per employed worker.

16. 1970 for the US and 1973 for the UK.
17. Its significance may of course differ across countries. Thus in Italy, the overall unemployment rate would actually be lower if the relative shares had remained the same in the past two decades. This may be due to the different labour market institutions responsible for youth unemployment.

REFERENCES

Barro R. and X. Sala-i-Martin (1990), 'World Real Invest Rates', NBER, *Macroeconomics Annual*.

Berman, Eli, John Bound, and Zvi Griliches (1994), 'Changes in the Demand for Skilled Labor within U.S. Manufacturing: Evidence from the Annual Survey of Manufacturers', *Quarterly Journal of Economics*, **109**, 367-97.

Blanchard, Olivier E. (1996), 'Macroeconomic and Policy Implications of Shifts in the Relative Demand for Skills', *Unemployment Policy: How Should Governments Respond to Unemployment?*, (eds). Dennis J. Snower and Guillermo de la Dehesa, CEPR.

Bonatti, Luigi (1996), 'The Persistence of a 'Low-skill, Bad-job Trap' in a Dynamic Model of a Dual Labor Market', *Discussion paper* No. **3**, Universita degli Studi di Trento.

Davis, Steven J. (1992), 'Cross-Country Patterns of Changes in Relative Wages', *NBER Macroeconomics Annual*.

Erickson, Christopher L. and Andrea Ichino (1992), 'Wage Differentials in Italy: Market Forces, Institutions, and Inflation', *Differences and Changes in Wage Structure*, (eds). Richard Freeman and Lawrence Katz, Chicago University Press.

Gottschalk, Peter (1993), 'Changes in Inequality of Family Income in Seven Industrialized Countries', *American Economic Review*, **83**.

Gottschalk, Peter (1996), *The Impact of Changes in Public Employment on Low Wage Labor Markets*, paper prepared for the conference on Demand-Side Strategies and Low-Wage Labor Markets on the 26-27 June 1995 in New York.

Hoon, H.T. and Edmund S. Phelps (1992), 'Macroeconomic Shocks in a Dynamized Model of the Natural Rate of Unemployment', *American Economic Review*, **82**, 889-900.

Juhn, C., Kevin M. Murphy and R. H. Topel (1991), 'Why Has the Natural Rate of Unemployment Increased over Time?' *Brookings Papers on Economic Activity*, **2**.

Juhn, Chinhui and Kevin M. Murphy (1995), 'Inequality in Labor Market Outcomes: Contrasting the 1980s and Earlier Decades', *Economic Policy Review*, 26-32.

Katz, Lawrence F. and Kevin M. Murphy (1992), 'Changes in Relative Wages, 1963-1987: Supply and Demand Factors', *Quarterly Journal of Economics*.

Krugman, Paul (1994), *Past and Prospective Causes of High Unemployment*, The Federal Reserve Bank of Kansas City Symposium.

Murphy, Kevin M. and R. H. Topel (1987), 'The Evolution of Unemployment in the United States: 1968-1985', *Brookings Papers on Economic Activity*.

Nelson, Richard R. and Edmund S. Phelps (1966), 'Investment in Humans, Technological Diffusion, and Economic Growth', *American Economic Review*, **56**, pp. 69-75.

Nickell, Stephen and Brian Bell (1996), 'Would Cutting Payroll Taxes on the Unskilled have a Significant Impact on Unemployment?', *Unemployment Policy: How*

Should Governments Respond to Unemployment?, (eds). Dennis J. Snower and Guillermo de la Dehesa, CEPR.

Nickell, Stephen and Brian Bell (1996), 'Changes in the Distribution of Wages and Unemployment in OECD Countries', *American Economic Review*, **86**, 302-308.

Nickell, Stephen (1996), *The Collapse in Demand for the Unskilled: What Can be Done?*, paper prepared for the conference on Demand-Side Strategies and Low-Wage Labor Markets on the 26-27 June 1995 in New York.

Parmentier, Klaus et al. (1996), 'Beschaftigungssituation und -perspektiven von Hochschulabsolventen', *Arbeitspapier*, Institut fur Arbeitsmarkt- und Berufsforschung, Nurnberg.

Phelps, Edmund S. (1994), *Structural Slumps*, Harvard University Press, Cambridge Ma.

Sachs, Jeffrey D. and Howard J. Shatz (1994), 'Trade and Jobs in U.S. Manufacturing', *Brookings Papers on Economic Activity*, **1**, 1-69.

Saint-Paul, Gilles (1994), 'Unemployment, Wage Rigidity, and the Returns to Education', *European Economic Review*, **38**, 535-43.

Shapiro, Carl and Joseph Stiglitz (1984), 'Equilibrium Unemployment as a Worker Discipline Device', *American Economic Review*, **74**, 433-44.

Wood, Adrian (1994), *North-South Trade, Employment and Inequality: Changing Fortunes in a Skill Driven World*, Clarendon Press, Oxford.

van Ark, Bart (1990), 'Comparative Levels of Manufacturing Productivity in Postwar Europe: Measurement and Comparisons', *Oxford Bulletin of Economics and Statistics*, **52**, 343-73.

APPENDIX

Sources of Data

1. Unemployment rates and labour force.
Source: Canada; Statistics Canada, France; INSEE, Germany; Institute for Employment Research and the Central Statistical Office, Italy; ISTAT, UK; General Household Survey, US; Bureau of Labor Statistics.
2. Direct taxes.
The ratio of direct taxes to total household income. Source: OECD.
3. Social security contributions.
The ratio of social security contributions to the total private sector wage bill. Source: OECD.
4. GDP deflators.
Source: International Financial Statistics.
5. Price of oil.
Ratio of US PPI for crude petroleum to overall US PPI. Source: Robert Barro.
6. Youth unemployment.
The rate of unemployment for workers between 15 and 24 years of age. Source: Labour Force Statistics, various issues.
7. Public employment.

Public employment as a percentage of total employment. Source: OECD, Public Management Development Report.

8. Public spending.

Source: OECD National Accounts and the SIPRI Yearbook, various issues.

9. Manufacturing employment.

Share of manufacturing in civilian employment Source: OECD Labour Force Statistics, various issues.

10. Labour productivity in manufacturing.

Hours per man-hour in manufacturing. Source: Bureau of Labor Statistics and Bart van Ark (1990).

11. World Real Rate of Interest.

The weighted average of real interest rates in the G7 using PPP-adjusted GDP as weights. These are Treasury Bill rates for all countries except France and Japan, where money market rates are used. Source: Robert Barro.

11. Labor Incentives and Manumission in Ancient Greek Slavery

Stanley L. Engerman[1]

I.

Slavery has been one of the most widespread and enduring of all human institutions, existing in almost all nations, going back to earliest known history, and persisting into the twenty-first century.[2] There were certain common characteristics in most cases of slavery: slaves were generally regarded as outsiders, coming from a different social groups than those owning the slaves; slaves were frequently military captives; and they were often used to provide labor on large-scale units in agriculture and mining, labor not generally performed willingly by free labor. There were also many similarities in debates about the role of slavery in different societies such as the morality of slave ownership; the treatment of slaves; the possibilities for slaves to obtain freedom; the relative productivity of slave and free labor; and the ability to influence the productivity of slave labor by the judicious use of punishments and rewards.

The most distinguished of twentieth-century scholars of ancient slavery, Sir Moses Finley, has described what he considered to be the major slave societies of the ancient and modern worlds.[3] In these societies, he argues, not only were slaves a significant proportion of the population, but the entire social, legal, political, and economic system was strongly influenced by the presence of slavery. The Greeks were the first of the major slave societies, followed by the Romans, and then, centuries later, Brazil, the Caribbean, and the United States South. In the case of the Greeks, it is estimated that slaves accounted for one-third of the total population, roughly the same proportion as in Rome, Brazil, and the United States. The islands of the non-Spanish Caribbean were an unusual case, with the slaves representing over 90 per cent of the population. Given that Greece was a major slave power, many of the problems that were to confront later slave societies were first dealt with by the Greeks, often in a quite sophisticated manner, and they influenced subsequent treatment of these problems.

In this paper, I will discuss two related economic issues relating to slavery, problems that have existed in most slave societies. One is the question of incentives to labor in a system where coercion presumably was not consistent with any positive incentives or with differential rewards to laborers. Second, is the issue of manumission, the freeing of individual slaves, the means of its accomplishment, and what roles were performed by the newly freed within society. Manumissions were granted in a number of different ways: as a gift from owners, or by the states; they may have required payments by either the slave or by others on his or her behalf, but with master approval granted. As we shall see, the problems of incentives and manumissions are related since the opportunity to be manumitted was generally based on the behavior and work performance of the slave.

II.

Perhaps the most frequently quoted remark on the issue of incentives to slave labor has been that of Adam Smith in *The Wealth of Nations*. Smith contended that slave labor was relatively inefficient because the slaves were lacking incentives. The incomes of slaves were not related to either their inputs and/or their outputs, since whatever the slaves were to be given to consume was provided by their masters. Smith claimed 'that the work done by slaves, though it appears to cost only their maintenance, is in the end the dearest of any. A person who can acquire no property, can have no other interest but to eat as much, and to labour as little as possible'. And 'a slave...who can acquire nothing but his maintenance, consults his own ease by making the land produce as little as possible over and above that maintenance'.[4]

The problem of incentives was, of course, not unique to slavery, serfdom, and other forms of coerced labor. Rather, anyone using labor will be concerned with obtaining desired amounts of work effort and labor intensity. Indeed the same argument concerning the relative productivity of slave and free labor was used by the Scotch economist, James Anderson, to proclaim the advantages of piece wages over time-based wages.[5]

As presented Smith's remark indicates how little he had learned about plantation operations. All planters knew about the need for incentives, positive as well as negative, and often provided benefits such as more food, cash payments, time-off from labor, travel passes, and related rewards, each of which could be done on an individual basis. Many of the guides aimed at planters as well as various contemporary newspapers and journals included advice and

opinions on slave management. Actually, Smith did discuss the better management of their slaves by the French planters in the West Indies compared to
the British, attributing this mainly to the greater protection of slaves by the
magistrate in countries where the rule is arbitrary rather than free.[6] Thus he
did acknowledge some systematic differences in the management of slaves
and resulting differences in their output.

There are differences in the incentive schemes aimed at slaves and those
aimed at free persons. The use of coercion and of incentives were aimed at
solving two different, albeit related, problems for users of labor. The first is
the attraction of labor to a specific workplace location. The second is, once
individuals are in a workplace, how can they be induced to become highly
productive workers. The first of these, given the disutility of certain occupations and locations, can lead to coercion and slavery, as free workers were not
willing to undertake certain types of work or to live in certain climates or
locations. The second problem, incentives to produce, provides some similarities for slave and free. These points were noted by several Greek writers
who discussed some proposed solutions.

Incentives based on providing rewards in the long-run were proposed by
Xenophon and by Aristotle, both of whom suggested that there were similar
problems for all labor, slave and free. Xenophon, for example, claimed that:[7]

> Slaves need some good things to look forward to no less, in fact, even more than
> free men so that they may be willing to stay.

And Aristotle argued that:[8]

> Every slave should have before his eyes a definite goal or term of his labour. To set
> the prize of freedom before him is both just and expedient; since having a prize to
> work for, and a time defined for its attainment, he will put his heart into his la-
> bours. We should, moreover, take hostages (for our slaves' fidelity) by allowing
> them to beget children; and avoid the practice of purchasing many slaves of the
> same nationality, as men avoid doing in towns. We should also keep festivals and
> give treats, more on the slaves' account than on that of the freemen; since the free
> have a fuller share in those enjoyments for the sake of which these institutions
> exist.

Xenophon also had proposed an ingenious system of providing incentives to
slaves in the short-term, relating consumption to productivity even when payments were made in kind. He also compared the teaching of slaves unlike that
of free workers, with the training of wild animals:[9]

> And in the case of human beings it is possible to make them more obedient merely
> by talking to them, pointing out that it is to their advantage to obey. But for slaves

the method of training that is accepted for wild animals is very effective in teaching obedience. For if you gratify their desires by filling their bellies, you may get a great deal out of them. Those who are naturally ambitious become even keener with praise; for some natures hunger for praise as much as others do for food and drink. These methods, then, are exactly the ones that I use myself, because I believe that I shall have more obedient people in my employ as a result, and I teach them to those I wish to appoint as foremen. And I also help them in the following ways: I make sure that the clothing and the shoes which I must supply for the workers are not identical, but some are of inferior quality, and others superior, so that I can reward the better workers with superior garments and give the inferior ones to the less deserving. For Socrates', he continued, 'I'm convinced that good workers become very discouraged when they see that although they have done all the work, nevertheless those who are unwilling to work or, when necessary, to run risks, earn rewards equal to their own. I, myself, then, by no means think that better workers should receive the same treatment as worthless ones. And when I know that the foremen have distributed the best things to the most deserving workers, I praise them; but when I see someone favored beyond the rest as a result of flattery or some other worthless service, I am not unconcerned, but I reprimand the foreman, and try to teach him, Socrates, that favouritism is not beneficial, not even to himself.

More general is the argument that the best way to insure high output is for the master to be kind and reasonable. Plato's proposal for avoiding the various troublesome aspects of slavery was:[10]

Two remedies alone remain to us – not to have the slaves of the same country, nor if possible, speaking the same language; in this way they will more easily be held in subjection: secondly, we should tend them carefully, not only out of regard to them, but yet more out of respect to ourselves. And the right treatment of slaves is to behave properly to them, and to do to them, if possible, even more justice than to those who are our equals; for he who naturally and genuinely reverences justice, and hates injustices, is discovered in his dealings with any class of men to whom he can easily be unjust. And he who in regard to the natures and actions of his slaves is undefiled by impiety and injustice, will best sow the seeds of virtue in them; and this may be truly said of every master, and tyrant, and of every other having authority in relation to his inferiors. Slaves ought to be punished as they deserve, and not admonished as if they were freedmen, which will only make them conceited. The language used to a servant ought always to be that of command, and we ought not to jest with them, whether they are males or females – this is a foolish way which many people have of setting up their slaves, and making the life of servitude more disagreeable both for them and for their masters.

Xenophon offered similar general advice to the estate-manager, pointing to the need for both rewards and punishments:[11]

And when the master shows that he lacks concern, it is difficult for a slave to be concerned. In short, I don't think I've ever come across a bad master with good slaves: on the other hand I've seen bad slaves belonging to a good master; however they, at least, didn't escape punishment. But the master who wants to make his men be concerned must be in the habit of supervising their work and inspecting it, be prepared to reward any slave who is responsible for work that's well performed, and not hesitant to impose the due punishment on any slave who lacks concern. 'I think' he added, 'that the well known reply of the foreigner is very relevant: I mean, when the king had acquired a good horse and wanted to fatten him up as quickly as he could, he asked one of those who had a reputation as an expert on horses 'What fattens a horse most quickly?' They say that he replied, 'his master's eye.' This applies to everything, I think, Socrates: the master's eye produces beautiful and good work.'

Aristotle's advice contains elements of several different elements, and he was quite aware of the problems of incentives and of coercion:[12]

In our intercourse with slaves we must neither suffer them to be insolent nor treat them with cruelty. A share of honour should be given to those who are doing more of a freeman's work, and abundance of food to those who are labouring with their hands. And whereas the use of wine renders even free men insolent, so that in may countries they too refrain from it – as, for instance, the Carthaginians do when they are on campaign – it follows that we must either deny wine to slaves altogether, or reserve it for rare occasions.

We may apportion to our slaves (1) work, (2) chastisement, and (3) food. If men are given food, but no chastisement nor any work, they become insolent. If they are made to work, and are chastised, but stinted of their food, such treatment is oppressive, and saps their strength. The remaining alternative, therefore, is to give them work, and a sufficiency of food. Unless we pay men, we cannot control them; and food is a slave's pay.

Slaves, again, are no exception to the rule that men become worse when better conduct is not followed by better treatment, but virtue and vice remain alike unrewarded. Accordingly, we must keep watch over our workers, suiting our dispensations and indulgences, to their desert; whether it be food or clothing, leisure or chastisement that we are apportioning. Both in theory and in practice we must take for our model a physician's freedom in prescribing his medicines; observing at the same time that food differs from medicine in that it requires to be constantly administrated.

These excerpts present a short guide to the ideas of slave management that were advocated by leading Greek philosophers.[13] They may bear little relationship to actual practice, but they do indicate that there was some awareness of the problems of slave management and the need for incentives considerably before the arguments presented on this question by Adam Smith. It also shows that even though a slave was considered to be an outsider to Greek society, and could be regarded as 'a living tool', 'a tame animal', or 'a slave by nature', clearly there was a belief in the slave's humanity and the ability to respond to the manner of treatment accorded him.

III.

Until the late eighteenth century there were no sustained political or intellectual attacks on slavery as a system, certainly none that led to the legal emancipation of all of the enslaved.[14] While there were no movements leading to the freeing of all slaves in an area, whether for political, moral, or economic reasons, yet all slave societies did recognize the rights of individual slaves to be manumitted and to obtain their own freedom. Manumissions were granted with the permission of the slave's owner, and were recognized by other members of society as changing the legal status and rights of those formerly enslaved. There was considerable variation in the terms of manumission and the time in which freedom would be recognized. Some manumissions were granted by the state, usually for military and other services but most were granted by private owners. Some manumissions meant immediate freedom, some deferred. Some manumissions were conditional on other events or patterns of behavior, some unconditional. In some cases manumissions were granted, free of cost, to the slaves, but in many cases the right to manumission meant the right to purchase yourself by payments to the slaveowners.[15] While the price to be paid could be subject to negotiation, in describing manumission in ancient Greece, the French historian Yvon Garlan states that it was 'a price that presumably corresponded roughly to the market value of the slave'.[16]

As described above, manumissions were frequently a purchase, by the slave of him- or herself from the slaveowner, not a gift or grant to the slave. And, based upon a study of Delphi from 201 BC to 1 BC, by Keith Hopkins, prices did increase over time, and they differed systematically by age and gender of the manumitted.[17] As in most other slave societies, more females than males were manumitted, and more adults than children. Prices for full freedom for adult females were about 80 percent those for adult males, girls were evaluated at lower prices than boys, while the female-male price ratio was higher for children than for adults, and children were generally worth about one-half the value of adult males. Those ratios resemble those found for later slave societies. Given the time required to earn sufficient funds for self-purchase, manumissions tended to be disproportionately at higher ages.

Manumission provisions did exist in most slave societies, although their numbers and importance varied depending on a variety of factors. In some places manumission was held out as a form of incentive to the slaves, as discussed above, with the possibility of purchasing oneself leading to labor in occupations in which it was possible to earn sufficient money, either for increased consumption or to save for subsequent emancipation. In the Americas, the Catholic colonies of Spain and Portugal had higher manumission rates than did the Protestant colonies of Great Britain and the United States.[18] This reflected some difference in religious beliefs and practices, but it may also have been influenced by economic differentials. High slave prices generally meant that self-purchase was more expensive, and would require more time and/or effort to earn the money needed for the transaction. Slave earnings were, however, related to slave prices, and the basic relationship between the level of slave prices and manumission rates is not obvious. In general, however, manumission rates have been argued to have been higher in places where slavery had been less profitable and slave prices lower. In a model to explain manumissions, based on Sir Alfred Zimmern's discussion of Greek slavery, Ronald Findlay points to the trade-off of costs of supervision and costs of incentive payments.[19] The ability to purchase oneself could be based on prior savings by the slave, including loans from associations established for that purpose. All of this implies some set of legal arrangements which protected some rights of the enslaved.

The size of the urban sector in Athens indicated that agriculture was sufficiently productive to feed city populations. Greek slavery demonstrates a point made by the first major theorist of slavery, H.J. Neiboer, the early twentieth-century Dutch ethnographer.[20] Poor, unproductive societies would not have a well-developed slavery, since there was little surplus above subsistence to justify large-scale ownership of other people. For slavery to be important a surplus to be captured by slaveowners was necessary. Thus the presence of a large number of slaves indicates a relatively rich, not a poor, society consistent with direct evidence about the Greek economy.

The granting of manumission was often encouraged within slave societies, and it was considered to be an indication of the goodness of the slaveowners. Some have argued that manumissions leading to a free ex-slave population represented a basic contradiction and an ultimate threat, ideologically and militarily to the slave societies. Nevertheless, the frequency with which manumissions occurred and the lack of any relation between rates of manumission and the timing of legal emancipations ending slavery suggests that whatever role manumission played, it was consistent with the maintenance of slave societies. As noted above, rates of manumissions in the New World colonies of the Iberian nations exceeded that of the British and French colonies, as well as of the United States. Yet Cuba and Brazil were the last two countries in the New World to experience emancipation, about 50 years after the British had ended slavery. The British, as did many other nations, had emancipation with compensation paid to slaveowners in cash or labor time. The payments of cash were, however, not paid by the slaves, who did pay in part by extended labor, but by the governments. While individual manumissions were paid for by the slaves, this cash payment was seldom discussed as a policy for slave and serf emancipation. Prior to legislated emancipation in 1863, the Dutch had proposed a program under which slaves would pay cash for their freedom, but this was not undertaken. Haitian ex-slaves, several decades after their successful revolution, were made to compensate the French for their loss of slaves, but this was done as part of a bargain for recognition and trading rights. In many cases, however, emancipation was delayed, the slaves being required to work a number of years after the legislation to both be educated for work in a new labor system and to provide some income to slaveowners that would otherwise had been lost with immediate emancipation.

In Greek society, as in later societies, there was some variation in the rights provided to the freed slave. In some societies manumitted slaves were given the same rights as those already free, while in others they had limited rights, the state not granting them full citizenship so that they became in effect wards of the state or of their former owners. Since Greek society did not necessarily grant rights of citizenship upon emancipation, there were limits to the maintaining of freedom and the extent to which it differed from slave status. Nevertheless, since there were apparently few cases of freemen reselling themselves to become slaves again, it may be presumed that freedom, however limited, was a preferred status.

The discussions of manumission indicates that freedom provided an important incentive to slave labor, a point clear to the enslaved and to the slaveowners. The fact that many manumissions were not by gift but by self-purchase suggests that Greek society was willing to put a price on freedom, and that bargaining over this price was allowed. Slaves could be permitted to buy themselves, free people could buy slaves from other free people, and slave-produced commodities that were sold in markets. Clearly market forces played some role in the ancient Greek economy.

NOTES

1.   Much that I know about Greek slavery I learned from sitting in on a course on 'Slavery', taught by Paul Cartledge and Walter Scheidel at the University of Cambridge, Michaelmas term 1998. I have further benefited from reading several books and numerous articles by Paul Cartledge relating to Greek slavery.
2.   For a recent collection of readings on slavery with bibliographic information, see Stanley L. Engerman, Seymour Drescher, and Robert Paquette (eds), *Slavery* (Oxford: Oxford University

Press, 2001.)

3.   Moses I. Finley, *Ancient Slavery and Modern Ideology* (expanded edition; Princeton: Markus Weiner: 1998), 147-148. See Keith Hopkins, *Conquerors and Slaves* (Cambridge: Cambridge University Press, 1978), 100-101. Both included Cuba as the only Caribbean area, it having a share of slaves equal to 30 per cent of the population, an amount comparable to the other four areas listed. The exclusion of the French, British, Dutch, and Danish West Indies, with slave shares of 80 to 90 percent is not fully explained, but was perhaps due to their being (as, however, was Cuba) colonies and not independent nations.

4.   Adam Smith, *The Wealth of Nations* (Oxford: Oxford University Press, 1976; 1st published in 1776). The quotes are from p. 387 and p. 389.

5.   James Anderson, *Observations on Slavery* (Manchester: J. Harrap, 1789), pp. 7-11.

6.   Smith, pp. 586-588.

7.   Xenophon, *Oeconomica: A Social and Historical Commentary*, tr. Sarah Pomeroy (Oxford: Clarendon Press, 1995), p. 133.

8.   Aristotle, *Oeconomica*, tr. C. Cyril Armstrong (Cambridge, MA: Harvard University Press, 1962), p. 339.

9.   Xenophon, pp. 177-179.

10.   Plato, 'Laws', in *The Dialogues of Plato*, tr. B. Jowett (4th edition; Oxford: Clarendon Press, 1953), **IV**, pp. 345-346.

11.   Xenophon, p. 175.

12.   Aristotle, pp. 335-339.

13.   For other excerpts from the writings of contemporaries on all aspects of Greek slavery, see Peter Garnsey, *Ideas of Slavery from Aristotle to Augustine* (Cambridge: Cambridge University Press, 1996). On a related issue, at a later time, Salvian, Bishop of Marseilles in the mid-fifth century anticipates current approaches to slavery by arguing: 'If slaves obey their masters according to their own judgement they are not obedient even when they obey. When a slave performs only those of his master's commands which he likes to perform, he is not following his master's will, but his own' (pp. 71-72). See also Thomas Weidemann, *Greek and Roman Slavery* (Baltimore: The Johns Hopkins University Press, 1981), particularly pp. 122-153, which includes Roman works.

14.   See the works of David Brion Davis, particularly *The Problem of Slavery in Western Culture* (Ithaca: Cornell University Press, 1966).

15.   For a wide-ranging survey of manumission in many slave societies, see Orlando Patterson, *Slavery and Social Death* (Cambridge, MA: Harvard University Press, 1982), pp. 209-296.

16.   Yvon Garlan, *Slavery in Ancient Greece* (revised and expanded edition; Ithaca: Cornell University Press, 1988), pp. 73-84. On Greek manumission see also N.R.E. Fisher, Slavery in Classical Greece (Bristol: Bristol Classical Press, 1993), pp. 67-70. See also pp. 65-66 on incentives.

17.   Hopkins, pp. 133-171.

18.   See the classic work of Frank Tannenbaum *Slave and Citizen* (New York: Vintage Books, 1946).

19.   Ronald Findlay, 'Slavery, Incentives, and Manumission: A Theoretical Model', *Journal of Political Economy*, **83** (October 1975) pp. 923-933. See also Alfred Zimmern *Solon and Croesus* (London: Oxford University Press, 1928) Chapters 4 and 5.

20.   H.J. Nieboer, *Slavery As An Industrial System* (The Hague: Martinus Nijhoff, 1910).

PART IV

Game Theory and Applications

12. Agency Games

Neelam Jain[†] and Leonard J. Mirman[‡]

1. INTRODUCTION

In this chapter, we study the effect of information in a simple principal-agent model. This is done by comparing several models with different market structures involving Cournot competition between firms in which at least one of the firms is in an agency relationship. To provide a benchmark, we also present the typical agency model in which the agent is a monopolist. The models presented here differ from each other not only in terms of their market structure but also in terms of their informational structure. In particular, different agents are assumed to possess different information in the various models. Indeed, the purpose of this paper is to examine the effect of these informational differences on the equilibrium contract, especially the effect that information has on the outputs of the different types of agents. In the process, we apply some of the results in this paper to the problem of non-linear pricing. In particular, we provide a simple duopoly version of non-linear pricing.

The motivation for this paper comes from the work of Jain, Jeitschko and Mirman (JJM), who, in a series of papers (JJM1, JJM2 and JJM3), study the effect of entry in the context of an agency relationship. One of the more important aspects of these models is the effect of information on the contract that a principal (a bank) offers to an agent (a firm with costs unknown to the principal), when the latter faces a threat of entry. These papers show that the informational aspects of the model, as well as the assumptions about the beliefs of the entrant, play an important role in determining the equilibrium contract, especially since the information is important for the second period contract. While JJM focus on the specific effects of potential entry on the equilibrium contract between the incumbent and the lender and vice-versa, a

† Jones Graduate School of Management, Rice University, MS#531, PO Box 1892, Houston, TX 77251-1892. Tel: 713-348-5392, Fax: 713-348-5251, Email: jain@rice.edu
‡ Department of Economics, University of Virginia, 114 Rouss Hall, Charlottesville, VA 22903. Tel: 804-924-6756, Fax: 804-982-2904, Email: lm8h@virginia.edu

general feature of all three papers, introduced first in JJM1, is the notion of a game in the second period of the dynamic agency problem. Indeed, there are several results in these papers that are due to the specific structure of a game within an agency relationship and not due to the dynamic nature of these models. Thus, these results transcend the questions addressed by JJM and are interesting in their own right. In this chapter, we develop these results further and explore implications of agency models with games in several different settings.

JJM1 assumes that demand is non-stochastic. This assumption implies that at the end of the first period, there is perfect information revelation since the output of the firm is either observable or can be deduced from the separating contract. Thus, all information is revealed for the second period. In contrast, in JJM2 and JJM3, the relationship between entry and the agency problem is studied under the assumption that the output of the firm is not observable and cannot be deduced. To do this, noise that hides the actions of the firms is introduced in the demand function.

Information, which becomes significant in the presence of noise, has an important effect on the results in this integrated agency-game model. While JJM1 (with non-stochastic demand) also has a game in the second period, the effect of perfect information revelation is that the two possible markets are segmented. In contrast, in JJM2 and JJM3, the existence of a game changes the outputs of both agents, as determined by the principal. In particular, the good agent no longer produces the first best level even if the notion of the first best level is made consistent with Cournot equilibrium. This is significant since in a standard agency problem, the good type agent is always required by the principal to produce the efficient or first best output and is offered a rent in order to induce this firm to self-select. The reason for this change is simple. In the standard agency relationships, the markets – or quantities – of the different types of firms are segmented. However in JJM2 and JJM3, the two markets are not segmented due to the informational assumption made, namely that the competitor firm knows only what the principal knows. Indeed, the output of the competitor connects the two markets. Thus the outputs of all the firms – the competitor and the two types of agents – are determined simultaneously.

This chapter explores the extension of this result by analyzing several models based on different informational assumptions and market structures. It is the purpose of this paper to study the effect of information on the optimal contract in the simplest setting. In order to do this, we present four variants of a simple example and show how different informational assumptions affect the solution of the agency-game problem. This is done in the context of a simple market in which the principal may be thought of as a bank – in the spirit of the JJM papers – and the agent is a firm that borrows from it. In contrast to the JJM papers, in this chapter only the static case is considered. In this static model the competitor is assumed to be in the market and thus entry is not an issue. Another difference between the model here and the model in the JJM papers has to do with the object of the informational asymmetry. While in the JJM papers, the unknown parameter is the cost of production, here the unknown parameter is the intercept of the demand function. This is done for simplicity. We assume that the intercept of the demand function is unknown to the principal but known to the agent.[1] We refer to the high intercept as the good market and the low intercept as the bad market.

As a benchmark, the first model assumes that the two possible agents are monopolists in their markets. This model represents the typical adverse selection agency problem (see Harris and Townsend, 1981, and Laffont and Tirole, 1993, for example). Thus the usual results apply for the separating equilibrium. That is, the good agent produces its most efficient output (i.e., its first best output) and the bad agent produces less than the first best level. In order to give the good agent an incentive to produce the first best, it receives a rent which forces the low type to produce less than its first best.

The second and the third models assume that the agent competes with another firm in a Cournot setting. However, the informational assumptions in these models differ. In the second model, it is assumed that the competitor and the agent have the same information, so that both the competitor and the agent know the intercept of the demand function. In the separating equilibrium in this informational structure, the two markets are segmented – as in the monopoly case. While the agent continues to produce the first best Cournot output in the good market, an interesting effect arises. The existence of a competitor affects the rent payment to the good agent and thus affects the output of the bad agent. Of course, the profits of all the agents are also affected.

In the third model, we assume that the competitor has the same information as the principal, so that the competitor does not know the value of the demand intercept (as in the papers of JJM discussed above). It is further assumed, in this context, that the competitor has the same beliefs about the unknown parameter as the principal. The results are different from the usual agency models as well as from the second model. Indeed, in this case it is no longer optimal for the principal to set the output of the good agent at the first best level. This is due to the fact that the information structure no longer implies that the markets are segmented, as in the first two models. In this case, the markets are connected through the reaction curve of the competitor, since the competitor does not know the value of the demand intercept and, therefore, must produce the same output in both markets. The competitor's output depends on his expectations of the outputs of the two types of agents. Thus, the first best output of the good agent cannot be supported in the Cournot equilibrium. Again, this result leads to a change in the rents paid to the good agent and the output of the bad agent, as well as the profits of all agents.

In the fourth and last model, we analyze the case in which there are two principals, each having their informed agents compete in a Cournot game. That is, we add a second principal to the second model described above. We show that the markets remain segmented and both agents produce the first best level of output in the good market and less than the first best level in the bad market. We also show that the rents and payments to the principals are affected by the addition of the other agency relationship. Finally, we show how an agency contract is similar to non-linear pricing. First, the benchmark monopoly model is reinterpreted to correspond to a Disneyland monopoly model of Oi, 1971. For example, the principal is now interpreted as the monopolist charging an entry fee and a marginal price to the two types of consumers. Using this interpretation, we apply the fourth model to provide a simple example of the duopoly version of non-linear pricing.

In each model, we calculate the difference in outputs of the two types of agents as a measure of the effect of asymmetric information between the principal and the agent. Interestingly, we find that this difference is identical between the benchmark monopoly model and the third model in which the competitor has the same information and beliefs as the principal. The intuition is simple. Since the uninformed competitor produces the same output regardless of the market, the agent's rent in the good market is only a function of his output in the bad market, just as in the monopoly model. Hence the outputs in the good and the bad market are set equally apart. On the other hand, in the second model, where the competitor has the same information as the agent and the markets are segmented, the principal sets the outputs apart by a different amount. In fact, the outputs are set closer compared to the monopoly and the uninformed duopoly model. Finally, in the fourth model, the outputs are set closer than in the informed duopoly model if the probability of bad market is not as 'high'. However, the output difference is less compared to the monopoly model and the uninformed duopoly model.

The chapter is organized as follows: in section 2, we present the model; in section 2.1 we present the monopoly model, in section 2.2, we present the informed duopoly model, section 2.3 contains the uninformed duopoly model, section 2.4 contains the two-principal-two-agent model, and finally in 2.4.1, we lay out the analysis of non-linear pricing for the monopoly and the duopoly cases.

2. THE MODEL

Consider a model in which there is Cournot competition between two competitors. The market is characterized by a demand curve, $\alpha - bq + \varepsilon = p$. Here p is the market price and q is the quantity or output. The slope, $b > 0$ and the intercept $\alpha \in [\overline{\alpha}, \underline{\alpha}]$. Here, $\overline{\alpha}$ is the good type (market) and $\underline{\alpha}$ is the bad type (market). ε is a random variable with mean 0 and density $f(\varepsilon)$. It is assumed that one of the competitors is in an agency relationship with a principal. The principal does not know the value of the intercept, α, i.e., the type of the market, but the agent does. The other duopolist in the model may or may not know the value of intercept parameter. It is further assumed, for the sake of simplicity, that both firms can produce the outputs with no costs. This is a static model and we study only a separating equilibrium.

It is further assumed that the principal believes that the market is bad with probability and good with probability $1 - \rho$. The objective of the principal is to design a contract that maximizes its expected profits and yields an incentive for each of its possible client firms to produce the amount that the principal intends for that firm. This contract must pay each firm enough so that both produce, i.e., the individual rationality constraint must be satisfied. Finally, each firm must produce the amount intended for that firm i.e., they must self-select. It is assumed that the normal profits for this industry are zero, so the individually rational profits are zero. Further we focus on expected repayments from each type of agent, $\overline{R}$ and $\underline{R}$ [2] rather than the repayment schedule for each observed price. [3]

In order to set ideas and to facilitate comparisons, we study four models based on different market structures and different informational structures. The purpose is to study the effects of market structure and information on equilibrium outputs and pay offers. In the first subsection, we study the simple case when there is only a monopolist in the market. This monopolist is assumed to be the agent of the principal.

2.1. Monopoly

The objective of the principal is to choose payments $\overline{R}$ and $\underline{R}$ to maximize the expected revenue generated by the contract, i.e., $(1 - \rho)\overline{R} + \rho\underline{R}$. Using standard arguments it follows that only the individual rationality constraint of the 'bad' agent binds and only the incentive compatibility constraint of the 'good' agent binds. Hence, the profits of the bad firm are,

$$\underline{R} = (\underline{\alpha} - b\underline{q})\underline{q} \,,$$

while the binding incentive compatibility constraint is,

$$(\overline{\alpha} - b\overline{q})\overline{q} - \overline{R} = (\overline{\alpha} - b\underline{q})\,\underline{q} - \underline{R} \,.$$

Here in order to deceive the principal into believing that it is the bad firm, the good firm must produce $\underline{q}$. Hence, the expected profits of the principal are,

$$\rho(\underline{\alpha} - b\underline{q})\underline{q} + (1 - \rho)\left[(\overline{\alpha} - b\overline{q})\overline{q} - (\overline{\alpha} - b\underline{q})\underline{q} + (\underline{\alpha} - b\underline{q})\underline{q}\right]$$

or

$$\rho(\underline{\alpha} - b\underline{q})\underline{q} + (1 - \rho)\left[(\overline{\alpha} - b\overline{q})\overline{q} - (\overline{\alpha} - \underline{\alpha})\underline{q}\right].$$

The first order condition with respect to $\overline{q}$ is,

$$\overline{\alpha} - 2b\overline{q} = 0$$

i.e.,

$$\overline{q} = \frac{\overline{\alpha}}{2b} \,.$$

This is the usual condition requiring the good type agent to produce the first best monopoly output. Next, the first order condition with respect to $\underline{q}$,

$$\rho(\underline{\alpha} - 2b\underline{q}) - (1 - \rho)(\overline{\alpha} - \underline{\alpha}) = 0 \,, \tag{2.1}$$

which yields the following output for the bad type firm,

$$\underline{q} = \frac{\underline{\alpha}}{2b} - \frac{(1 - \rho)(\overline{\alpha} - \underline{\alpha})}{2\rho b} \,, \tag{2.2}$$

where the appropriate assumptions on $\underline{\alpha}$, $\overline{\alpha}$ and ρ are made in order to ensure that $\underline{q} > 0$.

Proposition 1. *The agent produces the first best level in the good market and less than the first best level in the bad market.*

This is the usual result, that the principal makes the bad firm decrease its output from the monopoly level, reducing its profits. The principal, in order to reduce the bad firm's rents to zero, while at the same time allowing the good firm a rent in order to self-select and produce its efficient output, chooses the output for the bad firm as in equation 2.2. An interesting measure of the effect of the informational difference between the principal and the agent is the difference between the two output levels, $\overline{q}$ and $\underline{q}$. If the true value of the intercept term α is known then the difference between the two outputs is simply, $\dfrac{\overline{\alpha}}{2b} - \dfrac{\underline{\alpha}}{2b}$ but with the principal imposing a self-selection condition the difference becomes,

$$\overline{q} - \underline{q} = \frac{\overline{\alpha}}{2b} - \frac{\underline{\alpha}}{2b} + \frac{(1-\rho)(\overline{\alpha} - \underline{\alpha})}{2\rho b} \tag{2.3}$$

2.2. Informed Competitor

In this subsection, we allow a second firm in the market. This firm again, for simplicity, has no costs. It is also not entered into an agency relationship. It makes its output decisions in order to maximize its profits. However there are now two scenarios concerning the information of this firm. Specifically, it could have the information that its competitive firm has – it knows the value of the intercept term. Second, it knows as much as the principal and, in this case, it has the same beliefs as the principal. In this subsection it is assumed that the Cournot competitor knows the true state of the market, i.e., it knows the value of α. Let the quantity of the competitor be given by $\overline{q}_c$, if $\alpha = \overline{\alpha}$, and $\underline{q}_c$, if $\alpha = \underline{\alpha}$. The Cournot competitors compete in each market separately under this assumption. However, the introduction of a competitor has an important effect on the outputs of the firms (especially the 'bad' firms) as well as the payoffs to the firms and the principal. The objective of the principal is the same in this situation i.e., to maximize the expected revenue Cournot competition has an effect on the constraints of the two types of firms. The individual rationality constraint for the bad type, which remains binding, is now given by,

$$\underline{R} = (\underline{\alpha} - 2b\underline{q} - b\underline{q}_c)\underline{q}$$

and the incentive compatibility constraint for the good firm is,

$$(\overline{\alpha} - b\overline{q} - b\overline{q}_c)\overline{q} - \overline{R} = (\underline{\alpha} - b\underline{q} - b\underline{q}_c)\underline{q} - \underline{R}$$

which becomes,

$$\overline{R} = (\overline{\alpha} - b\overline{q} - b\overline{q}_c)\overline{q} + (\underline{\alpha} - b\underline{q} - b\underline{q}_c)\underline{q} - (\overline{\alpha} - b\underline{q} - b\overline{q}_c)\underline{q}$$

or,

$$\overline{R} = (\overline{\alpha} - b\overline{q} - b\overline{q}_c)\overline{q} - \left[(\overline{\alpha} - \underline{\alpha}) - b(\overline{q}_c - \underline{q}_c)\right]\underline{q}$$

Substituting the values of $\overline{R}$ and $\underline{R}$ in the expression for the expected revenue of the principal, the objective of the principal is to maximize,

$$\rho(\underline{\alpha} - b\underline{q} - b\underline{q}_c)\underline{q} + (1 - \rho)\left[(\overline{\alpha} - b\overline{q} - b\overline{q}_c)\overline{q} - \left[(\overline{\alpha} - \underline{\alpha}) - b(\overline{q}_c - \underline{q}_c)\right]\underline{q}\right]$$

The first order conditions are then,

$$\overline{\alpha} - 2b\overline{q} - b\overline{q}_c = 0, \tag{2.4}$$

and,

$$\rho(\underline{\alpha} - 2b\underline{q} - b\underline{q}_c) - (1 - \rho)\left[(\overline{\alpha} - \underline{\alpha}) - b(\overline{q}_c - \underline{q}_c)\right] = 0. \tag{2.5}$$

The reaction curves for the competitor firm, from the profit maximization for each state, for the good and the bad market, respectively, are,

$$\overline{\alpha} - b\overline{q} - 2b\overline{q}_c = 0 \tag{2.6}$$

and,

$$\underline{\alpha} - b\underline{q} - 2b\underline{q}_c = 0. \tag{2.7}$$

Since the markets are segmented, the equilibrium for each market is determined independently by solving the two pairs of equations, (2.4) and (2.6) for the good market and (2.5) and (2.7) for the bad market. Notice that the only effect of the agency solution is in the bad market because the agent firm is required to produce less in order to make the good firm self-select. Therefore, the competing firm could produce more (this is at least true for the most reasonable parameter values e.g., ρ near one). The reaction curves for the agent and its competitor, from (2.4) and (2.6) are, respectively,

$$\overline{\alpha} = 2b\overline{q} + 2b\overline{q}_c \,,$$

and

$$\overline{\alpha} = b\overline{q} + 2b\overline{q}_c$$

The outputs in the good market are then,

$$\overline{q} = \overline{q}_c = \frac{\overline{\alpha}}{3b} \qquad (2.8)$$

The reaction curves in the bad market from (2.5) and (2.7) are, respectively,

$$\underline{\alpha} = b\underline{q} + 2b\underline{q}_c$$

and, with $\overline{q}_c = \dfrac{\overline{\alpha}}{3b}$

$$\underline{\alpha} - \frac{2}{3}(1-\rho)\overline{\alpha} = 2\rho b\underline{q} + b\underline{q}_c \qquad (2.9)$$

Again the appropriate assumptions on $\underline{\alpha}$, $\overline{\alpha}$ and ρ are made in order to ensure that the right side of (2.9) is positive, in particular, $3\underline{\alpha} > 2\overline{\alpha}$. This yields,

$$\underline{q}_c = \frac{3(1-2\rho)\underline{\alpha} - 2(1-\rho)\overline{\alpha}}{3b(1-4\rho)} \qquad (2.10)$$

$$= \frac{\underline{\alpha}}{3b} - \frac{2(1-\rho)(\overline{\alpha} - \underline{\alpha})}{3b(1-4\rho)} \qquad (2.11)$$

and,

$$\underline{q} = \frac{4(1-2\rho)\overline{\alpha} - 3\underline{\alpha}}{3b(1-4\rho)} \qquad (2.12)$$

$$= \frac{\underline{\alpha}}{3b} - \frac{4(1-\rho)(\overline{\alpha} - \underline{\alpha})}{3b(1-4\rho)} \qquad (2.13)$$

The positivity of $\underline{q}_c$ and of the left-hand side of equation (2.9) together imply that $\rho > \dfrac{1}{4}$. Further, positivity of $\underline{q}$ and equation (2.9) imply that $\rho > \dfrac{1}{2}$. This leads to the following proposition:

Proposition 2. *The agent and the informed competitor produce the first best output in the good market. The agent produces less than the first best level whereas the competitor produces more than the first best output in the bad market.*

The results are intuitive. Since the two types of markets are segmented, the presence of an informed competitor has no effect on the nature of the contract offered by the principal. That is, the principal still requires the agent to produce the efficient (i.e. Cournot) output in the good market and less than the Cournot output in the bad market. Clearly, the informed competitor's output in the bad market is larger than the Cournot output since it is a decreasing function of the rival's output.

As in the case of monopoly an interesting measure of the effect of asymmetric information is the difference between the outputs for the two possible agent firms. This difference in this duopoly case, with the competitor knowing what the agent firm knows, is,

$$\bar{q} - \underline{q} = \frac{\bar{\alpha}}{3b} - \frac{\underline{\alpha}}{3b} - \frac{4(1-\rho)(\bar{\alpha} - \underline{\alpha})}{3b(1-4\rho)} \tag{2.14}$$

By $\rho > \frac{1}{4}$, this difference is positive. Further this difference is smaller than the one in monopoly.

Proposition 3. *When the competitor is informed, the principal sets the outputs of the agent in the bad market closer compared to the monopoly case.*

The intuition for this result has to do with how the presence of a rival affects the rent of the agent in the good market. From a comparison of equations (2.1) and (2.5), it follows that the marginal effect of $\underline{q}$ on the good agent's rent is reduced due to the presence of the informed competitor.[4]

Thus the distortion in $\underline{q}$ is reduced, resulting in a lower difference between the agent's outputs in the two types of market.

2.3. Uninformed Competitor

In this subsection, we consider the agency problem studied above but under the assumption that the competitor form does not have the information that the agent has but knows only what the principal knows. In this case suppose that the beliefs of the principal and the competitor are the same, i.e., ρ for the bad market and $1 - \rho$ for the good market. Since the competitor produces only one output under this scenario, regardless of the type of the market, let the competitor's output be denoted by q and let,

$$\hat{\alpha} = \rho\underline{\alpha} + (1 - \rho)\overline{\alpha} \text{ , and } \hat{q} = \rho\underline{q} + (1 - \rho)\overline{q}$$

The maximization problem for the competitor is,

$$\max_{q} \ (\hat{\alpha} - b\hat{q} - bq)q$$

with the corresponding first order condition,

$$\hat{\alpha} - b\hat{q} - 2bq = 0 \tag{2.15}$$

The maximization problem for the principal is the same as in the previous cases i.e., maximize $\rho\underline{R} + (1 - \rho)\overline{R}$. Here,

$$\underline{R} = (\underline{\alpha} - b\underline{q} - bq)\underline{q} \ ,$$

and,

$$\overline{R} = (\overline{\alpha} - b\overline{q} - bq)\overline{q} + (\underline{\alpha} - b\underline{q} - bq)\underline{q} - (\overline{\alpha} - b\underline{q} - bq)\underline{q} \ .$$

Hence, the principal chooses $\overline{q}$ and $\underline{q}$ to maximize,

$$\rho = (\underline{\alpha} - b\underline{q} - bq)\underline{q} + (1 - \rho)\left[(\overline{\alpha} - b\overline{q} - bq)\overline{q} + (\underline{\alpha} - b\underline{q} - bq)\underline{q} - (\overline{\alpha} - b\underline{q} - bq)\underline{q} \right]$$

or,

$$\rho(\underline{\alpha} - b\underline{q} - bq)\underline{q} + (1 - \rho)\left[(\overline{\alpha} - b\overline{q} - bq)\overline{q} + (\overline{\alpha} - \underline{\alpha})\underline{q} \right]$$

The first order conditions are,

$$\overline{\alpha} - 2b\overline{q} - bq = 0 \tag{2.16}$$

and,

$$\rho(\underline{\alpha} - 2b\underline{q} - bq) - (1 - \rho)(\overline{\alpha} - \underline{\alpha}) = 0 \tag{2.17}$$

The three equations (2.15), (2.16) and (2.17) must be solved simultaneously in order to determine the outputs q, $\overline{q}$ and $\underline{q}$. These are given by,

$$q = \frac{2(1-\rho)\overline{\alpha} + (2\rho-1)\underline{\alpha}}{3b}$$

$$= \frac{\hat{\alpha}}{3b} + \frac{(1-\rho)(\overline{\alpha} - \underline{\alpha})}{3b},$$

$$\overline{q} = \frac{(1+2\rho)\overline{\alpha} - (2\rho-1)\underline{\alpha}}{6b}$$

$$= \frac{\overline{\alpha}}{2b} - \frac{1}{6b}\left[2(1-\rho)\overline{\alpha} + (2\rho-1)\underline{\alpha}\right]$$

$$= \frac{\overline{\alpha}}{3b} + \frac{(2\rho-1)(\overline{\alpha} - \underline{\alpha})}{6b},$$

and, finally

$$\underline{q} = \frac{-(3+2\rho)(1-\rho)\overline{\alpha} + (3-2\rho)\underline{\alpha}}{6\rho b}$$

$$= \frac{\underline{\alpha}}{2b} - \frac{1}{6\rho b}\left[(3+2\rho)\overline{\alpha} - (3-2\rho)\rho\underline{\alpha}\right]$$

$$= \frac{\underline{\alpha}}{3b} + \frac{(3+2\rho)(1-\rho)(\overline{\alpha} - \underline{\alpha})}{6\rho b}.$$

Proposition 4. *When the market is bad, the agent produces less than the first best Cournot duopoly output, the uninformed rival produces more than the first best Cournot duopoly output, while in the good market, the agent no longer produces the first best output.*

This proposition shows the effect of information on outputs. In contrast to the monopoly and the informed competitor cases, here the agent in the good market does not produce the first best output. Thus the presence of a rival, in contrast to the informed competitor case, affects the nature of the contract offered by the principal to the agent by requiring the good agent to distort output. This result is due to the fact that the good and the bad markets are no longer segmented since the uninformed competitor must produce in response to the expected output in the two types of markets, thus connecting all outputs. Thus information of the rival matters.

Finally, the difference between $\bar{q}$ and $\underline{q}$ is given by,

$$\bar{q} - \underline{q} = \frac{\bar{\alpha}}{2b} - \frac{\underline{\alpha}}{2b} + \frac{(1-\rho)(\bar{\alpha} - \underline{\alpha})}{2\rho b},$$

$$= \frac{(\bar{\alpha} - \underline{\alpha})}{3b} + \frac{(3-2\rho)(\bar{\alpha} - \underline{\alpha})}{6\rho b}$$

Note that the first expression for the difference is the same as the monopoly case, given in equation (2.3). The intuition is simple. The uninformed competitor produces the same output regardless of the market. Thus the agent's rent from misrepresenting the size of the market does not depend on the competitor's output. Thus the difference between outputs of the agent in the two types of market remains the same although each output changes. The last expression can be used to study the effect that information has on the principal's choice of outputs by comparing it to the results contained in equation (2.14) for the informed competitor case.

Proposition 5. *In the uninformed duopoly, the principal sets the outputs of the agent as far apart as in the monopoly case and further apart than in the informed competitor case.*

Intuitively, as argued in the previous subsection, when the competitor is informed, his output is different in the two types of market. Thus the agent's rent from misrepresenting the intercept of the demand function depends not only on the output in the bad market but also on the difference in outputs of the competitor. Now since $\rho > \dfrac{1}{2}$, the competitor produces more in the good market than in the bad market. This in turn implies that the negative effect of $\bar{q}$ on the principal's profits is lower and, thus, the principal sets the outputs less apart than in the monopoly model.

2.4. Agency Duopoly

Finally, we consider the case of competition between two principals, each deriving a contract for an unknown agent, both operating in the same market. From an informational point of view, this case is similar to the monopoly case since both of the agents know the true value of the intercept parameter but the principals have (common) beliefs over the value of the intercept. On the other hand, the outputs do change in this example because both principals need to alter the output for the bad type market in order to make their agent self-select. The market structure is assumed to be exactly like the above markets. The objectives of the two principals are also the same, to maximize expected profits.

The maximization problem for the generic principal is,

$$\rho \underline{R}_i + (1-\rho)\overline{R}_i$$

$i = 1, 2$. Now,

$$\underline{R} = (\underline{\alpha} - b\underline{q}_i - b\underline{q}_j)\underline{q}_i$$

$i \neq j, i, j = 1, 2$, and,

$$\overline{R} = (\overline{\alpha} - b\overline{q}_i - b\overline{q}_j)\overline{q}_i + (\underline{\alpha} - b\underline{q}_i - b\underline{q}_j)\underline{q}_i - (\overline{\alpha} - b\underline{q}_i - b\overline{q}_j)\underline{q}_i$$

Again the markets are segmented. This is seen in the first order conditions for the good market,

$$\overline{\alpha} - 2b\overline{q}_i - b\overline{q}_j = 0,$$

$i, j = 1, 2. i \neq j$. Hence for the good market,

$$\overline{q}_1 = \overline{q}_2 = \frac{\overline{\alpha}}{3b}.$$

For the bad market the reaction curves are,

$$\underline{\alpha} - \frac{2}{3}(1-\rho)\overline{\alpha} = 2\rho b \underline{q}_i + b \underline{q}_j$$

$i, j = 1, 2, i \neq j$. Thus,

$$\underline{q}_1 = \underline{q}_2 = \frac{\underline{\alpha} - \frac{2}{3}(1-\rho)\overline{\alpha}}{(2\rho + 1)b}$$

$$= \frac{\underline{\alpha}}{3b} - \frac{2(1-\rho)(\overline{\alpha} - \underline{\alpha})}{3b(2\rho + 1)}$$

Proposition 6. *Both agents produce the first best Cournot output when the market is good and less than the first best when the market is bad. Further, each agent's output in the bad market is larger than in the case of the informed competitor.*

This result is interesting in that when the informed competitor is also an agent of a principal, its output in the bad market is lowered which in turn has a positive effect on the output of the other agent. In contrast, when the informed competitor is not entered into an agency relationship, its best response to the agent is to produce more than the first best thus pushing the agent's output lower.

Here again an interesting measure of the effect of the asymmetry of information is the difference between the two outputs for the agents of the two possible types for each of the principals i.e.,

$$\bar{q}_i = \underline{q}_i = \frac{\overline{\alpha}}{3b} - \frac{\underline{\alpha}}{3b} + \frac{2(1-\rho)(\overline{\alpha} - \underline{\alpha})}{3b}. \tag{2.18}$$

Proposition 7. *Each principal sets outputs further apart than in the informed duopoly case if $\rho > \dfrac{3}{4}$. However, compared to the monopoly case, each principal sets outputs closer.*

2.4.1. An Application to Non-Linear Pricing

In this section, we show how the two-principal case can be used to derive an interpretation for non-linear pricing in the context of duopoly. Typically non-linear pricing has been studied for monopolies. For example, the Disneyland monopolist in Oi, 1971, faces two possible demand curves – a good demand and bad demand. But the monopolist cannot tell which type a customer is and maximizes its profits by setting a non-linear price which includes an entry fee and a marginal price for each ride. Hence, there are different entry fees which are coupled with marginal prices that the different types of consumers self-select from. However in reality one sees such non-linear pricing in other market structures, for example in duopolies. An example of such a market structure is the auto rental industry. Here there are several (two in this example) firms, each offering cars for rent – their demand curves are generally complements. Each firm faces either high or low demand and in order to maximize profits designs a non-linear pricing scheme that includes two choices of a fixed fee and a marginal price – e.g., various combinations of weekly rates or daily rates and marginal mileage charges including the free mileage option.

We start with the monopoly case. The context is essentially the same as in section 2.1. However, we interpret the relationship between the agent and the principal as the relationship between a consumer and the seller. The consumer is of two types leading to two different demand functions for the seller-monopolist. We interpret payments from the agent to the principal as a non-linear price for the good consumed. The objective of the monopolist is to maximize expected revenue (equal to the expected profits since costs are assumed to be zero), i.e., $\rho \underline{R} + (1-\rho)\overline{R}$. Here R is the total revenue from the type being considered. Again for the bad type, the individual rationality constraint is binding and the monopolist sets the entry fee equal to the entire consumer surplus. However, the good type's self-selection constraint holds with equality and thus the monopolist is not able to extract the entire surplus.

Let $\overline{E}$ and $\underline{E}$ denote the entry fee for the two types of consumers and $\overline{p}$ and $\underline{p}$ denote the price per unit of the good consumed. By the IR constraint,

$$\underline{E} = \frac{(\alpha - \underline{p})^2}{2b} \quad \text{and} \quad \underline{R} = \underline{E} + \underline{p}\left(\frac{\alpha - \underline{p}}{b}\right),$$

and by the ICC for the good type,

$$\frac{(\overline{\alpha} - \overline{p})^2}{2b} - \overline{E} = \frac{(\overline{\alpha} - \underline{p})^2}{2b} + \underline{p}\left(\frac{\overline{\alpha} - \underline{p}}{b}\right) - \frac{(\alpha - \underline{p})^2}{2b} - \underline{p}\left(\frac{\alpha - \underline{p}}{b}\right),$$

or

$$\overline{E} = \frac{(\overline{\alpha} - \overline{p})^2}{2b} - \frac{(\overline{\alpha} - \underline{p})^2}{2b} + \frac{(\alpha - \underline{p})^2}{2b}.$$

Hence, the objective for the monopolist is,

$$max\ \rho\left[\frac{(\alpha - \underline{p})^2}{2b} + \underline{p}\left(\frac{\alpha - \underline{p}}{b}\right)\right] + (1-\rho)\left[\frac{(\overline{\alpha} - \overline{p})^2}{2b} - \frac{(\overline{\alpha} - \underline{p})^2}{2b} + \frac{(\alpha - \underline{p})^2}{2b}\right].$$

The first order conditions are,

$$\left(\frac{\overline{\alpha} - \overline{p}}{b}\right) + \frac{\overline{\alpha} - 2\overline{p}}{b} = 0,$$

or

$$\overline{p} = 0,$$

and

$$\rho\left[-\frac{(\bar{\alpha}-\bar{p})}{b}+\frac{\alpha-2\underline{p}}{b}\right]=-(1-\rho)\left(\frac{\bar{\alpha}-\alpha}{b}\right),$$

or

$$\underline{p}=\frac{(1-\rho)}{\rho}(\bar{\alpha}-\alpha).$$

The entry fee for the good agent, $\bar{E}$, is,

$$\frac{\bar{\alpha}}{2b}-\frac{1}{2b}\left(\bar{\alpha}^2-\alpha^2-2\frac{(1-\rho)}{\rho}(\bar{\alpha}-\alpha)^2\right)=\frac{\alpha^2}{2b}+\frac{1}{2b}2\frac{(1-\rho)}{\rho}(\bar{\alpha}-\alpha)^2.$$

Thus the monopolist charges zero (the efficient) price to the high-valuation consumer and a positive price (above the first best) to the low-valuation consumer. Further the low-valuation consumer is kept at its reservation utility through the entry fee whereas the high-valuation consumer earns a rent.

Next, we consider non-linear pricing for duopolies. The basic set up is the same as in this section on two principals and two informed agents. Just as in the monopoly case, we now interpret the principals as the duopolists and the agents as the consumers that have private information about their demand. Here the demand curves for the two principals corresponding to the two types of consumers are,

$$\underline{p}_1=\alpha-\alpha\underline{p}_2-b\underline{q}_1,$$

and

$$\bar{p}_1=\bar{\alpha}-\alpha\bar{p}_2-b\bar{q}_1,$$

for firm 1. The demand curves for firm 2 are,

$$\underline{p}_2=\alpha-\alpha\bar{p}_1-b\underline{q}_2,$$

and

$$\bar{p}_2=\bar{\alpha}-\alpha\bar{p}_1-b\bar{q}_2.$$

Here, $\bar{p}_i$ and $\underline{p}_i$ are the prices charged by the duopolist i, $i=1,2$, corresponding to high and low demand consumers respectively. Let R_i and E_i

denote the total payment and the entry fee to duopolist i, $i = 1,2$ by the consumers. The analysis is very similar to the monopoly case. We present the essence of it below. The total payment for the low types are,

$$\underline{R}_i = \underline{E}_i + \underline{p}_i(\alpha - \alpha\underline{p}_j - \underline{p}_i)/b$$

where,

$$\underline{E}_i = (\alpha - \underline{p}_i) + (\alpha - \alpha\underline{p}_j - \underline{p}_i)/2b$$

The ICC for the good consumer is,

$$(\overline{\alpha} - \overline{p}_i)(\overline{\alpha} - \alpha\overline{p}_j - b\overline{p}_i)/2b - \overline{E}_i = (\overline{\alpha} - \underline{p}_i) + (\overline{\alpha} - \alpha\overline{p}_j - b\underline{p}_i)/2b - \underline{E}_i .$$

Rearranging and substituting for $\underline{E}_i$ yields,

$$\overline{E}_i = (\overline{\alpha} - \overline{p}_i)(\overline{\alpha} - \alpha\overline{p}_j - \overline{p}_i)/2b - (\overline{\alpha} - \underline{p}_i) + (\overline{\alpha} - \alpha\overline{p}_j - b\underline{p}_i)/2b +$$

$$+(\alpha - \underline{p}_i)(\alpha - \alpha\underline{p}_j - b\underline{p}_i)/2b$$

Duopolist i chooses $\overline{p}_i$ and $\underline{p}_i$ given $\overline{p}_j$ and $\underline{p}_j$ to maximize,

$$\rho\left((\alpha - \underline{p}_i)\frac{\alpha - \alpha\underline{p}_j - \underline{p}_i}{2b} + \underline{p}_i\frac{\alpha - \alpha\underline{p}_j - \underline{p}_i}{b} \right)$$

$$+(1-\rho)\left(\begin{array}{c} (\overline{\alpha} - \overline{p}_i)(\overline{\alpha} - \alpha\overline{p}_j - \overline{p}_i)/2b - (\overline{\alpha} - \underline{p}_i)(\overline{\alpha} - \alpha\overline{p}_j - \underline{p}_i)/2b \\ + (\alpha - \underline{p}_i)(\alpha - \alpha\underline{p}_j - \underline{p}_i)/2b + \overline{p}_i(\overline{\alpha} - \alpha\overline{p}_j - \overline{p}_i)/b \end{array} \right)$$

The first order condition with respect to $\overline{p}_i$ yields,

$$\frac{1}{2b}(1-\rho)(\overline{\alpha} - \overline{p}_i + \overline{\alpha} - \alpha\overline{p}_j - \overline{p}_i) = \frac{1}{b}(\overline{\alpha} - \overline{p}_i - \alpha\overline{p}_j)$$

This yields,

$$\overline{p}_i = \overline{p}_j = 0 .$$

The first order condition with respect to $\underline{p}_i$ yields,

$$\rho\left(-\frac{1}{2b}\left\{\underline{a}-\underline{p}_i+\underline{a}-\alpha\underline{p}_j-\underline{p}_i\right\}+\frac{1}{b}\left\{\underline{a}-\alpha\underline{p}_j-2\underline{p}_i\right\}\right)+$$

$$+(1-\rho)\frac{1}{2b}(2\overline{a}-\underline{p}_i-\alpha\overline{p}_j-\underline{p}_i-2\underline{a}+\alpha\overline{p}_j+2\overline{p}_i)=0.$$

This gives

$$\underline{p}_i=\frac{(1-\rho)}{\rho}(\overline{\alpha}-\underline{\alpha})+\frac{p_j}{2\rho}.$$

Using the symmetry property, i.e., $\underline{p}_i=\underline{p}_j$, we obtain,

$$\underline{p}_i=\underline{p}_j=\frac{2(1-\rho)}{2\rho-1}(\overline{\alpha}-\underline{\alpha}).$$

Once again, the high-valuation consumer pays the efficient price of zero whereas the low-valuation consumer pays a positive price provided $\rho>\dfrac{1}{2}$. The low valuation consumer is again kept at the reservation utility whereas the high-valuation consumer is charged just enough in entry fee so as to prevent it from misrepresenting its valuation.

NOTES

1.   In the absence of uncertainty, an observation of price reveals the intercept to the principal, making the static contracting problem trivial. To address this, we assume that the demand is uncertain.

2.   In what follows, all variables with an overbar are associated with the good market and all variables with an underbar are associated with the bad market.

3.   See Jeitschko, Mirman and Salgueiro (2001) for an example of how the equilibrium repayment schedule is derived.

4.   This is because the rival produces more in the good market than in the bad market provided $\rho>\dfrac{1}{2}$.

REFERENCES

Harris, M. and R. Townsend (1981), 'Resource Allocation under Asymmetric Information', *Econometrica*, **49** (1), pp. 33-64.

Jain, N., T.D. Jeitschko and L.J. Mirman (2000) (JJM1), Financial Intermediation and Entry-Deterrence, Working Paper.

Jain, N., Jeitschko, T.D. and L.J. Mirman (2000) (JJM2), Strategic Experimentation in Financial Intermediation with Threat of Entry, Working Paper.

Jain, N., Jeitschko, T.D. and L.J. Mirman (2000) (JJM3), Financial Contracting, Signal Jamming and Entry-Deterrence, Working Paper.

Jeitschko, T.D., L. Mirman and E. Salgueiro (2001), 'The Simple Analytics of Information and Experimentation in Dynamic Agency', *Economic Theory*, **19**, 3, pp. 549-570.

Laffont, J.J. and J. Tirole (1993), *A Theory of Incentives in Procurement and Regulation*, Cambridge, MA, MIT Press.

Oi, W. (1971), 'A Disneyland Dilemma: Two-Part Tariff for the Mickey Mouse Monopoly', *Quarterly Journal of Economics*, **85**, pp. 71-96.

13. The Role of Beliefs, Knowledge, and Rationality in Non-Cooperative Games

James W. Friedman and Claudio Mezzetti[*]

1. INTRODUCTION

In the last 30 years non-cooperative game theory has had a major impact on economic analysis and game-theoretic terminology has become an important part of the economist's basic vocabulary. Even phenomena that require no game theory to be explained or analyzed are often described using its language. Besides being extensively used in many areas of economics, game theory has also been widely applied in other social sciences.

Nash equilibrium is the fundamental tool of analysis and basic equilibrium concept in non-cooperative game theory. In this chapter we examine the beliefs, the knowledge, and the level of rationality that are typically required of players who choose Nash equilibrium behavior, and we compare this with the requirements of various related equilibrium concepts. The hallmarks of Nash (1951) equilibrium are (i) that each player exactly and correctly predicts what other players will do and (ii) that the strategy of each player maximizes her payoff relative to these exact and correct beliefs.

Some of the concepts with which Nash equilibrium will be contrasted, such as perfect equilibrium (Selten 1975) and, in general, the refinements of Nash equilibrium such as proper equilibrium (Myerson 1978) and sequential equilibrium (Kreps and Wilson 1982), are more demanding than Nash equilibrium. Equilibria satisfying these refinements must satisfy all the conditions of Nash equilibrium plus some additional ones. Typically these refinements arise because in certain circumstances Nash equilibrium seems to permit equilibria that are based on intuitively unacceptable beliefs about what rival players might do.

* Department of Economics, CB# 3305
University of North Carolina
Chapel Hill, NC 27599-3305, USA

Other concepts are less stringent than Nash equilibrium such as rationalizable behavior (Bernheim 1984, Pearce 1984), quantal response equilibrium (McKelvey and Palfrey 1995, Chen et al 1997), and random belief equilibrium (Friedman and Mezzetti 2001). These concepts arise because in some games assuming exactly correct beliefs and payoff maximization without errors seems unrealistic and often at odds with field and/or experimental data.

Rationalizability places minimal requirements on what a player believes about the choices other players will make. Essentially, a player assumes that rivals will not do anything irrational where, roughly speaking, the criterion of irrationality is that a player will not choose a strategy that is strictly inferior to some other available strategy, given that the other players are not irrational themselves. In other words, rationalizability simply requires that the rationality of all players be common knowledge.

Random belief equilibrium relaxes Nash equilibrium by assuming that players have less exact beliefs in equilibrium than Nash players are assumed to have. However, beliefs are parameterized in a way that depends on what other players do and, as with Nash equilibrium, at equilibrium each player is maximizing her payoff relative to her beliefs about others.

Quantal response equilibrium can be interpreted in two different ways. In one of these each player's payoff structure is subject to random errors. At equilibrium each player is supposed to know the expected strategy choice of other players and to maximize her own realized payoff given these beliefs. The other interpretation supposes boundedly rational choice by the players. In general, all pure strategies are played with positive probability at equilibrium; however, the higher the expected payoff of a strategy, the larger the probability associated with it. The equilibrium conditions implicitly assume that players correctly predict what their rivals will choose.

The remainder of the chapter proceeds as follows. In Section 2 we set up a basic model and then characterize Nash equilibrium. In Section 3 we examine rationalizability. Perfect equilibrium is introduced and examined in Section 4. Then, in Section 5 we introduce and discuss random belief equilibrium. Section 6 describes quantal response equilibrium, and concluding comments are in Section 7.

2. THE GAME MODEL AND NASH EQUILIBRIUM

Our attention will be limited to finite games. These are games in which the number of players is finite and in which each player has a finite number of pure strategies. Denote by $N = \{1,...,n\}$ the set of players. For each player i

the set of pure strategies, or actions, is $A_i = \{1,\ldots,m_i\}$, the set of mixed strategies is $S_i = \left\{ s_i \in \Re_+^{m_i} \middle| \sum_{h=1}^{m_i} s_{ih} = 1 \right\}$, the set of pure strategy profiles is $A = \times_{i \in N} A_i$, and the set of mixed strategy profiles is $S = \times_{i \in N} S_i$. Each player i has a payoff (i.e., utility) function $P_i: S \to \Re$ and a payoff profile is $P = (P_1,\ldots,P_n)$. A game can then be represented by $\Gamma = (N,S,P)$.

After the saddle point theorem of von Neumann (1928) for two-person zero-sum games the next landmark result in game theory was the Nash equilibrium (non-cooperative equilibrium) of John Nash (1951). The underlying idea of Nash generalizes that of von Neumann to games having any number of players and in which there need not be any special relationship between the payoffs to one player and those of any other players. This advance opened the way for very important applications to economics and other social sciences.

A **Nash equilibrium** is a strategy profile, $s \in S$, such that for each player i, s_i maximizes the payoff of player i given that the other players are choosing $s_{-i} \in S_{-i} = \times_{j \in N \setminus \{i\}} S_j$. Nash equilibrium puts very stringent knowledge and belief requirements on the players. With respect to knowledge, in general it is supposed that each player knows all about the structure of the game; that is, each player knows the strategy set of each player and the payoff function of each player (i.e., **complete information**). Furthermore, every player knows that everyone has this information (i.e., **common knowledge**). This knowledge makes it possible for a player to figure out the outcome to any player resulting from a particular strategy profile. Basic, minimal rationality requires that a player choose a strategy that maximizes her own payoff; however, which strategy s_i maximizes the payoff of player i cannot be determined in a vacuum. The best strategy is, in general, a function of the choices of other players. For each $s_{-i} \in S_{-i}$ we define the **best reply mapping of player** i as

$$B_i(s_{-i}) = \left\{ s_i \in S_i \middle| P_i(s_i, s_{-i}) \geq P_i(s_i', s_{-i}) \text{ for all } s_i' \in S_i \right\}$$

Thus a Nash equilibrium s is characterized by the condition that $s_i \in B_i(s_{-i})$ for all players; that is, each player uses a best reply to the choice profile of the others. Defining $B(s) \times_{j \in N} B_i(s_{-i})$ we may say s is a Nash equilibrium if and only if $s \in B(s)$.

It is natural to think of each player as choosing a strategy that maximizes her payoff subject to her beliefs (i.e., her conjecture) about the strategies to be simultaneously chosen by the other players. Bringing beliefs explicitly into Nash equilibrium, it appears inescapable to conclude that when a Nash equilibrium $s^* \in B(s^*)$ is actually selected then each player i holds the belief that each other player j will choose s_j^*. That is, Nash equilibrium implies that each player has correct beliefs about the choices other players will make and that each player selects a payoff maximizing strategy given those beliefs. We refer to these beliefs as **Nash beliefs**.

3. PERFECT EQUILIBRIUM

At first thought it would seem that players with Nash beliefs are as correct and rational as one might ever expect; however, examples can be found in which even Nash equilibrium can be accused of permitting players to do something unreasonable, perhaps irrational. In this section we will present two examples; one is an extensive form game and the other is in strategic form. They each present Selten's (1975) **perfect equilibrium** in a distinct and interesting light.

We will not describe the extensive form in any detail, but will rely on the example in Figure 1 along with minimal explanation. The circle at the bottom of the figure, marked with '1' is the starting point of the game. Player 1 moves at this point and can choose L or R. This move is observed by player 2 who is then at one of the two circles marked with '2' where he can select either L or R. Following the choice of player 2 the game is over and the payoffs shown at the final location indicate what the players receive. The top payoff is for player 1 and the bottom payoff is for player 2. A pure strategy for player 1 is an element of {L, R}; however, a pure strategy for player 2 is an element of {(L, L), (L, R), (R, L), (R, R)}. That is, player 1 has only the choice of L or R while player 2 can choose conditionally on which of his two decision points is reached. Thus each of the four strategies of player 2 consists of a pair, for example, (L, R) where the first entry is what player 2 chooses when player 1 selects L and the second entry is what player 2 chooses when player 1 selects R.

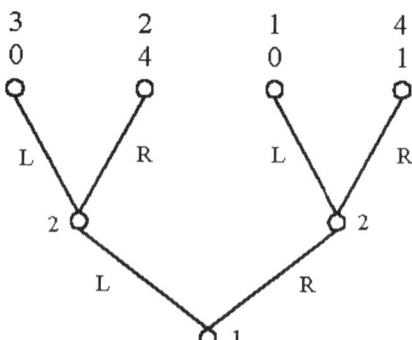

Figure 1. Extensive Form Game

In a finite extensive form game with perfect recall, a mixed strategy of a player can be represented by a probability distribution over the moves that the player can make at each point where he has a choice (i.e., for any mixed strategy there is an outcome equivalent behavioral strategy).[1] Thus player 1 would have a probability distribution over R and L at the beginning. This can be summarized as $p \in [0, 1]$ where p is understood as the probability of choosing R. For player 2, there are two places where he moves and he can have a different probability distribution for each. Thus his strategy can be represented as (q_L, q_R) where q_L is the probability of choosing R after player 1 has chosen L and q_R is the probability of choosing R after player 1 has chosen L. If $p \in (0, 1)$ then there is a positive probability of reaching each of the decision points of player 2; however, if p is either one or zero, then one of the two decision points cannot possibly be reached.

In general in an extensive form game a strategy profile may be such that certain decision points cannot possibly be reached. One might think that the way the players' strategies direct that the game would be played starting from some decision point that cannot be attained would be irrelevant; however, this is not the case. The way players would behave on a part of the game that will not be reached could affect the way earlier decisions are made at points that will be reached. This will be illustrated with the example.

This game has three pure strategy equilibria: [R, (L, R)], [R, (R, R)], and [L, (R, L)]. The first two lead to the payoff profile (4, 1) where player 2 receives 1 and the third leads to (2, 4) where player 2 receives 4. Obviously player 2 would prefer the third equilibrium and one might imagine player 2 telling player 1 that she will choose L if player 1 chooses R. If player 1 believed this, then he would certainly choose L so as to end up with a payoff of 2 rather than 1; however, player 1 has good reasons not to believe player 2. If player 1 chooses R then player 2 is left with an unchangeable fact and, in the face of it, would be better off choosing R than choosing L. Choosing L in response to R will never occur under the strategy profile [L, (R, L)], because this equilibrium profile calls for L to be selected by player 1. The specification by player 2 of choosing L in response to the choice of R by player 1 makes it better for player 1 to choose L. However, this specification can be viewed as a non-credible threat. Non-credible because, if player 1 did actually choose R, then it would not be optimal for player 2 to carry out the plan of choosing L. Player 1 might well reason this way and decide to choose R anyway. In supporting this third Nash equilibrium, a crucial element is that, in a circumstance that will not arise under equilibrium play, player 2 will supposedly do something irrational. As this decision point is not reached, player 2 is not called upon to behave irrationally. Any Nash equilibrium that depends on such irrational behavior (i.e., a non-credible threat) is suspect.

In a game like the one above perfect equilibrium requires the strategy profile of each player to be optimal for that player when looked at starting from
any decision point in the game where the player moves. Thus, for the Nash
equilibrium to be perfect, the game starting at any of the three points at which
a player makes a move must involve Nash equilibrium play from that point
on. This must hold whether or not the strategy profile could ever bring the
players to that point. The third equilibrium would never reach the right hand
node where player 2 moves (following R by player 1), but perfection requires
optimal play by player 2 at this point anyway. The intuition for such a requirement is that player 2 should not be expected to behave in an obviously
irrational way and player 1 should be capable of taking this into account.
When player 1 does this, he discounts the possibility of player 2 choosing L
following R by player 1 and instead has player 1 believing that only R could
be expected. This, in turn, eliminates the third Nash equilibrium from serious
consideration. It also eliminates the equilibrium first equilibrium [R, (R, L)].
Only the second equilibrium, [R, (R, R)] is perfect.

The example in Figure 1 is a game of perfect information, which means
that when a player moves, the player always knows precisely which decision
point has been reached. Perfect equilibrium in finite games of perfect information can be found by backward induction.

Table 1. Normal Form Game

	L	R
T	1,1	0,0
B	0,0	0,0

The second illustration is a strategic game, shown in Table 1, where there are
two pure strategy Nash equilibria: (T, L) and (B, R). Perfect equilibrium in
strategic form games is often referred to as **trembling hand perfect equilibrium**. In keeping with this name, suppose that each player has a small probability, ε, of making a mistake. If we characterize the mixed strategy of
player 1 by p, the probability of choosing T and for player 2 by q, the probability of choosing L, then the possibility of mistakes means that the strategy
set of each player is $S_{i\varepsilon} = [\varepsilon, 1-\varepsilon]$ rather than $S_i = [0, 1]$. If the game in
Table 1 were called G when mistakes are not part of the game, then we may
denote the game with ε mistakes as G^ε. Suppose that s^ε is a Nash equilib-

rium for G^ε; then $s^0 = lim_{\varepsilon \to 0} s^\varepsilon$ is a perfect equilibrium of G. In the game in Table 1, only (T, L) is perfect. This is easily seen by noting that for any $q < 1$ the payoff to T is q and the payoff to B is zero. The possibility of errors implies that $q \geq \varepsilon > 0$; therefore, the best reply of player 1 is to choose the largest possible value of p namely $p = 1 - \varepsilon$. Similarly for player 2. So if a strategy profile is never optimal in the presence of small mistakes, it fails to be perfect. Subgame perfection is appealing on practical grounds; real life players are fallible, even when they know exactly what they intend, and can make mistakes. Seen in this way perfectness is a robustness property.

In the presentation above we have not made completely precise the role of mistakes in the specification of trembling hand perfect equilibrium. Suppose a general strategic form game and suppose that the error probability associated with choosing the kth pure strategy of player i is ε_{ik}. Then this means that $s_{ik} \geq \varepsilon_{ik}$. The vector $\varepsilon_i = (\varepsilon_{i1}, \ldots, \varepsilon_{im_i})$ is the error structure of player i and $\varepsilon = (\varepsilon_1, \ldots, \varepsilon_n)$ is the error structure of the game G^ε. Let $s(\varepsilon)$ be a Nash equilibrium of the game G^ε. In the game G the strategy profile s is a perfect equilibrium if there exists a sequence of error structures $\{\varepsilon^\mu\}_{\mu=1}^{\infty}$ that converges to the zero vector and such that the sequence of Nash equilibria $\{s(\varepsilon^\mu)\}_{\mu=1}^{\infty}$ has s as a point of accumulation. Thus if any such error sequence can be found, then s is perfect. The only limitation on ε^μ is that it specifies a positive error probability for each pure strategy of each player.

Other refinements have similar flavors. For example sequential equilibrium in extensive form games is almost, but not quite, identical to perfect equilibrium. Proper equilibrium, which is a refinement of perfect equilibrium in strategic form games, adds a constraint on the error sequence $\{\varepsilon^\mu\}_{\mu=1}^{\infty}$. If the pure strategy k of player i results in a payoff below the best reply payoff and pure strategy h results in a lower payoff than strategy k, then ε_{ih}, the error associated with choosing h must go to zero an order of magnitude faster than ε_{ik}, the error associated with choosing k. More precisely, $\varepsilon_{ih}/\varepsilon_{ik}$ must go to zero as ε goes to zero. The rationale for this is that more costly errors should have a lower probability of occurring than less costly errors. While this sounds plausible, it is by no means clear that the particular formulation used in proper equilibrium is inherently sensible. In any case, proper equilibrium arises in a way analogous to perfect equilibrium. Namely, by the use of carefully selected examples, perfect equilibrium can be made to look rather unreasonable in a way that proper equilibrium can cure.

4. RATIONALIZABILITY

We turn now from refinements of Nash equilibrium to a coarsening of it. Nash beliefs are very stringent and can easily seem unreasonably demanding. Consider, for example, the game of matching pennies. Suppose that money measures utility, and the players engage in matching pennies for $10. The two players simultaneously select either heads (H) or tails (T). Denote by p the probability that player 1 chooses H and by q the probability that player 2 chooses T. Player 1 wins if the coins match and player 2 wins if they do not. It is well known that this game has a unique Nash equilibrium of (0.5, 0.5). It is true that if player 1 chooses $p = 0.5$ her ex ante expected payoff is zero, the equilibrium payoff; however, if she expects player 2 to choose $q = 0.5$ then $p = 1$ or $p = 0$ or any other value of p is as good as $p = 0.5$. Likewise, as she sees that she has some justification for any value of p, she can see that player 2 will have some justification for any value of q. This, in turn, means that she might project any particular value of q as player 2's choice and select the best reply to that value. The upshot of this line of reasoning is that any strategy of player 2 is defensible and any strategy of player 1 is defensible even though the game has a unique Nash equilibrium. To put it differently, Nash beliefs go far beyond the minimal requirements of rationality.

The minimal requirements of rationality are essentially those of Bernheim (1984) and Pearce (1984), which are formalized in what they call **rationalizable behavior**. Let $Z_i \subseteq A_i$ be the set of rationalizable actions of player i, and let $Z_{-i} = \times_{j \in N \setminus \{i\}} Z_j$. An action α_i is rationalizable (i.e., $\alpha_i \in Z_i$) if it is a best reply to a belief of player i (a probability measure over the action profiles of the player's opponents) whose support is Z_{-i}. That is, a rationalizable action must be a best reply to beliefs that only put positive mass on rationalizable action profiles of the other players. In matching pennies all strategies are rationalizable, because for player 1 each $p \in [0,1]$ is a best reply to some $q \in [0,1]$ and conversely for player 2. In general, in a game $\Gamma = (N,S,P)$ if, for each player i and each $\alpha_i \in A_i$ there is some $s_{-i} \in S_{-i}$ to which α_i is a best reply, then all actions are rationalizable; that is, the set of rationalizable action profiles coincides with A.

If an action α_i is strongly dominated (i.e., if the player has an alternative strategy s_i such that, $P_i(s_i,s_{-i}) > P_i(\alpha_i,s_{-i})$ for all $s_{-i} \in S_{-i}$, then it is not rationalizable. If correlated beliefs are allowed in the definition of rationalizability (i.e., if a player is allowed to believe that the opponents correlate their actions), then finding the complete set of rationalizable action profiles in a game can be accomplished by the iterated elimination of strictly dominated actions. To carry this out, define for each i $A_i^0 = A_i$, $S_i^0 = S_i$ and then define A_i^k and S_i^k recursively as follows:

$$S_i^k = \left\{ s_i \in \Re_+^{m_i} \middle| \sum_{h=1}^{m_i} s_{ih} = 1, s_{ih} = 0 \text{ if } h \notin A_i^k \right\}$$

$$A_i^k = \left\{ \alpha_i \in A_i^{k-1} \middle| \alpha_i \in \bigcup_{s_{-i} \in S_{-i}^{k-1}} B_i(s_{-i}) \right\}$$

This recursive process is continued until $A_i^{k^*} = A_i^{k^*-1}$ for all i. Then, A^{k^*} is the set of rationalizable action profiles and S^{k^*} is the set of rationalizable strategy profiles.

There is intuitive appeal to the idea that players need not correctly and precisely figure out how their rivals will behave in a game and that it is suffi-cient to believe that other players will not do something irrational. Rationalizability requires that each player choose a strategy that is a best reply to a belief that only attaches positive probability to those profiles of actions of the remaining players that they might rationally choose. That is, each player chooses something that is a best reply to rationalizable choices of the rivals.

5. RANDOM BELIEF EQUILIBRIUM

As with rationalizable behavior, random belief equilibrium (Friedman and Mezzetti 2001) weakens the beliefs held by players as compared with Nash beliefs. Random belief equilibrium (RBE) appears at first glance to be inter-mediate between Nash equilibrium and rationalizability; that is, one might expect any RBE to be rationalizable. This is not so for a subtle reason that will be explained below after RBE is developed. In place of the Nash beliefs we suppose that each player i does not know how any other player j will behave; however, player i is assumed to have beliefs represented by a probability den-sity function f_i^j defined on S_j.[2]

The equilibrium beliefs of player i are sensitive to the actual strategy choice of player j by means of a parameterization of the beliefs. Denote by $\phi_j \in S_j$ the **focus** about player j. The focus of player i about player j is some measure of central tendency of the density function f_i^j, such as the mean or mode; the parameterized density is written $f_i^j(\phi_j)$ and the density associated with some specific $s_j \in S_j$ is written $f_i^j(\phi_j)(s_j)$. There are two essential requirements on the beliefs of player i about player j. First, the density function is continuous with respect to ϕ_j and second, for any $T_j \subseteq S_j$

$$\int_{T_j} f_i^j(\phi_j)(s_j)ds_j > 0$$

if and only if T_j has positive Lebesgue measure. This latter condition means, essentially, that player i believes that any strategy of player j might well be used. In particular, even strictly dominated strategies of player j might be used. This is precisely where an RBE can be shown to fail rationalizability; an RBE may attach positive probability on actions that are not rationalizable. Of course it is possible to reformulate RBE so that strictly dominated strategies are iteratively eliminated, it is then assumed they always have zero probability, and the positive measure condition is then applied to the surviving rationalizable sets $S_j^{k^*}$. To represent the beliefs of player i about the other players jointly let $f_i^{-i}(\phi_{-i}) = \times_{j \neq i} f_i^j(\phi_j)$.

At a random belief equilibrium we require that the strategy of each player be a best reply to the beliefs of that player when the focus of all other players represents their actual choice. To express this, consider specific beliefs for player i and examine each of her pure strategies in turn. Let $D_i(\alpha_i)$ be the subset of of S_{-i} on which α_i is a conventional best reply of player i. Thus

$$D_i(\alpha_i) = \left\{s_{-i} \in S_{-i} \middle| \alpha_i \in B_i(s_{-i})\right\}$$

Under relatively mild assumptions $D_i(\alpha_i) \cap D_i(\alpha_i')$ has Lebesgue measure zero for any two distinct pure strategies.[3] Under this condition the best reply correspondence of player i, B_i, is essentially equivalent to a single valued function.[4] Thus, the expected best reply of player i to beliefs $f_i^{-i}(\phi_{-i})$ is given by

$$\psi_i(\phi_{-i}, \alpha_i) = \int_{D_i(\alpha_i)} f_i^{-i}(\phi_{-i})ds_{-i} \quad \text{for all } \alpha_i \in A_i$$

Thus $\psi_i(\phi_{-i}, \alpha_i)$ is the probability that player i plays her pure strategy α_i and the mixed strategy of player i is

$$\psi_i(\phi_{-i}) = (\psi_i(\phi_{-i}, 1), \dots, \psi_i(\phi_{-i}, m_i)) \in S_i$$

so that the strategy profile that is an expected best reply to ϕ is

$$\psi(\phi) = (\psi_1(\phi_{-1}), \ldots, \psi_n(\phi_{-n})) \in S$$

The function $\psi(\phi)$ is thus a mapping from S to S.

The expected best reply can be interpreted in this way: suppose each player i randomly draws a Nash belief about s_{-i} according to the density $f_i^{-i}(\phi_{-i})$ and then chooses a best reply to this belief. Then, the expected mixed strategy of player i prior to making this random draw is $\psi_i(\phi_{-i})$ and the expected strategy profile is $\psi(\phi)$. A random belief equilibrium (RBE) is a strategy profile $\phi^0 \in S$ such that $\psi(\phi^0) = \phi^0$. Thus at a random belief equilibrium the expected strategy of player i equals the central tendency of the belief that each other player j holds about player i.

The connection between RBE and Nash equilibrium is that, for Nash equilibrium, the belief measures must, at equilibrium, be degenerate with mass point at the focus. This connection can be made both more precise and more transparent by adding a parameter to the belief densities. Suppose that the belief of player i about the strategy choice of player j is given by the probability density $f_{i\varepsilon}^j(\phi_j)$ where $\varepsilon > 0$ is a parameter such that $f_{i\varepsilon}^j(\phi_j)$ varies continuously with ε and, as $\varepsilon \to 0$, $f_{i\varepsilon}^j(\phi_j)$ converges to the degenerate density corresponding to a mass point at ϕ_j. That is, as $\varepsilon \to 0$, beliefs converge to Nash beliefs, which implies that any accumulation point of an associated sequence of random belief equilibria is a Nash equilibrium. We call such an accumulation point a **robust equilibrium**.

By means of examples it is easily demonstrated that robust equilibria need not be perfect if there are at least three players (for two-person games we can show that any robust equilibrium must be perfect), and that some perfect equilibria are not robust. The distinguishing feature of robust equilibria, apart from being Nash equilibria, is that each pure strategy α_i in the support of a robust equilibrium is a best reply to a subset of S_{-i} that has positive Lebesgue measure. More precisely, a Nash equilibrium s^0 is robust if and only if for each α_i in the support of s_i^0 the intersection of $D_i(\alpha_i)$ and any small ball around s_{-i}^0 has positive Lebesgue measure. One implication of this characterization is that weakly dominated strategies never appear in the support of robust equilibria; indeed, they never appear in the support of an RBE. The same holds for an undominated strategy that can be mimicked by a convex combination of other strategies. The pure strategy α_i can be mimicked if there is some s_i, distinct from α_i, such that $P_i(\alpha_i, s_{-i}) = P_i(s_i, s_{-i})$ for all

$s_{-i} \in S_{-i}$. That a pure strategy is a best reply to a set of profiles having positive Lebesgue measure is a robustness property and one might regard precisely these strategies as robust strategies. A robust equilibrium is then a Nash equilibrium in which only robust strategies appear in the support of the equilibrium. Of course, robustness of a strategy is only necessary, but not sufficient, for being in the support of a robust equilibrium.

6. QUANTAL RESPONSE EQUILIBRIUM

Quantal response equilibrium (QRE) has been proposed by McKelvey and Palfrey (1995). In their interpretation of QRE players have some uncertainty concerning their own payoffs. The same mathematical structure has been interpreted by Chen et al (1997) as representing a form of boundedly rational behavior. It is the latter interpretation that will be made here. We will restrict attention to the logistic version of QRE; McKelvey and Palfrey (1995) and Chen et al (1997) contain a more general formulation.

The basic idea is that players always put positive probability on all of their pure strategies at equilibrium even if some strategies have higher expected payoffs than others. To be specific, for a given strategy profile s define

$$P_i(\alpha_i,) = \sum_{s_{-i} \in S_{-i}} P_i(\alpha_i, s_{-i}) \prod_{j \in N \setminus \{i\}} s_j \quad \text{for all } i \in N \text{ and } \alpha_i \in A_i$$

In the logistic QRE, the probability that player i will chooses action α_i when her opponents use the strategy profile s_{-i} is given by

$$Q_i(\alpha_i, s_{-i}) = \frac{exp(\lambda P_i(\alpha_i,))}{\sum_{\alpha_i' \in A_i} exp(\lambda P_i(\alpha_i',))} \quad \text{for all } i \in N \text{ and } \alpha_i \in A_i$$

where $\lambda \geq 0$ is a parameter whose interpretation will be discussed below. Then $Q_i(s_{-i}) = (Q_i(1, s_{-i}), \ldots, Q_i(m_i, s_{-i}))$ is the logistic quantal best reply of player i to s_{-i}, and $Q(s) = (Q_1(s_{-1}), \ldots, Q_n(s_{-n}))$ is the logistic quantal response function of the game. A logistic quantal response equilibrium (logistic QRE) is a fixed point of Q.

The parameter λ can be interpreted as indicating the level of rationality of a player. If $\lambda = 0$ then player i puts probability $1/m_i$ on each pure strategy irrespective of the payoff structure. As λ increases the probability associated with the best replies rises and, in the limit, as $\lambda \to \infty$, only pure strategies that are best replies will have positive probability. Thus as $\lambda \to \infty$ any accumulation point of a sequence of quantal response equilibria will be a Nash equilibrium. As with robust equilibrium, such a limit need not be perfect (not even for two-person games) and not all perfect equilibria can be obtained as a limit of logistic QRE.

7. CONCLUDING COMMENTS

In comparing the various equilibria that have been discussed, first consider the extremes: Nash equilibrium (with or without refinements) and rationalizability. Typically a game will have a finite number of Nash equilibria whereas there will be an uncountable infinity of rationalizable strategies for each player. This appears closely related to the belief requirements of the two concepts. With Nash equilibrium, beliefs are exact and correct and a player chooses a best reply to these exact and correct beliefs. With rationalizable behavior, a player may choose a best reply to a strategy profile very different from that which the other players choose; it is only necessary that the beliefs about other players not be absurd. While the set of rationalizable strategies of a player depends on the structure of the game, what is rationalizable for a player has little connection with the actual choices of other players. Any profile in which each player uses a rationalizable strategy is consistent with rationalizable behavior. In contrast, at any Nash equilibrium the strategy of a player has a very specific connection to the strategies chosen by the other players; that strategy must be a best reply to the choices of the others. Clearly this difference will generally mean that rationalizable strategies are much more numerous than Nash equilibrium strategies.

Now consider either RBE for fixed belief distributions (and hence a fixed ε) or QRE for a fixed λ. In terms of the number of equilibria, one should expect one or several as with Nash equilibrium. The reason is that RBE and QRE satisfy a best reply condition analogous to that of Nash equilibrium and a player's strategy in an equilibrium profile bears a precise relationship to the strategies of the other players by means of a best reply condition. QRE for fixed λ, RBE for fixed belief distributions and Nash each use a different sort of best reply, but an equilibrium strategy profile must exhibit mutual consistency mediated through a collection of n coordinated best reply conditions. Where RBE and QRE part company with Nash equilibrium regarding the multiplicity of equilibria is through their parameters λ and ε. For each $\lambda \in [0, \infty]$ there is at least one QRE and for each $\varepsilon \in (0, \infty)$ there is at least one RBE. So the sets of RBEs and QREs of a game vary with these two parameters. Because of this, RBE and QRE yield a statistical framework for estimation using either field or experimental data. For examples of applications to the analysis of experimental data, the interested reader should consult McKelvey and Palfrey (1995) for QRE and Friedman and Mezzetti (2001) for RBE.

NOTES

1.   To illustrate the difference between a mixed strategy and a behavioral strategy, for player 2 a mixed strategy is a probability distribution over the four pure strategies (L, L), (L, R), (R, L), and (R, R) and a behavioral strategy is a pair of independent probability distributions, one over R and L for the decision following L by player 1 and one over R and L for the decision following R by player 1.

2.   The model used in Friedman and Mezzetti (2001) is more general than the one used here. In particular, probability measures that need not be representable by density functions are allowed and beliefs with positive probability mass on atoms are permitted. The exposition here captures the essence of the model in a way that permits easier exposition.

3.   In Friedman and Mezzetti (2001) it is shown that $D_i(\alpha_i) \bigcap D_i(\alpha_i')$ has measure zero as long as player i has no duplicate strategies. The strategies α_i and α_i' are duplicates if $P_i(\alpha_i', s_{-i}) = P_i(\alpha_i, s_{-i})$ for all $s_{-i} \in S_{-i}$.

4.   Specifically, the mapping B_i is multi-valued on, at most, a set of measure zero.

5.   More precisely, for any $T_j \subseteq S_j$

$$F_i^j(\phi_j)(T_j) = \int_{T_j} f_i^j(\phi_j)(s_j) ds_j$$

is the probability that player i attaches to the belief that the strategy of player j will be in the set T_j. Define $T_j(\delta)$ to be a ball of radius δ around ϕ_j. Then, for any $\delta > 0$, as $\varepsilon \to 0$, $F_i^j(\phi_j)(T_j(\delta)) \to 1$.

REFERENCES

Bernheim, B. Douglas (1984), 'Rationalizable Strategic Behavior', *Econometrica*, **52**, pp. 1007-1028.

Chen, Hsiao-Chi, James W. Friedman, and Jacques-Francois Thisse (1997), 'Boundedly Rational Nash Equilibrium: A Probabilistic Choice Approach', *Games and Economic Behavior*, **18**, pp. 32-54.

Friedman, James W. and Claudio Mezzetti (2001), *Random Belief Equilibrium*, University of North Carolina, Chapel Hill, NC, unpublished.

Kreps, David M. and Robert Wilson (1982), 'Sequential Equilibrium', *Econometrica*, **50**, pp. 863-894.

McKelvey, Richard D. and Thomas R. Palfrey (1995), 'Quantal Response Equilibria for Normal Form Games, *Games and Economic Behavior*, **10**, pp. 6-38.

Myerson, Roger (1978), 'Refinements of the Nash Equilibrium Concept', *International Journal of Game Theory*, **7**, pp. 73-80.

Nash, John F.Jr. (1951), 'Non-Cooperative Games', *Annals of Mathematics*, **54**, pp. 286-295.

Pearce, David G. (1984), 'Rationalizable Strategic Behavior and the Problem of Perfection', *Econometrica*, **52**, pp. 1029-1050.

Selten, Reinhard (1975), 'Reexamination of the Perfectness Concept for Equilibrium Points in Extensive Games', *International Journal of Game Theory*, **4**, pp. 25-55.

von Neumann, John (1928), 'Zur Theorie der Gesellschaftsspiele', *Mathematische Annalen*, **100**, pp. 295-320.

14. The Economics of Research Joint Ventures

Yannis Katsoulacos and David Ulph

1. INTRODUCTION

It is well known that there are potentially significant market failures in the innovation generating process. At least since the seminal analysis of Arrow (1962) it is recognised that these stem fundamentally from the appropriability problems that arise from the public good nature of knowledge. In the absence of *any* form of policy intervention these problems imply that the private rate of return to investments that aim to generate knowledge would be extremely low, and consequently there would be considerable under-investment in new knowledge creation and thus in innovation generation.[1] To address these problems most governments operate a system of protection of intellectual property rights (IPRs) – the central component of which is patent protection. However, while policy intervention in the form of a patent system provides some correction of the basic market failures, it generates its own distortions, essentially because patents reward firms for discovering information but not for sharing it.

The main objective of the present chapter is to provide a general treatment of the role of Research Joint Ventures (RJVs) in addressing these problems. Following an overview (Section 2) we describe a general model based on our recent contributions (Section 3) and then discuss the main results emerging from this model and compare them to the existing literature (Section 4). Apart from R&D subsidies, the promotion of RJVs is the major policy instrument used to try to correct these market failures. Indeed 'promoting technological cooperation' has underlined the Commission of the European Union's technology policy in its attempts to improve European competitiveness and integration for over 20 years. We review the issue of RJVs Vs R&D subsidies in Section 5 and we conclude in Section 6.

2.   INNOVATION MARKET FAILURES, PATENTS, LICENSING AND RJVs: AN OVERVIEW

To understand better the market failures that are present in the innovation process it is useful to think of innovative activity as involving a three-stage sequence of decisions by firms:

- The first is whether to operate an R&D lab and, if so, what research path this lab should follow. We call this the *research design* decision. We assume that firms have open to them many possible research paths. Two different research paths, chosen by two firms, may be *duplicative* or they may be *additive, in terms of the knowledge (discoveries) generated by them*. If research paths are *duplicative* (or what Katsoulacos and Ulph (K&U), 1998a, called *perfect substitute*) i.e. lead to duplicative research discoveries,[2] that is, the research that all firms are doing effectively leads to the same discovery, then if two firms both make a discovery, there will be nothing to be gained by sharing information – information sharing is only beneficial in this case when one firm has discovered and the other has not. If, on the other hand, research paths are *additive* (or what K&U called *complementary*) i.e. lead to complementary research discoveries, if two firms discover, then if they share information, they will be able to make more progress than they can achieve on their own.

    Of course, if firms choose exactly the same among many different complementary research paths the result will be the same as if the firms had chosen two different but perfect substitute research paths.

    The literature has assumed either that the set of research paths available to the firms involves perfect substitute or that it involves perfect complementary research paths.
- The second is the amount of R&D to do on the chosen research path – the R&D decision.
- Finally, if a firm makes a discovery, it has to decide how much information about this discovery it should share with other firms. We call this the *(research outcome) information-sharing decision.*

In thinking about innovation market failures we want to contrast the decisions that would be made by firms on these three issues when they are acting independently in a competitive market environment, with the decisions that would be made by a social planner.

    Consider first a policy system in which:

(i)   any form of collaboration between firms is prohibited and so there are no RJVs;

(ii)   there is no mechanism such as licensing to allow firms to get rewarded for sharing information;

(iii) patents are completely effective and can prevent all involuntary information leakages or spillovers.

For the moment, suppose also that:

(iv)   firms are producing substitute products – an assumption made in much of the literature on innovation, spillovers and RJVs;

Then, as is well known from the Industrial Organisation literature,[3] given the above assumptions, there will be a number of innovation market failures, which we can group under the above headings.

1. Research Outcome Information-Sharing

There will be insufficient research outcome information-sharing. Because goods are substitutes, firms will have no incentive to voluntarily share information with their rivals. However, the social optimum would always involve full research outcome information-sharing: (a) because this diffuses the new ideas throughout the market; (b) because this consequently makes the market more competitive, thus increasing output and lowering prices. Notice that if research paths are duplicative (or, if firms choose exactly the same among many complementary research paths) then the lack of research outcome information-sharing will be important only when one firm discovers: if both firms discover there will be nothing to be gained by sharing information. On the other hand, if research paths are complementary and firms choose different research paths, the lack of research outcome information-sharing is important even when both firms discover since in this case information sharing would increase the progress made by both firms through the exploitation of complementarities – there is what we call an *under-exploitation-of-complementarities effect*.

2. R&D Investment

It turns out that there are four different market failures here:

(a)   Even perfect patents cannot correct all appropriability problems. Thus firms will not usually be able to appropriate the extra consumers' surplus from their innovations. By not taking into account consumers' surplus in their objective firms tend to under-value the returns to R&D, and so will **under-invest** in R&D. We refer to this as *the under-valuation effect.*

(b)   An additional reason for **under-investing** in R&D is that in deciding how much R&D to do firms take into account only the benefit of the R&D to themselves. Thus they ignore the potential benefit that the outcome of their R&D could bring to others (if the results of their R&D were shared). This is called the *stand-alone effect.*

(c)   A major reason for a firm's investment in R&D is to gain a *strategic advantage* by innovating ahead of one's rivals and so having a superior product or technology. This leads firms to **over-invest** in R&D since, from the point of view of society, it does not matter who innovates first. This over-investment is most dramatic in the case of what is known as tournament (race) models, but also arises in non-tournament models where firms choose R&D prior to the output stage of the game. We call this the strategic *over-investment effect.*

(d)   The above hold irrespective of the nature of research paths. In the case where the research paths are complementary there is an additional effect on (failure of) R&D investment: the possibility that firms fail to share research outcome information and hence to fully exploit the complementarities in research design will lead them to under-value the benefits of undertaking R&D and hence to **under-invest** in R&D. Call this the *under exploited-complementarities under-investment effect.*

Notice that an implication of this discussion is that we cannot say whether **at the level of the individual firm** there is over-investment or under-investment in R&D.

3. Research Design

When research paths are complementary but firms are acting independently and when competition policy prevents any collusion, it may be extremely difficult for firms to fully co-ordinate their decisions on which directions of research will maximise the complementarities that could be later exploited. Call this the *under-developed complementarities effect.*

Also because firms anticipate that there will be insufficient research outcome information-sharing, they realise that the only way that they can get access to the new technology or product is to set up their own R&D lab and try to discover it themselves. In many cases, especially when research paths are duplicative, it will be socially optimal to operate a smaller number of labs and have these laboratories fully share the information. Thus we have *excessive duplication* of R&D effort – an excessive number of R&D laboratories operate. Other things being equal this produces a consequent tendency for **over-investment in R&D at the market level**.

Now drop assumption (iv) and assume that firms are producing complementary products. Each firm now gains rather than loses when other firms make progress. This has two important implications. First firms will now have private incentives to give away free of charge any information about discoveries that they have made. The market failures arising at the research outcome information-sharing stage will therefore disappear. Secondly the magnitude of some of the R&D effects discussed above will now be altered. In particular the strategic investment effect will now be negative, further exacerbating the problem of under-investment in R&D. Notice that the research design problems will still arise because these are associated with an inability to co-ordinate such decisions.

Consider now the implications of dropping assumption (iii) and allowing for the possibility of spillovers – defined as *involuntary, unpaid* leakages of information. These spillovers are a form of externality, and, when firms act in isolation, they will fail to internalise them. These spillovers will change the magnitude of some of the effects referred to above, but, more importantly, introduce a new market failure in the R&D decision that we call the *spillover effect*. In the case where firms are producing substitute products this unambiguously leads to **under-investment** in R&D. There are two reasons for this. If a firm succeeds in innovating when its competitors do not then it will have less to gain from its discovery since some of the information will leak out to others. However if a firm fails to innovate, while some of its rivals succeed, then it will gain from their discoveries, and so has less to lose from a failure to innovate. The discussion is somewhat modified when firms are producing complementary products, for now the first of the above effects is positive, since a firm gains from any progress made by the other firms.

Before turning to the implications of dropping assumption (ii) notice that what we have learned is that, in the absence of any mechanisms or policies for promoting information-sharing, patents – and IPR systems more generally – by no means resolve all the market failures associated with innovation. Notice that this is true even if the patent system works perfectly and there are no spillovers.

Three other conclusions emerge from the above discussion.

(i) Many of the failures arise because, under a patent system, firms are rewarded for creating information, but not necessarily for sharing it. Under our assumptions so far, whatever information passes from one firm to another is unrewarded and, in the case of substitute products, involuntary.

(ii) There are two types of information that may need to be shared by firms. There is *research design information* that may need to be shared before any R&D is undertaken. This is necessary for firms to be able to co-ordinate their research design strategies and maximise the extent of complementarities that might be exploited. It may also be necessary in order to avoid duplication of research effort. There is also *research outcome* information that is shared after firms have made discoveries.

(iii) The failures are quite complex – some point to under-investment, and some to over-investment.

Now let us drop assumption (ii) and allow for the possibility of **licensing**. The important point about licensing is that it now gives firms a direct financial reward for sharing information – though notice that this will only apply to *research outcome information*. To consider the implications of allowing for licensing, consider again the three sets of innovation decisions that have to be made.

1. Research Outcome Information-Sharing

The ability to license will potentially give firms incentives to share information when they are producing substitute products, and will reward them for sharing information that they would have been prepared to give away free when producing complementary products.

Now it is well known that licensing may not induce firms to share information. There are two problems. First licensing is problematic when there are more than two firms, since the price any one firm is willing to pay to acquire a license will depend on how many other licenses are sold, and it may be difficult for licensor to commit to decisions on this. Second, even when there are only two firms involved, licensing will only take place when the maximum amount the buyer is willing to pay exceeds the minimum price the seller is willing to accept – and, as is well known, this condition will not always be satisfied. In particular, licensing may not occur when firms produce substitute products and the innovation is sufficiently large.

2. R&D Investment

It is important to recognise that even when licensing induces firms to fully share information, it still has all the R&D market failures. In particular, the *strategic investment effect* is still present since firms are keen to be the first to discover and so receive rather than pay the licence fee. In the particular case of complementary products this means that whereas the *strategic investment effect* would have been negative in the absence of licensing, it is now positive.

Against this background let us now drop assumption (i) and allow firms to form a Research Joint Venture (RJV). A research joint venture (RJV) is a mechanism whereby firms are able to take decisions about *all* aspects of innovation – information-sharing; R&D; research design – in a collaborative/co-operative fashion. Throughout the chpter we will follow much of the literature and simply assume that firms operating in an RJV are unable to collaborate on pricing/output decisions. This is not to deny that this is potentially a serious problem. However the aim of this paper is to show that even in the absence of this consideration, RJVs may be more problematic than much of the academic and policy discussion has typically recognised.

To simplify the discussion we will follow the bulk of the literature and in the rest of this paper we concentrate on the case where there are just two firms.

Now intuitively, by operating in a co-operative fashion an RJV can potentially address almost all of the market failures referred to above. Let us consider these in turn.

1. Research Outcome Information-Sharing

By acting cooperatively firms will have incentives to share R&D outcome information that they would not have shared when acting individually – as in the case of substitute products without licensing. In much of the literature it is just *assumed* that RJVs will fully share information. However, as we will see, it turns out that if RJVs can *choose* whether or not to share information then they may not do so. Indeed information will be shared inside an RJV under precisely the same circumstances as it will be shared under licensing. In this sense RJVs confer no information-sharing advantages over licensing. One case where there will be powerful incentives to share information arises when there are complementarities to be exploited, so RJVs will typically eliminate the under-exploited *complementarities effect*.

2.   R&D Investment

RJVs can ameliorate almost all the market failures associated with R&D.

- RJVs can eliminate the *stand-alone effect*, since the firms in the RJV will base decisions on the benefits to the group rather than to the individual firm.

- An RJV can reduce the *strategic effect*, since firms will no longer be trying to innovate ahead of their rivals.
- An RJV can eliminate the *spillover effect* since it will be able to internalise any externalities.
- RJVs can eliminate the under-exploited *complementarities under-investment effect* by fully anticipating the benefits to be had from exploiting complementarities.

Notice that the only R&D market failure not addressed by the RJV is the *undervaluation effect*. As we will see, this turns out to be crucial in appraising the performance of RJVs.

3. Research Design

An RJV can in principle choose to operate a single laboratory, and so, when research discoveries are duplicative or perfect substitutes then it can avoid duplication of effort.

On the other hand when research discoveries are complementary then an RJV can operate two laboratories and can design the research paths that each pursues so as to maximise the potential complementarity that can later be exploited.

Given these potential benefits, it is not surprising that RJVs have received considerable attention.[4] However when one examines the theoretical literature on the subject, it turns out that, while it has provided some useful insights, nevertheless there are a number of weaknesses in the way it typically models RJVs, and consequently the analysis fails to fully address many of the above issues.[5] The major weaknesses of this literature are as follows.

(i)   The only type of information flows considered are exogenous involuntary spillovers. These are either the same in the cooperative equilibrium as in the non-cooperative equilibrium or else it is *assumed* that they are greater in the cooperative equilibrium. In neither case does the theory *explain* how cooperation might lead to greater information sharing between firms.[6]

(ii) Research discoveries by firms are assumed to be perfect complements. This means that in both the cooperative and the non-cooperative equilibrium, it is assumed that information gained from other firms just adds to the progress that a firm makes on its own. This ignores the possibility of needless duplication of research, and also that one of the benefits of an

RJV is that it exploits better complementarities.

(iii) A related problem is that equilibria are assumed to be symmetric. In particular, in both the cooperative and the non-cooperative equilibrium all firms are active in R&D, and all do the same amount of R&D. This ignores the possible cost savings by concentrating R&D in a smaller number of labs.

(iv) The non-cooperative equilibrium is taken to be one in which no licensing is possible. Since many of the models assume that there are just two firms, it would seem sensible to allow the possibility of licensing – particularly if one wants to understand the full benefits of cooperation versus non-cooperation[7] – given that licensing provides a mechanism for information sharing to non-cooperating firms.

In two recent papers (Katsoulacos and Ulph, 1998a,b) we have tried to correct some of the weaknessess of the existing literature by using models in which:

(i) Information-sharing is endogenous in both the cooperative and non-cooperative equilibrium.

(ii) A general degree of complementarity/substitutability is allowed between research discoveries.

(iii) The number of research labs that will be active in the cooperative equilibrium[8] is endogenously determined and the equilibrium may be asymmetric.

Further the framework developed in the K&U (1998a) paper allows for firms that belong in the same or in different industries and also allows for process or product innovation. However none of these papers provides a welfare evaluation of RJVs. Also, they do not take into account the possibility of licensing in the non-cooperative equilibrium. Welfare analyses of RJVs have actually appeared in DeBondt and Wu (1997), Kamien et al (1992) and Martin (1994),[9] though none of these tackles any of the weaknesses just mentioned which we believe is crucial in analysing RJVs and the welfare consequences of RJVs.[10] Katsoulacos and Ulph (1999) contains an welfare evaluation of RJVs incorporating features (i) – (iii) albeit for the case of substitute products (firms belonging to the same industry) and perfect substitute research paths. Gravenitz and Ulph (2000a) also incorporate features (i) and (iii) in an analysis of the case of perfectly complementary research paths. Gravenitz and Ulph (2000b) extend this analysis by allowing firms to choose the degree of complementarity in research paths and by considering subsidies. The last three papers in addition allow for licensing in the non-cooperative equilibrium. In the next section we describe a general model that is based on the Katsoulacos and Ulph

(1998a,b;1999) and Gravenitz and Ulph (2000b) papers and then in the following sections we use it to examine how RJVs perform under alternative assumptions.[11] We also examine how RJVs fare in relation to the second policy that has attracted attention, that of R&D subsidies.

3. THE MODEL

In addition to the three stages in the innovation decision-making process referred to above, there is a final fourth stage – the market stage – that determines the equilibrium output and prices that each firm obtains conditional on the outcome of the innovation process. In this sub-section we will state the assumptions that are made at each of these four stages. We will work backwards.

3.1. Stage 4: The Product Market Equilibrium

There are two firms. The products they produce can be either substitutes or complements. The two firms spend money on R&D in order to make a discovery. R&D determines the probability of making a discovery, and each firm's discovery probability is independent and depends solely on the amount of R&D that it does. For the moment we can think about the discovery that a firm makes being either a process innovation or a product innovation, though, for simplicity, much of the later discussion will focus on process innovation.

For much of the paper we do not need to be very explicit about the nature of the market equilibrium – e.g. whether it is Cournot or Bertrand. The crucial point is that we assume that the nature of the market equilibrium is exactly the same however decisions get taken in the innovation stages. Thus we rule out the possibility that if firms cooperate in innovation decisions they will cooperate on pricing and output decisions. We also rule out the ability of the social planner to set prices and output.

Let $\pi(t,\tilde{t})$ denote the operating profits that a firm will make when the total amount of progress it has made in cost reduction or quality improvement is t while that of the other firm is $\tilde{t}$. We make the following assumptions:

A(i) $\dfrac{\partial \pi}{\partial t} > 0$, so firms always benefit from any increase in their own progress;

A(ii) $\dfrac{d\pi(t,t)}{dt} > 0$ so if both firms equally improve the amount of progress they make then each will be better off.

We have said nothing about the sign of $\dfrac{\partial \pi}{\partial \tilde{t}}$. We distinguish between the case where firms are producing *substitute products* in which case $\dfrac{\partial \pi}{\partial \tilde{t}} < 0$ and the case where they produce *complementary products* in which case $\dfrac{\partial \pi}{\partial \tilde{t}} > 0$.

We also let $\Sigma(t,\tilde{t}) = \pi(t,\tilde{t}) + \pi(\tilde{t},t)$ denote the joint profits of the two firms. We assume

A(iii) $t \geq \tilde{t} \Rightarrow \dfrac{\partial \Sigma}{\partial t} > 0$, so joint profits always increase in the progress of the leader.

Notice that it follows from A(ii) that $\dfrac{d\Sigma(t,t)}{dt} > 0$ so joint profits increase when both firms equally improve the amount of progress. We also assume:

A(iv) $\dfrac{\partial^2 \Sigma}{\partial t^2} > 0$, $\dfrac{\partial^2 \Sigma}{\partial \tilde{t}^2} > 0$ so joint profits are convex in the progress of each firm.

Finally we let $S(t,\tilde{t})$ denote social surplus. Obviously $S(t,\tilde{t}) = \Sigma(t,\tilde{t}) + CS(t,\tilde{t})$, where $CS(t,\tilde{t})$ represents consumer surplus. We assume

A(v) $\dfrac{\partial CS}{\partial t} > 0$, $\dfrac{\partial CS}{\partial \tilde{t}} > 0$, $\dfrac{\partial S}{\partial t} > 0$, $\dfrac{\partial S}{\partial \tilde{t}} > 0$ so both consumer surplus and total surplus increase whenever either firm makes more progress.

3.2 Stage 3: The Information Acquisition and Sharing Technology

We need to relate the total amount of progress that each firm makes to the amount of usable knowledge that it acquires as a result of any discovery it makes itself – denote this by s – and to any usable knowledge that it might acquire as a result of a discovery by the other firm – denote this by r.

We assume that if a firm has not discovered then $s = 0$, while, if it has discovered, then $s = q$, where $q > 0$ is an exogenously given parameter reflecting the rate at which new ideas are arriving in the industry.[12]

The amount of useable knowledge that firm i receives from the other firm depends on three things:

- whether the other firm has discovered;
- the fraction of its knowledge that the other firm chooses to share – which we denote generically by σ, $\underline{\sigma} \leq \sigma \leq 1$, where $\underline{\sigma}$ reflects the extent of information spillovers – unintended and unrewarded leakages of information;
- the 'usefulness' of the information it receives from the other firm – denote this by κ, $0 \leq \kappa \leq 1$. κ will generally depend on whether or not i has itself discovered and, if it has discovered, on the degree of complementarity between the research paths chosen by the two firms.

Obviously, if the other firm has not discovered then $r = 0$. If the other firm has discovered then $r = \kappa.\sigma.q$.

In Katsoulacos and Ulph (1998a) we introduced a very general technology $t = \tau(s,r)$ relating the way in which these two types of knowledge could be combined to determine the overall progress that a firm makes, where the function $\tau(s,r)$ takes the form:

$$\tau(s,r) = \begin{cases} s+t & \gamma = \infty \\ \left[s^{\frac{1+\gamma}{\gamma}} + r^{\frac{1+\gamma}{\gamma}} \right]^{\frac{1+\gamma}{\gamma}} & , \quad 0 < \gamma < \infty \\ MAX[s,r], & \gamma = 0 \end{cases}$$

$\gamma = 0$ is the case referred to above as that for which research paths or discoveries are *perfect substitutes* or *duplicative*. $\gamma = \infty$ corresponds to the case where research discoveries are what we have called above *additive* or *perfect complements* – for here any useful knowledge received from the other firm simply adds to the total amount of knowledge generated by the firm in question. This is the case that has been dealt with in most of the literature.

It is useful to split this case into two sub-cases. The first is that of *weak complementarity* where a firm can learn something useful from the other firm's discovery whether or not it itself has discovered. This is the case considered by Katsoulacos and Ulph (1998a) and Gravenitz and Ulph (2000a). The second case is that of *strong complementarity*, where a firm can learn something useful from the other firm *only* when it itself has discovered. This is the case considered in Gravenitz and Ulph (2000b).

In what follows we will focus on the two extreme cases where research discoveries are *perfect substitutes* and where research discoveries are *strongly complementary*. These two cases give most of the insights about how the nature of the information-sharing technology affects the performance of the RJV.

In order to do this we need to say more about the 'information-sharing' and 'information – usefulness' parameters (σ and κ) in various situations. Obviously, when neither firm discovers there is no information to be exchanged. In the case where only one firm discovers, we are interested in the fraction of information that this firm shares with the firm that has not discovered – denote this by σ^{10}, $\underline{\sigma} \leq \sigma^{10} \leq 1$. In the case where both firms discover we are interested in σ_j^{11}, $j = 1, 2$; $\underline{\sigma} \leq \sigma_j^{11} \leq 1$ the fraction of the information discovered by firm j that it shares with the other firm.

To specify the 'information – usefulness' parameters we need to consider separately more carefully the cases of *perfect substitute* and *strong complementary* research discoveries. In the case of *strongly complementary research discoveries* where we assume that a firm can use the other firm's discovery only if it itself has discovered, it is natural to assume that $\kappa^{01} = 0$, where κ^{01} measures the usefulness to the firm that has not discovered of the innovation that the other firm has. If we let κ^{11} to denote the usefulness to each firm of the other firm's innovation when both have discovered then we assume that $\kappa^{11} = \delta$, $0 \leq \delta \leq 1$ where δ, $0 \leq \delta \leq 1$ is a variable that reflects the *degree of complementarity* between research discoveries that has been obtained through the choice of research paths at the research design stage. We will discuss this in more detail below. In this case, when both firms discover, the total progress that each makes is $t_1^{11} = q + \sigma_2^{11}.\delta.q$, $t_2^{11} = q + \sigma_1^{11}.\delta.q$. If only one discovers its progress is $t^{10} = q$ while the progress of the other firm is $t^{01} = 0$, which is independent of σ^{10}, the fraction of information shared by the firm that has discovered. Obviously if neither discovers then $t^{00} = 0$.

In the case of *perfect substitute* research discoveries it is natural to assume that since firms are effectively discovering the same thing, $\kappa^{11} = 0$ and $\kappa^{01} = 1$. In this case, if both firms discover then $t_1^{11} = t_2^{11} = q$ irrespective of how much information is shared by the firms. If only one firm discovers then $t^{10} = q$, $t^{01} = \sigma^{10}.q$. Notice that in the case where research discoveries are *perfect substitutes* then the amount of information that is shared only matters in the case where only one firm discovers, while, in the case of *strong complementary* research discoveries the amount of information that is shared matters only in the case where both firms discover.

3.3 Stage 2: The R&D Technology

We assume that the probability of each firm making a discovery depends solely on the R&D that it does.[13] Denote this R&D technology by the cost function $C(p)$, p, $0 \leq p \leq 1$ denotes the probability of discovery.

Assume

C (i) $C(0) \geq 0$; $C'(0) = 0$; $C'(p) > 0$; $0 < p < 1$;

C (ii) $C''(p) > 0$; $0 \leq p \leq 1$;

C (iii) $p \to 1 \Rightarrow C'(p) \to \infty$.

Assumption C(i) allows for fixed costs in R&D though we assume that these are sufficiently small that both firms would undertake R&D in any non-cooperative equilibrium. The assumption that the marginal cost at zero p is zero guarantees that any lab always does some R&D. Assumption C(ii) reflects diminishing marginal productivity in R&D, while C(iii) is made to ensure that no firm ever ends up discovering for sure.

3.4 Stage 1: Research Design

There are two research design issues.

(i)   The number of laboratories

We assume that in the non-cooperative equilibrium each firm operates a single lab, whereas both the RJV and the social planner can decide whether there should just be a single lab.

(ii) Choice of research path

We set out below a simple way of illustrating the idea that the choice of research path will affect the *degree of complementarity* between their discoveries that firms will be able to obtain. Assume that firms have open to them many possible research paths. We describe these paths by the amount of progress that a firm can achieve in each of two dimensions (x, y) through its own discovery. It is assumed that the set of feasible research paths that each firm has open to it is

$$F = \left\{ (x, y) \mid x, y \geq 0, \; x + y = q \right\},$$

where $q > 0$ is as defined above. Thus a firm's research path is completely determined by specifying the value of x, $0 \leq x \leq q$ that it chooses. Notice that all research paths result in the same total amount of progress so that, if there were only one firm, it would be indifferent as to which path it chooses.

Suppose now that firm j, $j = 1, 2$ has made progress $(x_j, q - x_j)$ in each of the two dimensions. Suppose that both firms fully share information, and assume that discoveries made in the same dimension are *perfect substitutes* for one another – as specified above. Thus if the two firms share their knowledge on the x dimension the total progress each makes is $MAX[x_1, x_2]$, while if they share their knowledge on the y dimension, the total amount of progress that each makes is $MAX[q - x_1, q - x_2]$. As a result of sharing knowledge each firm will have made progress by an amount $z = q + k$, where $k = |x_1 - x_2|$.

We can then define $\delta = \dfrac{k}{q}$, $0 \leq \delta \leq 1$ as the *degree of complementarity* between their discoveries that firms have achieved by the choice of research paths. The following diagram illustrates.

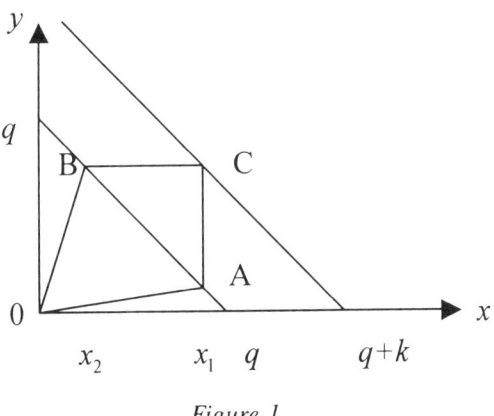

Figure 1

Here research outcomes $(x_1, q - x_1)$ and $(x_2, q - x_2)$ are represented by the points A and B respectively, while point C represents the outcome that can be achieved by sharing. This has a number of implications.

- If the two firms choose identical research paths – so $x_1 = x_2$ and $k = \delta = 0$

– then the two paths are *perfect substitutes*, and, as above, there is nothing to be gained by sharing information.

- The maximum degree of *research path coordination* that firms can achieve is $k = q$. This is obtained when the two firms specialise completely – each in a different dimension.

3.5 The Profit Functions

We can now draw the above assumptions together and define the payoffs to the various decision makers in the following general way.

(i) *Neither firm discovers*

Let $\pi^{00} = \pi(0,0)$ be the profits of each firm; $\Sigma^{00} = 2\pi^{00}$ their combined profits; and $S^{00} = S(0,0)$ the social surplus.

(ii) *Only 1 firm discovers*

Let:

$\pi^{10}(\sigma^{10}) = \pi(q, \sigma^{10}.\kappa^{01}.q)$ be the profits of the firm that has discovered;

$\pi^{01}(\sigma^{10}) = \pi(\sigma^{10}.\kappa^{01}.q, q)$ be the profits of the firm that has not discovered;

$\Sigma^{10}(\sigma^{10}) = \pi^{10}(\sigma^{10}) + \pi^{01}(\sigma^{10})$ be the combined profits of both firms;

$S^{10}(\sigma^{10}) = S(q, \sigma^{10}.\kappa^{01}.q)$ be the social surplus.

It follows from our assumptions A(i) – A(v) that $\pi^{10}(\sigma^{10})$ is a strictly decreasing function of σ^{10} if products are substitute, and a strictly increasing function if products are complements; that $\pi^{01}(\sigma^{10})$ and $S^{10}(\sigma^{10})$ are both strictly increasing functions of σ^{10}, while $\Sigma^{10}(\sigma^{10})$ is a strictly convex function of σ^{10}.

(iii) *Both firms discover*

When both firms discover and research paths are perfect substitutes then $\kappa^{11} = 0$, and the total progress of each firm is q irrespective of how much information is shared, so the payoffs are $\pi^{11}(q)$, $\Sigma^{11}(q)$ and $S^{11}(q)$ for the independent firm, the RJV and the social planner respectively.

Let $\pi_j^{11}(\delta,\sigma_1^{11},\sigma_2^{11}) = \pi(q+\sigma_i^{11}.\delta.q, q+\sigma_j^{11}.\delta.q)$, $i,j = 1,2$, $i \neq j$ be the profits of firm j as a function of the *degree of complementarity* and of the fractions of information shared by the two firms.

Let $\Sigma^{11} = \pi_1^{11}(\delta,\sigma_1^{11},\sigma_2^{11}) + \pi_2^{11}(\delta,\sigma_1^{11},\sigma_2^{11})$ denote aggregate profits.

Let $S^{11}(\delta,\sigma_1^{11},\sigma_2^{11})$ denote social surplus.

Notice that it follows from A(ii) and A(v) that if $\delta > 0$ then $\pi_j^{11}(\delta,1,1) >$ $\pi_j^{11}(\delta,\underline{\sigma},\underline{\sigma})$; $S^{11}(\delta,1,1) > S^{11}(\delta,\underline{\sigma},\underline{\sigma})$ so full information-sharing by both firms dominates no voluntary sharing, both for individual firms – and hence the RJV – and for the social planner. Also note that since an increase in δ increases the progress made by firms, from A(iv) and A(v), Σ and S are increasing functions of δ.

Finally notice that the two cases of *perfect substitute* discoveries and *strong complementary discoveries* can be thought of as special cases of all these formulae: perfect substitute research discoveries corresponds to the case where $\kappa^{01} = 1$; $\delta = 0$ whereas strong complementarity corresponds to the case $\kappa^{01} = 0$; $\delta \geq 0$.

3.6 Comparison with Alternative Models

Having described in detail our model it is useful to compare it once again to alternative models. The model that provided the starting point for much of the literature on RJVs in the last 15 years or so is that by D'Aspremont and Jacquemin (1988). This model does not itself consider the social optimum though our remarks apply to straightforward extensions of it that make social welfare comparisons. The D'Aspremont and Jacquemin model has the following main characteristics (similar characteristics to D'Aspremont and Jacquemin are present in much of the rest of the literature):

- It neglects the stage of research design – it is thus unable to examine neither the under-developed complementarities nor the under-investment in R&D due to this market failures, and cannot capture the fact that RJVs will perform better than the non-cooperative equilibrium with respect to these market failures.
- It neglects the stage of information sharing – it is thus unable to examine the insufficient information sharing market failure in both the coopera-

tive and non-cooperative equilibria and the fact that this may lead to excessive duplication of R&D effort when research paths are perfect substitutes (a case not examined at all) or to under-exploited complementarities when the research paths are perfect complements (the case examined by D'Aspremont and Jacquemin). Again by neglecting this stage it is not possible to capture the fact that RJVs may perform better than the non-cooperative equilibrium with respect to these market failures.

- Given the above two characteristics it is then reasonable to make a number of other assumptions (in particular, symmetry in equilibrium, no licensing and substitute product markets) that in a richer (four stage) framework are not innocent at all and their relaxation sheds new light on the relative efficiency of RJVs and non-cooperative equilibria.

In the D'Aspremont and Jacquemin model the main prediction is that RJVs will invest more on R&D than independent firms when spillovers are sufficiently high but the reverse will occur when spillovers are low.

4. THE MAIN RESULTS

Let us now turn to describe the decisions that are made by the various decision-makers at each of the three innovation stages of our model.

4.1 Stage 3: Research Output Information Sharing (Choice of σ)

4.1.1 The social planner

As noted in section 3.5 above S^{10} is a strictly increasing function of σ so there will be full information sharing if one firm discovers (remember that under our assumptions, if only one firm discovers, information sharing is relevant only with perfect substitute research paths, since with strong complementary paths if only one firm discovers the firm that does not discover cannot gain from the discovery of the other firm). When both firms discover information sharing is irrelevant with perfect substitute research paths whilst with strong complementary paths, from section 3.5, no information sharing will never be optimal. Since as it is easily shown (see, for example Gravenitz and Ulph 2000b) welfare will be higher if *both* firms shared information than if *only one* shared, it follows that:

Result 1: The social planner will always pursue *full* information sharing.

4.1.2 The RJV

Again, we start by noting that information sharing is not relevant if both firms discover and research paths are perfect substitutes. If both firms discover and research paths are strong complements, then, from section 3.5 above, the RJV will never opt for no voluntary information sharing. The only issue is whether the RJV would be better off still if only one firm fully shared information than if they both fully shared. It is easily shown (see Gravenitz and Ulph, 2000b) that:

Result 2: For as long as both firms discover and are active in the equilibrium full information sharing is optimal for the RJV.

If one firm discovers (so information sharing is only relevant with perfect substitute research paths) then, as we have seen, Σ^{10} is a strictly convex function of σ^{10} and firms will agree that the successful firm will fully share information if joint profits are higher than if it did not voluntarily share information. This will arise when the successful firm is unable to sufficiently exploit any advantage it obtains by being the sole firm with the new product or technology that it can push industry profits close to the maximal profits that arise under monopoly. So:

Result 3: With process innovation and substitute products full information sharing is optimal for the RJV when one firm discovers if the innovation is sufficiently small and/or the level of involuntary information leakage, $\underline{\sigma}$, is sufficiently high.

4.1.3 The non-cooperative equilibrium

From section 3.5, $\pi^{10}(\sigma^{10})$ is a strictly decreasing function of σ^{10} if products are substitute, and a strictly increasing function if products are complements and $\pi^{01}(\sigma^{10})$ is a strictly increasing function of σ^{10}. Thus, even in the absence of licensing, if one firm discovers (and research paths are perfect substitutes) there will be full information sharing when products are complements but there will be no information sharing when products are substitutes. From 3.5, $\pi_j^{11}(\delta, \sigma_1^{11}, \sigma_2^{11}) = \pi(q + \sigma_i^{11}.\delta.q, q + \sigma_j^{11}.\delta.q)$, $i, j = 1, 2$, $i \neq j$ so given our assumption A(ii) the same conclusion holds when both firms discover and the research paths are strong complements.

If licensing is allowed then firms can bargain over whether or not information should be voluntarily shared. But we know that when firms bargain they will wish to achieve an efficient outcome – i.e. one that maximizes joint profits – with the size of the license fee determining how any gain is split between the parties. Thus the information-sharing decision will be exactly the same as for the RJV as is noted for perfect substitute research paths in Katsoulacos and Ulph (1999) and for strong complementary research paths by Gravenitz and Ulph (2000b).

Thus we have:

Result 4: When licensing is allowed, then, in the non-cooperative equilibrium, the amount of information that is shared between firms will be exactly the same as in the RJV.

Corollary: In the non-cooperative equilibrium with licensing firms will fully share information when both firms discover; when only one discovers and products are substitute full information-sharing will take place as long as the innovation is sufficiently small and/or the level of involuntary information leakage, σ, is sufficiently high.

The importance of this result is that it shows that when licensing is allowed then, in terms of the *quantum* of information that is shared, RJVs have no advantages over the non-cooperative equilibrium. However, as we will see below, the way in which information is shared still matters as far as the R&D decisions are made. In particular, licensing still gives firms an incentive to over-invest in order to be the first to discover.

4.2 Stage 2: R&D Investment (Choice of p)

The value to firm i, $i = 1, 2$ of engaging independently in R&D is

$$p_1 p_2 \pi^{11} + p_i(1-p_j)\pi^{01} + p_j(1-p_i)\pi^{01} + (1-p_1)(1-p_2)\pi^{00} - C(p_i), \quad j \neq 1,$$

so, in the non-cooperative equilibrium, firm i takes p_j, $j \neq 1$, as given and maximizes this expression with respect to p_i. We then seek a non-cooperative Nash equilibrium. In an RJV firms jointly choose p_1 and p_2 to maximize expected joint profits $p_1 p_2 \Sigma^{11} + p_1(1-p_2)\Sigma^{10} + p_2(1-p_1)\Sigma^{10} + (1-p_1)(1-p_2)\Sigma^{00}$ $-C(p_1) - C(p_2)$. Finally the social planner will choose p_1 and p_2 to maximize expected social surplus $p_1 p_2 S^{11} + p_1(1-p_2)S^{10} + p_2(1-p_1)S^{10} + (1-p_1)$ $(1-p_2)S^{00} - C(p_1) - C(p_2)$. In writing these expressions we have used the fact that $\Sigma^{10}(S^{10}) = \Sigma^{01}(S^{01})$.

It is straightforward to show that when two labs are operated,[14] then, whatever decision-making environment we are considering, the only equilibrium solution is the symmetric one in which both labs have the same probability of discovery. Moreover, whether the decision-maker is the social planner, the RJV, or the individual firm in a non-cooperative equilibrium, the equilibrium probability of discovery in each lab is characterized by the same first order condition:

$$p.CT + (1-p)PI = C'(p) \qquad (1)$$

Here CT is what is known as the *competitive threat* and is the difference between the payoff (to whomever is making the decision) from having one of the labs make the discovery and the payoff if that lab does not make the discovery *conditional on the other lab having already discovered*. PI is what is known as the *profit incentive* and is the difference between the payoff (to whoever is making the decision) from having one of the labs make the discovery *conditional on the other lab NOT having discovered*.

The LHS of (1) is just the marginal benefit from an increase in the probability of discovery by one lab, given the probability of discovery by the other lab. This marginal benefit is a linear function of p and is increasing (resp.decreasing) according as the CT is greater than (resp. less than) PI. The RHS of (1) is the marginal cost of an increase in the probability of discovery by a single lab.

In discussing CTs and PIs in the various decision-making environments we will use the following notational convention. First we will not explicitly show the variable q in the payoff functions. Then, when only one firm discovers (we are in state 10) we will write the payoffs as functions of the single information sharing parameter (as already mentioned the value of κ is in this case known, $\kappa^{01} = 1$ with perfect substitute and $\kappa^{01} = 0$ with strong complement research paths). When both firms discover (we are in state 11) the payoffs are functions of the two information sharing parameters and of $\kappa^{11} = \delta$. Thus we will use the convention of writing the payoffs when both firms discover as functions of the two information sharing parameters and of δ. If we let $\hat{\delta}$, δ^c, δ^n denote, respectively, the degree of research discovery complementarity achieved by a social planner, a research joint venture, and independent firms, then, if research discoveries are perfect substitutes we can say that $\hat{\delta} = \delta^c = \delta^n = 0$.

The profit incentives and competitive threats of the various decision makers in various situations can now be determined, and are set out in the table below.

Notice that as shown in section 4.1 above when both firms discover (state 11) there will be full information sharing irrespective of the decision-making environment. Also notice that the licence fee (F) depends on the size of the information spillover, $\underline{\sigma}$. For example, if the bargaining strengths of the two firms are equal then

Table 1

	Profit Incentive	Competitive Threat
1. Social Planner: Full Information Sharing	$S^{10}(1) - S^{00}$	$S^{11}(\hat{\delta},1,1) - S^{10}(1)$
2. RJV: Full Information Sharing in 10	$\Sigma^{10}(1) - \Sigma^{00}$	$\Sigma^{11}(\delta^{c},1,1) - \Sigma^{10}(1)$
3. RJV: No Information Sharing in 10	$\Sigma^{10}(\underline{\sigma}) - \Sigma^{00}$	$\Sigma^{11}(\delta^{c},1,1) - \Sigma^{10}(\underline{\sigma})$
4. Independent firms: Full Info – sharing in 10	$\left[\pi^{10}(1) - \pi^{00}\right] + F(\underline{\sigma})$	$\left[\pi^{11}(\delta^{n},1,1) - \pi^{01}(1)\right] + F(\underline{\sigma})$
5. Independent firms: No Info-sharing in 10	$\pi^{10}(\underline{\sigma}) - \pi^{00}$	$\pi^{11}(\delta^{n},1,1) - \pi^{01}(\underline{\sigma})$

$F(\underline{\sigma}) = \frac{1}{2}\left[\Sigma^{10}(\underline{\sigma}) - \Sigma^{10}(1)\right]$, so the two firms just share the gains from information-sharing.

To better understand the implications of these formulae, notice first that when only one firm discovers but full information-sharing does take place then each firm is in a symmetric duopoly with progress q – which is precisely the outcome when both firms discover and the degree of research discovery complementarity is 0. When firms act independently the firm that makes the discovery gets the profits arising from this symmetric duopoly plus the license fee, while the firm that fails to innovate gets these profits minus the license fee. It follows that

$$S^{10}(1) = S^{11}(0,1,1) ; \quad \Sigma^{10}(1) = \Sigma^{11}(0,1,1) ; \quad \pi^{10}(1) = \pi^{01}(1) = \pi^{11}(0,1,1).$$

If we substitute these expressions into the above table and do some re-arranging we get the following.

Notice first that when research discoveries are perfect substitutes and so $\hat{\delta} = \delta^{c} = \delta^{n} = 0$ then the competitive threats facing the RJV and the social planner are both zero. However when research discoveries are perfect complements then both these competitive threats are positive.

This table clearly illustrates all the R&D market failures that we introduced in the earlier part of the paper. To understand these we undertake a systematic comparison of rows 2-5 of the table with row 1.

By comparing row 2 with row 1 we see that since $\hat{\delta} = \delta^{c} = 1$ (see section 4.3 below) a full information-sharing RJV suffers from just a single innovation market failure – the *undervaluation effect*. As explained above this reflects the fact that the objective of firms is profits and so they ignore the gain in consumer surplus from some new technology or product. Compared to the social optimum this means that the profit incentive is too low, as is the competitive threat when research discoveries are complementary. So we have:

Table 2

	Profit Incentive	Competitive Threat
1. Social Planner: Full Information Sharing	$\left[\Sigma^{11}(0,1,1)-\Sigma^{00}\right]+$ $\left[CS^{11}(0,1,1)-CS^{00}\right]$	$\left[\Sigma^{11}(\hat{\delta},1,1)-\Sigma^{11}(0,1,1)\right]+$ $\left\lfloor CS^{11}(\hat{\delta},1,1)-CS^{11}(0,1,1)\right\rfloor$
2. RJV: Full Information Sharing in 10	$\Sigma^{11}(0,1,1)-\Sigma^{00}$	$\Sigma^{11}(\hat{\delta},1,1)-\Sigma^{11}(0,1,1)$
3. RJV: No Information Sharing in 10	$\left[\Sigma^{11}(0,1,1)-\Sigma^{00}\right]+$ $\left[\Sigma^{10}(\underline{\sigma})-\Sigma^{11}(0,1,1)\right]$	$\Sigma^{11}(\hat{\delta},1,1)-\Sigma^{11}(0,1,1)$ $\left[\Sigma^{10}(\underline{\sigma})-\Sigma^{11}(0,1,1)\right]$
4. Independent firms: Full Info – sharing in 10	$\frac{1}{2}\left[\Sigma^{11}(0,1,1)-\Sigma^{00}\right]+$ $F(0)-\left[F(0)-F(\underline{\sigma})\right]$	$\frac{1}{2}\left[\Sigma^{11}(\delta^{c},1,1)-\Sigma^{11}(0,1,1)\right]$ $+F(0)-\left[F(0)-F(\underline{\sigma})\right]$ $-\left[\pi^{11}(\delta^{c},1,1)-\pi^{11}(\delta^{n},1,1)\right]$ $-\left[\pi^{01}(\underline{\sigma})-\pi^{01}(0)\right]$
5. Independent firms: No Info-sharing in 10	$\frac{1}{2}\left[\Sigma^{11}(0,1,1)-\Sigma^{00}\right]+$ $\left[\pi^{10}(0)-\pi^{11}(0,1,1)\right]$ $-\left[\pi^{10}(0)-\pi^{11}(\underline{\sigma})\right]$	$\frac{1}{2}\left[\Sigma^{11}(\delta^{c},1,1)-\Sigma^{11}(0,1,1)\right]$ $+\left[\pi^{11}(0,1,1)-\pi^{01}(0)\right]$ $-\left[\pi^{01}(\underline{\sigma})-\pi^{01}(0)\right]$ $-\left[\pi^{11}(\delta^{c},1,1)-\pi^{11}(\delta^{n},1,1)\right]$

Result 5: a full information- sharing RJV will invest too little in R&D.

From row 3 we see that if the RJV chooses not to fully share information then there is a *strategic information-witholding* market failure that will raise the profit incentive but lower the competitive threat. Thus:

Result 6: we cannot say (at the general level we are operating) whether the RJV that chooses not to fully share information will under- or over-invest in R&D.

Of course even if a no information sharing RJV performs better in R&D than an information sharing RJV this does not in general imply that social welfare will not be higher in the latter, since the level of social welfare will depend on R&D investment AND information diffusion (for an explicit comparison of the levels of social welfare under alternative decision-making frameworks albeit for perfect substitute research paths, see Katsoulacos and Ulph, 1999[15]).

If we now consider row 4 (full information sharing non-cooperative equilibrium) and compare this with row 2, then we will learn what market failures independent firms are subject to *in addition* to the *undervaluation effect*. These are as follows.

- If we consider the first terms in both the competitive threat and the profit incentive, then we notice that these are precisely half the corresponding terms for the RJV. This reflects the *stand alone effect*. Thus, in making their R&D decisions firms take account solely of the effect on their own profits and ignore the fact that, if their discovery were shared, the industry could benefit. *Ceteris paribus* this leads to under-investment in R&D relative to a full information-sharing RJV.
- The second term in both the profit incentive and the competitive threat is the license fee that would prevail if there were no spillovers. This captures the *strategic investment incentive* with firms competing to be the first to innovate and so be the firm that gets the licence fee rather than the one that has to pay it. *Ceteris paribus* this leads to over-investment in R&D.
- The third term in both the competitive threat and the profit incentive is the difference between the licence fee when there are no spillovers and the licence fee with the prevailing level of spillovers, $\underline{\sigma}$. This captures the idea that to the extent involuntary information leakages – spillovers – reduce the value added from voluntary information sharing and hence the licence fee, then the strategic incentive will be smaller with spillovers than it would otherwise have been. This is the *spillover effect* and, *ceteris paribus*, leads to under-investment.
- The final term in the expression for the competitive threat captures the *underdeveloped complementarities effect*. This shows that if independent firms are unable to fully co-ordinate their choice of research path ($\delta^n < 1$, see also section 4.3 below) and so are unable to obtain the maximum degree of complementarity, then this could again lead to an undervaluation of the benefits of R&D and hence to under-investment in R&D. This term will be zero if research discoveries are perfect substitutes or if independent firms do in fact achieve maximum complementarity.

The above imply that:

Result 7: a full information sharing non-cooperative equilibrium may or may not come closer to the social optimum R&D than a full information sharing RJV.

More specifically, the prediction of D'Aspremont and Jacquemin that with sufficiently low involuntary spillovers (low σ) in the non-cooperative equilibrium firms will invest more on R&D may well not hold in this richer framework. Also their result that with sufficiently high involuntary spillovers (high $\underline{\sigma}$) in the non-cooperative equilibrium firms will invest less on R&D than in the RJV will not hold in our framework Indeed, Gravenitz and Ulph (2000b) show that:

Result 8: if research paths are strong complements and if the non-cooperative equilibrium achieves full research design coordination ($\delta^n = 1$) then it will invest more on R&D than a (full information sharing) RJV and will welfare dominate the RJV.[16]

However, Katsoulacos and Ulph (1999) show that:

Result 9: with perfect substitute research paths full information sharing RJVs may welfare dominate full information sharing non-cooperative equilibria (even if the latter outperform the former in R&D investment terms) because of the excessive duplication market failure in non-cooperative equilibria.

Finally notice that when independent firms do not share information (row 5 in Table 2) then they are subject to exactly the same market failures (due to the strategic incentive and spillover effects) as when they do. The only difference is that the precise magnitude – though not the sign – of these effects may differ between the profit incentive and the competitive threat.

Thus a very important implication of this analysis is the following:

Result 10: The nature of R&D market failures does not depend on the *quantum* of information that is shared so much as on the *mechanism* through which it is shared.

Thus when firms act independently, they are subject to exactly the same market failures when they choose not to share information as when they fully share it through the mechanism of licensing. All that happens is that the precise expressions for some of the market failures are just somewhat different. On the one hand both independent firms and a research joint venture can result in full information-sharing, yet independent firms can be subject to up to four additional market failures – though it is hard to say in general whether independent firms will do more or less R&D than if they were operating as an RJV.

4.3 Stage 1: Research Design (Choice of κ)

Notice that since we are only dealing with the cases of perfect substitute and strong complementary research paths and we know that in the first case always $\kappa^{11} = 0$ and $\kappa^{01} = 1$ and in the second case $\kappa^{01} = 1$ and $\kappa^{11} = \delta > 0$, the only research design variable that we have to determine is δ. Now δ, $0 \leq \delta \leq 1$, is a variable that reflects the *degree of complementarity* between research discoveries that has been obtained through the choice of research paths at the research design stage, for the case where both firms have discovered and research paths are complementary. From section 3.5 above, joint profits (Σ) and social welfare (S) are increasing functions of δ, so if we let $\hat{\delta}, \delta^c, \delta^n$ denote, respectively, the degree of research discovery complementarity achieved by a social planner, a research joint venture, and independent firms, then, if research discoveries are perfect complements:

Result 11: $\hat{\delta} = \delta^c = 1$.

Further, as shown in Gravenitz and Ulph (2000b):

Result 12: while it is possible that independent firms can also achieve full complementarity, there are circumstances where they will not, and we will have $\delta^n < 1$.

5. RJVS vs R&D SUBSIDIES[17]

A major weakness of the literature that is based on the D'Aspremont and Jacquemin framework is that it can give very misleading policy advice. To see this, consider the following result obtained recently by Hinloopen (1997a, b; 2000)[18] within the same framework as that of D'Aspremont and Jacquemin. So spillovers are fixed and are the same in both the non-cooperative and cooperative equilibria.[19] The number of laboratories is fixed as are research designs. Thus the only difference between cooperative and non-cooperative behaviour lies in the amount of R&D each lab does (in short, the research design and information sharing decisions are ignored). Hinloopen shows that R&D subsidies *alone* are sufficient to achieve the social optimum. The intuition is clear – whether firms act cooperatively or non-cooperatively it is possible to choose a subsidy that achieves the first-best. There is only one policy target – R&D – so only one instrument is needed.

Let us now revert to the framework of this paper and suppose that there is an additional stage 0 to the game at which the government has two policy instruments: it can allow or disallow firms to form research joint ventures; and it can impose an R&D subsidy. We assume that if the government allows firms to form an RJV, then the R&D subsidy is not conditioned on whether firms choose to form an RJV. It is clear that in that case, if firms are allowed to join an RJV they will always choose to do so.

Since we wish to focus on how the (equivalence) result of Hinloopen (1997a, b; 2000) is affected by our alternative specification of how an RJV performs, we will follow him in ignoring the distortionary costs of funding an R&D subsidy.

The following conclusions are obtained by Gravenitz and Ulph (2000b) for the case of strong complementary research paths:

- In all cases where the non-cooperative equilibrium achieves full research design co-ordination in the absence of a subsidy, full co-ordination is also obtained when the optimal subsidy is imposed – so allowing the non-cooperative equilibrium to achieve the full social optimum.
- It appears that the various effects that a subsidy has on research design co-ordination pretty well cancel each other out in the sense that in virtually every case examined the research design co-ordination decision is the same when there is no subsidy as when the 'optimal' subsidy is imposed.
- There is one case where the imposition of the R&D subsidy improves both the research design co-ordination decision and the R&D decision, allowing the non-cooperative equilibrium to achieve the full social optimum.
- However there remain cases where the imposition of the subsidy does not induce full research design co-ordination, and so an R&D subsidy, by itself cannot induce the full social optimum.

These conclusions suggest that:

Result 13: when research paths are complementary the use of R&D subsidies and the promotion of cooperation are highly complementary policies and the government can achieve desirable outcomes with both policies that it cannot achieve with each alone.

However:

Result 14: Result 12 cannot be reproduced for perfect substitute research paths.

The policy implications of perfect substitute research paths have been examined by Katsoulacos and Ulph (1998b). Here, on the one hand, we show that again the Hinloopen result may not hold, in particular when the market equilibrium (cooperative and non-cooperative) does not generate the right amount of (research outcome) information sharing and also does not generate the right amount of R&D. However now we may not get the socially optimal outcome *even* with a combination of RJV promotion and subsidies because the information sharing failure will arise under exactly the same circumstances in the non-cooperative and the cooperative (RJV) equilibria[20] (while with strong complementary research, RJV promotion may be used to correct the research design failure in the non-cooperative equilibrium and then the subsidy to correct the R&D investment failure).

6. CONCLUSIONS

The innovation process suffers from a large number of market failures. RJVs have attracted considerable attention from economists in the last 15 years as a means of dealing with many of these market failures. A very large literature has developed most of which takes as its starting point the analysis of D'Aspremont and Jacquemin (1988).

We have argued in a number of contributions in the last four years that this literature has produced largely misleading results because it has neglected two very important aspects of the innovation decisions of firms:

a)   The research design decision
b)   The information sharing decision.

Neglecting these two decisions seriously distorts the comparison between RJVs and the non-cooperative equilibrium as well as the comparison between these and the social optimum and the consequent policy implications. In the present paper we have produced a synthesis and generalization of our previous contributions and those of Greanevitz and Ulph. This has allowed us to provide a very succinct account of exactly how RJVs differ from non-cooperative equilibria and of their relative performance in relation to the social optimum.

NOTES

1. As in almost all of the economics literature on technical change we will use the terms 'technical progress', 'discoveries', 'innovation', and 'new knowledge' interchangeably to indicate the output of the knowledge generating process and we will assume that R&D investment is the sole input to this process.
2. We will use the terms 'research path' and 'research discovery' interchangeably.
3. See the collection of articles in the *Handbook of the Economics of Innovation and Technological Change* (1995), edited by P. Stoneman.
4. See the collection of articles edited by Poyagou-Theotoky (1997).
5. Of course not every paper suffers from every one of the weaknesses we identify. However most of them arise in the paper by d'Aspremont and Jacquemin (1988) which has become a classic reference in the literature.
6. In DeBondt and Wu (1997) a distinction is made between involuntary leakages and voluntary information flows but the latter is captured by an exogenous parameter that varies between the non-cooperative equilibrium and the RJV.
7. The exception here is Martin (1994); see also below.
8. Each firm operates its own lab in the non-cooperative equilibrium.
9. Also Katz (1986), Poyagou-Theotoky (1995) and Combs (1993) contain welfare analyses of the size of RJVs an issue that will not concern us here.
10. In some ways Martin (1994) is the closest to Katsoulakos and Ulph (1999). However his results are rather special emerging from the fact that due to the pure tournament model used only one firm can ever innovate in the non-cooperative equilibrium and in the RJV firms always are assumed to fully share information. Features (i) – (iii) above are not captured.
11. It is finally worth noting that in all subsequent analysis we assume that firms behave non-cooperatively in the product market – RJVs are assumed not to influence competitive behaviour in the product market. For an analysis that attempts to link RJVs to product market collusion see Martin (1995).
12. This ignores the possibility that a firm can only use its own discovery if the other firm has also succeeded in making its discovery. This is an interesting issue that has received some preliminary attention by Ulphand O'Connell (2000) in recent unpublished work but warrants.
13. This is very general. A distinction is sometimes made between 'R&D output spillovers' (or 'discovery spillovers') and 'R&D input spillovers'. A model of the type presented here is then said to be one that focuses only on 'R&D output spillovers' and ignores 'R&D input spillovers'. However, in general all spillovers are output spillovers – a firm has to have discovered something in order to share it with another firm. The real question is whether there are intermediate discoveries that can be shared before going on to make subsequent discoveries. The model discussed here could be applied to intermediate discoveries, with all the values to which we refer being the values of these intermediate discoveries.
14. The decision as to whether or not to close a lab is examined in detail in Katsoulacos and Ulph (1998a) and in Katsoulacos and Ulph (1999).
15. Gravenitz and Ulph also contain welfare comparisons for strong complementary paths but in this case RJVs will always fully share information.

16. Also, their simulation results suggest that a full information sharing RJV will outperform a full information sharing non-cooperative equilibrium sufficiently so that even if the latter does not achieve full research design coordination it will welfare dominate the RJV.

17. This section is based on Gravenitz and Ulph (2000b) and Katsoulacos and Ulph (1998b).

18. Hinloopen (1997a, b; 2000) obtains the same result in a somewhat different framework – but the intuition is the same.

19. Hinloopen also considers how cooperative outcomes might be affected if one *assumes* that RJVs can fully share information.

20. This last statement requires that we allow for licensing in the non-cooperative equilibrium, even though in the 1998b paper we had not allowed for licensing.

REFERENCES

Arrow K. (1962), 'Economic Welfare and the Allocation of Resources for Invention', in the *Rate and Direction of Inventive Activity: Economic and Social Factors National Bureau of Economic Research*, Princeton University Press.

Beath, J., Katsoulacos, Y. and D. Ulph (1995), 'Game-Theoretic Approches' in P. Stoneman (ed.), *Handbook of the Economics of Innovation and Technological Change*, Oxford, Basil Blackwell.

Beath, J., Poyago-Theotoky, J. and D. Ulph (1998), 'Organization Design and Information – Sharing in a Research Joint Venture with Spillovers', *Bulletin of Economic Research*, 50, 47-59.

Bernstein, J.I. and Nadiri, M.I. (1988), 'Interindustry R&D Spillovers, Rates of Return and Production in High-Tech Industries', *American Economic Review*, 78, (Papers and Preceedings), 429-434.

Combs K.L (1993), 'The role of information sharing in cooperative research and development', *International Journal of Industrial Organisation*, 11, 451-602.

Crepon, B., Duguet, E., Encaoua, D. and Mohnen, P. (1992), 'Cooperative, Non-cooperative R&D and Optimal patent life', *INSEE Discussion Paper* 9208.

D'Aspremont, C. and A. Jacquemin (1998), 'Cooperative and Non-cooperative R&D in a Duopoly with Spillovers', *American Economic Review*, 78, 1133-1137.

DeBondt R. and Changqi Wu (1997), *Research Joint Venture Cartels and Welfare* in Poyagou-Theotoky (Ed).

Geroski, P. (1995), 'Markets for Technology: Knowledge, Innovation and Appropriability', in P. Stoneman (ed.), *Handbook of the Economics of Innovation and Technological Change*, Oxford, Basil Blackwell.

Gravenitz G. and Ulph D. (2000a), 'A Comparative Welfare Analysis of Research Joint Ventures and Licensing under Strongly Additive R&D', *mimeo*, University College London.

Gravenitz G. and Ulph D. (2000b), 'Technology Policy with Complementary Research Paths: The complementary Roles of RJVs and R&D Subsidies'. *Programme CNRS: Les Enjeux Economiques De l'Innovation*, Cahier No. 00020.

Griliches, Z. (1995), 'R&D and Productivity: Econometric Results and Measurement Issues', in P. Stoneman (ed.), *Handbook of the Economics of Innovation and Technological Change*, Oxford, Basil Blackwell.

Hinloopen, J. (1997a, b; 2000), 'Subsidizing Cooperative and Non-cooperative R&D in Duopoly with Spillovers', *Journal of Economics*, 66, 151-175.

Hinloopen, J. (1997a, b; 2000), 'Subsidizing Cooperative and Non-cooperative R&D: an equivalence result?', *Economics of Innovation and New Technology*, **9** (4), pp. 317-329.

Hinloopen, J. (2000), 'Subsidizing R&D Cooperatives' (mimeo).

Kamien, M., Muller, E. and Zang, I. (1992), 'Research Joint Ventures and R&D Cartels', *American Economic Review*, 82, 1293-1306.

Katsoulacos, Y. (1993), 'EC R&D Support: Effects on the Cooperative Behaviour of Firms', European Community Office Publications, Luxembourg.

Katsoulacos, Y. and Ulph D. (1998a), 'Endogenous Spillovers and the Performance of Research Joint Ventures', *Journal of Industrial Economics*, 46, 333-357.

Katsoulacos, Y. and Ulph D. (1998b), 'Innovation Spillovers and Technology Policy', *Annales d'Economies et Statistiques*, 49/50, 589-607.

Katsoulacos, Y. and Ulph D. (1999), 'Endogenous Information Sharing and the Welfare Evaluation of Research Joint Ventures' (mimeo).

Katz, M. (1986), 'An Analysis of Cooperative Research and Development', *RAND Journal of Econonmics*, 17 (Winter), pp. 527-543.

Katz, M. and Ordover, J., 1990, 'R&D Cooperation and Competition', Brookings Papers, Microeconomics, 137-203.

Kesteloot, K. and De Bondt, R. (1993), 'Demand-Creating R&D in a Symmetric Oligopoly', *Economics of Innovation and New Technology*, 1993, 2, 171-183.

Kesteloot, K. and Veugelers, R. (1997), 'R&D Cooperation between Asymmetric Partners', in J. Poyago-Theotoky (ed.), *Competition, Cooperation, Research and Development*, Macmillan, Basingstoke.

Martin S. (1994), 'Private and Social Incentives to Form R&D Joint Ventures', *Review of industrial Organisation*, 9, 157-171.

Martin S. (1995), 'R&D Joint Ventures and Tacit Product Market Collusion', *European Journal of Political Economy*, 11, 733-741.

Motta, M. (1992a), 'Cooperative R&D and Vertical Product Differentiation', *International Journal of Industrial Organisation*, 10, 643-661.

Motta, M. (1992b), 'National R&D Cooperation: a Special Type of Strategic Policy', mimeo, CORE, Louvain-la-Neuve.

Poyago-Theotoky, J. (1995), 'Equilibrium and Optimal Size of a Research Joint Venture in an Oligopoly with Spillovers', *Journal of Industrial Economics*, 43, 209-226.

Poyagou-Theotoky J.A. (eds) (1997), *Competition, Cooperation, Research and Development: The Economics of Research Joint Ventures*, Macmillan Press Ltd, London.

Rosenkranz, S. (1996), *Cooperation for Product Innovation*, WZB, Editions Sigma, Berlin.

Stoneman P. (eds) (1995), *Handbook of the Economics of Innovation and Technological Change*, Basil Blackwell Ltd., Oxford.

Suzumura, K. (1992), 'Cooperative and Non-cooperative R&D in an Oligopoly with Spillovers', *American Economic Review*, 82, 1307-1320.

Index